South African Revie

South African Review II

Edited and compiled by
SARS (South African Research Service)

Ravan Press   **Johannesburg**

Published by
Ravan Press (Pty) Ltd.,
P.O. Box 31134, Braamfontein 2017, South Africa

First Published 1984

Cover Design: The Graphic Equalizer

Typesetting & reproduction: Hamiltons Typographical Services (Pty) Ltd
Set in 10 on 12 pt. Times Roman

ISBN 0 86975 238 3

Printed by Galvin and Sales (Pty) Ltd., Cape Town

Contents

SECTION 1: POLITICS AND RESISTANCE

SECTION 2: LABOUR

Usages and abbreviations

In this issue of the *South African Review*, the term 'black' refers collectively to all racially oppressed groups, i.e. Africans, Indians and coloureds. The use of 'racial' or 'ethnic' categorisation reflects a certain reality in apartheid society, and is accordingly necessary in contemporary writings. However, the editors of the *Review* reject the racism implicit in such categorisation.

Many abbreviations used in the text of the *Review* are spelled out in full on first usage. In the case of trade unions, the following abbreviations are commonly used:

AFCWU	– *African Food and Canning Workers Union*
BAMTWU	– *Black Allied Mining and Tunnel Workers Union*
BAWU	– *Black Allied Workers Union*
BCAWU	– *Building, Construction and Allied Workers Union*
BMWU	– *Black Municipality Workers Union*
CCAWUSA	– *Commercial, Catering and Allied Workers Union*
CTMWA	– *Cape Town Municipal Workers Association*
CUSA	– *Council of Unions of South Africa*
CWIU	– *Chemical Workers Industrial Union*
EATU	– *Electrical and Allied Trades Union*
EAWU	– *Engineering and Allied Workers Union*
EPSFAWU	– *Eastern Province Sweet, Food and Allied Workers Union*
FBAWU	– *Food, Beverage and Allied Workers Union*
FCWU	– *Food and Canning Workers Union*
FMU	– *Federated Mining Union*
FOSATU	– *Federation of South African Trade Unions*
GAWU	– *General and Allied Workers Union*
GAWU	– *Glass and Allied Workers Union*
GWU	– *General Workers Union*
GWUSA	– *General Workers Union of South Africa*
JGU	– *Jewelers and Goldsmiths Union*
LDCDWU	– *Laundry, Dry Cleaning and Dyeing Workers Union*
MAWU	– *Metal and Allied Workers Union*
MACWUSA	– *Motor Assemblers and Component Workers Union*
MAGWUSA	– *Municipal and General Workers Union of South Africa*
MWASA	– *Media Workers Association of South Africa*
MWU	– *Mine Workers Union*

NAAWU	–	National Automobile and Allied Workers Union
NGWU	–	National General Workers Union
NFW	–	National Federation of Workers
NISMAWU	–	National Iron, Steel, Metal and Allied Workers Union
NUSMRE	–	National Union of Sugar Manufacturing and Refining Employees
NUTW	–	National Union of Textile Workers
NUM	–	National Union of Mineworkers
OVGWU	–	Orange-Vaal General Workers Union
PWAWU	–	Paper, Wood and Allied Workers Union
SAAWU	–	South African Allied Workers Union
SABS	–	South African Boilermakers Society
SACLA	–	South African Confederation of Labour
SACWU	–	South African Chemical Workers Union
SAMWU	–	South African Mine Workers Union
SATU	–	South African Typographical Workers Union
SATWU	–	South African Transport Workers Union
SEAWU	–	Steel, Engineering and Allied Workers Union
SFAWU	–	Sweet, Food and Allied Workers Union
TAWU	–	Transport and Allied Workers Union
TGWU	–	Transport and General Workers Union
TUCSA	–	Trade Union Council of South Africa
UAMW	–	United African Motor Workers (Natal and Transvaal)
UAMAWU	–	United African Motor and Allied Workers Union (Natal)
WPSFAWU	–	Western Province Sweet, Food and Allied Workers Union

In the case of newspapers referred to in both text and notes, the following abbreviations are used:

CP	City Press
CT	Cape Times
DD	Daily Dispatch
DN	Daily News
EPH	Eastern Province Herald
FM	Financial Mail
NM	Natal Mercury
NW	Natal Witness
RDM	Rand Daily Mail
Sow	Sowetan
SE	Sunday Express
ST	Sunday Times
ST Extra	Sunday Times Extra
S Trib	Sunday Tribune
S Trib Herald	Sunday Tribune Herald
CH	Cape Herald

Introduction

This is the second annual *South African Review* produced and co-ordinated by the Johannesburg-based Southern African Research Service (SARS).

Over thirty social analysts — academics, lawyers, journalists and researchers — were asked by SARS to contribute specific studies on current South and Southern African issues. These studies, linked by general introductions to each section, form the basis of the *Review*.

Authors are responsible for their articles only and SARS bears responsibility for the *Review* in conceptualisation and final form. But the project is in certain important ways a collective one. Many of the contributions were discussed at a meeting of editors and authors held during January 1984, and rewritten in the light of comments made at this editorial seminar. The collective effort of some forty people involved in the *South African Review* is an important component of the project. Apart from the writers themselves, mention must be made of the section editors and co-ordinators:

Section One (Politics and Resistance) was edited by Peter Hudson and co-ordinated by Glenn Moss;

Section Two (Labour) was edited by Nicholas Haysom and Eddie Webster, and co-ordinated by Merle Barsel;

Section Three (South Africa's International Relations) was edited by Peter Vale and co-ordinated by Glenn Moss;

Section Four (Rural Areas and Bantustans) was edited by Alan Mabin and David Webster, and co-ordinated by Gerhard Maré.

Isabel Hofmeyer edited a number of contributions, and the SARS office staff, authors and Ravan Press' Kevin French proofread sections of the book. SARS is indebted to all those mentioned for their continuing support for and involvement in the *Review*.

Introduction

Peter Hudson

It is premature to suggest that the emergence of the United Democratic Front has been the most important political development since the publication of *South African Review One*. Any survey of politics and resistance in South Africa over the last year must however allocate a central place to the UDF's formation, and to the debates over theory and strategy which its formation has stimulated. For this reason this section of the *Review* opens with Howard Barrell's analysis of the UDF's origins, its strategy, and its relations to the other principal political and trade union organisations representing the dominated classes.

The UDF's strategy seeks to co-ordinate the multiple points ˙of resistance and struggle which have emerged in recent years (eg. trade unions, community, student, youth and women's organisations). In this way the UDF aims to construct a national democratic resistance to the state. This is based on the assumption that structures of racial oppression facilitate the formation of alliances between black dominated classes. This assumption underlies and makes viable the UDF project to construct a political alliance linking together a plurality of dominated black classes.

The strategy is not new. But the emergence of the UDF as an above-ground legal, national political movement has given new currency to this strategy and revived debates over its coherence. Tom Lodge suggests in his survey of the ANC that it is about to direct its energies away from armed struggle towards internal underground political organisation. If this is so, then questions concerning the possibilities and problems of class alliances will become even more central to political debate in South Africa.

In their analysis of state policy with respect to the endemic problems of the transport industry, McCarthy and Swilling consider the effects of this policy on relations between the black petty bourgeoisie and working class. They identify the roots of the current transport crisis in the great distances which increasing numbers of workers are forced to travel as a result of apartheid policies. This increases the costs incurred by the transport monopolies which have, up until now, received a subsidy from the state and employers. Employers are however reluctant to increase their contribution and workers' wages are insufficient to cover any substantial increase in fares. On top of this, current state ideology favours the elimination of subsidisation and the stimulation of market forces. The Welgemoed Commission, which reported in 1982, had as its task the formulation of a policy making it possible for the transport monopolies to maintain existing levels of profitability without having to introduce drastic fare increases. Fare hikes run the risk of sparking off politically explosive bus boycotts. The Commission recommended the eventual elimination of subsidisation. The transport monopolies could offset increased costs by capturing a larger share of the market. This is to be achieved by state curtailment of the operations of black taxis and small bus companies. This section of the black petty bourgeoisie is thus opposed to the state's new transport policy. So, argue McCarthy and Swilling, is the black working class. This new policy satisfies none of its demands concerning the poor quality and high price of the transport service offered by the monopolies.

On one level state policy is bringing black petty bourgeois and working class interests into alignment. Both are opposed to the recommendations of the Welgemoed Commission. On the other hand, these are still separate classes with their own specific interests, engaged in conflict with each other. McCarthy and Swilling point out that during past bus boycotts the black petty bourgeoisie involved in the transport industry has taken advantage of the lack of competition from the monopolies and the consequent vulnerability of boycotting commuters, and raised fares. This section of the black petty bourgeoisie derives its revenue largely from fares paid by working class commuters. This is an intrinsically conflictual situation. Neither the fact that these two classes are both politically dominated, nor their common opposition to current state transport policies, can eliminate this.

The relationship between the working class and this section of the black petty bourgeoisie is thus a complex one. It is a relationship of conflict and, potentially at least, a relationship of alliance. The emergence of such an alliance is clearly only a possibility, as the relationship of conflict might preclude the formation of this alliance. The creation of a multi-class national democratic movement as envisaged by the UDF does

not therefore entail merely the co-ordination of hitherto separate struggles. It also involves uniting classes which are at one level already engaged in conflict. Of course — and this is stressed by McCarthy and Swilling
— the basis of an alliance is being created by state policy. But it must also
be stressed that the realisation of this potential alliance requires more
than overcoming the absence of co-ordination of struggles waged by the
dominated classes.

Another important obstacle in forging a multi-class national
democratic resistance movement is the problem of creating an organisational framework which both facilitates unity and accommodates the
specific modes of mobilisation, organisation and struggle of quite distinct
organisations. Many feel that the UDF does not represent such an
organisational framework. In his article, Barrell refers to the position of
David Lewis, general secretary of the General Workers Union, on the
structure of the UDF. For Lewis, the fact that trade union leaders depend
on a mandate from union members for every policy decision taken
precludes trade unions from becoming part of the UDF. Most of the
organisations affiliated to the UDF do not operate in this way. The UDF
is thus, Lewis argues, able to take unmandated decisions, which is impossible for an authentic trade union.

Grest and Hughes's analysis of state strategy with respect to black local
government throws further light on the complexity of relations amongst
black dominated classes. The general thrust of state policy in black local
government involves granting 'autonomy' to black local authorities. This
entails the entrenchment of apartheid through the creation of separate Indian, coloured and African local authorities, and the extension of the
powers currently enjoyed by black local authorities. In recent years,
recession and rapid urbanisation have resulted in an intensification of opposition in black areas to rising rents, tariffs and rates. There has also
been mounting protest against the poor quality of the services offered.
The state hopes, suggest Grest and Hughes, that this situation will be
defused by the granting of 'autonomy' to racially separate local
authorities. According to the strategy being pursued by the state these
bodies will come to be seen as responsible for the situation in black areas.

On the basis of the analysis undertaken by Grest and Hughes it is possible to identify two contradictory effects of this strategy on relations between black dominated classes. On the one hand, black local authorities
are for the most part located in dormitory suburbs. They accordingly
have no possibility of being able to finance better services. They are crea-
tions of the racially oppressive state which tightly circumscribes their

'autonomy'. The institutions of black local government are as a consequence perceived as impotent and without legitimacy. This has given rise to a boycott strategy supported by sections of both the black working class and the black petty bourgeoisie.

On the other hand, the creation of separate black local authorities with increased powers provides an opportunity for certain groups in the black dominated classes to further their specific interests. For aspirant or new members of the black petty bourgeoisie participation in the institutions of black local government can offer some opportunities to achieve or consolidate membership of this class. This can be done through, for example, control of the granting of licences, permits and contracts. As Grest and Hughes point out, the issues that are tackled with most vigour and enthusiasm by black local authorities generally reflect the specific interests of the black petty bourgeoisie. Participation in the local government system by members of the black petty bourgeoisie brings them into political conflict with those who suffer most from rent and tariff increases imposed by local authorities, i.e. the black working class.

The possibility cannot therefore be ruled out that the state's black local government strategy will lead to an entrenched and durable political division within the dominated classes. This questions those analyses which argue that national domination constitutes the central structural political cleavage in South African society. It also weakens the claim that the specific structure of South African society privileges the emergence of multi-class national democratic struggle as the dominant form of resistance to the South African state.

There is no warrant for assuming that the dominant line-up of political forces in South Africa is likely to be along the white power bloc/black oppressed majority axis. Political polarisation might occur along these lines, but this should not be seen as implied by the structure of South African society. National and class domination both exist as distinct yet linked structures of oppression. Neither is in a position of automatic and necessary dominance over the other. A multi-class national democratic movement can only become the principal opposition to the state if strategic and organisational forms are found to overcome the impediments which obstruct the formation of such a movement.

The United Democratic Front and National Forum: Their Emergence, Composition and Trends

Howard Barrell

The new constitution and the Koornhof Bills[1] were major factors stimulating the formal rebuilding of a broadly based national democratic resistance inside the country. The two leading vehicles of this development were the United Democratic Front (UDF), launched nationally on 20 August 1983, and the National Forum (NF), which met on 11–12 June 1983.

These two loose coalitions took on the character less of organisations than of mechanisms for consultation and/or co-ordinated action between existing organisations. They brought together a wide variety of predominantly black[2] political, community, labour, student, professional and pressure groups of varying strengths. Some organisations were to participate in both the UDF and NF.

Their 'unity' was based on the perceived need to combine their different localised struggles and address the central political question of state power. They aimed to resist the government's new plans and, ultimately, to satisfy their shared interest in ending apartheid.

The UDF in particular succeeded — at least temporarily — in nullifying the government's attempt to attract black support for the new constitution and Koornhof Bills.

The UDF viewed the new constitution and the Bills as part of the same attempt to modernise apartheid. The government, it said, 'cannot rule us in the old way . . . we have become too strong for them to do that anymore'.[3] The new constitution was a fraudulent attempt to draw the so-called coloured and Indian portions of the black population into a political alliance with the white minority — to put 'Africans on the one side, coloureds and Indians with the whites on the other'.[4] The Koornhof Bills were seen in a similar light but, in addition, they strengthened apartheid's function of labour and security control. The Bills would further 'divide African townspeople from migrant workers' and tighten the pass law barricades around those who 'starve in the homelands'.[5] In the case of the new black local authorities, the Bills would 'make (the government's) puppets stronger' in the townships, said the UDF.[6] The NF and its prime mover, AZAPO, expressed a similar view on the new legislation.

The UDF viewed the moment as a 'critical stage in our struggle for a free, democratic and non-racial country'. More than ever before 'unity and organisation' were necessary, particularly the creation of 'one united force for freedom'.

Far from creating and entrenching divisions within the black population, the new legislation seems, so far at least, to have stimulated joint black political resistance to a formally organised level not seen since the 1950s and the Congress Alliance.

The UDF was the most visible force working for this unity, although important parallel campaigns against government manoeuvres were conducted outside its ranks, notably by the Federation of South African Trade Unions (FOSATU), the two Food and Canning Workers' Unions and AZAPO.[7]

Debating organisational forms

The structure and programmes of the UDF and NF prompted vigorous debate on how the central issue of state power should be addressed, particularly how a broad democratic alliance should relate to working class organisation and interests. In this respect, some attention was also given to the appropriate political vehicle for distinctly working class interests. A second debate arose around the concept of 'the nation' and the compatability of non-racial democratic principles and ethnically orientated political organisation. In the same vein, argument persisted over what role democratic whites could play in the struggle against apartheid. A third debate centred on what organisational methods developed by the trade unions could be adapted by community and political groups to ensure more persistent mass participation in their affairs and programmes.

Three broad ideological currents emerged out of these debates: progressive nationalism (also known as progressive democracy), left- and
right-wing black exclusivism, and what can be called the independent
worker position.[8] There was some overlap between them. Rhetorically
at least, all three currents shared the position that the working class
should lead the political struggle. Essentially, they differed on how this
working class leadership should relate to race or national issues.

Progressive nationalists stressed the potential involvement of most sections of the community, regardless of race or class origins, in a broad
political struggle against apartheid. They argued that all oppressed sections of the community had an over-riding interest in the destruction of
apartheid, and they allowed white participation where whites identified
with this national struggle. This current combined elements of traditional
nationalism with the view that the working class should lead the political
struggle. But the progressive nationalists expressed the view that at this
stage distinct class mobilisation should largely be subsumed within the
broader national democratic struggle. They argued that the trade unions,
although a critically important factor, were not the only form of working
class organisation. Unions were limited in their capacity to represent
working class political interest.

Left- and right-wing black exclusivism shared an emphasis on the exclusion of white democrats from their organisations despite a commitment to the 'development of one national progressive culture in the process of struggle'.[9] They repeatedly concerned themselves with the concept of 'the nation'. The left emphasised 'the historic task of the black
working class and its organisations to mobilise the urban and rural poor
together with the radical sections of the middle class in order to put an
end to the system of oppression and exploitation by the white ruling
class'.[10] The right regarded a privileged role for the working class with
increasing suspicion and emphasised the more traditional political-
ideological component of black national liberation.[11]

The independent worker position stressed the need for the trade
unions, as forms of working class organisation, to maintain their
autonomy outside the broad national democratic movement at least at
present. Two broad internal trends within this position were evident. One
view was that the working class should enter organisational alliances
with other classes and groups only once it could stand distinctly at the
centre of the broad democratic movement. It held that working class
political confidence was not yet sufficiently developed to allow this. A
second view stressed the need for an independent working class political

party, closely derived from factory floor organisation. Such a party would exclude other classes and, possibly, also reject political alliances with these other classes. Both these internal trends insisted that working class struggle should have a non-racial character, even under apartheid conditions.

The UDF, although concentrated around the progressive nationalists, was to contain, or be treated sympathetically by, pockets from within the other strains.

The National Forum was concentrated around the left and right of black exclusivism contained mainly within AZAPO, but some members of progressive nationalist organisations attended its meeting.

During the year, adherents of the independent worker position attempted to construct a larger progressive trade union federation whose future core seemed likely to comprise FOSATU, the two Food and Canning Workers' Unions, the General Workers' Union (GWU), the Commercial, Catering and Allied Workers' Union (CCAWUSA), and the Cape Town Municipal Workers' Association (CTMWA).

UDF is conceived

The immediate impetus for the UDF arose out of the Anti-South African Indian Council campaign (Anti-SAIC), one of the most successful anti-apartheid election boycotts. At the Transvaal Anti-SAIC (TASC) conference in Johannesburg in January, two needs were identified. The first (more limited) need was to create an organisation able to 'convert into programme and action' the political work done in the Anti-SAIC campaign. As a result of this the Transvaal Indian Congress (TIC) was resuscitated. The second need was to translate a whole range of economically, geographically and ethnically specific struggles into 'one national struggle forming alliances with groups sharing similar interests' in order to address the central political issue of state power.[12]

Against the background of the President's Council proposals (which formed the basis of subsequent constitutional legislation), World Alliance of Reformed Churches president Dr Allan Boesak called for a 'united front'. He said:

> There is . . . no reason why the churches, civic associations, trade unions, student organisations and sports bodies should not unite on this issue, pool our resources, inform people of the fraud that is about to be perpetuated in their name and, on the day of the election, expose their plans for what they are.[13]

Boesak's call was widely endorsed at the conference, among others by South African Allied Workers' Union (SAAWU) president Thozamile Gqweta.

The conference appointed a commission to investigate the feasibility of a united front. The commission presented a statement to the conference. This was adopted and formed the basis for the initial regional UDFs. It laid down guidelines including dedication to the 'creation of a non-racial, unitary state undiluted by racial or ethnic considerations as formulated in the bantustan policy', the adoption of a non-racial form of organisation and the need to consult with 'all democratic people wherever they may be'.[14] Although TASC itself endorsed the Freedom Charter, adopted at the Congress of the People in 1955, the commission statement on the formation of a front did not lay down the Charter as the basis for UDF unity.[15] Successive rounds of consultations with other organisations and activists ensued and it was decided to form regional UDFs before proceeding to a national body.

Within days of the TASC conference, debate opened up around the issue of 'the nation' and ethnic organisational forms. AZAPO called the decision to revive the TIC a 'retrogressive step'. The UDF, claimed AZAPO, would be a 'conglomerate of ethnically orientated groups' whereas 'the oppressed should be rallied together in a single organisation which is not structured on an ethnic basis.[16] These criticisms were subsequently given more form at the NF by Dr Neville Alexander, a former Robben Island prisoner with political origins in the Non-European Unity Movement (NEUM) tradition. Alexander exerted strong theoretical influence within black exclusivist organisation during the year.[17]

TIC president Dr Essop Jassat countered that the revival of TIC had been sound for 'historical and practical reasons', and enjoyed a reputation as an 'honourable organisation'. Although it organised primarily among the Indian section of the black population, it had sought to forge non-racial unity among all the oppressed during the Congress Alliance − 'the greatest amount of joint action ever seen in this country'.[18] According to 'Terror' Lekota, subsequently UDF national publicity secretary, this form of organisation was not intended to legitimate racial separation. Instead, it was a realistic response to the fact of separation and race consciousness where it existed, and an attempt to bring people together into non-racial unity through joint activity − 'You cannot just declare non-racialism; you must build it'.[19]

A series of formal and other approaches[20] by the central activists involved in launching the UDF failed to attract AZAPO into the Front.

On 14 May a Natal regional UDF was constituted out of more than 40 organisations. The Transvaal followed a week later when 28 organisations committed themselves to a UDF, although this was only formalised subsequently. A Western Cape region of the UDF was formed on 24 July out of 22 organisations, some of them federations. By the year's end, regional UDFs had also been constituted in the Border and Eastern Cape, and a North Cape UDF was at an advanced stage of development.[21]

Men off the Island

At a time when many black consciousness adherents were finding political homes in the progressive nationalist camp,[22] AZAPO gained some much-needed vigour in December 1982 when a number of black consciousness leaders jailed in the lengthy SASO-BPC trial of 1974–76 were released from Robben Island. Prominent among the former trialists – and convenor of the National Forum – was Saths Cooper, who had been elected AZAPO vice-president shortly after his release. Another former trialist, Muntu Myeza, became AZAPO secretary general.

The Forum, as its name suggests, did not constitute itself as an organisation. Instead it was a mechanism for consultation between existing organisations. AZAPO was its driving force and the intention of the forum was to broaden AZAPO's base as the political vanguard of the 200 organisations attending.[23]

The meeting on 11–12 June reflected the dominance of the new left wing tendency within black exclusivism. The gathering was presented with the outline of a document, entitled the 'Manifesto of the Azanian People'. This was referred back to organisations present for 'consideration', 'review' and possible adoption at the next meeting of the forum – scheduled for the 1984 Easter weekend.[24] The document sparked off acrimonious exchanges as members of progressive nationalist organisations who had attended the forum disclaimed responsibility for it.

Issued partly in response to the 'implications of the Botha government's "new deal" strategy', the Manifesto expressed a distinctly socialist and internationalist commitment. It declared that the people's struggle was directed against 'the system of racial capitalism which holds the people of Azania in bondage for the benefit of the small minority of white capitalists and their allies, the white workers and the reactionary sections of the black middle class'. Apartheid would be 'eradicated with the system of racial capitalism'.

The black working class was the 'driving force of the struggle' and its 'historic task (was) to mobilise the urban and rural poor together with the radical sections of the middle classes in order to put an end to the system of oppression and exploitation by the white ruling class'. Reference was made to unidentified 'opportunistic "leaders"' who should be prevented from turning the struggle against the people. The Manifesto demanded the 'establishment of a democratic, anti-racist worker Republic in Azania'.

The Manifesto did not explicitly exclude white democrats from this struggle though it spoke of 'non-collaboration with the oppressor and its political instruments' and 'opposition to alliances with ruling class parties'. Only 'representatives of the oppressed' were allowed to attend the forum as delegates.[25] In effect, this meant the continued exclusion of white democrats in the view of AZAPO and the majority at the Forum. Nonetheless, Alexander told the Forum that some place would have to be found for genuine white democrats within the envisaged struggle.

A National Forum Committee, in whose name the meeting had been held, was charged with organising the next meeting of the Forum. Widely divergent political positions were represented on the committee.[26] A number of black exclusivists confided dissatisfaction with the new left-wing emphasis, but said the 'moment' was not right for a counter-offensive.[27]

Critics argued that there were reasons to doubt AZAPO's determination and ability to give concrete meaning to its own and the Forum's rhetorical commitment to working class leadership.[28]

UDF is born

In late July, the UDF ad hoc national secretariat took a decision to launch the organisation nationally. The date was set for 20 August. One of the most extensive propaganda campaigns in the history of resistance to apartheid followed. More than 400 000 UDF newsletters, posters and pamphlets were distributed nationally to advertise the launch. The gist of the propaganda was to inform people of the national political dimension of their fractured struggles and the need to reconstruct formal countrywide resistance to the new government manoeuvres.

The inaugural conference at Rocklands outside Cape Town brought together more than 600 delegates from over 320[29] political, trade union, youth, sport, religious, professional and other organisations from many areas of the country. An estimated 100 more organisations sent observers. The subsequent people's rally comprised about 10 000 people.[30] Organisers had to keep them under cover of the centre and a large adjoining marquee to comply with a government ban on outdoor political meetings.

The inaugural conference stated that the UDF did not 'purport to be a substitute movement to accredited people's liberation movements'. The conference gave all regional formations and member organisations 'complete independence provided their actions and policies were not inconsistent with those of the UDF. Any organisation was eligible for UDF membership if committed to the UDF policy declaration.[31] Provision for individual UDF membership came under consideration later in the year.[32]

The UDF committed itself to 'uniting all our people, wherever they may be in the cities and countryside, the factories and mines, schools, colleges, and universities, houses and sports fields, churches, mosques and temples, to fight for our freedom'.[33] This broad, inclusive approach was repeatedly tempered by a declared commitment to the primacy of the working class in the national democratic struggle. Announcing the national launch, the interim UDF leadership stated that 'the main thrust of the organisation is directed towards the participation of the working people in the workplace, in communities, wherever (they) may be'.[34] The inaugural conference expressed its belief in 'the leadership of the working class in the democratic struggle for freedom' and resolved to 'strengthen the unity between genuine democratic trade unions and freedom loving people in the struggle for political rights for all'.[35]

Trade unions: in or out?

Trade union membership of the UDF included the Council of Unions of South Africa (CUSA), which also attended the Forum, SAAWU, the General and Allied Workers' Union (GAWU) and the Motor Assemblers and Component Workers' Union (MACWUSA) among 13.[36] Interestingly, the Western Cape region of the Media Workers' Association of South Africa (MWASA) and the Eastern Cape region of the African Food and Canning Workers' Union affiliated to the UDF whereas their national bodies were to remain outside its ranks. MWASA split in early 1984, among others, over the issue of its Western Cape region's participation in a non-racial form of organisation.

The decision of the 'independent worker' unions to remain outside the UDF precipitated the debate on how a broad national democratic alliance should be related to the working class. There was deep concern within the UDF that those unions representing the most cohesively organised sector of the black working class should choose to remain outside the Front. These unions — centred around FOSATU, the two Food and Canning Unions and GWU — gave qualified support to the UDF and publicly encouraged individual participation by their members.[37] But they aimed important criticisms at the UDF's structure and nature.

The structure of UDF regional general councils and national conference allowed two delegates and two votes from each affiliate regardless of its organised strength (with the exception of the Western Cape region where the system was loaded in favour of the larger organisations). Most of the regions also established UDF area committees, whose membership was generally loosely constituted. In Natal, these committees had two votes on the regional general council, whereas in the Western Cape and Transvaal this was not the case by the end of the year.[38]

A central 'independent worker' objection was that this structure could not adequately reflect the strength of the trade unions and the necessary primacy of working class political interests.

The Food and Canning Unions stated that their first priority was a larger union federation 'for the working class to take the lead in the struggle for a united, democratic South Africa'.[39] FOSATU general secretary Joe Foster added that a portion of FOSATU's membership was politically hostile to the UDF and therefore, in the interests of unity, FOSATU could not join.[40] This was an apparent reference to shop floor support for the independent worker position, and to FOSATU's partial overlap with Inkatha membership in Natal and the NEUM tradition in the Western Cape. GWU general secretary Dave Lewis stated among others that democratic working class organisations could not submit their memberships to political decisions taken by a loose coalition such as the UDF consisting of organisations whose own structures sometimes did not ensure democratic answerability. While Lewis said it was unlikely GWU would join the UDF under any circumstances he did not rule out a subsequent alliance between a powerful independent trade union centre and broadly based political organisations.[41]

Lewis's criticisms accompanied the realisation in some quarters of the UDF that organisational methods might have to be adapted from the trade union experience to ensure more persistently active mass involvement in community and other organisations.[42]

Some supporters of the 'independent worker' position argued that the UDF was being dominated by a 'radical petty bourgeois' emphasis on national oppression without the necessary emphasis on class exploitation. But the criticism was sometimes couched in the compliment that the UDF had 'opened a whole new vista of struggle' and the hope that it was possible to build a UDF 'under the leadership of the working class'.[43]

UDF leaders responded that the structure had answered the initial needs of the Front's formation, but they told 'independent worker' union leaders and shop stewards that it was 'negotiable' and could be amended to meet these unions' requirements. They added that, in order for the working class to lead the national democratic movement, organisations of this class had necessarily to participate in full strength in that movement. But these leaders expressed their understanding of union hesitancy and the hope that future co-operation could establish a basis for eventual unity.[44]

UDF campaigns

The UDF's ability to mount political campaigns around its programme was hindered by a number of factors: the difficulties created by repressive conditions, problems of communication over long distances, the diffuse nature of its affiliates and their uneven strengths. The adoption of common positions and the implementation of agreed programmes were complicated as a result.[45] Nonetheless, a number of successful campaigns were mounted over the year.

The UDF's 'people's weekend' — which comprised rallies in most main centres voicing opposition to the new constitution and Koornhof Bills on the eve of the November whites-only referendum — drew about 30 000 people.

The Front and its affiliates mounted boycotts of elections for the new black local authorities (provided for in the Koornhof Bills). Thousands of pamphlets were put out and house-to-house campaigns undertaken in some African townships. Despite new government efforts to break the tradition of boycott and election apathy within the townships, percentage polls were generally lower than the 1978-79 elections for the former community councils.[46]

UDF affiliates working in the coloured and Indian portions of the black population could also claim much of the credit for the view, apparent even among Labour Party and South African Indian Council members

towards the end of the year, that referenda among these sections on the
new constitution would meet either an overwhelming boycott or a
massive 'no' vote.

Unions both within and outside the UDF combined with the Front on
20 September to condemn general repression and the banning of SAAWU
'by the Ciskei puppet government' — an issue of distinct working class
importance which the 'independent worker' unions had no difficulty taking up. The UDF also did much to stimulate awareness of the situation
in the Ciskei and to jolt the bulk of the commercial press out of its torpor
on the subject.[47]

White responses

The response to the UDF from the state (and unidentified right-wing
agencies) appeared erratic. Police briefly held scores of UDF supporters
for handing out UDF propaganda on the national launch and some were
charged for allegedly attending an illegal gathering. About 40 000 copies
of *UDF News* were confiscated by police in the Western Cape but released under threat of legal action. In major centres, a number of bogus pamphlets appeared. These said that the UDF national launch had been
postponed and tried to exacerbate ideological differences with other
organisations. Lekota was briefly interrogated by police and told he might
soon be banned. UDF president Oscar Mpetha and other leaders received threats and the car belonging to a UDF supporter in Port Elizabeth
was blown up. A Transvaal UDF activist died in a mysterious stabbing,
prompting UDF allegations that he had been assassinated. A Western
Cape UDF activist and former Robben Island prisoner was shot dead at
his home in January 1984, which renewed suspicions of an assassination
campaign. Further bogus pamphlets, aimed at alienating the Indian portion of the black population from the UDF, appeared in Johannesburg in
early 1984 at the instigation of an unidentified group of white men in a
car with false number plates. At about the same time, a statement purportedly from the outlawed South African Communist Party was issued
under a UDF letterhead and posted to some of its activists. And, as if
a precursor to strong state reaction, some government spokesmen and
pro-government commentators branded the UDF a 'front of the ANC'.[48]

Following the banning of a number of UDF gatherings — among them
a meeting of its ten-member national secretariat — the UDF wrote to
Prime Minister PW Botha. The UDF demanded an end to the banning

of its meetings, non-implementation of the new constitution and for heed to be paid to 'this voice of reason'. Botha should 'respond to the urgency of this moment in our country's history and abandon (his) present disastrous course'. The UDF had received no reply by the end of the year.[49] But, following his victory in the whites-only referendum on the new constitution, Botha responded on SATV to a question on the UDF. He said his government opposed 'all forms of radicalism' and was prepared to talk only to 'reasonable leaders' of the black population. In this context, he had ruled out discussion with the UDF.

Inkatha president Gatsha Buthelezi initially welcomed plans for the formation of the UDF. However, his movement was excluded from affiliation. By the end of the year, relations had soured to bitter enmity. At a time when talks between the UDF and Inkatha were a prospect, Inkatha-student clashes occurred at the University of Zululand which left at least five dead and more than 100 injured. The public UDF reaction did not match the shrillness of the bantustan leader's accusations. The UDF he claimed, planned to have him killed. The Front did, however, respond strongly to Inkatha's and Buthelezi's behaviour over Zululand University.

The white liberal establishment expressed some sympathy for the UDF and hailed its development as significant. But this was couched in reservations. *The Star* appealed to the UDF not to adopt 'an uncompromisingly radical stance' that would 'alienate possible support among moderates, both black and white'.[50] *The Rand Daily Mail* suggested the UDF's choice of patrons invited 'questions about (its) motivation'. In this respect it singled out the UDF's election of an unnamed jailed communist as a patron – an apparent reference to Dennis Goldberg.[51]

Recent developments

The UDF held its first national conference in Port Elizabeth in mid-December, mainly to decide on its response if the state called referenda for the coloured and Indian sections of the black population. By that stage, the Front was claiming more than 560 affiliates[52] and some newspapers estimated its membership and support through affiliates at about 1,5 million people. Delegates were divided at the conference over whether to call for participation and a 'no' vote, or to boycott any ethnic referenda. There was, however, agreement that there could be no participation by affiliates in the bodies created under the new constitution.

The referendum decision was referred to the UDF national executive committee which was charged with following the recommendations of the regions and affiliates. The result, in early 1984, was a compromise. The UDF called for a non-racial referendum, said it would not participate in any ethnic referenda, but left the way open for affiliates to take part in ethnic referenda if this was appropriate in terms of 'local conditions'.[53] The Transvaal and Natal Indian Congresses then announced their intention to participate in any Indian referendum and call for a 'no' vote.[54]

The UDF entered 1984 by embarking on a 'Million Signatures Campaign' which sought to test both opposition to the government manoeuvres and support for the Front. The major aims behind the campaign were political education and a strengthening of the Front, but the UDF also recognised the propaganda value locally and internationally of such a register of opposition.[55]

AZAPO began 1984 with its annual congress, at which it renewed its attacks on the UDF and prepared for the second National Forum which, again, was not intended to result in the formation of another political organisation.[56]

The major progressive trade unions again concerned themselves largely with the construction of a larger national federation.

In spite of the persistence of disagreements amongst these three currents, they undeniably progressed during 1983 towards the unification of a wide range of previously fractured struggles. The rigour of the debates – particularly those waged at the level of leadership – indicated a keen attention to what forms of organisation were appropriate under South African conditions rather than any deep-seated differences over publicly declared strategic objectives.

The broad democratic movement markedly increased and improved its capacity to mobilise its support.

Notes

1 The Koornhof Bills refer to the Orderly Movement and Settlement of Black Persons Bill, the Black Local Authorities Act and the Black Community Development Bill.

2 The term 'black' is used to denote all sections of the oppressed – African, coloured and Indian people.

3 *UDF News*, 1(1), August 1983.

4 *UDF News*, 1(1), August 1983.

5 *UDF News*, 1(1), August 1983.

6 *UDF News*, 1(1), August 1983.

7 FOSATU conducted a one-man, one-vote campaign at the time of the whites-only referendum on the new constitution. FOSATU and Food and Canning Workers' Union members were prominent in mobilising opposition to the Labour Party's decision to participate in the new constitution. AZAPO also campaigned for a boycott in the black local authorities elections.

8 Black consciousness can no longer be treated as a homogeneous entity. Its original principles of black self-reliance and cultural enrichment have prompted adherents into divergent political directions. What is being isolated here is that strand of latter-day black consciousness distinguishable by its persistent racial exclusivity.

The independent worker position is most difficult to characterise adequately and my attempt to do so is tentative. Pejorative labels given it by its critics, such as 'workerist', do not in my view add to an understanding of it at this stage.

9 Manifesto of the Azanian People.

10 Manifesto of the Azanian People.

11 Confidential interviews with the author.

12 N.G. Patel's 'The Road Ahead', speech at the TASC conference, 22–23.01.83.

13 Speech at the TASC conference by Dr Allan Boesak.

14 Statement by the 'Commission on the Feasibility of a United Front against the Constitutional Reform Proposals', at TASC conference.

15 The TASC conference's endorsement of the Freedom Charter, which came at the same time as the Commission statement on the formation of a united front, might explain the fairly widespread confusion that arose over whether or not the Charter was the intended basis for unity in the Front.

16 AZAPO publicity secretary Ismael Mkhabela, quoted in *The Leader*, 28.01.83.

17 See *Work in Progress*, 26, August 1983, for Alexander's account.

18 *FM*, 04.02.83.

19 Author's interview with Lekota.

20 Author's interviews with AZAPO president Mabasa, secretary general Myeza, publicity secretary Mkhabela, and UDF's Lekota.

21 Author's interviews with Lekota and regional UDF leaders.

22 I refer, in exile, to the visible cases of Barney Pityana, Mongezi Stofile and Tenjiwe Mtintso while, inside the country, to the ideological changes in the Azanian Students' Organisation (AZASO) and the positions of Diliza Mji, Aubrey Mokoena and Rev. Frank Chikane, among others.

23 Author's interviews with Mabasa and Myeza on AZAPO's intentions. The figure of 200 organisations was that given by the NFC.

24 Author's interview with Myeza.

25 Author's interview with Myeza.

26 It includes both left- and right-wing black nationalist tendencies, some based in Christian theology, some purportedly on scientific socialism.

27 Confidential interviews with the author.

28 Author's interviews with progressive nationalists and adherents of the independent worker position.

29 Interim UDF national publicity secretary Zac Yacoob at a press briefing at midday on the day of the inaugural conference.

30 The author's estimate.

31 UDF Working Principles.

32 Interview with Lekota.

33 UDF Declaration.
34 Press conference statement, announcing national launch.
35 A resolution of the inaugural UDF conference.
36 *South African Labour Bulletin*, 8(9)/9(1), September/October 1983.
37 *South African Labour Bulletin*, 8(9)/9(1), September/October 1983.
38 Interviews with regional UDF officials.
39 *South African Labour Bulletin*, 8(9)/9(1), September/October 1983.
40 *South African Labour Bulletin*, 8(9)/9(1), September/October 1983.
41 Interview with David Lewis, 'General Workers' Union and the UDF', *Work In Progress* 29, October 1983.
42 Author's interviews with UDF activists, among them Lekota.
43 Isabella Silver and Alexia Sfarnas, 'The UDF: A "Workerist" Response', *South African Labour Bulletin*, 8(9)/9(1), September/October 1983.
44 Author's interview with Lekota.
45 Author's interviews with UDF activists.
46 *CP*, 11.12.83.
47 The commercial press was surprisingly hesitant about giving coverage to the situation in the Ciskei. See Nicholas Haysom, *Ruling with the Whip*, DSG/SARS, 1983.
48 See *Aida Parker's Newsletter*, 14, 1 September 1983.
49 Confirmed by UDF leaders.
50 *The Star*, editorial, 25.01.83.
51 *RDM*, editorial, 23.08.83.
52 Author's interviews with Boesak and Lekota.
53 Statement of UDF national executive committee, 25.01.84.
54 See *CP*, 29.01.84.
55 Interview with Lekota.
56 Author's interview with Myeza.

The African National Congress, 1983

Tom Lodge

During 1983 the African National Congress maintained low-intensity military operations inside South Africa while externally-based leadership structures underwent significant re-organisation. Increasingly aggressive South African regional policies presented fresh problems for the ANC's military strategists. The indifference or hostility of certain Western governments was only partially compensated for by sympathy shown to the organisation in China and Australia.

Police attributed 31 bomb attacks to the ANC during the year. The ANC denied responsibility for two of these. One involved an explosion in a Bloemfontein township administration board building. It took place at ten thirty-five in the morning, killing one and hurting seven work seekers lined up outside the building. In its denial the ANC's Lusaka office commented that 'injury of civilians was not a tactic used by the organisation' (*RDM*, 24.02.83). The ANC also disclaimed responsibility for a limpet mine attack which damaged a Johannesburg synagogue. In addition to successful bomb attacks, guerillas were arrested on three occasions before carrying out their missions, police defused bombs in at least four instances and ANC guerillas and police were involved in eight exchanges of fire.

Most sabotage attacks took place in Pretoria, Pietermaritzburg, Durban and on the Rand, and the previous year's emphasis on attacks in small towns or rural areas was not repeated. Only two attacks took place in the Cape but Bloemfontein emerged as a new centre for ANC activity. Targets most often chosen by saboteurs were the railways (six attacks) followed by electrical installations (five attacks). Township offices were hit four times and six government offices in city centres were also bombed. Two of this latter group were Ciskeian diplomatic offices.

Bombs exploded outside military premises twice, court buildings were damaged twice, an oil depot at Warmbaths was bombed and rockets missed the Secunda SASOL III refinery by three kilometres.

The most serious incident — and the one which generated most public discussion — involved the car bomb which exploded in the late afternoon of 20 May outside the South African Defence Force headquarters in Pretoria's Church Street. The car bomb's victims included 19 dead and 215 injured. Seven of the dead were military personnel and two others, according to the police, were ANC saboteurs who carried out the attack. The car bomb represented a tactical innovation for the ANC. Its timing (during the afternoon rush hour), its location (in a busy street in Pretoria's commercial centre), and the scale of the casualties inflicted, led commentators to view it as opening a new phase in the ANC's insurgency campaign.

The first ANC statement from Lusaka[1] tended to corroborate this belief. It claimed that the Church Street attack was a 'response to appeals by South African blacks for more action against minority white rule'. 'At last', the statement continued,

> ... the ANC has stopped blowing up walls. It's now doing the right thing. It can't make sense to continue blowing up pylons if we're going to get massacred for it and going to get hanged. It's not going to be possible for us to continue our action on the exclusive basis that no civilians shall be killed. That is implicit in our idea of intensifying the struggle ... people are very resentful and feel they want to hurt ... they somehow felt the ANC had been denying them this.

Later however, a senior ANC spokesperson denied that the bombing 'marked a change in strategy'. Certainly 'the loss of civilian life was a matter of regret' but he knew of 'no war which did not result in injuries to the innocent'.[2] Two years earlier ANC leaders had warned that in future there might arise 'combat situations' in which civilians could get killed.[3] ANC statements have generally stressed that the Church Street bombing involved a military target (*CP*, 22.05.83).

It is possible that the planners of the operation did not anticipate the extent of loss of human life. Umkonto we Sizwe operations since 20 May have more or less conformed to the previous pattern: explosive devices timed to detonate out of working hours usually at night in near-empty buildings. An exception to this was the attempt to place a bomb at the Pietermaritzburg Town Hall during a referendum meeting addressed by P.W. Botha. But even in this case the guerilla turned back because, according to his own account, 'I saw many people at the City Hall and realised that it would not be safe.' He had, he claimed, been instructed to ensure the bomb did not injure anybody (*RDM*, 15.12.83).

Attacks were less geographically dispersed than in previous years and, with the exception of the Church Street and Warmbaths attacks, less organisationally elaborate. The limited scope of the violent activity in 1983 testified to the increasingly stringent conditions under which Umkonto operated. Infiltrating insurgents through territories adjacent to South Africa has become more and more difficult (see below) and in the second half of the year ANC strategists have tried to expand guerilla training within the republic.[4] A senior ANC representative claimed in July 1983 that the ANC had an internal military and political organisational base, and this has been partly borne out by some trial evidence. For example Nobleman Shezi, on trial in Pietermaritzburg, apparently had an extensive understanding of timing devices on Soviet-made explosives despite never having left South Africa (*Star*, 03.11.83). The police version of how the Pretoria attack was mounted, if taken at face value, also indicates an increasingly localised organisation: according to police the insurgents were two well-known Mamelodi criminals and the car they used had been stolen in Pretoria some months previously (*RDM*, 03.08.83).

After Sobhuza's death in Swaziland an administration more amenable to South African influence and less sympathetic to the ANC was installed. This led in 1983 to a sharply reduced ANC presence in the Kingdom. Only 30 active ANC members were believed to be residing in Swaziland by mid-1983 and South African politicians regularly commended the Swazis on their steps to curtail the organisation.

Whereas Swazi politicians' attitudes have been influenced by South African business interests and the continuing possibility of a land transfer, the authorities in Lesotho have been more reluctant to meet South African security demands. After the failure of talks on 23 June border restrictions were imposed on the flow of Basotho work seekers into the Republic, Lesotho-bound arms shipments were impounded in Durban and a heavy Lesotho Liberation Army offensive was mounted with probable South African connivance. In August the Lesotho government capitulated and 20 ANC 'refugees' listed by the South African authorities left the country.

An air-attack on Mozambique in the wake of the Pretoria car bomb and an October raid on an ANC office in central Maputo demonstrated Mozambican vulnerability. The South Africans claimed in each case that the targets comprised important ANC strategic facilities: a logistical headquarters, a command post, offices housing the headquarters of

Umkonto's rural and urban Transvaal operations. They also claimed to have killed 41 ANC personnel (as well as 17 Mozambicans). Mozambique government spokesmen discounted such claims: the targets and casualties inflicted were civilian. In the case of the October attack the insurgents seemed unusually well-informed and may not have been South African (*Star*, 18.10.83). Mozambique experienced military incursions into its territory by both South African forces and their Mozambican proxies, economic dislocation resulting from the drought, and the increased influence of Western conservative administrations (itself an effect of economic difficulties). These were all factors which by the beginning of 1984 helped to prompt a more receptive Mozambican attitude to South African overtures. It seems likely that the Mozambicans will reluctantly have to follow the example of the Basothos and Swazis and discourage Umkonto units from operating through and from their territory. For the ANC the direction and supply of Umkonto units in the field will become increasingly difficult as a result of the inevitable lengthening of lines of communication and logistical support.

Perhaps in anticipation of these problems and also possibly in reaction to the relatively slow construction of an internal clandestine political network to complement the extensiveness of military structure, the ANC has re-organised and centralised its external bureaucracy. The Revolutionary Council, from 1969 responsible for the formulation of military strategy and staffed jointly by the ANC and the South African Communist Party (SACP), was abolished. It was replaced by a Military Committee, chaired by Umkonto's Commander, Joe Modise; a Political Committee, chaired by the former trade unionist, John Nkadimeng; and a coordinating Joint Committee. The changes emphasised the leading position of the ANC in the ANC-SACP-South African Congress of Trade Unions alliance, for the committees are tightly subject to the authority of the ANC's National Executive. They also represent a recognition of the need for more effective co-ordination and liaison between political and military activity undertaken by the ANC inside South Africa.

Some commentators have attributed an ideological function to this reshaping: Thomas Karis understood the abolition of the Revolutionary Council as underlining 'the pre-eminence of Africans in directing the struggle'.[5] This view was supported in a well-informed anonymous article in the *Sowetan* (29.06.83) which speculated that 'ANC leadership may try to restore a more traditionalist black African image'. Another interpretation of the restructuring links it to a change in strategy — an advance from the phase of 'armed propaganda' to the intensification of 'peoples' war'.[6]

Notwithstanding the Church Street attack which took place shortly after this re-organisation there does not seem much evidence to support the view that the ANC is poised to expand dramatically its military activities.

The ANC is confronted with an increasingly unfavourable international environment. American 'constructive engagement', the fears of Frontline States, and anti-terrorist legislation in the United Kingdom are instances of this. But an encouraging development for the movement has been a shift in Chinese policy. A successful visit by ANC president Tambo in June followed a Chinese call for blacks to unite with progressive whites in defeating apartheid. This was generally interpreted as a repudiation of the Pan Africanist Congress, previously a recipient of Chinese aid. Australia's new Labour government also provided grounds for ANC optimism by requesting the establishment of an ANC office.

1983 probably represents the close of a phase in the ANC's development — construction of a mass political following through armed propaganda. The phase now opening is one in which the ANC will have to channel this popular support into its underground organisational structures. Extensive and discreet political organisation will probably be accompanied by a decline in military activity. In the short term, at least, predictions of strategic retreat seem more sensible than the anticipation of an extension of armed struggle.

Notes

1 The contents of the statement were broadcast on *Capital Radio*, 05.07.83.

2 Text of interview published by AIM press agency (Maputo, August 1983).

3 See *The Times* (London), 13.04.81 and 14.04.81.

4 See Thomas G. Karis, 'Revolution in the making: Black politics in South Africa', *Foreign Affairs*, No 62207, Winter 1983/84, 386; and Carole A. Douglis and Stephen M. Davis, 'Revolt on the Veldt', *Harpers*, December 1983, 37.

5 Karis, 'Revolution in the making', 395.

6 See 'South Africa: People's war now', *Africa Now*, August 1983, 21.

Transport and Political Resistance: Bus Boycotts of 1983

Jeff McCarthy and Mark Swilling

Bus boycotts in various parts of the country during 1983 highlighted a fundamental contradiction in transport policy. On the one hand, the state has created apartheid's spatial separation between community and workplace. On the other hand, the state has to reduce the cost of subsidising millions of commuters who do not earn a living wage.

Proletarianisation in South Africa has been based on the systematic separation of the community and the work-place. This separation depends on a cheap transport system which will not substantially raise the cost of reproducing the work-force. Over a few decades, the South African state, a few transport monopolies, and employers formed an alliance to establish a capitalist transport system that met this requirement. The result was a relatively expensive and inefficient bus and train service that has frequently been the cause of important political struggles.

This article focusses particularly on bus transport. We will argue that severe structural pressures, together with the prolonged and highly politicised bus boycotts in Durban and East London, have thrown the entire transport system into an unprecedented crisis. A coherent solution within the present framework seems unlikely due to the serious contradictions that have broken out between the state, the transport monopolies, and capital. The Welgemoed Commission was given the task of preserving this alliance to prop up the crisis-ridden transport system.[1] But the commission's recommendations will probably precipitate further politicisation of bus transport.

Travelling back in time

The origins of the transport alliance began in the 1930s when the state intervened to reorganise and regulate the transport industry. The Motor Carrier Transportation Act, no. 39 of 1930, was used to squeeze African bus companies and many taxis out of business in Pretoria and on the Reef.[2] This measure not only revealed the racial bias of state policy, it also provided the framework for the monopolisation of the transport industry. By 1940 a cartel dominated the industry. In 1945 several companies merged to form the Public Utility Company (PUTCO). With the transport market safely in their pockets, the bus companies began to increase bus fares.

These hikes triggered the Alexandra bus boycotts of the 1940s. In addition, the Group Areas Act extended the distance between home and work. Together these factors forced the state to agree to subsidise black transport costs (Bantu Services Levy Act, no. 64 of 1952).

After the Evaton and Alexandra bus boycotts in the 1950s, transport policy as it exists today was entrenched with the Bantu Transport Services Act, no. 53 of 1957. This Act transferred responsibility for black transport subsidies from the (then) Native Affairs Department to the Department of Transport.[3] The subsidy has since come from a fund made up of compulsory contributions from employers and state funds.

Although the most serious problems for the transport industry are caused by the separation of work-place and community, the state's transport policy has accepted this as a given. During the 1950s and early 1960s, this policy had to cope with the relocation of inner-city locations. Duncan Village, Cato Manor, Lady Selbourne and Sophiatown, amongst others, were moved to the outskirts of towns, forcing workers to travel an additional 10–25 km to work. In response to these changed conditions, the state evolved the 'frontier commuter' programme. After Umlazi was built as the first 'homeland' town, a new method of reversing African urbanisation became official policy in the late 1960s (General Circular no. 27 of 1967). As a senior state official put it:

> The white man must not govern the black man. That's when the trouble starts. If you could bring the homelands within commuter reach of the growth points, you are solving the so-called problem of urban blacks. You could accommodate them in a homeland where they can own property and govern themselves.[4]

The Riekert Commission encouraged this process on condition that commuters would not have to travel more than 70 km a day. By 1979 there

were nearly 700 000 frontier commuters − an increase of 147% since
1970.[5] 51,7% of these commuters travel by bus. Only 17,8% use the train
and a further 18,5% use various other modes of transport. 46,5% of all
frontier commuters work in the Pretoria, East London and greater Durban areas.[6] The last two areas saw extended bus boycotts in 1983.

Transport policy today

There is evidence to suggest that the state was oblivious to the effects that
the relocation of three-and-a-half million people between 1960 and 1980
would have on the transport system. There was even a serious suggestion
in 1970 that South Africa's entire proletariat be located in the bantustans
from where they could be ferried to employment areas by a sophisticated
high-speed transport system.[7] It was utopian experiments like these that
blew up in the face of the state's transport planners when they began to
count the cost of transporting labour over increasingly greater distances.
In 1982 officials in the Transvaal Provincial Administration reckoned that
R240-m a year was needed to solve South Africa's transport problems.
But only R50-m from the Urban Transport Fund was spent on projects
in the five major metropolitan areas (*Star*, 12.08.83). In July 1983 Don
Macleod, Durban's city engineer, predicted that Durban's entire
transport structure would collapse by the end of 1984. The central state
had promised R19,5-m for the improvement of transport facilities. Only
R6,5-m materialised (*DN*, 21.07.83). The growing commuter population,
which increased by about 70% between 1960 and 1980 exacerbated this
shortfall.[8] Noot surprisingly, the Welgemoed Commission's primary task
was to investigate this fiscal crisis in order to find ways of reducing the
cost of subsidisation which reached the R162-m mark in 1983.

Since 1957, the Department of Transport has subsidised transportation
of bona fide employees. The size of the subsidy is calculated on two factors: the operating costs of the company concerned, and the ability of the
commuter to pay the economic fare. The subsidy goes directly to the
transport company, not the consumer. The calculation of the economic
fare recognises the right of transport companies to make a profit. The
subsidy is equivalent to the difference between the actual fare paid by
bona fide workers for a weekly clip-card, and the economic fare. In 1982
the commuters paid an average of about 50% of the economic tariff,
employers paid 13%, and the state contributed 37% (a substantial amount
of this came from profits from the state-run liquor industry and the Dur-

ban–Rand pipeline service).[9]

The transport monopolies are the state's primary partners in the alliance that holds the transport system together. They are a mixture of publicly and privately owned undertakings that fall into four categories:

1. the state, through its South African Transport Services (SATS);
2. semi-state corporations, such as the Corporation for Economic Development which runs the Ciskei Transport Company;
3. local authorities which provide services within their own areas, like Durban and Johannesburg;
4. private operators which include giants like PUTCO in the Transvaal and Natal, Tollgate Holdings in the Cape, United Transport in the Transvaal and Natal, and small owner/operator undertakings in certain areas like Durban.

Except for certain concerns in Durban, the entire transport industry is regulated by the National Transport Commission (NTC). Each area has a Local Road Transportation Board (LRTB) which the NTC controls. The transport companies have to get permission from the LRTB to operate on particular routes. The NTC's policy has been to restrict competition by granting monopolies over particular routes. The NTC has followed this policy on the grounds that monopoly facilitates economies of scale and large revenues, which in turn keep fares down.[10] In reality the exact opposite is the case. To increase its fares, the bus company has to submit an application to the NTC or LRTB. It must support the application with latest running cost figures. The application is published in the government gazette and objections from the public are heard. The LRTB/NTC can then approve or refuse the fare increase, or recommend that the Department of Transport increase the subsidy to cover the new running costs. The two major transport companies, PUTCO and Tollgate Holdings, are monopolies which control a range of subsidiary companies that supply them with fuel, maintenance facilities, advertising, insurance and properties. Running costs may increase on paper, but the bus company pays these increased costs to subsidiaries of the same monopoly and hence there is no total loss of profits. This monopoly situation does not affect the transport companies' applications. Compannies continue to make profits and still receive subsidies.

For the year ending 30 June 1981, PUTCO's annual report reveals that it made a R5,5-m profit. In 1980 alone, the state gave PUTCO R40-m in formal subsidies (*Star*, 29.10.80). The annual benefit from dividends for

PUTCO's shareholders[11] was approximately 69%. City Tramways, which is wholly owned by Tollgate Holdings, enabled shareholders to receive annual benefits from dividends of approximately 67%. The stock exchange price for PUTCO's shares increased by 600% between 1976 and 1981.[12] But these profits come from the tax payers' money and the high fares from commuters. The burden of increasing fares has been shifted onto the commuters instead of the employers. As fares have risen, the proportion paid in by employers has steadily decreased while it has increased for commuters. Employers' approximate contributions decreased as follows:

1974–5: 32%
1976: 16%
1980–1: 14%
1981–2: 13%.[13]

Capital's minor role in subsidising transport ended in 1983, when the Black Transport Services Amendment Act was passed. This was designed to correct the imbalance between the employers' and Department of Transport's contributions. The Minister now has the power to increase the levy on employers after 12 months notice.[14] In October the chairperson of the NTC announced that employers' monthly contributions would increase from R1 to R3 per employee in certain areas. The Associated Chambers of Commerce objected, arguing that certain employers would have to retrench workers and resort to mechanisation. The total inadequacy of the measure is clear. The employers' contribution will increase, at most, by 3%, while there will be a downward pressure on wages.

The alliance that controls the transport system has been under severe strain. The underlying structural cause was the escalating cost of transporting an increasing number of commuters over longer distances. The state was faced with the need to reduce their share of the cost without restructuring the spatial separation of work-place and community. But any shift of the burden onto capital would either result in greater mechanisation or a downward pressure on wages.

The transport monopolies are not concerned how the subsidy is raised as long as it reaches them in the end. Either way their interests, which can always be backed up by the political threat to increase fares, do not coincide with the state's; nor are they in favour of an unconditional phasing out of the subsidy system. It is against this background that the Welgemoed Commission's recommendations must be understood. The commission chose to respond to three basic conditions inherent in the emergent socio-spatial formation: the problem of regional co-ordination;

the difficulties involved in regulating the costs of reproducing the transport system; and the historical implications for political legitimacy.

Regional co-ordination

Historically the problem of movement had been managed, at least at the level of bus transportation, by local authorities. (This was subject to the regulation of a national advisory body.) Both the Driessen Report (1974) and the Welgemoed Commission (1983) argued that this scale of operation was now too small. Travel to urban centres from far flung group areas or bantustans presents a problem for transportation planners. In a journey from home to work, a worker might have to travel through several national, regional and local government areas, each with its own public transport system and transportation policies. Hence, much of the Driessen Commission Report, and the bulk of the First Interim Report of the Welgemoed Commission dealt with problems of regional co-ordination between metropolitan bus services. To reorganise bus routes or adjust tariffs required consultation with bus companies from several local authorities in South Africa, and those from bantustans.

In the view of the Welgemoed Commission, the Department of Transport and the National Transport Commission should be responsible for resolving regional co-ordination. These bodies should form, and assume a directorship role of new Regional Transport Co-ordinating Boards and Metropolitan Transport Advisory Boards. These boards would assume the new tasks of co-ordination. Current trends in state policy reflect a tendency towards greater administrative centralisation bedevilled by an expanding contradiction: the fixed geographical units of reproduction established in the 1950s on the one hand, and the rapidly expanding geographical extent of urban production and exchange in the 1970s and 1980s on the other.

Costs of reproduction

The entire Second Interim Report of the Welgemoed Commission concerned itself with the problem of tariffs and subsidies. Surprisingly the commission did not emphasise further privatisation of bus services. It rejected ideas that subsidies will become redundant if all restrictions on passenger transport are lifted and the free market is allowed to determine

fares.[15] The commission steadfastly defended the principle of subsidisation. In particular, it argues that 'the Government began to pay subsidies
to the workers so as to enable them to be economically active while at
the same time retaining their family ties and so as to make sources of
labour available to the employers of the Republic of South Africa'.[16] The
argument, in short, is that the state must intervene to secure labour for
capital under conditions where the costs of reproducing workers outstrip
wages.

The Welgemoed Commission's interest in bus fares and subsidies did
not come simply from industrialists lobbying for efficient transport services for labour. Nor was it based on the irate cries of parliamentarians
about a budgetary item for which there is no political constituency. The
commission was influenced by memoranda from the bus companies
which pushed for fare and subsidy increases.[17] But much of the concern
about tariffs and subsidies derived from media and police warnings.
These highlighted the political significance of bus boycotts in response
to fare increases. The commission noted the effects of these boycotts with
apprehension.[18] The Second Interim Report, for example, adopted the
view that bus boycotts resulted in 'the politicisation of public transport',
and that this was the unfortunate result of the work of 'agitators':

> It is an unfortunate fact that in South Africa public transport, particularly public bus
> transport, is highly politicised. Because large numbers of people are brought together
> . . . in circumstances in which the group largely has a shared destiny, it is only to be
> expected that shrewd observers would see opportunities for making political capital
> from the situation.[19]

The commissioners, however, were not so naive to assume that bus
boycotts were caused exclusively by the work of activists bent on populist
foment. They also indicated some understanding of the structural context
of bus transportation as an object of popular struggle:

> For understandable reasons the entire question of tariff increases is one of the most sen-
> sitive aspects of the problem (of politicisation). If this potential for destabilisation is
> seen against the background of interaction between wage levels, the profitability of
> operation, quality of the service, user convenience, the human dignity of the user in
> particular and many other factors, each of which may contain the germ of possible
> dissatisfaction, it is laudable that users of many services make use of the services with
> so much understanding and responsibility. . . . In the South African set-up, further-
> more, there is the question of Group Areas within the country that is exploited to a large
> extent to whip up feelings and it appears that cross-border transport is also exploited
> and will become a greater source of conflict in the future than it is at present.[20]

The commission, however, offered no real solutions to these structural problems and implicitly favoured the use of repression to contain the activities of 'agitators'. On the question of subsidies, the commission found that 'each passenger should pay the whole of his economic fare himself'; and it reported that it was 'against the use of subsidies primarily for the redistribution of wealth and is of the opinion that subsidies should not be used for purposes other than economic ones where these are involved'.[21] The commission conceded that 'there is sufficient justification for the payment of subsidies to worker commuters who cannot pay their own transport costs'. Nevertheless it was 'of the opinion that it is necessary to phase out subsidies in the long term'.[22] In short, the outlook for workers with regard to bus fares in the future appears bleak.

Political implications

If the recommendations of the Welgemoed Commission with regard to bus tariffs and subsidies are adopted, they are likely to intensify the 'politicisation of public transport'. The commission's attack on black taxi operators will probably augment this politicisation. This move against taxis is meant to compensate transport monopolies if subsidies disappear. Should this prop be withdrawn, then the 'unhealthy competition' of taxis would be eliminated by legislation.[23] The transport monopolies support this suggestion because they are perturbed by the large number of commuters who use taxis.[24] The taxi associations have vociferously rejected the idea.[25]

The working class will be confronted with ever-rising fares and transport will continue to be a crucial site of struggle. But the petty bourgeois transport sector will not necessarily form an alliance with the working class as in the 1940s and 1950s.[26] Many workers in the trade unions point out that taxi drivers raised their fares during the bus boycotts. These workers see no reason why they should help the taxi operators now that they are in trouble. This does not rule out an alliance between commuters and taxi operators to resist the consequences of the Welgemoed Commission. But any such alliance between petty-bourgeois led community-based struggles and working class struggles would be politically vexed. In our view, this problem may be solved by a political culture which moves away from the work-place/living-place dichotomy imposed by the state. Transport may provide an objective site of struggle that links up oppression in the township and exploitation at the work-place by connecting them within the process of capitalist accumulation. The way these links are presented will depend on how progressive political and working class organisations pose the question of transport.

A number of surveys in recent years have revealed how dissatisfied black commuters are with the transport system.[27] The NITRR survey was based on 1 045 interviews with commuters from the Bophuthatswana towns surrounding Pretoria. The report documented high levels of dissatisfaction with bus transport, particularly cost, crowding and travel time. Transport consumes between 5% and 20% of working class incomes. Unlike food or clothing, travelling costs are a non-substitutable item in the domestic budget. Consequently, working class households maintain a fragile balance between food and clothing expenditures which must be reduced as bus fares increase. This balance becomes particularly strained during a recession. Real wage levels decline and bus companies experience downward pressures on profits and therefore press for fare increases. Within this context a bus fare increase can be the last straw for the working class.

In this light we can understand the working class experiences that lead to bus boycotts. Ever since workers have had to travel to work in large numbers, they have frequently identified the transport system as part of the cause of their exploitation.[28] A racially exclusive state that excluded the black petty bourgeoisie from the transport industry, has often united working class commuters and aspirant transport capitalists against the transport monopolies and the state.[29] In December 1982, bus boycotts broke out in the greater Durban area. They lasted until May–June 1983. This was followed by the more publicised East London bus boycott that began in July, and continued into 1984.

The Durban case

Durban's urban form resembles a 'T'. Industrial development stretches along the northern and southern coastal regions and an interior corridor extends up to the Pinetown-New Germany industrial complex. In 1976 there were approximately 475 600 blacks and 120 000 whites employed in the area. The large majority of blacks live in Indian group areas within the Durban municipal area and in large townships like Umlazi and KwaMashu which are part of KwaZulu. Durban's present urban form was the product of the drastic spatial restructuring that began in the 1950s. In the 1940s, for example, 90% of the 1 100-strong labour force in

Dunlop's Congella plant came from shack settlements and compounds within four miles of the factory. By 1965, two-thirds commuted from KwaMashu and Umlazi. In 1961, half of the work-force at the Kingsgate Clothing plant in Durban central were Indian workers living within three miles of the factory. By 1970, after the clearance of Cato Manor, no less than 22% of the staff lived in Chatsworth some ten miles from the factory.[30]

Today 368 829 black commuters use public transport each day. In 1978 there were about 201 309 bus commuters (84 000 at peak hours), and 167 520 train commuters (71 750 at peak hours).[31] In addition about 13 000 taxis and 5 500 private cars cater for the remaining transport needs.[32] The average commuting time from KwaMashu and Umlazi to the employment area is about 45 and 50 minutes respectively.[33] Excluding the considerable walking and queueing times (which can be as much as 50 minutes), commuters spend more than one-and-a-half hours each day getting to and from work. In addition, Durban's commuters experience further irritations. There are no time tables, buses are frequently late, wages are deducted for late arrivals, leisure time is diminished, buses wait longer than is necessary at bus stops to fill the bus, unofficial stops are made to pick up additional passengers, and no service is provided at night or on the weekends.[34]

Durban has a unique transport system. There are 200 different bus operators who own a total of 1 600 buses. The Durban Transport Management Board (DTMB) owns 386 buses and PUTCO owns 375 buses.[35] A few companies run 50 or more buses. But the majority are Indian owner/operator concerns with one or two buses. These small companies are extremely bitter about the Welgemoed Commission's recommendations that they should be incorporated into a rationalised monopoly of some kind.[36] In this case petty-bourgeois transport interests, including both small bus companies and taxis, share a serious objection with working class commuters to the Welgemoed Commission. In addition to this, the failure of the industrial decentralisation strategy to cope with burgeoning unemployment in the frontier towns has led to the expansion of squatter communities on the outskirts of many Durban townships. It was in these townships that the boycott tended to last longest (eg. Inanda).

The contradictions of the transport system appeared most clearly in Durban. On the one hand an extremely inefficient service had to extend its operation to keep pace with the growing distance between home and work. On the other, a multiplicity of overlapping state, municipal and bantustan structures have resulted in the inadequate provision of services. Durban's local authorities initiated an overarching revision of their transport policy to qualify for more funds from the central state. However, Umlazi and KwaMashu are not part of the Durban Metropolitan Transport Area. Improvement projects in these areas do not qualify for subsidies from the central state. One report concluded: 'If metropolitan transport planning is to succeed in Durban, this problem will have to be resolved.'[37] When the central state approved Durban's transport plans in 1980, improvements to the black bus service got a low priority.[38] Here lies the root cause of Durban's highly inefficient bus service.

The bus boycott that broke out in December 1982 affected Inanda, Clermont, Lamontville, Klaarwater, St Wendolins and KwaMashu. In each area a Local Commuter Committee (LCC) emerged to co-ordinate the boycott. These in turn united to form a Joint Commuter Committee (JCC). The demands of the JCC were: 1. full recognition of the JCC as the sole representative of the commuters; 2. that the DTMB and PUTCO agree to meet the JCC; 3. that the bus fare increases be dropped or else these companies must withdraw their services to make way for 'cheaper bus services of the people's choice' (presumably the Indian owner/operators).[39] Although the transport monopolies managed to win in the end, the boycott did make four significant gains. Firstly, the formation of LCCs in each area facilitated the growth of community organisations in the greater Durban area; secondly, the formation of the JCC was an important step towards forging inter-township unity; thirdly, a well supported petition managed to popularise the JCC leadership; fourthly, the extensive discussions, pamphleteering and participation generated a new political consciousness.

There are two significant features about the Durban boycott. Firstly, it generated the formation of progressive community organisations in areas that were previously unorganised. This provided the community leaders with a ready-made constituency that they have since managed to develop and enlarge. Ideologically, this movement unambiguously favours the United Democratic Front. Secondly, the JCC represents the interests of disempowered commuters and as such is a challenge to a system that consciously excludes them from the decision-making process.

It is arguable that a bus boycott broke out in the Durban area for four basic reasons. Firstly, after the greater Pretoria region, it has the largest frontier commuter population, who have suffered severe dislocations as relocation strategies have taken their course. Secondly, there are large numbers of marginalised poverty-stricken people who may not be commuters, but who live in the interstices of the frontier towns placing an added pressure on domestic incomes. Thirdly, DTMB and PUTCO offer particularly inefficient bus services. Fourthly, the large number of taxis and the owner/operator bus companies which provide cheaper services than the bigger companies, provide alternative transport for boycotters. This is a crucial factor for the success of any bus boycott. The relative absence of alternative transport in the Pretoria area may explain why a boycott did not break out there.

The East London case

The East London bus boycott began in July 1983. Its duration and the political consciousness of its participants, coupled with the failure of unprecedented state terror to break the boycott, make it one of the most important struggles of the year.[40]

East London is a minor port city that is based on a small crisis-ridden local economy dominated by the food and textile sectors. One of the most politically volatile regions in the country, it relies totally on the state's decentralisation strategies. It is located in an area where unemployment is as high as 40%, and it feels the political consequences of drastic population relocation measures. These are all underpinned by the notoriously coercive rule of the Ciskei administration.

These conditions have structured the nature of the East London working class. There are 51 613 workers employed in the industrial, commercial, domestic and services sectors.[41] Of these, 65% live in Mdantsane and 32% in Duncan Village. It is significant that a large number (47%) are industrial workers. The East London working class is unique in many ways. Its members earn the lowest wages in South Africa, this being directly related to the level of unemployment. Africans comprise a higher proportion of the work-force (78%) than other areas in the country. Most East London workers are drawn from the Xhosa language group. There is a fairly high proportion of Africans in skilled and semi-skilled jobs.[42] These factors help to explain the dramatic series of working class struggles of the last few years which shaped the democratic trade unionism associated with SAAWU in the region.

Duncan Village is located within a few kilometres of the major industrial concentration on the West Bank and Central Business District.

Mdantsane, where most of the working class lives, lies approximately 25 km from the major work zones. The reasons for the relocation of workers to Mdantsane are similar to those applicable to townships in many other South African cities. During the 1930s and 1940s hostility developed amongst East London's white residents towards the physical proximity of poverty-stricken black slums. This pressure resulted in several commissions of enquiry to consider conditions in Duncan Village and to establish a new peripheral 'location' (the Thornton and Welsh Commissions). When the Nationalist government came to power and implemented its twin race-space policies of group areas and 'homeland' development, the present Mdantsane site suggested itself. By 1963 the first houses were built in Mdantsane and relocation began. Mdantsane satisfied local authority demands for an 'invisible' black work-force and it was consistent with the central state's ambitions to contain urban black political aspirations to rural townships dominated by pre-capitalist elites (in this case those of the Ciskei).

An attitude survey conducted by the authors in Mdantsane in July 1981 found that 70% of all the working class respondents identified transport as their most serious problem. This was followed by crime (59%), housing (32%), educational facilities (19%) and services (17%). This contrasts drastically with the concerns of the petty-bourgeois respondents, 65% of whom identified crime and the general threat to property as their most serious problem. Only 36% of them identified transport as their most serious problem. In Mdantsane, in short, transport is a working class issue.

In 1982, 66,9% of the commuters travelling between Mdantsane and their places of work used the bus, whereas 22,7% used the train, 1,4% used taxis, 6,4% went by car or pirate taxi, and 2,5% used various other modes of transport.[43] The travail of travelling to work usually begins before dawn. Commuters walk for about ten minutes on crime-ridden streets to reach the nearest bus stop. They catch a bus to the central terminus in Mdantsane, where they join long queues for a second bus to East London. Every commuter spends two to three hours a day travelling to and from work. Transport is not merely a necessary inconvenience, but a daily struggle experienced by nearly 25 000 commuters who are processed en masse through a central terminus twice a day and get compressed into 276 buses. Matravers is correct when he concludes that the Mdantsane public transport system is 'a service to employers and not to travellers'.[44]

The bus company (the Ciskei Transport Corporation) is jointly owned by the Ciskei state and the Economic Development Corporation. It was formed in 1975 when the previous owners, Tollgate Holdings, were forced to sell out after a two month long bus boycott over fare increases. Sebe initiated a take-over bid of the crippled company believing that if the Ciskei state owned it, the people would support it. This assumption was refuted when vigilantes had to be used to break the boycott. Today the widely accepted rumour that Sebe is a director of CTC is evinced as proof that his terroristic actions to break the 1983 boycott were designed to protect his own interests.

The CTC bus service is notoriously inefficient. Buses are frequently late making commuters wait for up to two hours. To avoid arriving late at work, commuters are often forced to walk or spend extra money on a taxi fare in addition to the money they have already spent on weekly tickets. The buses are dirty and broken windows are left unrepaired. Rainy days are intolerable due to the lack of bus shelters. A further grievance is that the bus time table was drawn up without consulting the workers. This means that bus times do not always coincide with shift times. In 1980 SAAWU took up grievances associated with the bus service. Four demands were drawn up at a mass meeting and the union leadership was mandated to take them to the CTC. They were: 1. the provision of bus shelters; 2. scrapping of the weekly ticket and the provision of a ticket that was only invalidated when it was used; 3. students and pensioners should pay half price; 4. cushions must be put on the cold wooden benches. These demands were ignored.

Dissatisfaction with the bus service reached a head when the CTC increased the fares on 13 July 1983. The only people consulted were leading members of the Ciskei National Independence Party (CNIP), community councillors and various other unrepresentative bodies. The problem with this, one worker said, 'was that all the people who had been consulted do not use the buses'. The commuters elected representatives who formed the Committee of Ten. The CTC refused to meet this body and within a week a boycott began. During the first few days the commuters began to walk the 25 km to work. They sang freedom songs, taunted the police and many were drawn into the emotionally explosive atmosphere of solidarity. As police began to set up road blocks and harass people to stop what was in effect a mass demonstration the commuters began to use the trains.

The railway line runs along the outskirts of Mdantsane and forms the Ciskei's border with South Africa. The trains which are run by the South African Transport Services have been crucial for the success of the boycott. They provide the only legal public space where commuters can meet and discuss the daily progress of the boycott.

The Ciskei authorities used the police, army and hired vigilantes to try and break the boycott by forcing people to board the buses. Despite the murder of over 20 people, extensive harassment and victimisation of the innocent, arbitrary assaults, mass torture in the Sisa Dukashe Soccer Stadium and the mysterious disappearance of hundreds of people, the commuters have remained obstinate and defiant.

The turning point for the boycott came during the cold early hours of 4 August. Police and soldiers formed an armed human blockade at the Mount Ruth and Edgeton stations to prevent commuters from catching the train. After hesitating, the crowd advanced a few paces to be met by the threat of raised guns. They stopped and someone shouted: 'Don't shoot, we are not at war.' Without warning the police consciously fired into the crowd. Witnesses claimed that 15 were left dead and 35 wounded. Sebe had declared war and the workers were willing to take him on.

The 4 August massacre had an electrifying effect on the political consciousness of the people. Within hours the boycott was transformed from a rejection of fare increases into a political struggle against the Ciskei state. Many former CNIP supporters tore up their membership cards and vowed never to use the buses again. One worker commented: 'After the shooting, what people learnt was that the bus company has directors in the Cabinet. When the shooting took place, the bus company and the Ciskei Government had joined.' On the trains this summation of political and economic demands was reflected in the emergence of new slogans: 'Away with Sebe, Amandla!' became the main one. In December, after his release from detention, a Committee of Ten member summed up the mood: 'The people say the buses are full of blood and when they pass the buses they smell the blood . . . the people have realised that they need transport but the Ciskei Government must have no strings attached to it.'

The Ciskei state responded to this new mood by declaring a state of emergency on the same day as the massacre, followed by the banning of SAAWU a month later. The boycott continued unabated. The central state registered its concern with top level visits from Foreign Minister Pik Botha, police commissioner General Johan Coetzee and security police head Major-General Steenkamp. In the end it was not the boycott that began to crumble, but the Ciskei state itself. Seventeen of its top officials were detained including the head of the security police, Charles Sebe, and a number of cabinet ministers. Towards the end of September a number of petty-bourgeois elements set up a Committee of Twenty. These entrepreneurs had shops surrounding the central bus terminus which were seriously affected by the absence of the commuters. Their main objective was to find a conciliatory way to end the boycott after the release of the Committee of Ten on 4 November.

At a mass meeting in early December, the commuters resolved to continue the boycott. Their determination leaves little doubt that the CTC will never be able to operate 'normally' again. As the transport manager of the East London municipality admitted, 'I don't see the boycott ending, the people don't want to use the buses.' The Committee of Ten has demanded the formation of a new bus company. It is unlikely that the East London municipality or industrialists will be willing to take on such a task. Furthermore, it is estimated that by 1987 there will be 40 000 bus commuters needing 610 buses. This requires a doubling of the present size of the bus service for Mdantsane which will only be possible if the transport industry and the central state's transport policy is totally transformed. The long term solution to East London's transport problem, which is intricately bound up with the political struggle in the Ciskei, lies in the re-incorporation of Mdantsane into a unitary post-apartheid South Africa.

It remains to be seen what the effects of the new Ciskei transport policy will be. This policy is based on the recently completed Commission of Enquiry into the Economic Development of the Ciskei. Policy planners have accepted the commission's recommendation that development of private transport such as buses, minibuses, taxis and trucks should be unrestricted. This is based on the belief that deregulation of transport will depoliticise the issue. But these ideas contradict the Welgemoed Commission's recommendations that have been accepted by the central state and will be applicable to East London. It is unlikely that an aggressive free market transport policy cheek by jowl with a centralised pro-monopoly transport policy will depoliticise transport.

Conclusion

Workers and the state are on a collision course regarding bus transportation. The Welgemoed Commission, on the one hand, responded to an emerging fiscal crisis. It suggested phasing out subsidies; limiting competition from black transport entrepreneurs to make up for losses that transport monopolies would incur from waning subsidies; increasing centralisation of transport and increases in profits for transport monopolies. The Ciskei administration's transport policy is slightly different. It seeks to enlarge its base amongst the underdeveloped petty bourgeoisie which will be strengthened by a free market transport policy. But the final effect of the two policies will be the same — the maintenance of a disempowered commuter population.

Workers, on the other hand, have responded through mass direct action to express their dissatisfaction with both the economic nature of fare increases and the political nature of the state's reproduction policies. The future of this contradiction between the interests of workers and the state will depend to a large extent on two factors:

1. the way the transportation problem is posed and analysed by working class and progressive political organisations;
2. the degree to which the Welgemoed Commission's recommendations will succeed in reinforcing the alliance between the state, capital and the transport monopolies.

In the final analysis the solutions demanded by boycotting commuters in 1983 can only be met by the restructuring of the spatial relations between community and work-place that is only possible in a democratic post-apartheid society, based on new relations of production and reproduction.

Notes

1 Republic of South Africa, 'Commission of Inquiry into Bus Passenger Transportation in the RSA', (P.J. Welgemoed), 1982.

2 A.W. Stadler, ' "A long way to walk": Bus boycotts in Alexandra, 1940–1945', *Working Papers in Southern African Studies II*, edited by P. Bonner (Johannesburg, 1981).

3 E.M. Voges, 'Accessibility, Transport and the Spatial Structure of South African Cities: An Historic Perspective', (Technical Report, RT/9/83, National Institute for Transport and Road Research, CSIR, 1983), 33.

4 Quoted in B. Creecy, 'Urbanization in the Homelands', *Debate on Housing*, Information Publication 4, edited by DSG/SARS (Johannesburg, 1980), 50.

5 A. Lemon, 'Migrant Labour and Frontier Commuters: Re-organizing South Africa's Black Labour Supply', in *Living Under Apartheid*, edited by D. Smith (London, 1982), 83.

6 Computed from figures quoted in Lemon, 'Migrant Labour', 84.

7 J.J. Burger, 'Transport systems as a basis for the application of a policy of Separate Development, paper delivered to the South African Bureau of Racial Affairs Congress on 'Homeland Development — A Programme for the Seventies', 1970.

8 Republic of South Africa, 'Report of the Committee of Inquiry into Urban Transport Facilities in the Republic', (J. Driessen), RP60/74, 26.

9 Voges, 'Accessibility, Transport and the Spatial Structure', 34.

10 Report of the National Transport Commission, 1980, quoted in Human Awareness Programme, *Black Public Road Transport: An Assessment*, Special Report, 3, (Johannesburg, 1983), 23.

11 PUTCO is a public company with 400 shares. Gaetano, the managing director of the holding company owns 54% of them.

12 Legal Resources Centre, 'First Report of the Committee of the Urban Transport Project', (mimeo, 1983), 19–20.

13 Computed from figures quoted in *Survey of Race Relations in South Africa, 1983* (Johannesburg, 1983), 305, in combination with figures quoted in the Welgemoed Commission Report, 37.

14 *Survey of Race Relations, 1983*, 306.

15 Republic of South Africa, 'Second Interim Report of the Commission of Inquiry into Bus Transportation in the Republic of South Africa', (Pretoria, 1983), RP 103/1982, para 4.31.

16 RP 103/1982, para 4.34.

17 RP 103/1982, Annexure B, 81–83.

18 RP 103/1982, para 3.43–3.49.

19 RP 103/1982, para 3.44–3.45.

20 RP 103/1982, para 3.46–3.47.

21 RP 103/1982, 50–51.

22 RP 103/1982, 51.

23 Republic of South Africa, 'Final Report of the Commission of Inquiry into Bus Transportation in the Republic of South Africa', 1983, 24–5.

24 *NM*, 15.07.83.

25 *RDM*, D 19.07.83.

26 T. Lodge, *Black Politics in South Africa Since 1945*, (Johannesburg, 1983), 153–188.

27 Some of these surveys were conducted by: National Institute of Transport and Road Research (NITRR), *Pretoria Black Commuting Study*, (Pretoria, 1982); J.H. Ehlers, *Pendelaars in Kwa Ndebele*, Human Sciences Research Council, Navorsingsbevinding M-N-98 (Pretoria, 1982); *FM*, 25.03.83; evidence of the Legal Resources Centre to the Welgemoed Commission.

28 See R. Ellsworth, 'The simplicity of the native mind: Black passengers on the South African Railways in the early twentieth century', Paper presented at the African Studies Institute Seminar, (University of Witwatersrand, 25.04.83).

29 Stadler, 'A long way to walk'; and Lodge, *Black Politics*.

30 B.S. Young, 'Journey to Work Patterns and Labour Sheds in the Durban Region', *South African Geography*, 4(3), 1973.

31 Computed from figures quoted in Durban Metropolitan Advisory Board, *Interim Transport Plan, 1980–1985*, (Durban, 1980), para 1.3.10–1.4.1.

32 Durban Metropolitan Advisory Board, *Interim Transport Plan*, para 1.4.2.

33 Young, 'Journey to Work', 240.

34 Human Awareness Programme, *Black Public Road Transport*, 14–16.

35 Durban Metropolitan Advisory Board, *Interim Transport Plan*, para 5.1.3.

36 *UKUSA*, January 1983.

37 Durban Metropolitan Advisory Board, *Interim Transport Plan*, para 5.1.3.

38 A.B. Eksteen (Director General of the Department of Transport), to Director of Roads, Natal Provincial Adminnistration, 21 May 1980.

39 *UKUSA*, January 1983.
40 See M. Swilling, ' "The Buses Smell of Blood": The East London Bus Boycott, 1983',
   in *South African Labour Bulletin*, 9(6), 1984.
41 D. Jenkinson, 'East London-Mdantsane Commuter Transport Study', Report Number
   719/3667, May 1982, East London Municipality.
42 A. Hirsch and A. Kooy, 'Industry and Employment in East London', *South African
   Labour Bulletin*, 7(4/5), February 1982, 50.
43 Jenkinson, 'East London-Mdantsane Commuter Transport'.
44 D.D. Matravers, ' "It's all in a day's work" ', in *Mdantsane: Transitional City*, edited by
   G. Cook and J. Opland (Grahamstown, 1980), 40.

State Strategy and Popular Response at the Local Level

Jeremy Grest and Heather Hughes

The new constitution dominated the political scene in South Africa during 1983. The constitution makes local government an 'own affair' where it affects members of one race group only. When a local government matter affects the interests of more than one group, it falls under 'general affairs'.

One of the hallmarks of the local government system is the separation of Africans from whites, coloureds and Indians. The state acknowledges no common political future.

Rapid urbanisation and economic recession have sharpened local conflict in recent years. Different manifestations of the local state influence the shape which resistance and popular struggles take. The new local dispensation is in part a ruling class response to these struggles, which it seeks to contain and channel. These state initiatives have met with a varied response. Taken together, these initiatives and responses form the two main themes of this article.[1]

The state's gift to the people

Autonomy is a key concept in the state's planning for the local level. The question of autonomy assumes different forms for Black Local Authorities (BLAs)[2] and their coloured and Indian counterparts, the Local Affairs and Management Committees (LACs and MCs). For Africans, autonomy means the assumption of certain functions previously exercised by the administration boards and a few additional new ones. For coloured and Indian committees eventual separate municipal status is envisaged.

At the beginning of 1983, the government appointed a special cabinet committee to investigate the rights of urban Africans outside the 'homelands'. Its deliberations have not yet been made public but there were other indications through the year of the state's strategy for Africans in urban areas. During discussions in parliament on the Promotion of Local Government Bill, the PFP tried to move an amendment for African local authorities to be included within the ambit of the Bill. This was disallowed. Minister of Constitutional Development Chris Heunis stated flatly: 'The development of authority structures for the blacks (i.e. Africans) . . . will follow a different path' (*RDM*, 25.06.83).

The PC proposals advocated links between BLAs, metropolitan structures and also possibly bantustans or a confederation. Chairman of the Riekert Commission P.J. Riekert, of the Western Transvaal Administration Board, suggested a formal link between the BLAs and the bantustans. The purpose of BLAs, in his view, is 'to defuse pent-up frustration and grievances against administration from Pretoria' (*RDM*, 29.08.83). The 'autonomy' so heavily advertised as the main attraction of the BLAs will mirror in miniature the kind of 'autonomy' (called 'independence') offered at a higher level. The two are very closely associated in some official minds.

Predictions made at the start of 1983 that autonomy for Indian and coloured areas would be a reality within the year proved to be over-hasty (*NM* 21.01.83). 'Autonomy' has been rejected by most LACs, MCs and community groups. When Isipingo became autonomous, Prospecton, an industrial area nearby, was excised and reallocated to white-controlled Amanzimtoti. Albie Stowman, chairman of the Durban coloured LAC commented: 'I hate to think of any autonomous coloured local authority anywhere in South Africa. Our areas are purely residential dormitories' (*NM*, 21.01.83). It was felt that the areas in question were part of the cities concerned. They had contributed to their development and therefore should not be excised as the government intends (*NM*, 26.01.83). Civic associations reject autonomy on the grounds that residents will have to bear very heavy increases in service costs (*Leader*, 22.04.83).

Lenasia: fragmentation under apartheid

In Johannesburg the publication of the City Council's budget in June gave rise to speculation, denied by the city treasurer, that the municipality intended foisting autonomy on the coloured and Indian townships under its control (*Post*, 29.06.83). Lenasia, an Indian township about 30 km south-west of Johannesburg has been the scene of a developing confrontation between the civic group, the Federation of Residents' Associations (FRA), the various state-recognised local representative bodies and the several local authorities controlling the area.

Until December 1983, the Johannesburg City Council controlled most of Lenasia, and constituted the Lenasia Management Committee (LMC) as its representative body. Since February the Transvaal Peri Urban Board (PUB) took control of Lenasia extensions eight to eleven which fell outside the Council's boundary. The PUB constituted its own Consultative Committee (LCC) for this area. In addition, the Department of Community Development controlled all housing matters in Lenasia. The FRA called for the Johannesburg City Council to assume control over the whole area. It also campaigned against the high rates in extensions eight to eleven since the PUB take-over.

The LMC and LCC for their part rejected the idea of autonomy for Lenasia and called for extensions eight to eleven to be re-incorporated under Johannesburg City Council control. The LCC was also forced to take a stand against the high monthly water and electricity accounts served on residents by the PUB, and Chairman Mr Pillay denounced the Group Areas Act and separate development (*RDM*, 04.08.83). However, in November, the LMC voted to accept further delegation of powers from the Johannesburg City Council. The vote was taken in the face of warnings from the Transvaal Indian Congress and the FRA. These two organisations said that such moves would introduce autonomy 'by the back door' and would provoke a full scale campaign organised by these two bodies (*RDM*, 12.11.83).

In December the Johannesburg City Council, acting on instructions from the provincial administration, granted Lenasia autonomy. The LMC will now prepare an annual budget for approval by the City Council. It will also have greater powers over housing, grants-in-aid and financial assistance, shopping hours and licences. TIC President Dr Jassat has said that the decision still leaves real financial control in the hands of the City Council. He argued that LMC control over housing in the face of a critical shortage could open the way to mismanagement and corruption. 'The government has made it quite clear that a system of integrated local authorities is not possible under the new constitution and we see this as the start of ethnic local government,' commented Jassat on Lenasia's autonomy (*S Trib Herald*, 04.12.83).

48 Politics and Resistance

The future in the present?

Five Natal towns already 'enjoy' autonomy. A brief look at some salient features of these boards in 1983 may illuminate the future of autonomous bodies in other areas.

In Stanger, in what was heralded as an 'unprecedented move', the municipality decided to pay equal allowances to white councillors and LAC members (*NM*, 15.10.83). In Tongaat, for the first time all five Indian members of the multi-racial town board were to be elected. The election was called off after the 'surprise withdrawal' of the sixth candidate left the others unopposed (*NM*, 16.06.83). In Isipingo a rents protest meeting in September made it clear that all that autonomy had brought was the problem of ever-escalating rates because of lack of alternative sources of revenue (*Leader*, 02.09.83). The press claimed a 'high' 35% poll in the September elections for Isipingo, with a population of more than 20 000 of whom 4 475 were registered voters (*Post*, 17.09.83).

Verulam was returned to the status of a fully-elected local authority in 1983, two years after the dismissal of the previous board following a provincial commission of enquiry into its administration (*NM*, 24.03.83). Verulam has a population of over 30 000, of whom less than 3 000 were registered voters, apathy being cited as the cause by a former mayor (*NM*, 02.09.83).

In October the Administrator of Natal suspended the Umzinto Town Board and replaced it with a three-man Development and Services Board (*S Trib Herald*, 02.10.83). This decision was taken following the failure of the Board to elect office bearers in an election on 7 September when three out of nine sitting members contested their seats (*NM*, 29.09.83). The election came hard on the heels of a provincial commission of enquiry into the running of the board and the dismissed members claimed they were awaiting its results before proceeding (*NM*, 22.09.83). The evidence before the enquiry paints a picture of strained relations between officials and elected members of the board, dubious administrative practices, and strong personal antagonisms leading to vendettas and physical violence.

The experience of the town boards suggests that autonomous status has not enabled the state to develop a self-regulating system. Continued political intervention has been necessary due to the frailty of the economic base on which autonomy was erected.

Financing the deal

During 1983 the state attempted to create some finance for its political plans at the local level.

The sale of the century?
In March the government announced that it would be selling off 500 000 state-owned houses and invited capital to participate in the venture (*FM*, 11.03.83).[3]

Administration boards control housing stocks in African townships. In Indian and coloured areas housing falls under the city councils. MCs and LACs have no jurisdiction over housing. The different bases of control entail different fiscal realities. The position of the larger municipalities is healthier than that of the administration boards, which are constantly attempting to clear large deficits. Dr P.J. Riekert told a parliamentary select committee that the boards were 'busy going under' (*CP*, 17.04.83). The sale of township houses and the sale of administration board liquor outlets also announced during 1983 seemed to have been undertaken for two main purposes: firstly, to reduce board debts before the new local government structures are set in place and secondly, to acquire new houses. A figure of R385-m accruing from the housing sale has been mentioned.[4]

Conjuring the money
The thinking of the Croeser Working Group, set up to examine the Browne Report[5] began to emerge from its shroud of confidentiality in March. Croeser favours a system of metropolitan financing through combined local government organisations called Joint Services Committees which will provide 'hard services' to urban areas. As well as providing and operating the services they would have powers of taxation and financing. These bodies will be dominated by the wealthier local authorities since their composition is to be determined on the basis of financial contribution. Revenue would be derived from tariffs levied on a range of services.[6] Three additional sources of finance were proposed by Croeser. These were

  i. a levy on the turnover of all business enterprises, industries and service industries;
 ii. a percentage tax on wages of all employees to be collected from employers;

iii. an 'investment levy' on improvements and production equipment of
     business enterprises (*FM*, 11.03.83).

Capital's response has been to predict dire consequences for profitability.
A spokesman pointed out that the proposed taxes will only be levied in
the five major metropolitan areas. The taxes will discourage investment
there and favour decentralisation (*EPH*, 09.09.83). Some white local
authorities have voiced fears that their independent financial decision-
making powers will be usurped by the proposed joint institutions (*EPH*,
13.10.83).

The state has undertaken to pay the 'full agreed amount of assessment
rates' to local authorities on all government-owned property as well as
property of government business enterprise from 1984–5.[7] This
represents an additional source of finance for local authorities, but in
future local authorities will pay central government taxes from which
they have been exempt in the past (*EPH*, 09.06.83).

Our evidence suggests that adequate finance will never be available for
any of the black local bodies. Coloured and Indian areas might be able
to plug in to the metropolitan boards to maintain 'acceptable' levels of
services and industrial parks might be ceded to their control. But for the
foreseeable future Indian and coloured areas will be little better off than
their African counterparts. They are all effectively dormitory suburbs.

Legislation

The legislation enabling the creation of new town and village councils in
African areas is the Black Local Authorities Act (See *South African
Review One*, 130–1). Another Act which affects local government in
African areas is the Black Communities Development Act. It was introduced in parliament in 1983. It deals with the role of administration
boards (to be called development boards). They will remain intact under
the Department of Co-operation and Development (CAD) and will have
four main functions: influx control; local government in African areas;
housing; and acting as agents for other government departments in their
areas of jurisdiction (*CT*, 11.08.83).

The Promotion of Local Government Act, passed by parliament in
June, is of central importance to the future of local government. This Act
creates a Council for the Co-ordination of Local Government Affairs,
sets up Municipal Development Boards and provides for interim
measures to improve communication between coloured and Indian com-

mittees and white local authorities. The Act is a product of the work done by the President's Council and the Croeser Working Group. It creates the mechanisms for a greater concentration of power at the centre through the standardisation of local government functions and their 'rationalisation'.

Speaking in the second reading debate on the Bill, Heunis said that:

> The principal object of the Co-ordinating Council is, therefore, to bring about direct contact − around a table if you will − among representatives of white, coloured and Indian population groups so that they may deliberate with one another concerning local government affairs of common interest, and on that basis advise the Government.[8]

The second part of the Act provides for the creation of Municipal Development Boards. These will comprise technical specialists in various fields related to local government. Their task will be to facilitate the necessary conditions for autonomy at the local level as fast as possible.

The third part of the Act relates to the 'interim measures', and is a response to the President's Council findings that relations between white municipalities and coloured and Indian councils were poor. State policy is to create separate local authorities, but some sort of interim working arrangement is necessary until this can be achieved.[9]

The Association of Management Committees (ASSOMAC) accepted the major elements of the Bill after Heunis gave assurances that it was not intended to create separate local authorities (*CT*, 07.06.83). ASSOMAC chairman David Curry commented:

> Quite aside from any moral objections to such separation, we think it is unworkable. . . . Imagine every town and city having three separate councils, three separate town clerks, three separate treasurers, three separate engineers, and so forth. It's ridiculous (*Friend*, 06.06.83).

Curry's position is that direct representation is 'inevitable', and that 'economic realities' will force the government to bow to a new system in the end.

The constitutional proposals highlighted divisions within the ranks of the MCs and LACs. By accepting the constitution in January, the Labour Party was widely rejected in the Cape Peninsula, the Transvaal and Natal. Following the government threat to enforce the Group Areas Act more strictly, the Natal leadership called for the withdrawal of Labour's participation (*NM*, 20.10.83). The Labour Party chairman, David Curry, resigned his post in October following a dispute over participation tactics, thereby weakening an embattled leadership (*EPH*, 14.10.83).

In October the Natal Association of LACs (NALAC) became the first statutory body to reject the constitutional proposals (*NM*, 24.10.83). This decision caused a split within the association. Representatives of four LACs denied that the constitution in toto had been rejected (*ST Extra*, 30.10.83). The president of the Association argued that rejection of the local government issues only would mean continued support for most of the country's racial laws (*S Trib Herald*, 30.10.83). The NALAC move gained support from the National Ad-hoc Committee in the Transvaal led by Curry who had retained his position as head of ASSOMAC (*NM*, 31.10.83). It is possible that he will use his power base in ASSOMAC to negotiate with both the state and the Labour leadership from whom he is currently estranged.

Faced with a growing threat from below of militant community groups opposed to the Labour Party's participation Curry responded by raising the political stakes:

> We are not a body of yes-men. We know that stooge politics will get us nowhere. . . . We know that some people have labelled us as blind followers of government policy who offer no criticism. The years have taught us how to participate in politics (*CT*, 17.11.83).

Curry has also argued that the civic bodies which challenge his support at local government level have the same problems of 'delivering the goods' as the management committees. 'They won't survive if they can't get amenities and facilities because that is all our people care about' (*CH*, 01.01.83). He is articulating a politics of survival. It aims to control access to scarce resources, which will be denied to non-participants.

Resistance and participation

The main divide here is between those organisations willing to participate and those who boycott. On the participation side, a small band of willing candidates persist in offering themselves as agents of state policy. Many urban bantu council members of the late 1960s have participated in the elections for BLAs in 1983. The Labour Party's involvement in the Coloured Representative Council leading to its acceptance of the new tricameral structure is well known. The state has had little success over the years in expanding the core of participants.

The boycott position has attracted widespread support and has been instrumental in discrediting participation and spreading community organisation in the larger centres.

Rent struggles

The most unpopular form of revenue for boards and their community councils[10] has been rents and other tariffs. These have increased year by year in gross disproportion to tenants' incomes.

As the new 1983–4 financial year opened, the annual spate of rent and other tariff increases came up for discussion in council chambers. Friction built up quickly. On the one hand, councils bickered with boards (in cases where councillors, wary of the consequences, refused to support board-suggested increases). On the other hand, residents took on councils (in cases where councillors were convinced that the board hikes were justified). Across the country, angry residents accused councillors of self-interest. Councillors complained to boards of impotence. For example, in Kagiso (Krugersdorp), residents called a mass meeting in mid-February to protest against a 60% rent increase (R20,00 to R33,73). They demanded the resignation of the Council and agreed to boycott all businesses owned by councillors (*CP*, 20.04.83).

In the Pretoria townships of Atteridgeville/Saulsville, the Council rejected an increase of R13,63 due to be implemented in three phases, beginning in July. Chairman J. Tshabalala told his Council that it was facing a deficit of R1 861 674 on the 1983–4 estimates. The Council then recommended smaller increases later in the year — if the Black Local Authorities Act was implemented in its area (*RDM*, 21.01.83). Subsequently, the Council refused to meet the Administration Board over the issue and Tshabalala angrily suggested that Board officials themselves stand for elections should the government enforce the increase (*Sow*, 18.03.83).

Community councils and those upgraded to town or village status are in need of a sound financial base if they are to attract any degree of credibility. As Chris Dlamini, president of the Federation of South African Trade Unions put it: 'There is no reason for the community council to be there, when they have no financial resources to run the townships' (*CP*, 27.11.83).

Community vs council

Over the last few years civic bodies have proliferated in response to rent increases and related matters such as the availability and quality of housing. Because rent increases are perceived to be closely linked to councils (as agents of boards), civics have in many instances become ready alternatives to community councils. Residents choose them to voice their grievances and to negotiate with township authorities. In 1983, several civics were specifically established to oppose the councils. Examples include the Vaal Action Committee (*Sow*, 11.11.83), the Grahamstown Civic Action Association (*EPH*, 14.10.83), and the Joint Rent Action Committee (JORAC) in townships under the jurisdiction of the Port Natal Administration Board (PNAB).

Councillors began to feel sandwiched between the growing popularity of the civics and the hardline attitude of the boards. One Port Elizabeth councillor accused his council of being a 'dead horse' (*EPH*, 23.04.83). With decision-making bypassing them from both ends, their attempts to assert credibility became more desperate and the level of violence associated with township politics rose. Bomb attacks on councillors, death threats (even deaths), court cases alleging fraud, murder, theft, and assault punctuated the business of many councils.[11] Violence seemed to be directed both at rival participants and at councillors from outside parties. The *Sowetan* described the 'reign of terror' against councillors on the East Rand (04.08.83). Several council chairmen received death threats and Mamelodi (Pretoria) chairman W. Aphane went so far as to invite the police to tap his phone because of the number of threats to his life (*CP*, 03.04.83). The worst cases of violence were experienced in Lamontville (see below).

Two episodes in the West Rand townships did little to enhance the councils' image: the merger debacle and the Soweto Council's demolition of shacks. Early in 1983, the possibility of amalgamating the councils of Soweto, Diepmeadow and Dobsonville was mooted. The West Rand Administration Board and Soweto Council chairman David Thebehali supported the move, reasoning that a single body would be more rational. The other two Councils fiercely resisted the move, claiming that their finance would simply be used to pay off others' debts. The bitter disagreements were terminated in September, when Koornhof decided that the merger was off. In February, a legal ruling prevented the Soweto Council from demolishing further shacks. For a while, Council officials were forced to discontinue demolitions, until the Council successfully appealed against the ruling in April.

Some councils in the face of what must have seemed a hopeless situation collapsed altogether. The Drakensberg Administration Board, for example, had to assume direct control of Sobantu when that council was left without a quorum (*CP*, 04.12.83). Another response was simply to get on with the business of the councils for whatever benefit might be left. J. Mahuhushi, chairman of the Diepmeadow Council, allegedly allocated himself huge plots of land in the township (*Sow*, 07.07.83). Ephraim

Tshabalala, wealthy Soweto councillor, when asked why he participated in the Council, answered: 'I can't trade without a licence. The community council is my government' (*RDM*, 24.10.83). (This, he said, was his response to Soweto scholars in 1976 and added that 'they understood'.)

Lamontville: local crisis

The events in Lamontville threw into sharp focus all these trends and tensions.[12] Towards the end of 1982, Lamontville residents battled with the Durban Transport Management Committee (DTMC) over fare increases. A commuters' committee had been set up to negotiate with the DTMC but was flatly rejected because it was not a statutory body. A bus boycott began in December.

Hard on the heels of the fare increase came an announcement, in March, of a 63% rent hike in all townships and hostels controlled by the PNAB. This meant a rise from R18,32 to R29,85 for a basic house and R26,09 to R42,60 for a five-roomed house in Lamontville. There had been no consultation between the Ningizimu Community Council and the residents — with the one exception of Community Council member Harrison Msizi Dube, prominent in organising the commuters' committee and involved in the formation of JORAC, the Joint Rent Action Committee. JORAC was established soon after the announcement of the rent increases and rapidly gained popular support in all of the PNAB townships. In April, it declared itself willing to negotiate with the PNAB over the increases. It was told, however, that the increases were non-negotiable. The Ningizimu Community Council seemed to be completely immobilised — even the PNAB accused it of being 'extremely ineffective'. Then the highly respected Harrison Dube was assassinated on the night of 25 April. Crowds surrounded the house of Council chairman Moonlight Gasa, with whom Dube had had a longstanding dispute over their rights and roles in the Council. A bus was set alight and a liquor outlet and beer halls belonging to PNAB were damaged. The spiral of violence escalated when an alleged informer was killed at Dube's funeral and the police moved in with teargas and dogs. The eruption spilled over into nearby Chesterville, also under PNAB, where lives were lost and buildings damaged.

On 1 May, the PNAB announced that the May rent increases would be halved, while the remainder would be phased in over the next ten months. JORAC intensified its 'Asinamali' ('We have no money') campaign with a boycott of increases and a number of public meetings.

At the beginning of May, three councillors resigned and Gasa was moved from his house by PNAB officials after repeated threats and attacks. For several weeks,

> the Government moved in with its Police force and put Lamontville under a semi-military siege. There was throwing of teargas, beatings, insults, injuries to property and life. Brutality whether from the Police or people could not solve the situation. . . .[13]

Towards the third week of June, Lamontville calmed down. But peace was shortlived: shockwaves spread through the township when, on 23 June, Moonlight Gasa and one other appeared in court in connection with Dube's death. The following day they were joined by two more, and all four pleaded guilty. After preliminary hearing, three of the pleas, including Gasa's, were changed to not guilty. In later appearances, startling allegations about hired assassins and hit lists emerged. After their appearance in court, the PNAB offices in Lamontville were gutted and police sealed off the township.

At the end of June, JORAC met with PNAB officials and community councillors to discuss the situation. In the continuing turmoil, JORAC called on the city council to take over running of the townships from PNAB.

In the first week of July, two PFP MPs, Peter Gastrow and Harry Pitman, visited Lamontville to investigate allegations of police violence against residents. They submitted a comprehensive memorandum to parliament — but their evidence was hotly disputed by the Minister of Law and Order, Louis le Grange.

Towards the end of July, the Community Council and E. Ngobeni took the rent issue to court in an Inkatha-sponsored case. A review date was set for mid-August, when judgement was reserved. In November, the rent increase was declared in order.

An announcement certain to precipitate further unrest came at the end of August: Lamontville, Deputy Minister of CAD Dr Morrison said, would be incorporated into KwaZulu. Faced with the prospects of losing Section 10 rights and becoming 'migrants', residents' tempers flared. JORAC's Rev. M. Xundu outlined possible action:

> In the same way that the KwaZulu administration won its case against Pretoria over the Ingwavuma issue, claiming there was no consultation, so too will we claim there was no consultation with us over this shocking decision (*CP*, 04.09.83).

Inkatha and the Community Council, which had limped through the trouble, declared themselves in favour of incorporation into KwaZulu. In mid-October violence again broke out as meetings called both for and against the move were disrupted or broken up. Nearby hostel-dwellers (mostly migrant workers from KwaZulu) stormed into the township on one occasion and were halted on another. The migrants later resolved to withdraw money they had committed to a JORAC fund to fight the rent increases.

By December, the violence had died down but Lamontville remained tense, particularly when it became known that the PNAB was exerting pressure on employers to deduct money owing on rent increases.

While there were particular factors precipitating such severe unrest in Lamontville, some of the ingredients are shared by townships all over the country:

> The real crisis in Lamontville as anywhere in South Africa is the fact of undemocratic decision making by a minority over a majority; for as long as that obtains there will be a crisis.[14]

Committees for the management of own affairs

In practical terms there was little visible change in the position of LACs and management committees in 1983.

Their crisis of powerlessness continued, and this was perceived both by those who were involved and by those who opposed them. Prospective candidates remained unwilling to come forward to offer their services (*Leader*, 18.02.83), and vacancies had to be filled by nomination (*NM*, 03.05.83).

Relations between LACs, management committees and white local authorities continued to be tense.[15] The most widespread grievance of MCs and LACs was that they were not seriously regarded and that the areas they represented were neglected. The number of occasions on which these bodies either suspended themselves or threatened to do so points to their general sense of frustration.[16] Participants try to create more space in the system by these actions and threats. They do so in order to pursue their own interests. Their failure to achieve direct representation on city councils precludes the achievement of goals which participants consider central. Without direct representation they have little chance of gaining popular legitimacy.

Various civic organisations which have developed over the last few years tend to bypass these bodies, and seek to deal directly with the local authorities in matters affecting housing, transport and services.[17] The sorts of issues which LACs and MCs do take up are instructive. The

Westville LAC disbanded itself in 1980 over a dispute about rebates on property rates, and is currently taking up this question again (*NM*, 19.08.83).

The Durban City Council decision, supported by the Southern Durban LAC, to admit white-owned chainstores into Chatsworth was hotly contested by the local traders association on the grounds that they would be ruined by the competition.

The LACs and MCs do take up issues of a more popular nature.[18] However, certain questions are pursued with more enthusiasm than others and this must be an indication of the particular class interests LAC and MC members seek to defend and further through participation.[19]

'Democracy' at work?

Township elections in 1983 were the focal point both for those in favour of the new BLA Act and for political, civic, youth and other organisations predicting its failure. Elections in African urban areas had never attracted so much attention before — foreign press representatives displayed interest in the campaigns in Soweto.

In September, Koornhof announced that elections for the first 26 councils to be upgraded under the Black Local Authorities Act would be held in November and December (*EPH*, 09.09.83). None of these was in Natal, where the community council system had reached an advanced stage of disintegration.

Campaigns for the elections began earlier than usual, with rival groups vociferously attacking each other. Attention centred on Soweto, where 120 candidates were eventually nominated for the Soweto, Diepmeadow and Dobsonville Councils. Elections also met with the biggest-ever display of resistance, despite the new status. For different reasons, rejection was expressed by workers and various sections of the petty bourgeoisie, who were able to adopt a common 'Do not vote' position.

At the end of May, even before election dates had been announced, an Anti-Community Council Committee was formed in Soweto (*Sow*, 30.05.83). Initiated by the Soweto Civic Association, it had gained wide support by November from organisations such as the Council of Unions of South Africa; General and Allied Workers' Union; South African Allied Workers' Union; Motor Assemblers and Component Workers' Union; the Federation of South African Women; and the Azanian People's Organisation. The UDF backed the anti-community council campaign vigorously in areas where elections were scheduled (*CP*, 20.11.83).

The Federation of South African Trade Unions also called on its members to stay away from elections (*CP*, 27.11.83), and migrant workers in the Saulsville Hostel under the banner of the Saulsville Hostel Anti-Community Council Committee, SHACC, (a UDF affiliate) vowed to support the boycott (*CP*, 27.11.83).

Even Inkatha decided not to participate officially — a reversal of its earlier stance — although it stopped short of calling on members to refrain from involvement in their personal capacities.

In October, the Urban Foundation conducted a survey which found that 38–46% of eligible voters in Soweto would turn out at the polls (*Sow*, 28.10.83). Incumbent Council chairman David Thebehali predicted a 30–35% poll (*CP*, 27.11.83). A leader of the Soweto Anti-Community Council Committee, Amos Masondo, called the results of the Urban Foundation survey 'preposterous' — and he turned out to be right. The poll for the Soweto election on 3 December was 10,7%. Although this was some 4% higher than the previous poll, it indicated a massive rejection of the 'new deal' even before it had been tried.[20] Before the new local authorities had even been inaugurated, they had failed to attract some of the wider support the government had hoped for.

In September, management committee elections were held in the Cape. The Freedom Party decided to participate in the elections thus jettisoning its former non-participation stance (*EPH*, 23.06.83). An attempted merger between the Peoples Congress Party and the Freedom Party to form a common front against the Labour Party failed to materialise before the elections. Both parties have committed themselves 'in principle' to a merger, and are insistent that they will conduct joint discussions with the government on constitutional matters in future (*EPH*, 10.08.83).

The UDF launched a boycott campaign in the Western Cape to highlight the management committees as 'puppet bodies' (*CT*, 05.09.83). There was a poor turnout of voters in the Western Cape, which made the Labour Party victory a hollow one.[21] The secretary of the Western Cape UDF, Trevor Manuel, commenting on the elections said: 'The disaster is of course that the management committees will continue to exist and to claim they are representative of these communities' (*S Trib*, 11.09.83).

There was a greater degree of interest in the Eastern Cape elections which were contested by the Freedom Party. In Uitenhage, the Labour Party defeated the four Freedom Party and two independent candidates by a large majority on a 56% poll. In Despatch there was an 80% poll and three Independents defeated the Labour candidates. In other rural

Eastern Cape elections Labour Party candidates were elected, largely unopposed (*EPH*, 08.09.83).

The results of the elections show that Labour support has been effectively challenged in the Western Cape through the various civics. But in the Eastern Cape the party machine has maintained a firm grip on its voters. What is significant is the willingness of the Freedom Party to participate in the elections.

Conclusion

The state has responded to local crisis by modifying existing structures for participation and creating new ones, without conceding ground to opposition groupings. In some instances, these structures themselves have had the effect of displacing struggle. The state's announcement of Lamontville's incorporation into KwaZulu had the effect of diverting energy from the central issues of rents and housing into fighting the KwaZulu take-over. Similarly, autonomous local bodies will be charged with functions over which they have no real control. They face the prospect of being disrupted by struggles directed against them in their capacity as 'responsible' authorities.

Patterns of resistance and participation suggest that the state is not actively seeking allies. Instead participants present themselves to the state. The state needs allies to participate in its 'representative' structures but will probably dispense with its present set if more 'acceptable' ones make themselves available.

Local struggles have been uneven in their spread, intensity and effect. State initiatives have afforded community organisations an opportunity to strengthen their position. But none of them has succeeded in forcing the state to modify its structures fundamentally. Popular pressure will have to be more generalised before real changes in representation can be realised. For the moment, the state has been able to contain active resistance by using its repressive powers. It is likely that these powers will be used in future. It is also likely that capital will provide support, since it has become more deeply involved at the local level through the provision of services.

There is a link between the process of political concentration which has been taking place in local government within the Departments of Constitutional Affairs and Co-operation and Development and the fragmentation of structures at the local level. Greater powers have been taken at the centre, at the expense of the provinces. At the same time local political structures are being further fragmented through the mechanism of autonomy. A parallel economic process emerges from the plans to regionalise local government services. Financial resources will be more concentrated and there will be a correspondingly greater ability to control what were formerly local services. At the same time the newly created autonomous bodies will not be financially viable. Economic concentration at the metropolitan or regional level will allow the provision of services to continue under the political control of the wealthier white local authorities without any threat from fragmented autonomous coloured or Indian bodies. There is a logic to the contradictory trends of concentration and fragmentation at the local level.

Notes

1 For general background to the structures of the local state and a discussion of the underlying unity of local level politics despite its institutional appearance in the form of racially discrete structures see H. Hughes and J. Grest, 'The Local State', in *Same Foundations, New Facades*?, South African Review One (Johannesburg, 1983).

2 The term 'Black Local Authorities' (BLAs) is the one officially given to the new councils in African townships under the control of administration boards. It is used here for convenience.

3 We deal only in the briefest terms with this important event; further discussion needs the context of a thorough analysis of housing and related facilities, which is outside the ambit of this paper.

4 'Political Monitor', *Social Indicator* 1(2) (1983), 6.

5 For detail see Hughes and Grest, 'The Local State'.

6 — *Trading Services* (water, power, sewerage) to produce a profit;
  — *Economic Services* (libraries, caravan parks, licensing) to cover costs of administration;
  — *Subsidised Services* (zoos, halls, museums, fire protection);
  — *Community Services* (traffic, street lighting, etc.) to be financed from normal revenue and subsidies (*FM*, 11.03.83).

7 *Hansard*, col 4196-7 (30.03.83). In 1982 R43,6-m was budgeted, and for 1983-4 R60-m. These are not substantial sums when the overall needs of local authorities are taken into account. However, given that a large proportion of such property falls within the boundaries of the major white local authorities it could go some way towards allaying their fears about sharing costs.

8 *Hansard*, col 8288 (01.06.83).

9 The measures provide for, amongst other things; consideration of the council's budget before it is submitted to council, the creation of special liaison committees by city councils, the possibility of joint subcommittee meetings, the attendance of meetings without voting rights and the provision of a seat with voting rights on the council for chairmen of MCs and LACs (*EPH*, 24.05.83).

10 The system of financing as well as the relationships between boards and community councils are explained in Hughes and Grest, 'The Local State', 124–8.

11 For example, five candidates in the Port Elizabeth Community Council elections had their homes petrol-bombed (*S Trib*, 04.12.83); the Mbekweni councillors who appeared in court charged with stoning the house of another councillor (*CT*, 13.09.83); Thebehali's appearance in court charged with defeating the course of justice — subsequently acquitted (*CP*, 29.05.83) and his All Nation vigilante group the subject of a state probe (*CP*, 13.11.83); and the deputy chairman of the Katlehong Community Council questioned by police in connection with receiving stolen property (*Sow*, 12.10.83).

12 Not every detail has been referenced. For full coverage see *Daily News*, *Natal Mercury*, *Ilanga* and *Sunday Tribune* from April to December 1983.

13 M. Xundu, 'The Present Crisis in Lamontville', paper presented to Workshop on African Urban Life in Durban in the Twentieth Century, University of Natal, Durban, 26–27 October 1983, 5.

14 Xundu, 'The Present Crisis', 5.

15 The Eastern Cape presents a good example. Over the year, repeated accusations of ineffectualness were made. See *EPH*, 16.04.83; 14.09.83; 21.09.83; 21.09.83; 05.10.83.

16 Estcourt (*S Trib*, 24.04.83); Southern Durban LAC (*NM*, 05.08.83 and *Leader*, 16.09.83); Ladysmith (*Leader*, 09.09.83 and *NM*, 10.11.83).

17 On hearing the news that coloured townships in Durban would be faced with large rent increases in February 1984 and being asked whether the LAC would make representations to the National Housing Commission on behalf of the tenants, the chairman, Mr Stowman, indicated that the LAC was only an advisory body and had no say over rentals (*Leader*, 18.11.83).

18 See for example the questions of the sports complex at Heidedal (*Friend*, 12.04.83); evictions in Estcourt (*S Trib Herald*, 24.04.83); community facilities in Durban (*S Trib Herald*, 20.02.83); the second Chatsworth access route (*DN*, 04.08.83); housing (*S Trib*, 25.09.83, *Post*, 26.10.83).

19 Parity of allowances with those paid to city councillors is a case in point.

20 *City Press* reports (11.12.83) show that polls were generally lower than in the 1978–9 elections. For example, Dobsonville 42% to 23,5%; Diepmeadow 16% to 14,6%; Kimberley 37,6% to 26,9%. Only Soweto and Tembisa (15% to 17%) were higher in 1983. An interesting feature of the Soweto election was the unseating of David Thebehali by Sofasonke leader Ephraim Tshabalala.

21 It was reported that in Cape Town only an estimated 8% of coloured people are registered as voters. The highest poll was in Kensington with 11,8%, and the lowest in Athlone with 1,81% (*S Trib*, 11.09.83).

Political Trials and the Legal Process

Raymond Suttner

South African courts, previously much celebrated, locally and overseas, now face serious problems in maintaining or recapturing their image of impartiality and independence. The difficulties that they encounter are part of a wider challenge to the legitimacy of the state as a whole and the consequently escalating problems of law and order.

Until recently, the judiciary enjoyed a less tarnished reputation — in the eyes of many — than other state institutions. Yet its role in political trials, which are run according to rules that are heavily loaded against the accused, has made it increasingly difficult for courts to maintain this image.

Professor John Dugard has remarked that the political trial has become a 'regular and from the Government's point of view, necessary feature of the political process. ...'[1] There have been political trials throughout much of the history of white control in South Africa. Yet the form these trials have taken and their targets have undergone modifications at various times.[2]

Prior to the 1960s there was generally not a distinct political trial process. Political offenders were usually charged with common law offences and procedurally, the prosecution normally enjoyed no special advantages in bringing such cases to trial.[3] The 1960s saw the emergence of a distinct 'drastic legal process'. Political offenders were tried under widely defined offences, subject to heavy, sometimes mandatory penalties. This special process was partly a response to popular resistance and the emergence of guerilla struggle. To some extent these legal changes anticipated intensified opposition, which they hoped to curb or deter before it matured. That 'drastic process' has in turn undergone modification in the 1980s, consequent on the restructuring of the state.

This article outlines the characteristics of the modern South African political trial, indicating the goals of the state, the response of the accused and their supporters. A final section seeks to explain recent modifications in the trial process.

What characterises the political trial in South Africa?

Dugard writes that the 'main purpose of the political trial is to eliminate or discredit a political opponent according to established rules' (p. 206). This statement is not, I suggest, sufficiently precise to characterise the most typical political trial in South Africa. The motivations that Dugard outlines for political trials certainly do reflect the features of certain trials in South Africa. The prosecutions against Connie Mulder, Jaap Marais, Eschel Rhoodie and Eugene Terre' Blanche are examples. These trials reflect an attempt to use the courts for scoring victories against white political opponents, and for buttressing the Nationalists' hegemony over the white power bloc.

Yet the most enduring and characteristic form of political trial in South Africa has, of necessity, reflected less the intra-white conflict than the conflict between the white ruling bloc and the black masses whose right to self-determination has been denied. The typical political trial in South Africa is one where the state seeks to contain the resistance to the suppression of black aspirations. Equally, for the oppressed, the courtroom is a site of resistance, albeit under disadvantageous circumstances. Such trials are not generally aimed at *individual opponents* (though, as we have seen, these are sometimes prosecuted). In the most characteristic political trial, individuals are prosecuted because they have acted on behalf of organisations that challenge the basis of the South African state. In many cases these individuals were unknown outside their own families until they appeared in court. Their public significance derives from their identification with political struggles that enjoy widespread support.

Repressive aspects
A political trial seeks to punish those who challenge the existence of the South African state or who seek to mobilise resistance on a significant scale. It also aims at deterring others who might contemplate such activities. To facilitate these goals the prosecution receives various aids that are not available in ordinary trials.

Before discussing these, it should be noted that the 'ordinary trial' is itself procedurally loaded against blacks and poorer people.[4] One cannot conduct an adequate defence without a lawyer. Legal defence is a right, but it can only be exercised where one has significant financial resources. Bail may be allowed, but the amount is often set beyond the means of the average black and/or worker. In the case of Africans, Bantu languages are not 'official' languages. Proceedings are conducted through interpreters who, it has been claimed, often misinterpret nuances, to the detriment of the accused. Under the Criminal Procedure Act of 1977 the presiding officer may now put questions to the accused on their first appearance in court. Without legal representation, the accused sometimes make very damaging admissions.[5] These factors also operate in the case of political defendants, but they are supplemented by further specific disadvantages in both substantive and procedural law.

Detention: In a 'normal' case, the accused would only be arrested after investigation and questioning, unless he/she has committed an offence in the presence of a police officer.[6] In contrast, a crucial part of the process leading to a political trial is that the accused are usually first held for a lengthy period without being charged. While detained their case is continuously investigated. Detainees are repeatedly interrogated and lose the normal privilege against self-incrimination, the right of access to lawyers, etc. Following such interrogation, much of the evidence presented in court concerns statements made in detention or the evidence of alleged accomplices of the accused, who have themselves arrived in court as prisoners in detention.

Such confessions, evidence and admissions arise out of circumstances that have caused many lawyers and psychologists to question their reliability. Not only is solitary confinement considered to be a form of psychological torture, but there have also been repeated allegations of physical torture. Such allegations have sometimes been proved. But the detainee's access to outsiders is so curtailed that it is usually impossible to prove ill-treatment. Thus, one trade unionist, Mathews Oliphant, on his release from detention, remarked that detainees 'are either too scared to make complaints in case they are victimised or feel it is useless to complain because the men who visit us are part of the system that has detained us' (*RDM*, 25.05.82).

Most political trials rely heavily on the evidence of accomplices. There are considerable inducements for detainees to provide such evidence, leading one lawyer, Charles Nupen, to describe detention as a 'witness factory, a place where evidence is manufactured for court' (*RDM*, 12.08.82). When the court considers such evidence to be satisfactory, the witness will be indemnified against prosecution.

A wide range of people regard those who give state evidence with such displeasure that the state often tries to conceal the identities of their witnesses. This leads to a further characteristic of political trials — the regular practice of holding part or all of the proceedings *in camera*. Despite the heavy inducements, large numbers of people still refuse to testify for the state. The penalty for such refusal has been increased. In 1964 the sentence was a repeatable eight days (which was not applicable to accomplices). Since 1977 this has risen to a theoretically repeatable five years on each occasion (Dugard p. 265).

Yet in the eyes of many, the penalty for assisting state prosecutions may be heavier. Apart from the real danger of assassination, social ostracism is common.[7] When a leading African journalist, Thami Mazwai, refused to give state evidence, it was advanced on his behalf that if he gave evidence he, as a journalist, would have lost all credibility with the black community (*RDM*, 13.02.82). Others, such as Ms Nonkululeko Mazibuko, have rejected what they called the 'police offer to turn State witness to sell my brother' (*Sow*, 11.04.83). Or it has been said (by Phillip Dlamini) that 'it was written in The Good Book that a person should not give false evidence against a neighbour' (*RDM*, 14.01.83).

Bail: When a judge or magistrate adjudicates in a political trial, the accused normally arrive direct from detention. They have possibly been questioned at their first court appearance without the assistance of legal representation. Their right to a public trial may also have been curtailed. In addition, bail is often denied to political accused.

In some proceedings bail is not in the court's discretion. The attorney-general may 'issue an order' indicating that bail is not allowed.[8] Very few people have ever been allowed bail in such proceedings. For all practical purposes any accused facing the most serious political charges, which carry the death penalty in some cases, must conduct their defence preparations from prison. Defending oneself from prison places the accused at a considerable disadvantage. If he/she can afford a lawyer, there are nevertheless restrictions on communication that do not affect accused who are out on bail. If one is undefended, there are serious impediments in the way of interviewing, arranging for the attendance of witnesses and the general preparation of one's defence.[9]

The Detainees' Parents Support Committee has recently criticised this power of the attorney-general, indicating some cases where people were denied bail but were ultimately acquitted, often spending long periods in prison (*Star*, 28.11.83). On some occasions, politically prominent people have been arrested and denied bail for vague charges relating to events of some time earlier. Ultimately they have been acquitted.[10] These arrests often coincide with important annual commemorative events. The denial of bail keeps these activists 'out of the way' for that period. At the same time, their being in prison after being charged, has reduced the number of people who can be listed as *detained without trial* — a consideration that might be calculated to win favour with powers interested in 'constructive engagement'.

Definition of offences: The definition of offences under the now repealed Terrorism Act and General Laws Amendment Act ('Sabotage Act') was very wide. In addition to the prosecution of substantial threats to the state, it was also possible to try relatively minor offenders whose acts might equally well have fallen under the heading of less serious offences. After the 1976 rising, black teenagers were sometimes charged under the Sabotage Act for minor offences which could have fallen under lesser common law provisions relating to damage to property. The new Internal Security Act of 1982, drafted after recommendations by the present Chief Justice, seeks to attain narrower, more precise definitions. Many of these definitions nevertheless remain wide.

Procedural advantages regarding rules of evidence: The new Act, like the Terrorism Act, provides the prosecution with many procedural advantages. With certain offences ('Terrorism', 'Subversion'), once the state has proved the commission of certain acts likely to have furthered one of a series of widely phrased aims, the onus is on the accused to prove beyond reasonable doubt that he or she lacked the intention.

Peculiar penalties: Another characteristic of the political trial of the 1960s and onwards is the very heavy potential or mandatory penalties provided for in applicable legislation. After 1962 an increasing number of offences carried a potential death penalty. In addition, the now repealed Terrorism and Sabotage Acts and a clause of the previous Suppression of Communism/Internal Security Act provided for minimum penalties. Certain offenders who were charged with sabotage (five years minimum sentence) could as easily have been prosecuted for arson.[11] The police and prosecution were therefore able to jail people for lengthy periods for relatively minor acts.

The new Internal Security Act, although providing for heavy penalties, does not lay down minimum sentences. This change has, however, been offset to some extent by recent sentencing patterns, especially in the magistrates' courts. Some courts still appear to be imposing sentences with the previous minimum sentences as a guideline.[12]

Splitting of charges:[13] Under security legislation it is fairly common and permissible for political offenders to be charged with a number of separate offences where these form part of one act. Magistrates with limited jurisdiction have been able to sentence offenders to a series of periods of imprisonment. People were frequently punished separately for different aspects of the same political act. For example, in many trials in the eastern Cape in the 1960s people who attended ANC meetings, displayed the ANC badge and who subscribed to the funds of the ANC, were punished separately for each activity. Such trials were generally held before regional magistrates whose sentencing power was then limited to three years imprisonment on each count. But in sentencing people separately on each count, these courts were (and are still) able to impose lengthy periods of imprisonment.

Ideological aspects

In bringing accused to trial the state aims not only to punish the individual accused, but also to create wider ideological effects. Judicial proceedings enjoy greater legitimacy than merely administrative action. A court trial is a public ceremony which seeks to convince as many people as possible that 'justice has been done', and that what the accused did needed to be curbed and deserved to be punished. It is hoped that the public will accept the criminalisation of certain organisations and their activities.

The extent to which the ideological dimension is present may vary from trial to trial. In the 1960s, for example, after most of the ANC leadership had been gaoled, a whole series of trials were held against rank-and-file members. These were often staged in remote rural areas, with a minimum of press publicity.[14] These trials were possibly regarded primarily as 'mopping up operations' and were consequently almost entirely repressive in orientation.

Where the state has difficulties creating the ideological impact that it desires, as in times of 'unrest', it may hold large parts of a trial *in camera*[15] or it may hold the trial in a court far away from the accuseds' supporters. It is thereby conceded that it would be practically impossible to convince the people of the accuseds' home area that they acted wrongly and that state repression was justified.

South African 'security' legislation has suppressed previously non-violent, popular organisations and the state has considerable aid in securing conviction of those who resist this suppression. In this light how does the court convince the public that a trial is 'fair'?

The problem of trying to make the application of law, whose legitimacy is widely questioned, appear just, is not restricted to political trials. The way that courts cope with this problem in ordinary trials is in many respects applicable to political trials. In both instances courts rely on a strict definition of legally relevant issues. Court proceedings are depicted as contests merely between individuals or between the state and the individual.

In the conduct of a trial the court seeks to reconstruct a particular event or series of events. Such occurrences are abstracted from much of their history and context, though not all. There are certain 'relevant' defences and arguments that can be raised. Attempts to relate the dispute to factors beyond such 'legally relevant' issues are likely, according to the rules, to be called to order. Consequently court cases are denuded of much of their actual, most significant social context. The court cannot, in determining 'guilt', concern itself with whether X, by virtue of being black had no significant constitutional avenues open for political expression. Its job is to protect 'society' from such offenders. The way in which courts operate isolates accused people from their social and historical circumstances and attributes to them a moral guilt.

The court assumes the legitimacy of the existing order and by its treatment of offenders purely as individuals, it serves to negate the idea that there is any relevance in their being members of specific national groups or classes or their being associated with a popular national movement.

Obviously for the positivist, the fact that 'A' is an offence may be sufficient irrespective of the type of trial. Yet there are many others who may ask, especially in regard to a political trial, what preceded the law which made 'A' an offence. Before condemning the accused they may ask whether it was possible for this person to have made a meaningful contribution in any way other than the unlawful mode chosen. If the accused is convicted of violent acts they might well ask whether this person's acts were not preceded by acts of repression by the state and whether these might have led the accused to conclude, rightly or wrongly, that such acts were an appropriate response.

The court proceedings are not a debate of the rights and wrongs of such issues nor a reconstruction of the total history. The accused is charged with specific acts. Much of the proceedings are concerned with whether the accused has or has not done 'A' and with or without the required intention, which may or may not be presumed, depending on the legislation concerned. The legitimacy of making 'A' an offence is not an issue. Despite the accused's actions being socially motivated he or she is treated as an individual malefactor against 'society'. As a judge in the Pietermaritzburg treason trial of 1979 stated: 'Society cannot allow that a man who cannot resolve the position through constitutional means to do it (sic) in an unconstitutional manner.'[16]

The response of the accused and the public

Repressive dimension

The repressive aspects of trials aim, in the first place, at punishing an individual accused. But they, along with other means of repression, are also aimed at deterring others who might contemplate similar action.

In punishing an individual the court clearly achieves one of these aims. But such individual punishment does not appear to have served as a significant deterrent to others contemplating illegal action in support of the ANC and its allies. It is difficult to gauge how many people engage in any illegal action. Numbers obviously vary from year to year, but no one appears to doubt that many young people are leaving and will in the future leave the country to take up arms.

Ideological

There is an inherent danger for the state in mounting any public trial. To have the desired ideological effect it must appear fair. It must seem that the accused have had the opportunity of putting their side of the case. Once that is allowed the accused may act in a manner that nullifies the state's ideological objectives. Equally, a public trial runs the risk that the public may conclude that the accused were justified.

On the ideological level, then, the state's version of events does not go unchallenged. Many accused in political trials present their version and seek, wherever possible, to justify their actions. Such arguments of the accused have in the past been presented in a variety of forms. Until 1977 (after which the Criminal Procedure Act made it impossible), many political accused made unsworn statements from the dock. Some, such as those of Nelson Mandela and Andiba Toivo ja Toivo, became famous as statements of their political cause.[17] More recently, accused have explained their actions in evidence (for example, Barbara Hogan) or in mitigation (for example, Mogoerane, Mosololi, Motaung, Niehaus).

John Dugard has remarked on the fact that political accused have tended not to disrupt proceedings, as has happened, for example, in the United States. He explains this in terms of the 'mystique of the Bench and the professionalism of the Bar'. The Bench, he argues, has maintained its reputation as an 'isolated institution of objectivity and fairness'. This reputation, he feels, has validity even for 'some of the most vigorous opponents of the Government' (pp. 248–49). While this explanation may reflect the views of some sections of the opposition to apartheid, it is doubtful, I suggest, whether the 'mystique of the Bench' and even the 'professionalism of the Bar' has the same impact on blacks as it does on whites.[18] Certainly it is doubtful whether many political accused hold the Bench in the degree of awe that Dugard suggests.

Subsequent to Dugard's remarks, proceedings were in fact disrupted in the Pietermaritzburg Treason trial of 1979.[19] What happened, to distinguish this trial of Mange and others from previous political trials, was not a changed attitude towards the Bench, but that special circumstances arose in this trial. Much of the trial was held *in camera*. That is why the accused concluded that their side of the case could not be presented through conventional methods. According to a report in *Work in Progress*: 'Tladitsagae Molefe, the second accused, told the court that he was prepared to participate in the proceedings if the trial was opened to the public. When this was refused, he said that he would have nothing to do with the hearing. "Your worship can impose sentence on me now," he said' (10, November 1979, 43). Subsequent trials have generally been open to the public and the tactics of the Pietermaritzburg trial have not been repeated.

It is not only the accused but the masses in South Africa and democrats throughout the world who contest the ideological goals of South African political trials. Supporters of the accused have often demonstrated their support by shouting slogans and singing freedom songs in court. (Legislation now makes it possible to curb this and one prosecution is pending at present.)

When Mogoerane, Mosololi and Motaung were sentenced to death, the presiding judge spoke of their actions as 'premeditated terrible deeds',[20] that would not be approved by 'any decent Black person'.[21] The spectators were clearly unimpressed and one relative shouted: 'They were soldiers and will die like soldiers.'[22] When they were hanged church bells rang to signal mourning in Soweto. Far from the judicial version of their behaviour being accepted, they were regarded by ordinary people as heroes.

Internationally, such trials have been even less successful. In the UN, apartheid has been declared an international crime. The legitimacy of legal proceedings against opponents of apartheid is not accepted. There is also a growing body of legal opinion that holds that captured guerillas are entitled to Prisoner of War status.

Political trials in the 'new dispensation'

In most bourgeois societies the judiciary is relied on as a final repository of legitimacy. When the courts are invoked, it is hoped that their seeming impartiality will win wider acceptance than purely administrative acts. Consequently, great pains are taken to secure the reputation of the judiciary and to ensure that it is accorded appropriate respect. A crisis in confidence in the judiciary is a particularly serious matter.[23]

The image of the South African judiciary in the country and overseas appears to have been compromised in the eyes of some of its admirers, through the part which it has played in trials which are so obviously loaded against accused who represent political forces opposed to the social order. It is noteworthy, therefore, that there has been a recent tendency to 'normalise' the legal process. Charges have been framed under such common law offences as treason and murder in cases that might previously have been tried under the Terrorism or Internal Security or 'Sabotage' Acts. In addition, the new Internal Security Act attempts to narrow the definition of offences and make penalties less extreme.

These tendencies, as with much else in the current 'reform' programme, are not without contradictions. The removal of minimum penalties is to some extent undermined by excessive prosecution and sentencing practices. Also, the decision to prosecute violent activities under common law headings, coexists with an apparent widening of the scope of common law treason, to cover the non-violent activities of Barbara Hogan.[24]

Though contradictory, these tendencies are, I suggest, nevertheless significant. They may be explained by the following factors:
• The type of armed activity that has been committed in recent years can be successfully prosecuted under the normal common law of treason or murder or some other provision. These are sufficiently precisely

defined so that they cover violent activity *only* instead of using dragnet provisions which potentially encompass these acts and *also* the activities of people like the Dean of Johannesburg, black consciousness groups, etc.
• With the aid of pre-trial interrogation and various other procedural advantages, the prosecution still starts the case with very substantial advantages over the defence.
• In the prevailing domestic and international conjuncture the government might derive political advantages from such modifications. Present security legislation is very unpopular in the legal profession in South Africa, as well as overseas; it is criticised by the government's political friends as well as its opponents, locally and abroad. It is also a source of concern in business circles.

This government has launched a concerted attempt to convince sympathetic governments, such as the present US administration, that reforms are being introduced. It has also embarked on a concerted campaign to unify white public opinion and to win over petty-bourgeois blacks, especially coloureds and Indians, behind what is described as a total strategy. This 'toenadering' may be facilitated by 'normalisation' of the legal system.
• Such reforms might also be hoped to provide the additional advantage of increasing the value of judicial 'authentication'.[25] The judiciary can only attempt such a role if it appears to retain a measure of 'judicial space', i.e. where it continues to decide the most substantial issues in a particular case. Present rules for political trials have narrowed or excluded judicial discretion with regard to a number of issues. The less that the judiciary appears merely to be a rubber stamp for decisions taken elsewhere, the more that it may appear to be an 'impartial arbiter'.

Although the new security legislation makes only limited changes, it may nevertheless be hoped by the government that the move towards narrower definition of offences and the ending of mandatory sentences, by restoring elements of judicial discretion, will simultaneously restore some of the appearance of impartiality.

Both these reforms and the tendency to charge political offenders under common law provisions should in the final analysis be seen, I suggest, as attempts to depict these trials as 'normal' criminal trials. Presumably it is therefore hoped that, in consequence, a wider range of people will be more willing to accept the validity of the label of criminality that is appended to these offenders.

Notes

1 John Dugard, *Human Rights and the South African Legal Order* (Princeton, New Jersey, 1978), 212.

2 For a review of some of the earlier trials, see J. Dugard, *Human Rights*, 208 ff.

3 On the limited provision for special procedures in political trials, see J. Dugard, *Human Rights*, 252-3.

4 For full discussion, see R.S. Suttner, *The Role of the Judiciary in the South African Social Order* (unpub. 1983, currently being prepared for publication by Ravan Press), 24-37.

5 See, for example, the reports of the appearance without legal representation in the Pietermaritzburg magistrates' court of T.P. Ngcobo. He is reported to have confessed to responsibility for various bomb explosions and to have carried a bomb to a meeting that the prime minister was to address (*Star*, 15.12.83). At his trial, E. Wentzel SC, for the defence, told the court that 'a cornerstone of the whole system of law' was in question with the conditions under which Ngcobo pleaded guilty at a preliminary hearing in a magistrate's court (*RDM*, 09.03.84).

6 See J. Dugard, *Human Rights*, 254-5, and sections 39, 40 and 43 of the Criminal Procedure Act, no. 51 of 1977.

7 Both these factors were mentioned in mitigation by counsel when Phillip Dlamini refused to give state evidence in the Terrorism Act trial of Ms Lillian Keagile, (*RDM*, 14.01.83).

8 See section 30(1) of Internal Security Act, no. 74 of 1982.

9 See R. Suttner, *Role of the Judiciary*, 33-34 and notes 211, 212, p. 84.

10 Here, I have in mind trials such as that of George Moiloa, the Rev. Molefe Tsele and Amanda Kwadi, a leading figure in the Federation of South African Women who was arrested when she was due to speak on Women's Day in August 1983. See 'No case, say 3 freed in ANC trial' (*RDM extra*, 12.11.83).

11 See report of advocate's plea in case of J.M. Pantshwa in 'The Courts', *Work in Progress*, 5, June 1978, 67.

12 I have in mind, here, such cases as the sentence on two men found to have sung ANC songs at a concert and the man who had an ANC slogan engraved on his mug.

13 See J. Dugard, *Human Rights*, 241-2; 259-60.

14 J. Dugard, *Human Rights*, 215-6.

15 There are, of course, other reasons for holding trials *in camera*, including as already mentioned, the fear of reprisals against state witnesses.

16 Quoted in 'The Treason Trial: "Never on Our Knees" ', *Work in Progress*, 11, February 1980, 44.

17 Toivo ja Toivo's speech 'Here I Stand' is printed in *Forced Landing*, edited by Mothobi Mutloatse (Johannesburg, 1978), 192-198.

18 On possible attitudes of blacks to the Bar and Bench, see R. Suttner, *Role of the Judiciary*, 10-11 and generally.

19 See note 16 above and 'The Treason Trial', *Work in Progress*, 10, November 1979, 39-44.

20 See *Lawyers for Human Rights Bulletin*, 1, February 1983, 126.

21 At 124, 125.

22 'ANC Trio Sentenced to Death', *Drum*, October 1982, 25.

23 See *Selections from The Prison Notebooks of Antonio Gramsci*, edited and translated by Quintin Hoare and Geoffrey Noweil-Smith, (New York, 1971), 246.

24 See John Dugard 'Sentences in Political Trials', *Lawyers for Human Rights Bulletin*, 1, February 1982, 91–2.
25 See Otto Kircheimer's discussion of the judiciary's role as authenticator, in *Political Justice*, (Princeton, New Jersey, 1961), 6–7, 423–25; and Dugard, *Human Rights*, chap. 7.

Section 2: Labour

Introduction

Nicholas Haysom and Eddie Webster

1983 was a mixed year for labour. The emerging trade unions consolidated gains won in 1981 and 1982 and even expanded in some cases. But the overall economic condition of workers deteriorated. The economic recession deepened leaving large numbers of workers without jobs, and some close to starvation in the rural areas.

Recession allowed management to adopt an aggressive attitude to union organisation, to effect the disposal of surplus stock during work stoppages, and to make use of job insecurity to temper worker demands.

Management was reluctant to grant wage increases, and real wages for many black workers declined further in 1983. Deteriorating conditions in the 'reserves', compounded by drought and increased unemployment, forced employed black workers to carry a larger number of dependants. In these unfavourable circumstances, and with the persistence of anti-union attitudes and racist legislation, some unions have defensively resorted to industrial relations institutions such as industrial councils and the Industrial Court. In the case of the Industrial Court, unions have done more than protect their position. They have used 'unfair labour practice', legislation to significantly limit management's right to dismiss or retrench at will. At the end of 1983, however, there were distinct signs that both the traditional institutions of collective bargaining (industrial councils) and management were attempting to recapture their authority. This involved pressurising the state to clip the wings of the Industrial Court.

In spite of the recession, unions made further advances during 1983. Emerging unions now have an organised presence in over 756 workplaces and have signed 420 formal agreements. At the centre of this new force on the shop floor are the 6 000 shop stewards. Bargaining by these shop stewards is steadily widening. An increasing number of collective agreements have been concluded limiting 'managerial prerogative' to dismiss, discipline, retrench or deduct wages unilaterally. The rights of women workers have been increasingly recognised. The emerging unions have gone some way in establishing the right to strike as part of collective bargaining.

Issues such as health and safety were placed firmly on the industrial relations agenda during the year. The Machinery and Occupational Safety Act (not yet in force) is in part an attempt to side-step the unions in dealing with such issues. Inadequate policing of the inadequate official standards of health and safety means that there is likely to be a sharp conflict as labour attempts to upgrade working conditions in 1984. The most significant cases that surfaced in 1983 both involved the National Union of Mineworkers. One dealt with the refusal of gold miners to work in conditions where they feared for their lives. The other involved a comprehensive failure to comply with safety standards at Hlobane. This resulted in the death of 68 coal miners.

The organisation of mine workers is now proceeding rapidly, making up for the delay with which this industry has been opened to organisation.

The nature of working class politics continued to be a matter of debate during the year. It was given added impetus by the formation of the United Democratic Front and the National Forum. While most emerging unions stayed out of both UDF and NF, the question of class alliances was debated widely in political circles. The nature of working class politics was one of the questions raised: Should it concern itself with the marginalised unemployed in the bantustans? Does it deal with the immediate question of national democratic rights, and if so, in what way? How, if at all, should trade unions articulate with popular struggles?

The growing sophistication of collective bargaining was of immediate concern to the unions. At the end of the year Barlow Rand noted publicly that demands by certain unions for 'worker control' threaten the 'private enterprise' system. This remark was probably in response to union demands for information on company strategies and intentions on mergers, profits and closures. While management might have liked the 'one big family' analogy in the past, requests to account for their management appeared novel and impudent. Labour is likely to insist that such information is reasonable and legitimate, and indications are that bargaining in 1984 will be sharply contested.

The response of some bantustan governments to the emerging unions was a matter of growing concern. The overtly repressive response by the

Ciskei towards unions culminated in the September 1983 banning of
SAAWU. The Ciskei, like KwaZulu and Bophuthatswana houses African
workers who commute to nearby industrial centres. The response of
these bantustan administrations is partially explained by their ethnic and
authoritarian nature. This is threatened by non-racial democratic
organisations which express the dissatisfaction of bantustan subjects with
separate development.

Bophuthatswana's strategy is to prohibit and harass the operation of
unions which are not confined to their territory. The Venda minister, introducing that bantustan's Labour Act, which provides for liaison committees, echoed the sentiments of a Nationalist minister 30 years before him
when he stated: 'Our country is not at the stage yet to entertain trade
unions. We will only allow unions when we are sure they are free of outside influences.'

How are unions likely to deal with bantustan states that want no union
activity at all, or insist on 'ethnic' unions? These administrations reinforce the central state's attempt to entrench regional divisions within the
working class. The emerging unions aim to build nationwide industrial
unions. This cuts across state strategy to divide workers, and the issue
of unions in the bantustans is likely to emerge as a central issue in the
years to come.

The tentative moves towards trade union unity made minimal progress
in 1983. Formidable barriers posed by different organisational structures
(general, regional, industrial) have obscured the advantages of co-
operation which could avoid the disorganisation of workers caused by
competition between unions. Co-operation among industrially based
unions has now reached the planning stage, and a new federation of
unions may be built by the end of 1984.

New Force on the Shop Floor

Eddie Webster

In spite of the recession, 1983 was a year of consolidation and steady growth for the emerging unions. Although significant differences still remain between the general and industrial unions, most emerging unions are now winning similar rights for black workers on the shop floor. This new force on the shop floor has led to a managerial counter-offensive defending 'managerial prerogatives' against union demands for worker control.

Management's recognition of the permanence of unions for black workers has begun a process of redefinition of industrial relations in South Africa. Although major recognition battles continue (such as the one between the NUTW and Frame Group in Durban-Pinetown), unionism is becoming less of a struggle for recognition. Industrial relations in South Africa have begun to take on some of the familiar features that characterise collective bargaining in Europe and America. This has opened long standing debates on the nature of trade unionism within a capitalist society: are they essentially institutions of accommodation designed simply to protect the jobs of their members or do they have the potential for a more dramatic challenge to capitalism? A crucial element in this debate is the nature and objectives of the unions themselves. What are the structures, organisational achievements and potential role of the emerging unions in the post-Wiehahn period?

Structures

In the post-Wiehahn period, the emerging unions moved unequivocally to the centre of the industrial relations stage. These unions, which draw on predominantly African unskilled and semi-skilled workers, have grown rapidly since 1979. Initially, black workers did not join unions for the benefits they offered. These are usually modest, in most cases a R100 funeral benefit. Nor did most of them join because they were expecting to win wage increases. Most unions have only begun recently to engage in serious wage bargaining. The majority joined unions out of a desire to defend worker rights from what they see as arbitrary or unfair treatment by management. 'I joined the union,' one worker I interviewed said, 'because workers are not treated like human beings by management.'[1]

While recruitment has indeed been rapid in the post-Wiehahn period, membership is still small at approximately 400 000 signed-up members. Membership is spread between two national federations — FOSATU and CUSA — and at least another dozen independent unions such as SAAWU, FCWU and GWU. However, with an economically active population of ten million, their potential for growth is considerable. With a traditional union membership of 800 000, South Africa can be said to have a total union membership (registered and unregistered) of approximately 1 200 000, comprising about 12% of the total work-force. This gives South Africa the lowest percentage of workers unionised in the developed capitalist world. Sweden with 83%, has the highest, followed by the UK (50%), Germany (38%), Japan (33%), and the USA (20%).

South Africa's unions are still small compared to the 'giant unions' of the US and Europe. Of the 189 registered and unregistered unions operating in South Africa at the end of 1980, 73% had less than 5 000 members and 38% had less than 500. Only 13,7% had a membership of more than 20 000. The largest established union in South Africa, the SA Boilermakers' Society, has a membership of only 54 000.

The most dramatic and public demonstration of this new assertion of black worker rights is the increase in the number of strikes. Some of the main trends in recent strike activity among black workers were:

1. The number of strikes has increased dramatically since 1979, reaching its highest point ever in 1982. In spite of the economic downswing, the number of strikes did not decline as dramatically in 1983 as expected. Figures released by the Department of Manpower show that strikes decreased from 394 in 1982 to 336 in 1983. This accounted for almost half the number for the other 11 months of the year (*RDM*, 10.02.84).

2. The most important trend is the growing involvement of trade unions in the resolution of industrial conflict. Significantly, strikes were longest where union penetration was highest.

3. Not surprisingly, wages have emerged as the major demand among striking workers, followed by dismissals, then retrenchment.[2]
4. While strikes are becoming a normal part of the collective bargaining process, it is important to place South Africa in comparative perspective. In 1981–2, Sweden had the highest number of working days lost per annum per 1 000 workers, i.e. 105. The UK was second, with 45, the US third, with 32, while South Africa had 26. Germany and Japan had only one and two days respectively.
5. With some exceptions, such as the nationwide strike in Autoplastics in 1983, strikes tend to be single factory disputes rather than industry-wide.

The work-place location of organisation and action reflects an important feature of these emerging unions − their concentration on building shop steward structures in selected work-places. The emerging unions now have an organising presence in over 756 work-places, covering largely factories, but including newspapers, supermarkets, hotels and nursing homes. In 420 of these, formal agreements have been signed by unions. These take three main forms: recognition, procedural and substantive. Recognition agreements provide for recognition of the union's right to organise and represent workers: this includes regular meetings with management, time off for shop stewards' meetings, training and report-back meetings and union rights such as stop orders and access. Procedural agreements establish procedural rights in the case of retrenchment, dismissal and grievance handling. Substantive agreements provide for negotiating rights over wages and working conditions.

Shop stewards and their committees have become the pivot of the organisational structures of these new unions. Structuring of these committees and their incorporation in the constitution of the unions was a significant innovation in South African trade unionism. Each department in the work-place elects a shop steward and there are now over 6 000 shop stewards in the emerging unions. On average, there is one shop steward for every 60 signed-up union members. Those elected to the position of shop steward tend to be below the age of 35, have worked for some time in their current work-place, and have a strong sense of service to their fellow workers.

Shop steward committees meet regularly − at least once a month − although some meet as often as once a week. First and foremost, shop stewards represent the interests of union members in their department, protect the rights of workers against management and, if necessary, challenge their decisions. As members of the shop stewards' committee, they play a role in negotiating for the whole plant on wages and working conditions; and where an agreement exists, they must see that it is followed. However, shop stewards are also the key link between full-time union officials and members. Their function, as they understand it, is to establish a stable relationship between management and workers. As spokespeople for the workers in their department, it is their task to resolve grievances that are brought to them. 'He is,' one shop steward I interviewed said, 'a representative of the workers in the factory. His job is to maintain discipline among the workers under him, and to take workers' grievances to management and report back to workers.'

A shop steward is rooted in the work-place and his power and position are largely dependent on the continuing support of the members. Any suspicion that the shop steward has been 'bought' is likely to lead to an instant rejection by workers. An examination of strikes in the East Rand metal industry in 1981 showed that workers would stop work demanding that management remove a shop steward from the factory because he had become an 'impimpi' — an informer. The important point is that shop stewards are directly accountable to the shop floor. The system is, in other words, a form of direct democracy.

Worker control is maintained through shop steward representation on the central decision-making bodies of the unions. In FOSATU the Branch Executive Committees (BEC) consist of shop stewards from the different factories; in FCWU each factory elects a union committee which is then represented at branch level; in GWU, shop stewards elect a controlling committee which is the highest decision-making body.

One of the most significant organisational developments has been the way shop stewards have taken responsibility for organising local areas into their own hands creating structures by which this could be done. The principal means by which this has been accomplished in FOSATU is through the shop steward council. These councils bring together different industries and provide a focus for workers as a *class* around issues beyond the factory in that area. The Kathlehong shop steward council, for example, has concerned itself with opposing the East Rand Administration Board's demolition of thousands of township shacks housing many of its migrant workers. Councils have also emerged linking together shop stewards from different companies such as the shop stewards' committee at Barlow Rand, Metal Box and Dorbyl. In East London, the formation of the Committee of Ten by workers during the

1983 bus boycott is another example of shop steward involvement beyond the factory.

The focus on shop steward structures has led to an emphasis on factory-level bargaining. Wiehahn's strategy of incorporating the emerging unions into industrial councils (ICs) was seen as an attempt to pre-empt these emerging shop floor structures. Although no consensus on ICs has yet been established within the emerging unions, FOSATU, after long debate, clarified its position in 1982: provided that plant bargaining and recognition rights are not sacrificed, affiliates can enter ICs if it appears organisationally advantageous to the members of the union. In 1983, two FOSATU affiliates applied to join ICs — MAWU and the NUTW.

It remains to be seen whether these unions are able to achieve their objectives in the IC. Although MAWU was not able to win significant wage increases in the 1983 negotiations, it refused to sign the agreement and successfully mobilised membership nationwide over a demand for a R90-a-week minimum wage. In southern Natal, membership of MAWU actually increased as workers turned toward the union that had refused to accept the IC settlement.

MAWU was also able to open up important divisions within the Confederation of Metal and Building Unions, a traditional union caucus. These divisions were between those unions with a base largely or exclusively among white workers (such as the Amalgamated Engineering Union), and those like the Boilermakers' Society which are attempting to recruit large numbers of African workers. But the crucial test will be the extent to which MAWU will be able to retain its shop floor structures in the face of a growing centralisation of decision-making and the division of labour necessary to negotiate a complex industrial council agreement.

How have the approximately 800 000 workers organised into the traditional unions responded to this 'challenge from below' from the emerging unions? Amongst the traditional unions, the conservative SACLA has steadily declined in membership with its two major affiliates (SA Iron and Steel and the Mine Workers' Union) differing on how to respond to the new labour dispensation. Standing for traditional white worker privilege, the MWU's racist rhetoric is attractive to some white workers who feel their job security threatened by black advancement and the recession. Eager to establish itself as the 'champion' of the white worker, the MWU has expanded its scope of membership beyond mining, encroaching on areas occupied by some of the major traditional unions. SA Iron and Steel, by contrast, has shown a more pragmatic acceptance of the changes introduced by Wiehahn. Forced to negotiate side by side with FOSATU's black motor union (NAAWU) in the eastern Cape, they have had first-hand experience of the effect of NAAWU's tough bargaining and shop floor base. The union now runs courses to upgrade the bargaining skill and knowledge of its shop stewards. According to the secretary of SA Iron, white workers have been protected by job reservation, and their unions have generally not relied on tough bargaining on the shop floor; little attention has been paid to bargaining skills.

Most traditional unions, however, belong to TUCSA and welcomed the changes introduced by Wiehahn. Many applied for an extension of their scope of registration to include Africans or set up parallel unions. Benefitting by close links with management and the closed shop provisions of many industrial council agreements, TUCSA was able, by September 1983, to boost its membership to 478 420, including 139 567 Africans (29%).

However, 1983 was a troubled year for TUCSA. Shortly before the September annual conference its largest affiliate, the Boilermakers' Society, accused TUCSA of failing to respond adequately to the emerging unions. Although the National Executive Committee responded with a confidential memo on the role of TUCSA, and successfully steered a proposal through conference to substantially increase their range of services, the Boilermakers' Society resigned from TUCSA when their motion calling for a special conference was defeated. Underlying their dissatisfaction is TUCSA's failure to respond constructively to the emerging unions. Most TUCSA affiliates see the emerging unions as rivals who are 'poaching' their members. In fact, the 1983 conference went as far as proposing the banning of all unregistered unions.

The closed shop is at the centre of the battle between traditional and emerging unions. TUCSA affiliates defend it as a mechanism for protecting the job, while the emerging unions criticise it on the grounds that traditional unions are using it to gain or maintain unwilling membership with a minimum of effort. In fact, the FOSATU-affiliated PWAWU successfully challenged the TUCSA-affiliated SATU's closed shop in a number of printing works during 1983, enabling workers to join PWAWU.

In November, the Electrical and Allied Trades Union, a black parallel union, severed links with its white 'parent' in an attempt to establish a more independent position. The traditional unions will either have to adapt their structures to incorporate a stronger shop floor involvement, or else they will find their membership declining and will eventually disappear.

Organisational achievements

What are the organisational achievements of the emerging unions? The first and most important is the winning of certain rights in the work-place through an emphasis on work-place organisation and the establishment of plant agreements. Through the 420 agreements already signed, black workers are winning enforceable rights in their work-place, in areas where management has in the past exercised unilateral power. In May 1983, CCAWUSA negotiated an agreement with OK Bazaars establishing maternity rights for its members. This included the right to retain a job for up to 12 months after confinement. This has established an important precedent which has now been reproduced in at least seven other agreements.[3] The most immediate example of the extension of worker rights, is the successful demand to negotiate the nature and terms of retrenchment.

A second achievement is that these unions have laid the foundations for mass-based industrial unionism in the motor, textile, metal, retail, paper, chemical and food sectors. The current moves towards unity, although making little progress in 1983, are likely to accelerate the trend to industrial unionism as these unions begin to discuss the details of demarcation on a bilateral basis. In 1983, for example, the Glass and Allied Workers' Union merged with the CWIU, and EPSFAWU merged with the SFAWU. These mergers are the logical consequence of the centralisation within capital over the last two decades. In some industries one or two companies dominate. In the motor component industry where a section is owned by Autoplastics, NAAWU has established company bargaining. In the case of multinational companies such as Alfa Romeo, the union organiser for the industry in the Transvaal travelled to Italy, successfully putting pressure on the head office of the company to recognise the union.

Thirdly, the emerging unions have made a significant step in establishing the right to strike as a normal part of collective bargaining. South Africa experienced its first successful legal strike since the new labour dispensation, when the NUTW called for a nine-day overtime ban over wages on behalf of workers at Natal Thread. In January 1984 the first nationwide legal strike took place when AECI workers at all four plants went on strike over a wage demand. The strike at AECI led to dismissals. But the strike at Natal Thread led to an agreement that, in the event of a legal strike, the company would have to either dismiss all or none of the workers and it would have to re-employ all or none of the workers. This successful strike at Natal Thread was accompanied by a greater willingness to use conciliation boards to settle shop floor disputes (119 in 1983, as against 60 in 1982 and 21 in 1981) and the establishment of a mediation centre for the first time in South Africa.

The Industrial Court's growing role was one of the major labour trends in 1983. After having 20 cases referred to it in 1981, and 41 in 1982, the court had to deal with 170 cases in 1983 — a more than four-fold increase. Possibly the most significant decision made by the Industrial Court in 1983 was its temporary reinstatement of 17 NUM members who were dismissed at West Driefontein for refusing to work in an area they considered unsafe.

A fourth achievement is the contribution the emerging unions have made in establishing a working class leadership. The existence of over 6 000 shop stewards nationwide constitutes a significant cadre of working class leaders, most of whom are committed to non-ethnic and non-racial principles. An important indication of the emergence of an independent working class leadership was the highly successful public lectures given by FOSATU shop stewards in Johannesburg in July 1983.

Equally important, this leadership cuts across the migrant/non-migrant divide, challenging the state's strategy of dividing workers with permanent rights in the towns from those without rights. Often the emerging unions draw a substantial proportion of their membership, and indeed leadership, from migrant workers.

Nevertheless, the potential for the emergence of a 'labour aristocracy' of privileged insiders who have access to permanent residence in the urban areas and therefore stable employment and housing is a real one. The attempt by the bantustan governments to either outlaw some trade unions altogether (the Ciskei), or deal with them on a separate basis (Bophuthatswana), makes resistance to division more difficult for workers.

Finally, by establishing independent working class organisations, the emerging unions have created the embryo of a working class politics in South Africa. This is seen most clearly in the evolving shop steward councils which readily concern themselves with non-factory issues, pushing unions beyond 'pure-and-simple' trade unionism. The most dramatic example of political involvement beyond the factory in 1983 has been the bus boycott undertaken by workers in East London. This climaxed in September 1983, when the Ciskei government banned SAAWU. The most recent example of union involvement in politics was the demand by

FOSATU members for 'one-man-one-vote' in the recent referendum on the government's constitutional proposals.

Possibly the most significant political development for the trade unions in 1983 was the formation of the UDF and the affiliation of some unions to this new popular alliance. Most of the emerging unions have not joined the UDF; they argue that the priority at present is unity within the labour movement but they do not rule out a formal relationship between a national political centre and a national trade union centre at some future date.[4] Joe Foster, secretary general of FOSATU, addressed himself to this question when he spelt out some of the implications of workers expressing their own distinctive mark on the wider popular struggle. In a key speech at the FOSATU congress in April 1982, Foster stressed the need for workers to build a national presence within the trade union movement, to have their own newspapers, to build trained and accountable shop stewards, and to engage in community politics only to the extent that they can maintain their own identity. The workers' task, as Foster sees it, is to build their own powerful and effective organisation within the wider popular struggle. Foster's speech raises important questions that are beginning to be debated inside the unions. What, for example, is the actual content of this working class politics? Will it include the plight of the reserve army in the bantustans growing daily as more migrant workers are retrenched, unorganised workers, and the growing numbers of marginalised women?

Above all, the South African working class is not some collective *tabula rasa* waiting for the correct line — it contains its own traditions, political culture and consciousness which has to be confronted in any strategy to develop a working class politics. For many workers this political culture involves a conditional and qualified support for the national political tradition. A remark by a shop steward captures this: 'If we release Mandela, we can put Mandela as the prime minister — but he must be controlled by the workers.'

The nationalist tradition has, in the past, expressed itself most powerfully in the ANC, an organisation which symbolises for many the popular struggle against apartheid in the past, and its continuity into the present. But the logic of Foster's argument is to defer alliances between the working class and other oppressed classes until the working class has consolidated its own organisation. Is it possible to abstain from alliances and still retain leadership of the wider popular struggle or must the question of alliances be faced now? If workers are to enter an alliance, when are they to join with an alliance and who is to decide?[5] Or is the logic of Foster's argument that the working class requires its own separate political organisation?

The five organisational achievements identified above have increased the bargaining power of labour, opening up the opportunity for black people to participate democratically in organisations that have significant potential for change. By gathering together large numbers of workers and linking them together in production, monopoly capitalism has created the material conditions for mass-based industrial unionism. Their potential manpower, daily access to members and location in strategic sectors of the economy, have given the unions greater capacity for the mobilisation of power than any other organisation at present publicly active within the black population. This is well illustrated by the ability of the emerging unions to mobilise over 100 000 workers in the space of two days for a half-hour nationwide stoppage over Dr Neil Aggett's death in detention. These organisations are independent schools of democracy where substantial worker leadership has developed with the potential to play a central role in changing South Africa.

South Africa is at present at or near the head of the world's inequality league. Most real wage increases since 1970 took place between 1973–5. Since that period black incomes have remained relatively constant or perhaps even fallen.[6] Pleas by management that jobs need to be 'scientifically' evaluated and productivity increased before wage increases are given, are likely to lead to demands by workers for a 'living' wage and considerable scepticism about management productivity figures.[7] Management can expect a more sophisticated response to bargaining from the emerging unions in the future. Some may even be faced by a negotiating team, which includes full-time officials and senior shop stewards, knowledgeable about the economics of that industry and backed by research facilities. Unions are likely to respond to cries that profits are down by demanding greater financial disclosure by management. Management will find that issues previously not on the bargaining table now are — health and safety, child care, pensions and retrenchment. The significance of the post-Wiehahn period is that the emerging unions have laid the organisational foundations for a more systematic challenge to South Africa's inequality.

Notes

I would like to thank Merle Barsel for helping gather some of the factual information in this paper.

1 The information on shop stewards in this article is drawn from chapter 11 of my PhD thesis, 'The Labour Process and forms of Work Place Organisation in South African Foundaries', (University of Witwatersrand, 1983).

2 R. and L. Lambert, 'State Reform and Working Class Resistance, 1982', in *Same Foundations, New Facades?*, South African Review One (Johannesburg, 1983).

3 This is discussed in detail in J. Cock, E. Emdon and B. Klugman, 'Child Care and the Working Mother', Second Carnegie Inquiry, 1984.

4 Interview with D. Lewis, 'General Workers' Union and the UDF', *Work In Progress*, 29, October 1983.

5 During 1983 this debate began to widen beyond narrow circles, becoming a general debate within the left. See 'Class Alliances — the "Economic" and "Political" struggle',

6 J. Keenan, 'Trickle Up: African Income and Employment', in *Same Foundations, New Facades?*, South African Review One (Johannesburg, 1983).

6 J Keenan, 'Trickle Up: African Income and Employment', in *Same Foundations, New Facades?*, South African Review One (Johannesburg, 1983).

7 C. Meth, *A Challenge from FOSATU on Productivity*, Fosatu occasional papers, no. 6, 1983.

Union Unity

Doug Hindson

In August 1981, 11 unaffiliated unions and two federations[1] met at Langa, near Cape Town, to discuss ways of opposing bannings and detentions of union leaders and a common approach to the newly enacted Industrial Conciliation legislation. The new legislation offered to recognise African trade unions if they complied with certain requirements and registered with the Department of Manpower.[2] This was not the first attempt by the emerging unions[3] to unite, but the meeting marked the beginning of a new initiative to widen and strengthen ties between these unions.[4] At subsequent meetings the question of forming a new federation of independent unions was taken up and broad agreement was reached that this would be desirable in the near future, but this goal had not yet been reached by the end of 1983.

Between August 1981 and October 1983 there were six summit meetings to discuss ways of strengthening ties between unions. During these discussions the basis for co-operation, as well as the underlying differences between unions, was gradually clarified. The first part of this paper describes the summit debates and the second discusses the major obstacles to union unity.

Unity talks 1981–1983

Langa: August 1981

Much of the debate at the first Langa meeting focussed on the question of union registration with the Department of Manpower Utilisation. In order to register, unions had to submit their constitutions and, periodically, their finances to the Department. In return they would be granted official recognition — a right previously denied to unions with African membership.

Some unions felt that registration would inevitably lead to state control, a prospect they rejected in principle. For these unions the question of registration raised a larger political issue. They feared that subordination to state measures would lead to co-option and prevent the unions from serving the long term interests of workers.

Other unions, several of which were already registered, argued that registration was tactically expedient; its protection could be exploited to expand and strengthen a union. The extension of state controls could be resisted if a union developed strong democratic structures rooted in the shop floor.

The following statement was issued at the end of the meeting: 'We resist and reject the present system of registration insofar as it is designed to control and interfere in the internal affairs of a union.'[5] This statement reflected the wide opposition to registration expressed at the meeting. Nevertheless the statement was ambiguous as to whether registered unions should deregister, or unregistered unions register in the future if the terms of registration were changed.

Of the other matters discussed only one related directly to inter-union co-operation: the establishment of solidarity committees. The meeting resolved to establish ad hoc committees in each region of the country to discuss and initiate solidarity action.[6]

The solidarity committees set up after the Langa meeting met with little success in practice. They were attended mainly by union officials (as against worker delegates), many of whom appeared to have no clear mandate from their memberships. As a result the meetings tended to degenerate into bickering between union representatives and did little to solve the practical problems of fostering wider union unity in the regions.[7]

Wilgespruit: April 1982

The second unity summit was delayed until April 1982 as a result, amongst other things, of the spate of detentions which hit the leaders especially of SAAWU, AFCWU and GAWU.[8] This meeting, held at Wilgespruit on the West Rand, took up the question of the formation of a new federation of unions.

At the Wilgespruit meeting differences immediately arose over the policy principles of the proposed new federation. Some unions expressed the view that acceptance of a set of principles should be a prerequisite for joining. After a heated exchange, MACWUSA/GWUSA, a breakaway from a FOSATU affiliate, stated that it was not prepared to co-operate

with registered unions or unions which participated on industrial councils, and walked out calling on all unregistered unions to join it. Despite
this walkout the meeting ended on a constructive note with agreement
that the next discussions should focus on the practical details involved in
forming a new federation.

Some unregistered unions appeared to have answered the call from
MACWUSA/GWUSA. In the weeks following the Wilgespruit meeting
rumours circulated that a federation of unregistered unions was being
formed.[9]

Port Elizabeth: July 1982

When the unions reconvened in July in Port Elizabeth these rumours
seemed confirmed: a caucus of seven unregistered unions appeared at
the meeting. These were MACWUSA/GWUSA, SAAWU, BMWU
(MGWUSA)/SATWU, OVGWU and GAWU.[10] The group of seven unions was united over seven 'non-negotiable' principles which they felt
other unions had to adopt in toto before they were willing to join them
in a federation. These principles were non-registration, shop floor bargaining, federation policy to be binding on affiliates, worker control,
non-racialism, participation in community issues and the rejection of
reactionary bodies nationally and internationally.

All the unions present at the meeting shared at least some of these principles. But few had all in common, and only the caucus of seven unions
held that every principle should be non-negotiable. Unity on the basis of
the seven non-negotiable principles would have excluded not only the
majority of unions at the talks but also the vast majority of workers
organised by the emerging unions.

Other unions at the talks argued that differences over principles should
not be allowed to prevent wider unity. A strengthened workers' movement was more important than unanimity over a set of abstract principles.
Despite efforts to encourage the seven unions to modify their stand, they
stuck to their position, thereby precipitating a collapse in the talks.

The Port Elizabeth talks were a turning point in the unity initiative insofar as the influence of the group of seven unions was concerned. These
unions shared certain characteristics which marked them off from the
other unions. All were general unions in the sense of being open to workers from all economic sectors. Two of the general unions, MACWUSA
and BMWU (later renamed the MGWUSA), originally set out to
organise workers in a specific factory or sector, but sister unions were
created on paper to enable the unions to organise elsewhere. All were

regionally rather than nationally based. Most of these general unions were small new organisations with a presence in no more than one township and an organised membership restricted to a small number of factories. Only in two cases, SAAWU and MACWUSA, had the unions set up branches outside their original bases. These new branches remained regionally centred, operating for all intents and purposes as autonomous branches of the unions concerned. In view of these features these unions are best described as 'regional-general'.

All seven of the regional-general unions emerged in the late 1970s when industrial relations reforms coupled with a sharp economic upturn provided uniquely favourable conditions for rapid union growth. Organising through strike waves and mass meetings in the townships some of these unions gained large followings in a short space of time. But they failed to match their rapid gains in signed-up membership with consolidation on the factory floor. With the onset of the recession in mid-1982, weaknesses in this method of organising workers began to show.[11] In the face of retrenchments and mounting state attacks, all experienced heavy erosion of factory membership and a weakening of worker participation in union activities.

Despite this, the regional-general unions chose to continue recruiting new members, and in the first months of the recession they chalked up impressive figures of membership growth.[12] But these figures were based on a count of membership cards in the office files rather than paid up or active members, and obscured a process of erosion of the bases of the organisations. The strains brought about by recession, loss of membership and, in the case of SAAWU, the detention of leadership over long periods precipitated inter-regional tensions, splits and threatened splits within the regional-general unions in 1983.

The other unions at the unity talks have tended to organise workers within specific industrial sectors. However the organising scope of the industrial unions differs widely. At the one end of the spectrum was the GWU. Until just prior to the Port Elizabeth talks, it was theoretically open to all workers. However, as a result of its attempts to organise beyond its original base in the Western Cape, and as a step towards greater solidarity with other unions, it took a policy decision in June 1982 to demarcate its activities and concentrate on dock and transport workers. Other industrial unions such as MAWU and the TGWU also define their focus in broad terms, including workers from a wide range of economic sectors connected to metal and transport activities respectively. Although these unions are open to workers in a range of economic activities the core of their membership is drawn from one industrial sector.

At the other end of the spectrum are industrial unions which operate in narrowly defined economic sectors, such as FOSATU's Jewellers and Goldsmiths Union. Others, such as the Cape Town Municipal Workers Association are confined to one centre. All these unions, the broad and narrow, will be referred to here as industrial unions.

A significant development during the period under review was that several of the larger industrial unions expanded out of their home bases to establish a national presence. Some, such as NAAWU, MAWU and the FCWU established new branches in all the major industrial centres. Other unions such as FOSATU's SFAWU and WPSFAWU, which were organising workers in the same sector in different regions of the country, joined to form a single national union.

The growth of the industrial unions was perhaps less spectacular than that of the regional-general unions during the boom period. But the majority of industrial unions weathered the recession far better. All the larger unions suffered the effects of retrenchments, but the loss of factories as a result of inadequate servicing by officials was much less evident than in the case of the regional-general unions. By mid-1982 the industrial unions had taken steps to consolidate organisation in the factories, and some continued to organise new factories successfully through the period of recession. By the end of 1983 the larger industrial unions had gained more paid up members than they had lost over the year and their organisations were much stronger.[13]

An outcome of these developments was that the influence of the regional-general unions, which had been considerable up until the Port Elizabeth meeting, began to weaken. From the middle of 1982 onwards the larger industrial unions began to exert pressure to speed up the formation of the new federation.

Athlone: April 1983

The changed balance of strength within the union movement was evident nine months after the Port Elizabeth meeting, when the unions gathered at Athlone. In contrast to the previous summit which had been a small gathering mainly of union officials, the meeting at Athlone was swollen by large delegations of shop stewards from all the major industrial centres. With the exception of CUSA, which was represented by federation officials, all the industrial unions had elected worker representatives, in some cases from union branch level upwards. The regional-general unions, in contrast, were represented only by officials (and a number of volunteer organisers from SAAWU).[14] The presence of office bearers directly representing thousands of workers throughout South Africa injected the unity talks with a sense of determination which had been absent at Port Elizabeth.[15] The leadership of the regional-general unions were made aware through the participation of these workers in the meeting, of the depth of support within the industrial unions for a new federation. During the course of the meeting the spokespeople of the regional-general unions retreated from the position they had taken up at Port Elizabeth, finally accepting a proposal to form a federation including unibns with differing policies.

Most of the discussion at Athlone concerned the practical steps to establish a new federation. All agreed on the need for a federation of unions. The disagreement was over the correct approach and how soon the federation should be established. Two main positions emerged. The first, adopted by the regional-general unions was that there should be a return to regional solidarity action committees through which unity could be built 'from the base up'. A national federation of unions should only be entertained once inter-union unity had been achieved at the local level. The justification for this was that a federation should only be formed with the approval of the workers of South Africa as a whole. Since the majority of workers were still unorganised the first task of the unions should be to organise the unorganised. If this was not done first, it was argued, a federation would constitute an imposition on workers from 'above' by leaders, rather than an organic development from 'below'.

The second position argued for immediate practical steps to form a new federation. The mandate for such a move, it was argued, had already been secured from organised workers in the meetings to discuss union unity which had been held prior to the summits. Union unity would grow from the formation of the federation. Regional solidarity committees were too loosely constituted and insufficiently grounded in union structures to ensure effective unity action.

During the course of this debate the second position gained ground. By the end of the meeting all the unions present, with the exception of OVGWU (a member of the group of seven), agreed to participate in the formation of a new federation, or to seek the mandate to do this.[16]

The Athlone meeting concluded with an agreement to set up a steering committee to discuss proposals for the new federation.

Steering committee, Athlone: June 1983

When the steering committee met some two months later, again at Athlone, the question of the structure of the new federation was taken up. Some of the unions, notably those not already affiliated to a federation, argued for a simple federal structure comprising a single annual congress and an executive committee to deal with the affairs of the federation between congresses. FOSATU and CUSA described their own structures, the first comprising a tightly-knit system of national, regional and local bodies and the second a looser structure with considerable union autonomy.

Two other important issues were taken up: finances and demarcation. The majority of unions at the meeting, including the two federations, felt that outside financial support for the federation was imperative. A minority argued strongly that the federation should be financed solely by member unions, particularly for its running expenses. This was to ensure that control over the federation remained firmly in the hands of workers as against donor organisations or officials whose salaries were paid from outside sources. The question of demarcation was not pursued at the meeting but all participants agreed to submit audited reports giving paid-up membership and information on the industries and localities in which they were organised.

After the meeting hopes were high that the next steering committee would strengthen union co-operation by establishing a procedure to deal with problems of demarcation and union competition.

Steering committee, Johannesburg: October 1983

Hopes were dashed at the steering committee meeting held at Khotso House in Johannesburg. Four of the regional-general unions, MACWUSA/GWUSA, GAWU, SAAWU, and one union grouping, CUSA, failed to produce the necessary information on membership and the places in which they were organised. This information was essential for discussing co-operation over demarcation. Failure to produce the information raised doubts about the willingness or ability of these unions to continue in the unity initiative.

The meeting witnessed a polarisation between the regional-general unions on the one hand and FOSATU and the larger unaffiliated unions on the other hand, with CUSA representatives attempting to take an impartial stance. The conflict revolved around allegations of competitive organising and deliberate disorganising of workers. Several unions criticised SAAWU, in particular, of poaching, disrupting meetings and attempting to organise workers in factories and sectors where other unions were known to have achieved majority representation.[17]

Although most of the meeting was wasted in divisive argument, two questions of practical importance emerged: how to resolve the problem of organised workers being disorganised and how to ensure that unorganised workers were organised without undue conflict developing between unions. One suggestion, advanced by the FCWU, was that no union should attempt to organise a factory where another had majority representation and that a union which achieved majority representation in an industry, sector, or company should organise the rest of the workers in these categories free from competition from other unions. Another proposal, put forward by FOSATU, was that there should be a commitment to industrial unions, with a view ultimately to establishing one union in each industry. No general agreement was reached on these proposals.

After two years and six meetings the talks had deadlocked. But despite the conflict the unions were reluctant to declare that unity had collapsed and a further meeting was arranged for November. At the request of FOSATU this meeting was postponed until March 1984.

Obstacles to union unity

Policies and principles

Differences over principles were the major source of conflict during the first four unity meetings. No principle was accepted unanimously. Although all the unions stated that workers' control was a fundamental principle, CUSA defined this as black workers' control.

These differences reflected varying political positions within the unions, but it is not clear whether these positions emanated merely from leadership or were genuine expressions of demands formulated by union membership at general meetings. At times the debate over union principles appeared to be a conflict between leadership rather than an expression of different lines emerging out of different sections of the working class.

Certainly, there was no direct relationship between the principles set out by the various unions and their membership composition or methods of organising workers which could explain the intensity of conflict generated over this question. Many unions shared the principle of non-registration and non-participation on industrial councils. These unions

included the general unions, some CUSA unions and several of the unaffiliated unions. Only the seven regional-general unions insisted that
these principles should be non-negotiable prerequisites for federation
membership. In some cases the positions taken up by unions at the unity
summits had no clear connection with their organisational practices
within the factories. SAAWU (in the Transvaal and Natal), for example,
participated on an industrial council shortly after the Port Elizabeth
meeting, despite this union's stance on this question at the talks.[18]

Opposition to registration and participation on industrial councils cannot in all cases be attributed merely to the political preference of leadership. For example, opposition to registration within the AFCWU stems
from a long history of struggle against the racially divisive effects of this
policy as implemented from the 1940s to the late 1970s. Despite this opposition, the AFCWU and the FCWU, a registered union, have managed
to function as one union. The unions have a separate existence only on
paper; all committees and meetings are constituted as one.

The way the unions construed the principles of non-racialism/racial
exclusivity did not necessarily reflect the composition of their membership. The group of seven regional-general unions all insisted that non-
racialism was non-negotiable. Yet none of these unions had organised
significant numbers of workers across racial lines. On the contrary these
unions' greatest impact has been amongst African workers in industrial
areas where the majority speak one main language and are restricted to
one or a few major townships. The most striking example is SAAWU
which is strongest in Mdantsane, a township of settled urban people
bound together by a common language and the experience of state repression under the bantustan administration of the Ciskei. Other examples
are MACWUSA in Port Elizabeth and the National General Workers
Union in Pretoria. No regional-general union has to date made substantial progress on the Witwatersrand, which has the largest and ethnically
most heterogeneous African working class in South Africa.

Theoretical adherence to non-racialism did not decisively determine
which unions stood together and which apart. However those unions with
a history of organising workers of different races, such as some within
FOSATU, the FCWU/AFCWU and the CTMWA, moved closer together
over the period of the talks. There are also some indications that unions
which have organised racially selectively (in practice if not in principle),
such as CUSA and branches of SAAWU (in the Transvaal and Natal), co-
operated increasingly during the last months of 1983.[19]

Similarly, involvement in 'community issues' has not played an obvious role either as an obstacle or as an incentive to unity, apart from the friction generated over this as a theoretical question. Although the regional-general unions all listed community involvement as a non-negotiable principle, only SAAWU in East London (along with a number of industrial unions in that area) has played a significant role in community action. In the Transvaal MAWU has taken up community issues through its shop stewards' council and in the Western Cape both the FCWU and the GWU, often through their membership, have played an important part in community politics. For this reason it seems preferable to avoid the term 'community unions' which has been used widely, but incorrectly, to describe the regional-general unions.

The only principle accepted by all the unions at the talks was worker control, or, in the case of CUSA, black worker control.

This was a principle which should have helped cement relations between unions. But had the meaning of the term been debated, broad agreement would have been unlikely, particularly since the experience of worker control was highly uneven between the participant unions. The unevenness in the development of democratic structures within the unions constituted one of the most serious obstacles to union unity.

Industrial and general unions.
The major line of division which appeared during the period of the unity talks was that between the group of seven regional-general unions and the others. This division manifested itself, particularly at the Port Elizabeth meeting, in terms of an adherence to different sets of principles. But the methods of organising workers, rather than the belief in abstract principles, eventually emerged as the most stubborn obstacle.

It is usually easier for unions organising in different sectors than for those organising in the same sector to unite under a larger body because they are not in competition with each other. General unions find it difficult to unite with other unions, whether industrial or general, because they are actually or potentially in competition with all unions over all workers, organised and unorganised. Not surprisingly the majority of the industrial unions at the unity talks were already members of one of the two union groupings, while all the general unions were unaffiliated.

The different methods of organising workers also tend to result in different kinds of union structures making it difficult for industrial and general unions to combine. Organising workers in a restricted locality, across industrial sectors, gives the regional-general unions an advantage for a time. Their offices are more accessible than those of industrial unions whose membership may be dispersed over wide areas. It is easier to draw large numbers of workers to mass meetings in a single township than to organise many smaller meetings of workers in factories spread across the country.

Unions that have organised workers on an area rather than a sectoral basis have found it difficult to develop strong shop floor structures and branch executives. Organising through large, open, township-based meetings usually means that the problems affecting workers as township dwellers rather than as workers are given priority. Without regular factory and union branch meetings (closed to the rest of the public), the specific grievances of workers cannot adequately be taken up. The larger open meeting inhibits the participation of ordinary union members, who inevitably feel that the factory problems about which they can talk with confidence are not the concern of others at such meetings. While the open mass meetings have given these unions large followings in their home townships they have not encouraged the development of strong shop steward committees either on the shop floor or at branch level.

Particularly in the early stages of its development, an industrial union is unlikely to have a large impact on the politics of a township. Its membership will normally represent a small fraction of the township's population — except where one company dominates an industrial location and adjacent township. In sectors where factories producing the same commodities are distributed widely across the country, these unions at first experience great difficulties in setting up and maintaining branches. Union organisers spend much of their time travelling from factory to factory and financial resources are stretched thin. Factories or hostels, rather than union offices or city halls, are often the site of meetings.

However, as increasing numbers of factories join the union the advantages of organising workers within a particular industry accumulate. The high degree of monopolistic ownership within each industrial sub-sector in South Africa has resulted in particular patterns of ownership: workers across the country fall under the same management, and are increasingly linked directly through the interconnected nature of production. Workers' unity is continuously reinforced as different factories under the same management come together to take up practical issues of common concern on a regular basis, often without the assistance of union officials. The active participation of workers in joint action at the factory level fosters the development of strong shop steward committees, a sense of self-reliance vis-à-vis union officials and a tradition of direct worker control of union affairs at the branch level.

Industrial unions have the effect of uniting workers who are racially, residentially and regionally divided but occupy similar positions within production. It is only some of the larger industrial unions that have racially mixed membership and these, too, have been the only unions successfully to join substantial numbers of both migrant and settled African workers. In sharp contrast, the regional-general unions have gained followings mainly in townships which are racially and ethnically homogeneous and principally it seems amongst settled urban workers.

The attempt by the seven regional-general unions to resuscitate the regional solidarity action committees is explicable in the light of their method of organising workers and their structures. This approach held out the prospect of consolidating their positions in their home areas, thereby defending themselves against the larger industrial unions whose presence in any area, as against a sector, was usually small. At one time it seemed that SAAWU seriously considered expanding out of its home base in East London to become a national general union in opposition to the industrial unions, but its experiences since the onset of recession have made this increasingly unlikely.

The formation of a national federation of industrial unions would have severe implications for the regional-general unions. They would be obliged to focus on areas in which existing industrial unions have no significant presence and, in time, yield factories falling outside their lines of demarcation to other unions. In some areas this could involve the dismantling of union structures and the disappearance of these unions in their present form.

Of the seven regional-general unions only SAAWU has contemplated demarcation. Its intention was to reorganise its factories into separate industrial unions under the umbrella of the existing organisation. This, of course, meant that it would continue to stand in a competitive rather than a co-operative relationship to all other unions.

The alternative of forming a federation of regional-general unions would be unlikely to meet with success at this stage in the development of the union movement. The alliance of seven unions consists of six small unions, with a total membership of only a few thousand workers, clustered around SAAWU, which has a large following in one township but a relatively small base of organised workers in factories. The alliance appears to have been formed primarily at the level of union officials, and mainly as a defensive measure against the industrial unions. There have been few attempts to deepen this unity through meetings of the shop stewards. This means the alliance has not been rooted in strong democratic structures at the regional level. It would be unlikely to stand up to the organising power of a new federation of industrial unions.

Another difficulty facing the general unions is their tendency towards internal fracture. These unions maintain links between different branches principally by means of contacts between union leaders, as against, for example, the direct factory-to-factory links of the industrial unions. They have failed to produce strong worker executives at the branch level, although SAAWU has made serious attempts to establish such a foundation for its organisation in the East London area. These features of the regional-general unions have made them highly susceptible to splits along regional lines. Cases in point are the Pretoria branch of MACWU-SA/GWUSA, which split off to form the National General Workers Union after a dispute within leadership, and the conflicts which surfaced between the regional branches of SAAWU during 1983. The effects of these internal divisions, particularly in the case of SAAWU, are likely to ramify into the alliance of seven unions, weakening their chances of acting as a cohesive front during the unity talks in 1984.

The industrial unions have not escaped the problems of regionalism either. Few of these unions have as yet gained a presence in all the major industrial areas of the country. Even fewer have managed to organise all factories, let alone all workers, in their sectors. It is therefore not surprising that as these unions expand and set up branches in new regions, tensions and divisions in the formation of national structures take on a regional expression. Cases in point are the conflicts within MWASA and CCAWUSA. But by and large, the industrial unions have fared better in maintaining the cohesion of their organisations as they have expanded out of their home areas, or joined other unions organising workers in the same sectors in different industrial centres.

Levels of organisation

The most serious obstacles to union unity lie in the different organising practices and structures of the general as against the industrial unions. To some extent these differences can be explained in terms of the level of development of organisations, from local to regional to national, and particularly the development of democratic structures at each of these levels.

The lack of development of strong worker-controlled structures in the regional-general unions is clearly a function, in part, of their newness and lack of experience. However, with the exception of SAAWU in East London, there are few signs that these unions are successfully undertaking the difficult task of building up strong shop steward committees at branch (as against factory) level. This, in addition to some form of sectoral demarcation, would appear to be a necessary precondition for moving beyond the phase of recruitment-without-consolidation in which these unions have trapped themselves.

Despite the broad compatibility between the industrial unions, considerable difficulties arising out of their different levels of organisation and scope of activities have to be overcome in the course of forming the new federation. Some industrial unions remain essentially regionally based while others now operate nationally. Regionally based unions operating in the same sector will have to join to form a single national union. Competing national unions will either have to disband and reform as single unions or demarcate sub-sectors of activity. In achieving these changes, differences in policies, organising tactics and union traditions will have to be overcome.

The fact that two federations are already in existence presents advantages and obstacles to wider unity. The experience gained in inter-union co-operation within the groupings can be used to avoid repeating mistakes. However the reorganising of existing structures will in itself present problems. FOSATU gave a public commitment to disband just prior to the Wilgespruit meeting in April 1982. CUSA failed to attend the Wilgespruit meeting and has subsequently appeared equivocal about disbanding. However it is FOSATU that is likely to be the most resistant to disbanding when pressed. FOSATU is more tightly-knit and highly centralised than CUSA, and tends to operate in some respects like one large union. The degree of centralisation within FOSATU, and the lack of union autonomy, most marked in its weaker affiliates, will be questioned by the unaffiliated unions if FOSATU is discussed as a model for the new federation.

A particular difficulty relates to the regional structures of a future federation. At the Athlone meeting in June 1983, FOSATU described its regional structures. Some of the unaffiliated unions argued that these structures withdraw power from unions within FOSATU and concentrate it within federation structures. For a federation which will concern itself with social and political conditions affecting workers outside the factory, the need to establish structures which enable workers from different unions to come together to take up issues at a local level cannot be questioned. The shop steward councils within FOSATU, which bring together workers from different unions who live in one or a few townships in close proximity, may be a better model than FOSATU's regional structures which cover large areas of unconnected industrial and residential areas.

A further problem in the formation of a new federation is the question of finances. Both CUSA and FOSATU depend heavily on external financing for the maintenance of their federation structures. FOSATU has committed itself to financial independence and its affiliates have already achieved a considerable degree of independence. Some of the unaffiliated unions hold to the principle that a workers' organisation should be financed solely by workers, as this is an important means of ensuring that officials are made accountable to union members. In the case of both FOSATU and CUSA, the federation personnel who are dependent on external finances may be more resistant to dissolution than officials employed and paid by the unions. Particular problems may be encountered over the reorganisation of the regional structures within FOSATU and the various externally funded educational and other projects run by CUSA and FOSATU.

Conclusion

The first issue that has to be resolved at the unity talks in 1984 is whether and on what basis the regional-general unions will continue to participate in the unity initiative. Given the incompatibility of their method of organising workers and their structures with those of the industrial unions, it seems unlikely that regional-general unions will be able to unite with the others within a single federation in the immediate future.

In view of the fact that the vast majority of workers in South Africa remain unorganised, it is probable that the regional-general unions will continue to recruit membership for some time to come. But the space for this form of union organisation is likely to shrink as the industrial unions continue to expand. This expansion is already forcing the regional-general unions to narrow their sectoral focus and concentrate on areas not covered by industrial unions. Those which fail to make this transition, and continue to organise workers from all industrial sectors, will face increased rivalry with other unions, and growing internal difficulties. Those which demarcate and develop democratic branch structures will be attracted to a larger grouping of unions.

In the short term the regional-general unions may react to a new federation of industrial unions by formally constituting themselves as a federation. Such an organisation would, however, be prone to severe internal conflicts and would be unlikely to constitute a substantial alternative focus for the majority of workers.

If a wide new federation of industrial unions is ultimately formed, its impact will be considerable. It will strengthen the position of organised workers and speed up the process of organising the unorganised. The organisation of whole sectors across the country will place limitations on the capacity of management to exploit racial and regional differences in wages and working conditions. The federation will be better placed to take up non-factory issues at the local level by providing the means for workers from all sectors in an area to meet to discuss and take action on such issues.

Equally the federation will be better placed to press the demands of workers at a national level both in relation to capital and the state. For the first time it will bring the problem of the unemployed worker within reach of the workers' movement. This and the problems of employed and unemployed workers in border and bantustan areas will inevitably bring the union movement up against central state regional policy and the bantustan system, both of which are fundamental to the present 'reform' dispensation. For the first time in decades the possibility exists of the working class imprinting its specific demands and perspectives on the South African social and political process.

Postscript

The meeting of the Feasibility Committee on the 3–4 March 1984 released the following press statement:

> The view of the majority of organisations was that since it was decided in April 1983 to form a federation, little progress had been achieved. This was because some unions taking part in the talks are not ready or able to join a federation. The federation planned will be a federation of industrially demarcated unions, with the eventual aim of having one union for one industry. It follows that unions which are not demarcated along industrial lines or which have not yet formed industrial unions, are not ready to join a federation. It was decided to ask these unions to attend the meeting as observers, until such time as they are properly constituted along industrial lines. These unions did not accept the offer of observer status and left the meeting. However there is no hostility towards those unions and the offer to rejoin the talks as observers or as industrially constituted unions still stands.
>
> Considerable progress has been achieved in the talks and further meetings are planned in the near future.

The unions which left the meeting were MGWUSA, SAAWU and GAWU. The unions and groupings which remained were FCWU/AFCWU, GWU, CCAWUSA, CTMWA, FOSATU and CUSA. MACWUSA/GWUSA was not present.

Notes

1 The unaffiliated unions present at the Langa meeting were: FCWU/AFCWU, WPGWU (later renamed the GWU), SAAWU, CTMWA, BMWU (later to become MGWUSA and to form SATWU), GAWU, MACWUSA/GWUSA, SATWU, CCAWUSA and the OVG-WU. The two federations were FOSATU and CUSA. FOSATU affiliates were: MAWU, SFWU, PWAWU, CWIU, TGWU, NAAWU (previously three separate auto and allied workers unions), NUTW, GAWU (Glass and Allied Workers Union, later to join the CWIU), EAWU (later to disaffiliate) and the JGWU. CUSA affiliates were: BCAWU, LCDWU, SACWU, TAWU, FBAWU, SEAWU, UAMW (in Natal and the Transvaal) and the UAMAWU (Natal). The SATWU dropped out of the later talks, whereas MWASA, a union mainly of black journalists, attended the subsequent meetings as an observer. The OVGWU dropped out of the meetings after the Athlone summit in April 1983.
2 For a debate on the registration requirements see the *South African Labour Bulletin*, 7(1, 2, 3), September 1981.
3 There is no entirely satisfactory term to describe all the unions under consideration. The term 'emerging unions' is used in preference to 'independent' unions because it is not clear how or from what the unions are independent. Some of the unions at the unity talks, such as NAAWU and FCWU/AFCWU, were established long before the re-emergence of the union movement in the early 1970s. The Black Consciousness-oriented Black Allied Workers Union (BAWU) from which SAAWU and, later, GAWU split has not featured in the unity talks and it is not clear whether or in what form it now survives as a union.
4 A brief history of earlier unity initiatives is provided by K. Luckhardt and B. Wall, *Working for Freedom* (World Council of Churches, Geneva, 1981).
5 *South African Labour Bulletin*, 8(4), February 1983, 11–12.
6 The other resolutions are recorded in *South African Labour Bulletin*, 8(4), February 1983, 11–12.
7 An example is the committee set up in Johannesburg which after the detention of its chairman, Neil Aggett, met only once. Despite its name this committee played no role in organising the work stoppage to protest Aggett's death in detention, the most spectacular demonstration of worker solidarity in recent times, or in organising his subsequent funeral.
8 This meeting was to have been organised by CUSA, but arrangements were made at the last minute by other unions. CUSA failed to attend, as did CCAWUSA.
9 These unions formed a steering committee and established the South African Mine Workers Union (SAMWU).
10 *South African Labour Bulletin*, 8(4), February 1983, 13–14.
11 The BMWU collapsed after the Johannesburg Municipal Workers strike and has to date not managed to regain its following. *South African Labour Bulletin*, 8(1), September 1982, 89–94.
12 This practice is criticised in an article by Dave Lewis, 'Trade Union Organisation and Economic Recession', *South African Labour Bulletin*, 8(5), April 1983, 20.
13 For FOSATU affiliates see the *Annual Report of FOSATU 1984*. For CUSA affiliates see *Izwilethu*, 1(9,10), November/December 1983.
14 SAAWU had 12 unemployed workers acting as volunteer organisers, in addition to other officials.
15 *South African Labour Bulletin*, 8(6), June 1983, 9.

16 *South African Labour Bulletin*, 8(6), June 1983, 9.
17 *South African Labour Bulletin*, 9(2), November 1983, 1.
18 Interview with Herbert Barnabas, *South African Labour Bulletin*, 8(5), April 1983, 75.
19 Indications of growing co-operation between these unions are strong following their joint presence at an industrial council to negotiate wages. See the interview mentioned in note 18 above.

The Industrial Court: Institutionalising Industrial Conflict

Nicholas Haysom

It is strange that the debate[1] which was spawned by the introduction of the Labour Relations Act should have ignored the introduction of the Industrial Court. This institution has introduced a fairly radical departure from the existing legal framework governing the employer-employee relationship. The Court also represents a distinct shift in the form of regulating industrial conflict.

Until recently the industrial council system provided the model for the regulation of industrial conflict. The notions which underpinned this system were self-management of industry by employers and non-African unionists, and the separation of the rank and file from the collective bargaining process. This system provided a limited framework for determining the extent of managerial powers through collective bargaining. Under the new dispensation some areas of managerial power are subjected to the supervision of an institution outside the traditional collective bargaining forum. Industrial councils have begun to express considerable alarm at this invasion on their previous stronghold over collective bargaining.

The Amended Labour Relations Act

The Industrial Conciliation Amendment Act 94 of 1979, apart from introducing the Industrial Court, altered the definition of 'employee' in the Industrial Conciliation Act to include African workers, thus enabling trade unions with black members to 'register' and participate in the official bargaining machinery. The initial legislative intervention laid down a high price for the right of access to such machinery. Migrant workers were excluded. The Department of Manpower and the Registrar were granted powers of inspection and power to wind up unions, to vet their constitutions, to register them provisionally or in respect of racial groups or sectors. [2]

To the independent trade unions these provisions appeared as gratuitous restrictions for a dubious reward. In response to their uniform opposition to the bar on migrant worker membership, and the reluctance or refusal by some to enter into the framework created by the Act, several amendments have been enacted. These amendments and legal decisions have on the one hand stripped the Department of Manpower of its powers to register unions provisionally or for racial categories and have dropped the bar on migrant worker membership. On the other hand some of the remaining powers to monitor unions' constitutions and finances have been spread to cover unions which do not register. [3]

Context of the Act

There has been some debate on the advantages, disadvantages and the actual impact of registering in terms of the Act. But there was general agreement about the intended purpose of the legislative intervention and the context in which it was introduced. The Wiehahn labour 'reforms' were a product of the inability of the existing industrial relations framework to deal with industrial conflict, and in particular the growth of black trade unions operating outside of the official structures. The reforms were introduced at a time when there was disinvestment pressure and mounting overseas criticism of South Africa's racist and dual industrial relations legislation. It occurred in a context in which changes in the structure of industry and its labour requirements allowed for or needed a more settled and skilled labour-force. Furthermore the reforms were conceived and executed during a period of mounting political resistance to racial oppression.

The intention behind the 'reforms' was to exacerbate the divisions between rural and urban blacks; subject the independent unions to political controls and the general supervision of the Department of Manpower; and to reduce industrial conflict by drawing those unions into the official bargaining system. The latter objective is central to an understanding of the reforms. Overly political interpretations of the Act have tended to minimise the state's concern to reduce industrial conflict and particularly strikes. As in other Western countries, the South African state has intervened to bolster the framework of collective bargaining and to provide additional institutions of dispute-resolution.

The debate around the Act concentrated unduly on the often exaggerated good or bad consequences of registration per se. In reality managements were often ambiguous about enforcing registration of representative unions — except as a precursor to participation in the industrial councils. The difference between the position and status of registered and unregistered unions has narrowed and the most significant difference remains access to the councils. The logic of the reforms appears to be premised on the belief that participation in these councils is its own reward.[4]

Industrial Councils and Industrial Court

Industrial councils set the minimum conditions of service and wages in the industry and area in which they have jurisdiction. These conditions are negotiated between employer organisations and trade unions and are given the force of law. Attention has been drawn to the impact of the industrial council system on mixed and white unions. They have largely been accredited with the bureaucratisation and emasculation of these unions. Fine et al have correctly pointed to the danger of reading a similar necessary result on the independent and non-racial unions. The impact of industrial councils on these unions should be seen in the context of a racially divided work-force and the legacy of craft unions.[5] However in their present form the industrial councils are not neutral institutions. They are a particularly structured form of industry-wide bargaining. There are reasons why employers, established non-African and craft unions uphold this particular forum for negotiating wages, grievance and disciplinary procedures, and conditions of service. Here, reference is made to the following features: employee organisations are divided into a spectrum of craft and industrial and racially exclusive unions who have voting powers not based on representivity; negotiation is removed from membership muscle; bargaining seldom incorporates direct participation by union membership; the provisions of the Act and industrial council constitutions may hamper independent collective bargaining.

This is not to suggest that those unions which have sought to exploit the industrial councils will necessarily and inevitably become bureaucratised, or dependent on council patronage. There are divisions between sectors of industries too, and industrial councils are not homogeneous. Most importantly, industry-wide bargaining can be used to consolidate industry-wide strength, or to exercise that strength. Unions such as MAWU which have entered the industrial council do so with the express intention of exploiting the possibilities of an industry-wide forum and industry-wide organisation while minimising the tendency of the forum to imprint itself on its organisation.

The point here is that until the independent unions are strong enough to win effective representation in industrial councils or other industry-wide forum, the possibilities of using this institution to limit managerial powers in the interim are limited. In allowing Africans access to the industrial councils it was intended that industrial conflict would shift towards the regulating structure of the industrial council and away from the shop floor.

The Industrial Court however is an innovation of a different kind. While the civil courts have always determined conflicts of rights, the industrial councils and other forms of collective bargaining have resolved what have been termed conflicts of interests and determined the extent of managerial powers. The Industrial Court transgresses the previous rights/interests demarcation and has extended the rights of employees to encompass issues formerly not regarded as such. It subjects the hitherto legally unfettered discretion of management to manage in its own interests to the supervision of a legal agency standing outside the collective bargaining system. To understand fully the specific nature of this innovation, the framework within which the employment relationship is treated in law and in which managerial authority is inscribed should be examined.

Contract of employment and managerial authority

The employment relationship is regarded in law as a species of contract. Contract doctrine embodies a particular conception of society — atomised and juridically equal individuals who voluntarily bargain and agree on the terms of a contract — in this case the hire and letting of labour.

The employment relationship has not always been viewed as a simple contract. From feudal times to the eighteenth century it was regarded partly as a status and dealt with under the Law of Persons (as for children, wives etc.). Such a relationship could not be easily terminated. The extension of contract doctrine to the employment relationship facilitated the employer's ability to terminate at will the employee's contract to suit production requirements and to use dismissal as a mechanism of discipline. But the contractual framework also posed problems for the employment relationship — a distinctive aspect of which is the authority of the master over the servant. If the master commands and the servant is to obey how can the relationship be one of mutual agreement? The juridical reply was to ascribe to this species of contract the necessary term that the master has a right to direct activities — a right to command and the servant a duty of obedience — and ignored that these rights were not bargained but incident on ownership.[6] The concept of contract was adapted to suit the requirements of production.

Managerial authority — a broad power of command — is inscribed within the legal framework and enforced by the courts. The crucial control over the labour process rests on this legal platform. This legal power is not an abstract framework. It is a concrete and extensive power backed by the physical muscle of the state. This is the primary, but not only, example of the asymmetrical distribution of rights and duties in the contract.

Of particular relevance to a survey of the Industrial Court is the supposed reciprocal right to terminate the contract at will or summarily for breach of contract.[7]

Dismissal and discipline

In terms of the contract of employment, either employer or employee may terminate the contract on any whim or for any reason so long as due notice is given. This representation of the parties as equally affected by the termination of the contract is incorrect. Employees are dependent on employment and have an expectation that employment will continue. The common law gives no expression to this. Indeed it empowers employers to dismiss for even the most unfair or capricious reasons.

The state has historically intervened to limit this power but again only slightly and in exceptional cases. In the case of victimisation of union members the common law offers no protection. In statute there is some protection but the difficulty of establishing proof that union membership was the predominant reason for dismissal has rendered the protection ineffectual. Furthermore the tendency has been to confine the legal redress, even in cases where dismissal is statutorily unlawful, to an award of damages and not reinstatement.[8] This has effectively preserved the power to unilaterally terminate the employment by denying the worker the contractual remedy of remaining in employment. In any event civil litigation even for the dubious reward of damages was long-winded and expensive and could not provide effective protection against victimisation resulting in sudden unemployment.

The consequence of this wide power of dismissal has been to provide the employer with an effective mechanism, to enforce his commands, discipline his work-force, and maintain the 'work rules' his managerial prerogative empowers him to create. Within the factory the employer has the combined powers of a private despot and a judge. The only method employees had for containing or framing the boundaries of the exercise of this managerial power was through collective bargaining and collective agreements. But even here the very powers possessed by the employer could be used to decimate trade union membership and undercut trade unions. It should be mentioned that even employees lawfully withholding their labour in terms of the Labour Relations Act may be summarily dismissed for breach of contract. This is a strategy an employer can afford to use in South Africa where the unemployed are both numerous and hungry.

It is not suggested that managerial authority and control rests exclusively on this legal platform. A variety of factors such as the nature of the labour process, and the existence of an army of unemployed may affect the extent of the powers of the employer.

Unfair labour practice and the Industrial Court

The Industrial Court was introduced in the 1979 Act following the Wiehahn Commission recommendations. It was charged with a variety of functions which reflected the Commission's wishes that the Court should perform the task of resolving industrial disputes. Thus it was given the function of adjudicating not only as a conventional court of law on conflicts of right, but also of performing an arbitration function. The court was intended to attract conflict resolution because it would be 'uncomplicated, expeditious and very inexpensive'.[9] The novelty in the package was the 'unfair labour practice' and the Industrial Court was charged with determining such practices and remedying them. The Industrial Court was

intended to complement the other institutions in attracting industrial disputes towards conciliation machinery. In actual fact its impact has been
more ambiguous.

For unions the unfair labour practice was the main attraction. It offered
the possibility of penetrating the legal wall created by management's right
to rule on its own terms and the power to dismiss at will. Its novelty lay
in subjecting managerial practices to legal adjudication on the basis of
its 'fairness'. Observers might rightly question whether an objective test
of 'fairness' exists or could be applied by a tribunal of this kind. As it
stands, however, the departure from the common law position remains
fairly radical. For unions, the court's potential to protect job security and
to enforce collective bargaining would depend on the way it would approach

   i   the notion of 'unfairness' in relation to the framework of the contract
      of employment;
  ii   the remedies it would offer;
 iii   its power to order interim relief or more pertinently give expeditious
      relief to unions. The effect of an interim order would be to restore the
      parties to the status quo pending the resolution or settlement of the
      dispute.

An unfair labour practice has been defined broadly so as to achieve its
purpose — industrial peace. An unfair labour practice is essentially any
practice that prejudices industrial peace, the welfare or job security or
opportunities of employees or the business of an employer. In South Africa such a definition enabling extensive legal intervention is surprising.
At least one of the circumstances which prompted it was the need to reas-
sure white workers that attempts to reclassify skill categories or replace
them with cheaper labour would be protected by the Industrial Court. As
it happens, with the removal of racial distinctions in the Act the same
sweeping definition would have to cover all employees.

Development of the unfair labour practice

Faced with few guidelines, confusing definitions and ambiguities in its
brief, observers predicted that the Court might interpret its powers narrowly and overemphasise a legal formalism. This view appeared to be
confirmed in one of the first decisions it was confronted by — an applica-

tion for interim relief. It determined that it was not empowered to give interim relief.[10] The legislature eventually gave it express powers to grant interim relief in terms of section 43(1).[11] This provision significantly increased the number of cases. Thus in 1981 the court had to deal with 20 cases, in 1982 it dealt with 42, and in 1983 170 cases were referred to it. The Court has proceeded to issue decisions significantly affecting not only employees' rights but trade unions.

In the first place the Court has decided it is not bound by the principles of the common law contract of employment. Thus lawful dismissals — entirely within the rights of employers to perform — could still be an unfair labour practice. Secondly the Court has decided that it is not bound by the common law remedies and thus it was able to order reinstatement (or any other equitable remedy).[12]

It is in this area — dismissals — that 'unfair labour practice' determinations have been most concerned and where the decisions have had the greatest impact. Apart from the cases concerning legal procedures over 80% of reported cases deal with instances of dismissal.[13] The other area of concern has been the enforcement of collective bargaining. In both these areas the Court has functioned to prevent the incidence of strikes by bolstering collective bargaining structures. However, for the purposes of this article, the following general principle can be extracted from the reported cases:

i   *Victimisation.* The Court has declared that the onus of showing good reason for any dismissal rests with the employer. Secondly it will actually reinstate workers who have been victimised.[14] Thirdly it will rule against victimisation effected through retrenchment.[15] Significantly the Court has ruled that when a migrant's annual contract terminates the employer cannot refuse to renew that contract on the ground of the migrant's union membership. The Court has also held that a company may not dismiss a contract worker without good cause before the expiry of his contract — usually a year.[16]

ii   *Retrenchment.* The Court has made both interim and final rulings affecting management's right to retrench. Although the substance of the decisions has been primarily procedural they constituted a major check on disguised victimisation and unilateral retrenchment. The decisions boosted the status and powers of trade unions, and restricted unnecessary retrenchments.[17] In the most significant decision the Court ruled that where a union represented workers it should be consulted before retrenchment; that a fair procedure be adopted (last in, first out; those retrenched are to be the first to be rehired); that the union and company explore alternatives (short-time etc.), as well as issue prior proper warning.[18]

iii *Dismissal Procedures.* The Court has enforced agreed dismissal procedures and also declared it an unfair labour practice to dismiss an employee without a fair procedure where a representative union has sought to discuss the implementation of such a procedure.[19] There are a number of cases which suggest that a fair dismissal procedure is required in all cases i.e. a hearing and a chance to state one's case.[20] In the *Stobar* case the court appeared to approve of ILO recommendation No. 119 that dismissal be for 'good cause only' — either misconduct, incompetence or operational requirements.[21]

iv *Dismissal and safety at work.* The court has granted an interim order reinstating gold miners who were dismissed after they refused to work because of a real and reasonably held fear for their safety whether that fear was in fact correct or not.[22] The reasoning of this decision appears to backtrack on previous procedural rights but its implications are particularly significant for employees attempting to improve health and safety conditions.

v *Collective unfair labour practices.* It is apparent that these decisions supported trade unions indirectly by providing job security for members and protection against victimisation. Some of the decisions also gave unions direct support by insisting on the negotiation of appropriate procedural agreements with representative unions.

There is a clear decision relating directly to the question of negotiating with a representative union. The court has ordered an employers organisation to continue bargaining in good faith with the employees organisation.[23] In another instance the Court held it was an unfair labour practice to refuse to negotiate with a representative trade union.[24] Sweetheart unionism as an unfair labour practice is a crucial question which was confronted in a request for interim relief. In this case the court granted interim relief by ordering a company not to favour its sweetheart union over the rival union or compel members to join it pending a ballot or conciliation.[25]

Finally mention must be made of the significance of the powers of the Court to order the 'interim relief' referred to above. The purpose of these powers is to enable the status quo to be restored pending Industrial Court proceedings, industrial council hearings or other attempts at resolving the dispute. As such the powers are a significant advance on, say, the UK tribunals.

The advantage lies with the applicant in such proceedings in that the test for granting an order is less demanding than at the full and proper hearing. The test is whether the alleged practice would constitute an unfair practice if the facts alleged were true.[26] The basis for this is that the order merely maintains the status quo until the dispute is formally resolved. If this remedy were not available dismissed employees would be without income for lengthy periods and in some cases endorsed out of the urban area in terms of influx control or hostel regulations.

The status quo relief has been a significant aspect of the development of the Industrial Court. Its introduction must be seen as a result of the partial failure of the Court and the councils to induce the independent unions to enter the industrial conciliation machinery. Prior to its introduction few unions chose to litigate an 'unfair labour practice'. The provision of expeditious relief in 1982 opened the floodgates. It is clear that the extension of the powers of the court made a difference to union ability to use the court to achieve their ends. This would account for the fourfold increase in the use of the Court between 1982 and 1983.[27] However, in extending these powers the state added a twist − designed to bolster the centrality of the official conciliation machinery. It made access to the Court dependent on the submission of the dispute to an industrial council or conciliation board.[28] Thus between 1981 and 1983 the number of applications for conciliation boards increased 500%.[29]

The advantage of status quo relief to unions lies only partly in its speed (it still takes several weeks which is an improvement on the several months it takes to get a final hearing) but also in the greater facility with which unions may obtain a favourable ruling. Although such rulings are interim they significantly alter the balance of power − and few disputes proceed to the final determination.

The impact of the unfair labour practice

What this review indicates is that the rulings on unfair labour practices have significantly advanced the position of trade unions by giving them rights and a status that South African labour legislation and managerial power has denied them. In a matter of a few years workers have won rights through this institution that workers in Europe and the USA took decades to achieve and in some cases have not yet achieved. It did however require the provision of status quo relief to make the Court enticing.

In summary then the law of unfair dismissals has improved the legal position of both employees and their organisations by significantly protecting them from arbitrary dismissal and victimisation. It has further strengthened the status of trade unions by insisting that unwilling employers negotiate with representative trade unions. However the impact of these rules does not lie only with the few workers affected by these decisions. As these rulings are applicable in all similar cases, they have become an important negotiating weapon enabling numerous other cases to be settled out of court, or inducing employers to negotiate the requisite agreements. [30]

Direct contests of collective strength could and can achieve similar checks on managerial power and in regard to the actors themselves this process can consolidate organisation. There are however certain factors which have made the unfair labour practice law an important part of union strategies.

In the first place extremely high unemployment has made the workforce vulnerable particularly where workers are not skilled. The black unemployed in South Africa are impoverished due to inadequate unemployment insurance and the deterioration of economic conditions in the rural areas.

Secondly this feature has been exacerbated by the recession. In many cases management has been faced with surplus stock and a need to retrench. This has enabled management to adopt provocative and aggressive approaches to trade unions, and to use strikes to effect retrenchment via wholesale dismissals and selective re-employment.

Thirdly, the unions experienced a period of rapid growth in the 1978–1980 period and have needed to hold and deepen their organisation. Even now most industries are only partially organised and to establish effective industrial strength unions have also had to extend their presence into unorganised sectors and enterprises. Unions have been able to use the Court to secure industry-wide rights they would not have been able to obtain through the industrial councils at this stage.

Fourthly, union activities in South Africa have to take place within a context of an ensemble of repressive laws based on racial categories and attitudes that govern and control rights of association, movement, residence and expression. These laws hamper trade unions by banning open-air meetings, pickets, publications, and individuals. More particularly in the case of work stoppages workers can be repatriated or lose their rights to reside in urban areas and it is common practice for the employers to summon the assistance of police in 'resolving' disputes. The 'homelands' policy, influx control, deportations and rank hostility to worker organisation may well mean that access to institutions that protect job security and freedom of association is particularly significant. In more general terms, the use of the legal fiction of the equal legal subject can be a significant advance on the blatantly repressive and racial measures which state and management used against infant unions in the 1970s. This is one example of the danger of applying the postulate that 'legal formal equality enforces real inequality' to the concrete questions of extending organisation.

Thus the Industrial Court has been used by parties of very unequal power, in contests in which the considerable social power of management is reduced. The fact that an opponent is an emerging union or disenfranchised workers is less significant than it would be outside the Court.

All the factors listed above will explain how it is that management could now be bemoaning the absence of 'trial of strength' showdowns. The unions now using this forum cover the entire panorama of South African unions.

Employer responses

The response of employer organisations to the Industrial Court, more specifically to its ruling on unfair labour practice and status quo orders, has been to complain that the Court is a 'workers court'.[31] It has been argued that the determination of unfair labour practices has removed the resolution of conflicts of interest from the forum where it should be direct trials of strength through collective bargaining between employer and work-force. There has been astonishment and hostility towards those decisions which have tampered with management's previously inviolate prerogative powers. They have expressed alarm that they can be compelled to do battle in this forum where their bargaining muscle counts for little. More recently there have been requests that the Industrial Court's wings be clipped, in particular that the unfair labour practice be narrowly defined and that the power to issue status quo orders be scrapped.

Various industrial councils appear to be as concerned as employers with the growing use of the Court by unions and the ambit of unfair labour practice law. The reason for this concern appears to lie in the loss of jurisdiction of these bodies. Unions may get more joy out of the Court than the council and hence the passage of the dispute through the council is increasingly purely formal.[32] In the sense that the Court resolves disputes outside the industry-wide collective bargaining forum, and even independent of it, it undercuts it. It is this unintended contradiction in the function of the Industrial Court that the industrial councils now recognise.

Limits to unfair labour practice litigation

The unfair labour practice may well be a radical departure from the common law. It would be incorrect however to suggest that there are no limits to an inquiry into 'fairness' in this context. The foremost example of such a constraint is that the inquiry will always assume profitability of the enterprise. The implications of this are difficult to forecast. There have been few cases that have actually challenged the substantive control over the labour process and managerial decision making. In these cases we may expect argument concerning operational requirements to surface and prevail. The cases which have come close to such challenges are those dealing with retrenchment, and health and safety. As unions challenge managerial policies they are demanding access to information and books of account. But even here the base line will remain short term corporate profitability.

In general the Court, bearing in mind its legal nature, is always in danger of resolving such issues by resorting to a common law conception of the employer's right to manage according to the way he thinks best. A survey of the personnel of the Bench indicates that legal practitioners inducted into the Court have been most susceptible to such prejudices or premises (hidden or otherwise). Those from outside the legal profession have been better able to appreciate a broader conception of collective bargaining. The issue of fair work-place procedures is a more difficult question. A legal body such as the Industrial Court has been prepared to accept and enforce fair dismissal and other procedures. Such rulings have been an advance on the common law. However, there is a danger that an inquiry into the procedures followed at the work-place will replace an inquiry into the substantive fairness of the actual practices. The Industrial Court has in fact tended to follow the proceduralism of the British tribunal and current attempts to consolidate these legal rights and extend them seem to be endangered not so much by a blind proceduralism but a retreat towards managerial discretion. Apart from these constraints on the outreach of an inquiry into fairness it should also be mentioned that the Industrial Court has not been able to shed the legal formalism of the conventional courts and achieve the 'uncomplicated, expeditious and very inexpensive' relief that Wiehahn had recommended. Obtaining a determination of an unfair labour practice involves routing the dispute through an industrial council or conciliation board. Thereafter the parties commence with formal pleadings. When the matter is set down it may be over eight months later. The more expeditious status quo procedure may also take several weeks. The complexity of the law and the formal requirements has meant that few litigants would approach the Court without legal representation, and the whole process is not cheap.

The more substantial debate on the limits of the use of the Industrial Court concerns the debate over legalism versus collective action (organise, don't sue).

Legalism and the Industrial Court

The clear intention of the Industrial Court and unfair labour practice law was to contain industrial conflict − in its terms to preserve industrial peace − by providing an institution to deal with issues formerly only capable of resolution through collective bargaining or shop floor struggles. It has been argued out that where there is the development of shop floor organisation an individual dismissal becomes a collective issue. Indeed as Anderman puts it 'unfair dismissal law was not prompted entirely by considerations of individual employment law. They were produced in part to reduce strikes over dismissals.'[33] In South Africa dismissals also constitute a major cause of strikes.[34] The Industrial Court has the same potential to individualise dismissals by isolating each case and by relocating the power to reinstate from the union or the shop floor to the Court. This manoeuvre has its counterpart in the Machinery and Occupational Safety Act which intends to remove health and safety issues from the trade unions to safety committees.

Yet unions have not referred individual cases to the Industrial Court. In general the issues have been collective disputes involving organisational objectives. Furthermore the issues have been referred to the Court by unions − not individuals seeking private relief.

There is no doubt that some of the arguments against 'legalism' apply and will always apply in the use of legal institutions.[35] However the argument against legalism was not a polemic for the boycott of legal institutions per se. It was a specific intervention warning against the naïve worship of the law, implicit assumptions about its absolute neutrality, the substitution of legal suits when collective action was both more effective and organisationally desirable. The argument notes that the legal form tends to imprint its framework on organisation — constricting substantive collective demands into those of individual formal right, and inhibiting grassroots organisation, participation and control. This argument did not deny the importance of winning and defending rights in appropriate circumstances. On the contrary it warned against treating legal cases like a union benefit service. In this sense the 'legalism' debate was as much a call to establish shop floor organisation as it was a critique of legal practices. Victimisation cases are a good example. Unions advising victimised workers to pursue a legal remedy under the Wage Act effectively channelled this collective issue into a legal remedy that most unionists knew or should have known took a year or more to get to court and was seldom successful. It is no surprise that legalism is often the hallmark of lazy, bureaucratic and undemocratic unions.

These are important considerations. They demand that legal suits be undertaken with eyes wide open. However it is altogether a different proposition to inveigh indiscriminately against the use of legal machinery. To do so is effectively to reduce the law and legal institutions to the simple extension of a monolithic and coherent state apparatus. There is a failure to place the social bias of the judiciary next to the conflicting requirement that it stand above the competing claims of individuals. Such a position may result in abandonment of rights and options in a union's full range of tactics, some of which may be used in conjunction with other collective bargaining strategies.

What is required is an analysis of whether a particular legal institution will in the current circumstances advance or strengthen the union's objectives. In this regard consideration should be taken of the many laws and powers discussed earlier that render black workers vulnerable in South Africa.

At least part of such an analysis should take into account the contradictory functions of the Industrial Court. It would be incorrect to argue that there *must* be advantages in the unfair labour practice law simply because it was intended to draw unions into its conciliation machinery. Yet a review of its decisions and its potential to challenge managerial prerogative, to protect and extend rights at a time when the independent unions are still or especially vulnerable reveals that there are good reasons to explore the parameters of this institution. Whether this will continue to be possible is another question. There are concrete indications that the state intends to introduce amendments in 1985 to limit the unfair labour practice and the granting of status quo relief. Furthermore very recent decisions indicate that recent appointees to the Bench are trimming or cutting back the ambit of former decisions[36] and the terms of the Ministerial appointment of conciliation boards may in future exclude the categorisation of the dispute as an unfair labour practice and thus prevent the matter from reaching the Court.[37] However, as the unions consolidate their presence and if the much vaunted boom appears on schedule such a regression might backfire. Unions may well be in a position to pursue more direct assaults on the managerial prerogative.

Notes

1 See generally *South African Labour Bulletin*, 7 (1, 2, 3), 1981.
2 Section 12 of the Labour Relations Act 28 of 1956.
3 Amendments introduced by Labour Relations Amendment Act, Act 52 of 1981 and Act 51 of 1982.
4 Evidenced by the failure of Wiehahn Commission to even address itself to alternative collective bargaining systems.
5 *South African Labour Bulletin*, 7 (1, 2), 1981.
6 P. Selznick, *Law, Society and Industrial Justice* (Russell Sage, 1969), 137.
7 See Fox, *Beyond Contract* (Faber and Faber, 1974), 129. See also Selznick, *Law, Society and Industrial Justice* and O. Kahn Freund, *Labour and the Law* second edition (Stevens, 1977).
8 There has been some attempt to review this approach in *NUTW* v *Stag Packings* 1982 (4) SA 151(T). The court will also interdict an employer from victimising a union member where the victimisation has not already taken place.
9 Report of the Commission of Inquiry into Labour Legislation Part 1 Section 4.11.
10 *Moses Nkadimeng* v *Raleigh Cycles (SA)* 1981(2) *Industrial Law Journal* 34(1).
11 Labour Relations Amendment Act 51 of 1982.
12 *SA Diamond Workers* v *Master Diamond Cutters Association* 1982(3) *Industrial Law Journal* 87.
13 The available unreported cases confirm this ratio of cases which deal with dismissal.
14 The court in *MAWU* v *Stobar Reinforcing* 1983(1) *Industrial Law Journal* 84 and *MAWU* v *Fodens (Pty) Ltd* 1983(3) *Industrial Law Journal* 212.
15 *MAWU* v *Mauchle (Pty) Limited* 1980(3) *Industrial Law Journal* p227.
16 Foden's case.
17 G.A. Jaffee, 'Retrenchment Process and some social implications', *South African Review Two*, Ravan Press, 1984.
18 Foden's case. *Shezi and others* v *Consolidated Frame Cotton Corporation* unreported 18 January 1984.

19 Foden's case.

20 *Dlamini* v *Cargo Carriers Natal (Pty) Ltd*, unreported 1983.

21 *MAWU* v *Stobar*. See also *Van Zyl* v *O'Kiep Copper Co Limited* 1983(2) *Industrial Law Journal* p125.

22 *National Union of Mineworkers & Others* v *Driefontein Consolidated* (unreported 1983).

23 *Bleazard* v *Argus Printing and Publishing Co* 1983(1) *Industrial Law Journal*, 6.

24 Foden's case.

25 *NUTW* v *Frametex* 1983 (unreported).

26 There is one line of argument which suggests that the appropriate test is simply whether a dispute exists. See Paul Pretorius 'The Sacred Cow Tethered', in 1981(3) *Industrial Law Journal*.

27 Department of Manpower Statistics 1983.

28 Act 51 of 1982. See also P. Benjamin *'Labour Relations Act'* unpublished paper.

29 Department of Manpower Statistics 1983.

30 Jaffee, 'Retrenchment process and some social implications'.

31 *RDM*, 08.04.83; 09.05.83.

32 It should be mentioned here that the significant increase in applications for conciliation board in 1982/3 is presumed to be in satisfaction of this procedural requirement.

33 Anderman *Law of Unfair Dismissal* cited in P. Pretorius 'The Sacred Cow Tethered', 1983 3 *ILJ* p.183 n49.

34 See Pretorius, 'The Sacred Cow Tethered' 183 n49.

35 *Work in Progress*, 19, August 1981.

36 See the judgement of Landman in *NUM & Others* v *West Driefontein*.

37 As in the recent SACWU dispute with Pest Control, also NUTW dispute with Frame.

The Retrenchment Process

Georgina Jaffee

The recession revealed itself in widespread retrenchments of black workers as capital attempted to reduce production costs and adjust to lower demand. From November 1982, plants in most key sectors of the economy decreased productive capacity. The worst-hit sectors were motor vehicles, textiles, parts and accessories, glass and glass products. According to figures released in June 1983 by the Central Statistical Services, utilisation of total manufacturing capacity dropped from 89,1% in February 1982 to 84,5% in February 1983. The unused production capacity of the motor and spares industry in February 1983 was 22%, compared with the February 1982 figure of 12,6%. Unutilised capacity in textiles increased from 8,8% in February 1982 to 17,4% a year later. In clothing, it increased from 8,8% to 11,4% during the same period.[1]

This decrease in production led to the retrenchment of thousands of black workers, the reduction of the working week, short-time production and, in some cases, the closing down of factories. Accurate figures on the number of workers retrenched in each sector are not available, but the numbers involved are high. According to reports, 75 000 workers were retrenched in the steel and engineering industry; 13 000 in the textile industry since January 1982 (*RDM*, 14.01.83) and 24 000 in the South African Transport Services (SATS). More recently the *Star* (26.11.83) reported that SATS had reduced its staff complement from 279 000 in June 1982 to 242 700 in November 1983. Calculations from reports of the Institute of Industrial Relations indicate that since January 1983, 16 134 black workers were retrenched from the manufacturing industry, and 3 790 from mining.[2] In September 1983 the Central Statistical Services reported that the work-force in mining, construction, manufacturing, SATS, electricity and the post office dropped by 137 928 between May 1982 and May 1983.

The retrenchment process

Retrenchments and the strategies adopted by capital to reduce the work-force were influenced by a number of factors. Firstly, South African industry is increasingly mechanising and management took advantage of the reduction in the work-force to rationalise and consolidate new production techniques. Management dispensed with excess labour by weeding out the 'lesser quality workers', and introduced training schemes[3] and programmes to increase productivity and worker motivation. In addition, scientific methods of management were introduced such as new job evaluation systems and more sophisticated methods of control and discipline.[4] Secondly, the growing threat from the emerging trade unions led management to adopt repressive tactics whereby union members and activists were deliberately made redundant. Throughout this period many unionists complained that management had singled out union members for retrenchment.[5] The most blatant examples occurred at plants where unions had not yet signed recognition agreements or where recruiting drives were still embryonic. In other instances managements provoked strike action to provide an excuse for retrenchment and at the same time rid themselves of militant union members.

The shrinkage of the employed black work-force pushed unions into a defensive position. The organisation of new factories was curbed and substituted by negotiations on retrenchment procedures. This strategic retreat was necessary to protect already organised workers threatened with dismissal. Despite the risk of reducing their numbers, many of the unions faced with retrenchments were quick to adopt new methods and strategies of bargaining to protect their organised membership.

These union strategies arose from the arbitrary retrenchment procedures and lack of constraints on managerial prerogative. There are numerous examples of ruthless management actions. One firm instructed the factory doctor to examine all the workers. Those with minor ailments were the first to be retrenched. Some companies forced workers to take early retirement and others simply paid off workers telling them that there was no more work. Unions were consequently forced to use the Industrial Court to protect members. Notable test cases were taken up and won, and certain precedents tempered managements' behaviour. The threat of the legal weapon in other instances led to a number of out-of-court settlements.

The Industrial Court

The role of the Industrial Court became increasingly important as unions decided to take up unfair dismissals. For unions, the Industrial Court softened the retrenchment process and mitigated its effects on workers. There were important cases where the court ordered management to reinstate dismissed workers and negotiate retrenchment procedures. In some instances negotiations reduced the number of workers marked for redundancy. Most of the independent unions adopted similar retrenchment guidelines. These included the 'last-in-first-out' (LIFO) principle, extended notice, adequate compensation, consultation with the union, providing reasons for retrenchment and exact numbers involved, and provision for unemployment benefits. The unions also suggested an end to overtime and the recruitment of new workers.

In the case of *MAWU v Stobar Reinforcing* in January 1983, 51 workers were reinstated in terms of section 43 of the Labour Relations Act.[6] MAWU alleged that the workers had been sacked because the company was avoiding retrenchment negotiations with the union. In a number of cases the court ordered workers' reinstatement and even made management liable for payment during the period workers had been unemployed. In March 1983 Braitex, a Springs textile firm, was ordered to pay the NUTW R40 000 and to reinstate retrenched workers.[7] The union claimed that the company had unilaterally withheld workers' bonuses and retrenched 11 workers in June 1982. Braitex allegedly retrenched 60 more workers in December, without consulting the union or explaining retrenchments to the workers. Those retrenched received no severance pay. The Industrial Court ruled that management had to discuss impending retrenchments with the union.

In the case of *United African Motor and Allied Workers' Union v Fodens* in January 1983,[8] the Industrial Court enforced a previous settlement offer and also ordered that retrenchments be conducted in a fair manner and that the union be consulted. The court also ordered the company to pay one of the applicants – a retrenched contract worker – regular and overtime wages from the period of his dismissal until the end of his contract. As a result of this case, other instances of unfair labour practice were defined. These included failure to negotiate with a representative union; failure to negotiate a disciplinary code; and the dismissal of a contract worker before his contract was up.

After these successful cases, unions used legal machinery to curb management. In a case involving Datsun-Nissan and the United African

Motor and Allied Workers' Union, the union threatened the company
with court action over the retrenchment of 102 workers. In an out-of-
court settlement all the workers were reinstated. Datsun paid them 47%
of the difference between their pay and what they had earned since being
retrenched. The settlement cost the company more than R100 000. Alfa
Romeo also settled out of court over a dispute declared by NAAWU concerning the retrenchment of a union member and the failure of the company to recognise the union. Finally the union member was reinstated
and the union recognised.

There were also several cases where the threat of action from unions
forced companies to justify their retrenchment procedures. This was evident in a dispute between the NUTW and the Frame Cotton Corporation.
Workers had been transferred to another department, and then retrenched. The company claimed that the workers, who had been with Frame
Cotton for many years, were inefficient. The union argued that the
transference of these workers to a new department where they were un-
familiar with the work was unfair. If workers were to be retrenched, the
company should use the last-in-first-out principle. In December 1983 the
Industrial Court ordered the company temporarily to reinstate the retrenched workers, pending further hearings. At Sigma, negotiations
between management and the union involved (NAAWU) forced the company to trim its original numbers set for retrenchment from 341 to 237.

There were cases where the threat of legal action served to prevent entire plants from closing. Allied Cosmetics reversed its decision to shut
down operations when the SA Chemical Workers' Union threatened legal
action. In the closing down of Premier Biscuits, the Food Beverage and
Allied Workers' Union successfully negotiated training and transference
alternatives for 400 workers.

These cases affected capital's complacency about retrenchment and
created a general awareness and caution. But management reacted to
some of the judgements by closing loopholes. In January 1983 MAWU
threatened Dunswart Iron and Steel with legal action over the retrenchment of migrants whose contracts had not expired. The case was settled
out of court. But management introduced supplementary contracts which
the remaining workers were forced to sign. These validated the formal
contract only as long as work was available. From observations at two
labour bureaux in KwaZulu, new contracts were also stamped 'contract
valid provided availability of work'.

The unions' astute way of using the unfair labour practice clause in
labour legislation was important in disciplining companies during the

recessionary period. Outcomes of cases which appeared to favour labour may have been the result of the inexperience of the Industrial Court. However, it would be unrealistic to overestimate the court's overall effect in preventing management from carrying out non-negotiated retrenchments. Workers in unorganised industries — especially unskilled migrants — were the most vulnerable. The number of workers who were finally affected by the limited protections gained through the Industrial Court was probably a very small percentage of those retrenched.

When the Industrial Court did act in their favour, unions gained confidence. Certain precedents gave further credibility to the use of the legal system as a way of forcing management to consult unions on issues regarding the welfare of members. For the unions, the retrenchment crisis provided the opportunity for united action and consultation. For example, MAWU and GWU negotiated jointly with the Dorbyl group in March 1983 over the company's failure to provide severance pay to retrenched workers.

Solidarity between workers was also evident. Some GWU members voted that only workers with section 10 rights should be retrenched. This decision aimed to protect the more vulnerable contract workers without urban rights. Despite the defensive position of the unions, the gains made on the retrenchment question strengthened their hand in bargaining, and revealed their flexibility and growing power.

Migrant and contract workers

Retrenchments affected unskilled contract workers most heavily. As soon as they were signed off, they were endorsed out of urban areas. Before 1981, contract workers could be transferred without having to return to the rural areas to re-apply as work seekers. After 1981, thousands of contract workers, even if the company was willing to transfer them, had to return to the bantustans.[9] Many of these workers left the urban industrial centres without severance pay, leave pay, or provision of Unemployment Insurance Fund (UIF) benefits. In most cases no notice of retrenchment was given.

A study of 50 retrenched migrant workers from KwaZulu in January 1983 revealed that only 3% had received UIF benefits. Most of them had not received other payments such as pensions. Seventy-five percent of the families had no income coming into the household and were on the verge of starvation. Children had to be taken out of school and sent to the nearest towns to beg; families were forced to sell cattle and borrow money to buy food. Men who did apply for UIF had in some cases become too weak to walk to the nearest labour bureau often situated some 20 km from their homesteads.[10]

Retrenched migrant workers have little opportunity of finding alternative employment. New policies of labour allocation and control have ensured this. Influx control policies introduced shortly before the height of the recession softened control over urban Africans at the expense of stricter control over migrant and 'illegal' workers. Recruitment in the bantustans is also decreasing. Legislation allows greater mobility to urban workers and the state now encourages an 'unofficial urban labour preference policy'.[11]

The Unemployment Insurance Fund scandal

As applications for UIF[12] increased, the inadequacies and bureaucratic delays of the system emerged more clearly. Hundreds of men waited in queues to receive benefits both in urban and rural labour offices. Many of the workers had left their employer companies without their blue employment cards. These cards, which have to be produced to claim UIF benefits, carry information of employment history and reasons for dismissal. Some of the workers did not have enough money to return to their previous places of employment to collect their cards. Once back in the rural areas, retrenched workers have to report to the labour bureau monthly to remain eligible for UIF benefits. Payment of unemployment benefits often took so long that some claimants gave up. In the study mentioned above only five of the 50 people surveyed received UIF payments, and these were made eight months after application. Workers lived a long way from the labour office and some of them could not borrow enough money to pay for transport to sign the unemployment register. Payments were seldom correct and widespread corruption, petty theft and fraud were found in the circulation, claiming and cashing of UIF cheques.

Issues in the retrenchment of migrant workers

Both state and capital have benefitted from the expulsion of thousands of workers to the rural areas. This is particularly so when the black trade union movement is gaining momentum and urban-based political opposition is growing. Capital was able to rationalise industry and increase capital intensification with the removal of unskilled labour. The state displaced social and economic responsibility for the unemployed onto the bantustan government. Removing the unemployed from the urban areas undercut the probability of increased political expression or spontaneous resistance in the urban areas. In the rural areas the unemployed population has little opportunity for organised political action or for the effective demonstration of discontent.

At present it is difficult to assess the long term implications of the recession on the restructuring of the labour process. Industries which were deeply affected by the recession probably reorganised their workforce successfully. These changes may increase division within the working class by widening the gap between urban and rural workers.

The recession has caused unions to adopt defensive strategies in certain situations. But it has not had the expected effect of undermining recruitment of unorganised workers, and the more established unions have managed to maintain their organised presence in various industries. FOSATU, in its 1983 annual report, states that the total paid-up membership of its affiliated unions rose from 68 886 to 80 961 during the year, and signed-up membership reached 106 460. The report argues that despite the recession, unions not only survived and had considerable success in changing retrenchment practices, but also grew stronger.

A number of questions arise from this survey of the retrenchment process: What are the long term implications of increased landlessness and unemployment in the rural areas? Could this build-up of landless proletarians affect the politics of resistance in these areas? Some of the more recently retrenched workers have been exposed to the trade union movement and seem to expect relief from these organisations in the rural areas. Will those who return to the labour-force renew their ties with the trade union movement?

Crises such as the present recession have posed these and other questions not only for the trade union movement, but for all organisations which relate to the working class.

Notes

1 *ST*, 05.06.83.
2 Monthly reports from *Information Sheet*, Institute for Industrial Relations, Johannesburg.

3 Tax and cash concessions were granted to companies in order to encourage private training schemes. See *Star*, 22.11.82.

4 This has been shown in an in-depth study by I. Obery, 'Recession and Retrenchments — Responses of Capital and Labour in the East Rand Metal Industry, 1983', (unpublished BA Hons dissertation, University of Witwatersrand, 1983).

5 See the remarks by David Lewis, general secretary of GWU, in *Star*, 17.08.83; and by Sydney Mafumadi, general secretary of GAWU, in *Sow*, 09.05.83. Personal communications with CUSA, FOSATU and MAWU confirm this.

6 *MAWU v Stobar*, (1983) 4 *Industrial Law Journal*, 84.

7 *NUTW v Braitex*. This out-of-court settlement was made an order by the Industrial Court.

8 *United African Motor and Allied Workers' Union v Fodens*, (1983) 4 *Industrial Law Journal*, 212.

9 Personal communication with Black Sash, June 1983.

10 This study carried out by J. Keenan and G. Jaffee of the Department of Social Anthropology, University of Witwatersrand — in progress, 1984. The study entailed detailed interviews with retrenched workers and their families over a period of nine months in KwaZulu in the Bergville and Nqutu areas. The first set of interviews was completed in May 1983, with a follow up study in November 1983.

11 D. Hindson and M. Lacey, 'Influx Control and Labour Allocation: Policy and Practice since the Riekert Commission', in *Same Foundations, New Facades?*, South African Review One (Johannesburg, 1983).

12 The Unemployment Insurance Fund (UIF) provides benefits of 45% of a worker's average earnings for up to six months, provided the unemployed worker contributed to the fund for at least 13 weeks. R7,5-m was paid out in January 1983, this being twice the amount paid out in January 1982 (*Star*, 28.04.83).

The Recession and Its Effects on the African Working Class

Jeremy Keenan

In 1981 the South African economy entered one of its longest and deepest recessions. Growth in GDP for both 1982 and 1983 was negative, being –1,2 and –3,1 respectively. The outlook for the immediate future is gloomy with little likelihood of much recovery before 1985.

The extent to which this recession has affected workers cannot be considered solely at an economic level. Indeed, the distinctiveness of this recession is not just its economic magnitude, but a number of other economic, political and geographical features which together have given the recession its overall 'total character'.

On the wider economic front the last business cycle (1977–8 to present) has been marked by an intensification of capital restructuring towards a higher phase of monopoly capitalism, associated increases in structural unemployment, and, at least at the beginning of this period, apparent shortages of skilled/semi-skilled labour.

Neither can the last economic cycle be seen in isolation from the mounting political pressure that became increasingly prevalent in the latter half of the 1970s; namely, urban unrest and the reverberations of the 1976 disturbances, increasing African unemployment and the growing international pressure to eliminate unjust social, economic and political structures and practices.

Ideologically, this period has been characterised by the state's movement towards more monetarist policies and the advocation of the free market system. Free enterprise is seen as a means of deflating the appeal of communistic ideals to South Africa's 'lower-income groups' and is closely tied to the general 'reform' strategies of this period. On the economic front these reforms are alleged to be leading to an increase in the overall standard of living of the country's African population. This latter notion has helped create the impression that Africans have not necessarily suffered that severely as a result of the recession.

The strategies for controlling most of these problems were set out in the general recommendations of the Riekert and Wiehahn Commissions. On the one hand they sought to facilitate the transition to a higher phase of monopoly capitalism by removing several impediments to the movement and provision of certain categories of labour. On the other hand they attempted to establish a more 'stable' population in the urban areas of the Republic of South Africa. This more 'stable' population was to be created by granting it preference on the labour market, protecting it to some extent from the ravages of increasing unemployment, and providing it with improved living conditions. This strategy is being achieved by tightening up influx control with the result that the country's population is being divided even more rigorously into 'insiders' and 'outsiders'; the latter, and the majority of the population, being restricted to the impoverishment of the bantustans.

The effects of the current recession on the African population must be seen in the context of this divisive strategy, and the state's attempts to divert attention from its more restrictive and repressive dimensions. In this respect the state and capital have put forward a number of arguments to suggest that the effects of the current recession on the African population are not that severe.

The most common amongst these arguments are:

1. African wages have continued to rise during the course of the recession albeit more slowly;

2. utilisation of production capacity as recorded by the government's official statistics collected by the Central Statistical Services (CSS) has not fallen that much, the latest figure for the manufacturing sector which was for the second quarter of 1983 being 84,0%, down only 6,1% from the peak of the boom in 1981;

3. African unemployment has not risen that drastically. The total number of Africans unemployed in June 1983, according to the CSS is substantially less than during the previous recession. The latest available official unemployment figures for Africans show that in September 1983 only 8,1% of the economically active population was unemployed compared with 12,5% in October 1977;

4. much of the present suffering amongst Africans has not been caused by the recession, but by the drought which in some rural areas has now lasted four years.

Let us look briefly at the validity of each of these arguments:

1. It is true that earnings, which include pension contributions of both employers and employees, medical aid contributions, all bonuses, overtime, etc., have so far increased in real terms throughout most of the recession, at least until the latest available figures, which are for mid-1983. However, three important points must be made:

    (a) The rate of increase in earnings has fallen sharply over this period, and for 1983 as a whole will probably be flat or perhaps even negative. Earnings for the first two quarters of 1983 were actually lower than average earnings for 1982.

    (b) In some of the major sectors actual wage rates, as distinct from earnings, appear to have been negative in real terms throughout 1983. By November 1983, wage rates, as reported by the CSS, for lower-skilled operators and labourers in the mental and engineering industries, almost exclusively Africans, had risen by only 7,8% over the preceding 12 months. When inflation is taken into account this becomes a real decline of 2,3%.

    (c) These figures only apply to actual salary and wage earners. They do not apply to those out of work, and consequently mask the per capita income. The income lost to families through increasing unemployment over this period has far outweighed the very marginal increase in real earnings of those in employment.

2. The figures for utilisation of production capacity are questionable. Utilisation of production capacity has almost certainly fallen much more than 6% over the course of the recession. The reason for this anomaly is that many companies do not keep adequate records, or fail to complete CSS questionnaires correctly.

3. The government claims to record unemployment in accordance with internationally recognised and laid down criteria. To some extent this is true in the strict definitional sense. Without going into great detail we need merely note that for a man to be registered as 'unemployed' he must actively have sought work during the month. This means coming to the labour bureau and registering himself as a work seeker. In practice things are very different:

    (a) many unemployed workers live too far from and cannot afford to get to labour bureaux;

(b) the bureaux are usually part of the local magistrate's and/or local tribal authority offices. Presence at the bureaux may often involve harassment by some or other level of local authority;

(c) the worse the unemployment situation becomes, the more workers know that there is less chance of finding work. There is therefore even less point in going and registering at the bureau. In other words there is a tendency towards an inverse relationship between the real level of unemployment and the level of registered unemployment;

(d) unemployed workers rarely get the unemployment fund benefits to which they are entitled. Many of them do not know about their rights in this regard and consequently have even less incentive to register at a bureau;

(e) research into the administrative practices and recordings of data in certain labour bureaux earlier this year revealed three significant forms of worker-abuse and mal-administration:

(i) workers are often told not to keep on coming back and registering at the bureau each month as there is no work and the bureau will inform people when work is available. Just how it will inform people never seems to have been made clear. Workers consequently do not get registered as unemployed after the first month;

(ii) labour bureaux periodically write off several hundred registered unemployed workers. As the numbers build up, the clerks simply strike off 50% or more. In one such bureau the true number had risen to more than three thousand over the last few years, but each time the total figure rose to about one-and-a-half thousand the clerk would strike off between five hundred and a thousand;

(iii) clerks in some of these bureaux stated that they had received instructions from higher up not to record unemployment. They said that the reason for this was too few clerks and too many unemployed workers. It was becoming administratively difficult to keep registering them all.

One of the greatest misrepresentations in government statistics on unemployment is that they do not include the 'independent' bantustans in which an ever-increasing proportion of the country's population finds itself.

4. The drought which in many parts of the country has now entered its

fourth year, has caused considerable suffering in the bantustans. The drought is not the cause of rural impoverishment, it has merely exacerbated the suffering and poverty in these areas. The majority of the bantustan population have not been greatly affected by the drought in that they have no access to land and possess few if any livestock. For them, the major cause of impoverishment is the combination of low wages and increasing unemployment.

The effects of the recession on African workers

On the wage front the first 24 months of the recession saw real earnings increase for African workers. This increase was due to the decline in inflation which had effectively nullified wage increases in the boom period. But, for 1983 the rate of increase has been declining with the overall trend for real earnings now beginning to flatten out and perhaps even decline, with employers being reluctant to increase wages. Repeated worker defeats on wages during 1983 in conjunction with government tax policy has led to a decline in the African living standards. The government, as the *Rand Daily Mail* has commented, has shifted its policy over time to one of 'soaking the poor'. Instead of seeking revenue from the better-off, through company or income taxes, it is doing so through sales taxes — which hit the poor hardest (*RDM*, 28.02.84). Much of the decline in earnings is due to the significant drop in overtime, which according to the CSS, has fallen from a peak of 15% in August 1981 to about 8–9% now (overtime being measured as percentage of ordinary hours worked). People now work significantly less overtime than during the corresponding period of the last recession. This drop of about 40% in overtime pay has been a major loss to workers as many of them were dependent on this extra work to keep their families above the poverty level.

In the bantustans the situation is much worse. These workers are not included in CSS figures but research done in the 'independent' bantustans indicates that wages which were already abysmally low are now declining in real terms.[1] This has been a major contribution to the increasing poverty of the bantustans. For example, in the Bophuthatswana industrial complex at Babelegi, some workers who now work a three-day week are receiving R7,50 per week. Many others earn little more than R10 per week. At the new Bophuthatswana industrial growth point of Hysterkrand weekly wages of R12,50 are not uncommon.[2] In the agricultural sector of the bantustans, privatisation of many schemes over the last few years has also led to a significant increase in the rate of exploitation of workers as well as actual declines in their wages — sometimes by as much as 40%.

Unemployment

The major effect of the recession on the African population has been through the loss of employment. This is especially significant in view of the fact that the 1978–81 upswing was the first economic recovery in South Africa in which the rate of unemployment continued to rise. During this upswing the number of Africans in employment increased by only 208 000. It is generally estimated that at least 200 000 jobs a year have to be provided merely to halt the rate of increase in African unemployment. On this basis the 1978–81 boom saw African unemployment increase by a further 400 000. In the first year of the recession, the number of Africans in employment increased by only 7 000, thus adding another 200 000 or so to the ever-swelling ranks of the unemployed. During the year 1982–83 the number of Africans employed fell by 80 000, adding over another quarter of a million more to the number of unemployed.

The situation has deteriorated even more in the last six months with 2 000 workers being laid off in the car industry alone. One feature of the recession is that in many sectors of the economy it has both encouraged and facilitated a further rise in capital intensification which has been the root cause of the massive increase in African unemployment during the 1970s and 1980s.

Attempts to compare unemployment figures for this recession with those of the last recession are very misleading for they ignore one crucial difference between this recession and the last, namely, the re-orientation in the supply of labour to the mines. In 1974 the recruitment of foreign workers stood at a total of 763 675, of whom 231 666 and 227 619 were from Malawi and Mozambique respectively. By 1981 this figure had dropped to 301 758, of whom only 30 602 were Malawians and 59 391 were Mozambicans. In the mines, the number of foreign workers in the work-force fell from just on 80% in 1973 to barely 40% in 1979.[3] These foreign workers were replaced by 'local' workers. The transition from foreign to local labour mitigated the seriousness of unemployment during the last recession, especially in some of the deep rural areas of the bantustans from which the mines recruited labour. There are no such factors mitigating the enormous increase in unemployment in the present recession.

Research in a number of urban and rural communities has shown that this increase in unemployment has more than countered the modest increase in overall earnings. Studies in Soweto show that unemployment has risen at 5,5% per annum during the recession.[4] In the bantustans the situation is much worse. The recent Swart Commission on the Ciskei estimated that unemployment in the Ciskei is now at about fifty percent.[5] Research in parts of Bophuthatswana, Lebowa, KwaZulu and Gazankulu suggests that at least fifty percent of the potential economically active population in these areas is now unemployed. Surveys of 500 households in the Saulspoort area of Bophuthatswana, undertaken in 1977[6] and again in 1983–84,[7] showed an increase in unemployment from about eighteen to forty percent, giving an annual increase in unemployment of about twenty percent.

The increase in unemployment in both urban and rural areas has placed added burdens on those with jobs. While the incomes of those in employment may have risen over the course of the last business cycle, an increasing number of people depend on these wages. This has almost certainly resulted in a decline in the average per capita income for the African population as a whole with a concomitant increase in the level of absolute poverty and inequality. During the last few years there have been many sets of data showing that the inequality in the distribution of income between Africans and whites is declining. But this data applies only to 'recipients of income' and not the total population, many of whom, especially in the case of Africans, are no longer recipients of income and are consequently excluded from these statistics.

The situation is much worse for Africans in the bantustans for a number of reasons. Firstly, as already mentioned, many families have been hit by the drought.

Secondly, the significant increase in the commercialisation of agriculture in the bantustans since 1977 has led to thousands of Africans being dispossessed of their land. Numerous areas of better land in the bantustans have been taken over by the state and private capitalist concerns for commercial agricultural production. Compensation has rarely been given to those who lost land. Research in the Transvaal bantustans shows that hundreds of families have been dispossessed of their land in this way, and that for many of them the loss of cash income amounted to several thousand rands per year.

Thirdly, the increased powers of the tribal authorities in most bantustan areas are placing an increasing 'tax' burden on people. In some villages in Bophuthatswana, for example, residents may have to pay as many as

11 different local taxes/levies in addition to the various deductions made at their places of work.

Fourthly, the tightening up of influx control over the last few years means that Africans restricted to the bantustans have much less chance of finding employment than those with permanent rights in the 'white' urban areas. Research undertaken in Bophuthatswana in 1983 revealed that in most areas people hoping to find work outside the bantustan had to pay their tribal authority about R30–40 to get a work seeker's permit which in itself is no guarantee of employment. The situation is much worse for women. Several hundred women workers in the Bophutha- tswana villages in the hinterland of the industrial areas of Brits and Babelegi were interviewed and they revealed that to get work some were obliged to have sex with either or both the clerks at the labour bureaux and the company personnel officer or clerk. The refusal of women to be exploited in this way has further increased the level of unemployment.[8]

The determination of wages
Wages are now usually negotiated in accordance with changes in the cost of living (COL). This index is merely a measurement of the change in prices of goods and services over a specified period of time. It does not measure or reflect changes in the need or demand for any of these goods and services. In other words it is not related in any way to increasing unemployment, the loss of subsistence production in the bantustans, or the fact that urban-based families must provide more assistance for their kinsmen or other dependants in the rural areas.

If the decline in the overall standard of living of Africans is to be ar- rested, wage increases must reflect these other factors over and above changes in the COL itself. This would involve a reconceptualisation of wages and their determination. It would require the addition of indices covering such things as unemployment and dependency ratios, levels of rural subsistence production, etc. to that of the COL. Given the inade- quate state of research into these factors such indices could not be con- structed with any great reliability at this stage. Nevertheless, we can get a fairly good idea of the sort of figure that we would be talking about. Current research in Bophuthatswana, Lebowa, Gazankulu and KwaZulu, indicates that aggregate income from subsistence production (including livestock) in these areas, both marketed and non-marketed, has declined by at least 10% over the last couple of years, or at least 5% per annum. In the case of unemployment and dependency ratios we have relatively little to go on other than the Soweto and Saulspoort surveys mentioned above. Soweto is not very different in these respects from other Reef townships, which in turn have probably suffered less heavily from unemployment during the recession than most other parts of the country. We can thus take the 5,5% per annum increase in unemployment in Soweto as a reasonable and probably conservative indication of urban areas in general. Similarly, the 20% per annum increase in unemployment at Saulspoort is probably less severe than most other rural areas given the proximity of several mines, factories and Sun City. We can thus postulate, assuming perfect income distribution, that African workers need annual wage increases of between 23% and 37,5% to maintain the overall standard of living of the African population at its present level. These two figures are based on the addition of the above figures to the current increase in the COL of 12,5% and with both figures including the estimated 5% loss of income from subsistence production. Only a handful of workers will achieve wage increases of this magnitude this year.[9]

The response of management

Management's notion of wages tends to be based on one of two assumptions: either their workers, especially those from the rural areas, have alternative forms of income (e.g. familial support and rural subsistence) or their workers are fully urbanised and not affected by the exigencies and misfortunes that may befall the rural areas. Moreover, the general response of management is that it pays wages to an individual worker for work performed and is not responsible for the maintenance of his family.

These responses are flawed on a number of counts. Firstly, the relationship between the so-called urban and rural areas is extremely complex and cannot be discussed in great detail here. The assumption that workers have alternative or supplementary sources of income in the rural areas has been the fundamental historical basis for the extraction of cheap labour-power in South Africa. Today, even though it should be quite irrelevant to the determination of wage levels, this sort of thinking is still widespread amongst managements. Most families in the rural areas cannot support themselves and are almost wholly dependent on the earnings of migrant workers. On the other hand, supposedly fully urbanised workers frequently have kin ties and other responsibilities in the rural areas. Because of influx and other controls many African families are straddled willynilly between the urban and rural areas. Employers who assume that their workers are 'urbanised' and without rural links and obligations simply because they have section 10 rights, housing, etc., are probably mistaken. The flow of income from urban to rural households may be quite substantial, especially in times such as these when conditions in the rural areas are especially severe. Surveys undertaken in Soweto show that well over 50% of households make payments to dependants elsewhere, usually in the bantustans, and that the form and amount of assistance rendered to these persons varies considerably depending on the conditions in the rural areas, levels of employment, and so forth.[10]

Secondly, the idea that a wage is paid only to an individual worker for the work that he has performed is a simplistic and short-sighted view. It ignores the long term reproduction of labour-power for which capital must ultimately take responsibility. Employers who take this narrow view are acting against the long term interests of capital itself. If an adequate supply of labour-power is to be guaranteed for the future, wages must be more than sufficient to provide just for the worker's or his family's immediate needs.

Ideology and productivity

Capital has surrounded itself with a barrage of ideological 'data' which it is using to justify and rationalise its handling of the recession. Much of this data relates to 'productivity'.

The gist of capital's argument is that South Africa's labour productivity is far lower than any of its trading partners. It is also generally held that while African earnings have been increasing rapidly, there have been no significant gains in productivity. The implications of this sort of argument are:

(a) it justifies increases in the rate of exploitation during the recession, by speeding up the rate of production, or by other means;
(b) it justifies the current attempt to 'freeze' wage increases;
(c) it throws part of the blame for the recession, or at least its depth, onto the workers themselves;
(d) it is often used, as for example by the Minister of Finance, as an explanation for South Africa's exceptionally high rate of inflation, and can thus be used in legitimating the tighter monetarist policies which hit the African working class (including the surplus population) more severely than any other section of the country's population;

(e) it helps to justify management's strategies in handling the recession, particularly retrenchment practices. Many companies have argued that if African productivity had risen and/or unions had not pushed for and gained such big wage increases, management would not be in the position of having to retrench so many workers.

It is sufficient to make four points in rebutting these sorts of arguments:

(i) *Measuring productivity*
   Not only is productivity in general, and labour productivity in particular, extremely difficult to measure, but the concept of productivity is frequently used by capital in technically quite incorrect ways.

(ii) *Misrepresentation of data*
   On several occasions over the last two to three years capital has been found guilty of trying to equate real productivity with nominal wages.

(iii) *Ignoring cyclical tendencies*
   Capital has frequently argued that wages have risen more rapidly than productivity. This argument was frequently expounded around 1981, at the peak of the expansionary phase. At the end of an expansionary phase there is a tendency for wages to increase more rapidly than labour productivity, with the result that the labour costs per unit of production may rise during that period of the cycle. However, this is not usually enough for wages to catch up with earlier productivity gains. In other words it would have been quite within the normal expectations of the business cycle to see African wages running ahead of labour productivity around that time.

(iv) *Repudiation*
   The most important repudiation of capital's ideological stance on this subject has been produced by Charles Meth. In a study of productivity through the 1970s he claims that the government's official figures are wrong and that South Africa experienced both higher economic growth and much higher labour productivity than the official figures have shown.[11]

Finally, we should remind ourselves of some of the reasons why this recession has been so deep and so prolonged. Local factors such as the drought have played a significant part, but the major reason lies in the policies of Reagan and Thatcher which have sought to impose a solution on the international crisis of capitalism. Tight monetarist policies in conjunction with enormous US budget deficits have not only led to high interest rates, a strong dollar, and a consequent weakness in the gold price, but have possibly delayed as well as weakened the world recovery.

The ostensible victories of Reaganism and Thatcherism — lower inflation and recovery — have been at the expense of massive unemployment and the greater relative impoverishment of those affected by it. So too in South Africa the major burden of the recession has fallen on the African working class.

Notes

1 Research in progress. J. Keenan, forthcoming.
2 Research in progress. J. Keenan, forthcoming.
3 Marion Lacey, ' "Feudalism" in the Age of Computers', *Black Sash Annual General Congress*, March 1983.
4 J. Keenan, 'Trickle-up: African Income and Employment', in *South African Review One*, (Johannesburg, 1983), 184–92.
   J. Keenan, 'Boom for whom? The Socio-Economic Effects and Implications of the 1978–1983 Industrial Cycle for the African Population of South Africa', paper presented at the Symposium on Late Capitalism and Anthropological Studies in the 1980s, at the XIth ICAES, Vancouver, August 1983.
5 Commission of Inquiry into the Economic Development of Ciskei, (chairman: Prof. Nic Swart) (Potchefstroom University, 1983).
6 Lieb Loots, 'A Profile of Black Unemployment in South Africa: Two Area Surveys', *SALDRU* Working Paper No. 19, UCT April 1978.
7 Research in progress. J. Keenan, forthcoming.
8 Research in progress. J. Keenan, forthcoming.
9

	COL	Loss of income from subsistence agriculture	Effect of unemployment	Total
1st estimate (Soweto-based)	12,5%	5%	5,5%	23%
2nd estimate (bantustan-based)	12,5%*	5%	20%	37,5%

*COL for bantustans not adequately established, but possibly higher than in areas in which COL surveys are conducted.

10 see footnote 5 above and J. Keenan, 'The effect of the 1978–82 Industrial Cycle on Sowetan Household Incomes and Poverty Levels 1983', *SAIRR* forthcoming.
11 Charles Meth, 'A Challenge from *FOSATU* on Productivity', *FOSATU Occasional Publication* 6, 1983.

Health and Safety: An Emerging Issue on the Shop Floor

Jonny Myers and Malcolm Steinberg

1983 was an eventful year for industrial health and safety, and was characterised by a number of new developments. The year saw some legal fruits of ten years of intensified conflict between capital and labour — two new laws and one Bill concerned with health and safety were passed. Bad conditions together with increasing unionisation had focussed attention on health and safety as a field of conflict involving industrial relations and medical care at work.

This new legislation does not provide significant concessions to labour. The administration of health and safety at work is not intended to be tripartite (management, state, labour). The legal provisions serve rather to reinforce mutually beneficial state/management relationships and their joint domination of labour. Management's productivity concerns are evident in that the new laws do not permit work stoppages over unsafe work, do not promote workers' organisation in connection with health and safety issues, and attempt to exercise control over health and safety training and other activities at work. This is not to suggest an identity of interest as there has already been conflict between state and management over safety standards. The terms are perhaps more beneficial to the state, which is seeking to shift the burden of responsibility onto management, while management obtains principal control over the various levels of decision making about industrial health and safety (IHS).

The state

In 1976 the Erasmus Commission found much occupational disease in SA, lack of management concern about this, absence of a statistical data base, and fragmentation of health services, laws and safety provisions.

The Machinery and Occupational Safety Act (no. 6 of 1983) (MOSA) and the Basic Conditions of Employment Act (no. 3 of 1983) (BCOEA) were introduced to replace previously existing and rather ancient legislation embodied in the old Shops and Offices and Factories Acts. The fragmentation identified by Erasmus has been retained with the passage of MOSA, BCOEA, and the Occupational Medicine Bill (OMB). Conflict between the Departments of Manpower and Health, based on inter-departmental rivalry and/or professionalist interests, appears to have delayed the passage of legislation on health and safety at work, which has taken nine years since the Erasmus Commission to appear. In addition, two pieces of legislation (MOSA and OMB) have resulted which virtually duplicate each other. There has been no real systematic improvement in the collection of industrial health statistics, and management, the very party identified as being unconcerned with health and safety, is to have almost total power in terms of MOSA, BCOEA, and OMB.

The Basic Conditions of Employment Act
This Act was not really an improvement on previous legal provisions. This is particularly important as the Act is supposed to lay down minimal conditions, and as such should not exclude any category of workers. Those who have been excluded are generally isolated and unorganised workers. Such workers are most in need of the protection afforded by minimal standards, because they are most open to exploitation. They include workers in numerically and politically important economic sectors like domestic service, agriculture, state institutions, mines and works, people undergoing training, and seasonal workers who are important in the context of the food industry. Security guards are still discriminated against.

The basic working week is still much in excess of 40 hours at 46 hours. Provisions for overtime pay rates, sick leave, and annual leave are not improved. Uncertified sick leave has been further limited to two two-day episodes per eight-week period. While overtime is to be voluntary, management is not obliged to give advance notice. Special protection for women workers with regard to excessive overtime, overtime notice, and night shift work, has been removed under the guise of removing sexual discrimination from the Act. This represents a backward step where, instead of better conditions being extended to men, worse conditions apply for all. Control of continuous-activity shiftwork conditions is arbitrarily at the disposal of the Minister. There will be no consultation with workers, no guarantee of similar or equivalent conditions to non-shift workers, and no extra allowances to compensate for the inconvenience and ill-effects of shift work. In fact three-shift workers can be made to work a 48-hour week with no meal intervals.

The Machinery and Occupational Safety Act

This Act is a counter-challenge to trade union health and safety activity which, up to now, has been conducted through emergent shop floor structures, and has been largely free of legal strictures. Managements have been worried about work stoppages and the disorganisation of production over health and safety issues, and have been keen to institutionalise and control the handling of these issues. There is no real attempt to secure worker or trade union participation in the operation of legislation related to health and safety. New features of this Act such as management-selected health and safety committees and safety representatives are attempts to bureaucratise and professionalise health and safety at work. There are no real worker rights to information, access to facilities, time off with pay for training, or to stop hazardous work. The Act's new features, together with the weak character of workers' rights contained in it, serve to undercut shop floor safety activity and to divert conflict into bureaucratic management-dominated channels.

The fact that MOSA seeks to promote only state and management involvement in health and safety in the post-Wiehahn period is very interesting. On the one hand, concessions offered to labour would seem to amount to some technical improvements at work. On the other hand, the bipartite administration of health and safety at work envisaged in the legislation may have politically backward-tending results in terms of workers' organisation, especially shop floor organisation. It is in this sense that MOSA may be seen as a management offensive.

The autocratic and hierarchical orientation of the state Health and Manpower Departments is much in evidence. A body associated with the Workman's Compensation Commission, the National Occupational Safety Association, has already been helping management to implement the designs behind the legislation. They have recommended that those workers with a high educational level, and supervisory staff, be chosen by management as safety representatives. Trade unions are not considered to have any role in promoting worker health and safety. Such a selection procedure would bypass the shop stewards and their committees. It would also professionalise the health and safety structures at shop floor level by including educational and technical criteria in the selection of representatives. The presence of supervisors doubling as safety

148 *Labour*

representatives would also entrench a watchdog function for shop floor safety structures.

Other new aspects of MOSA are the advisory committee structures, including technical committees set up to pronounce on safety standards. Here again management and the state together with technical experts will predominate. The operation of these important bodies is virtually arbitrary, closed to public scrutiny, and not subject to appeal to the courts.

Another new provision is that workers may be fined up to R2 000 and 12 months in prison for failing to wear protective clothing provided by management. There is also a R4 000 fine and/or 24 months imprisonment for employers or machine users guilty of causing injuries in the use of machinery. A large proportion of cases brought to the court are likely to involve co-workers rather than management, judging from past records. Such a provision is unheard of in other countries and is a good example of victim-blaming. Personal protective equipment is generally recognised to be the last resort in the prevention of disease because of its poor efficiency relative to removing hazards at source — a principle enshrined in most countries' IHS Legislation. At the same time there is no legal duty on management to provide a safe working environment.

Some of the incoming regulations are already worse than prevailing practices in some work-places. Accident statistics will drop artificially, because in future only accidents resulting in loss of more than 14 days work-time will be reportable. Women have again been discriminated against by the dropping of the confinement allowance drawn from public funds.

The Occupational Medicine Bill (OMB)
The Bill ostensibly attempts to set up the rudiments of occupational health care and research facilities to promote better standards of IHS. It falls far short of this mark. No independent employment advisory service is to be set up to investigate problems on request. A committee structure will be set up to consider pertinent matters referred by the Minister of Health. There is no provision for input from workers or their organisations. The Bill duplicates the provisions of MOSA while envisaging no real linkage with the shop floor structures set up under MOSA. This will lead to confusion about the relative fields of operation of the two inspectorates that are to be established.

The Bill also attempts to institute state controls over all aspects of industrial health activity ranging from training of health personnel at all levels to the analysis of toxic substances. Another problem is that too many potentially useful innovations appear in the regulations where their very existence and usefulness are subject to the arbitrary power of the minister. Obligations relating to the disclosure of medical information to workers, for instance, would be better included in the provisions of the Bill itself. The Bill envisages medical examinations to monitor the health of certain groups of employees. These provisions are rather vague and may end up with workers being victimised, as there is no general obligation on employers to provide cover for disability contracted during the course of employment.

In general, wide Ministerial powers of exemption from provisions of these laws and their regulations are not subject to appeal to courts by workers. There is no provision for informing workers about laws, regulations, notices of exemption and other variations of conditions, or the way wages are calculated. Fines for management are still low.

It is obviously important not to fetishise the law which is just one aspect of a complex equation. The implementation of these Acts will depend upon the relative abilities of management, the state and workers to press their demands. Time will tell whether the more beneficial provisions of the Act will be applied maximally, and whether they may also serve to provide a more comprehensive set of minimum standards, particularly for unorganised workers. Similarly we shall have to wait to see whether the more draconian anti-worker measures will be applied, or whether they will turn out to be dead letters, of little use to management.

Management

The traditional area of interest for management in the area of health and safety has been 'loss control': their emphasis has been on minimising disruption of production resulting from accidents and illness rather than preventing ill-health in the work-force.

Management generally do not appear to be feeling too secure about their past record in health and safety at work. Their concern is that such issues may increasingly become part of negotiation with their workers. Their past failings might then result in expensive private compensation deals. They are also worried that democratically elected safety representatives exercising agreed-upon rights in the work-place would encroach on what is seen as managerial prerogative. Work stoppages as a result of dangerous production with attendant disputes could damage productivity.

In this regard, they would appear to have protected themselves by having their interests well represented in 1983's legislation. These laws ensure that management will have much greater say in the determination of safe working conditions than labour. They are under less of an obligation to provide safe working environments, and are, relatively speaking, less subject to punitive measures than workers.

Despite this it is interesting to note that the first set of draft regulations produced by the Department of Manpower, laying down standards under MOSA, were recently scrapped after management complaints. This reflects both easy management access to the state, and the clash of interests between the state and management over the setting of regulations.

After notable silence and inactivity in the field of health and safety, both before and after the Erasmus Commission, some managements have been surprisingly keen to implement the new provisions of MOSA, and thereby to remove the initiative from organised workers in terms of health and safety issues. In most cases, however, one suspects that management will simply ignore the new legislation, particularly where their workforces remain, with the majority of workers in South Africa, unorganised.

The unions

The emergent trade unions have experienced a significant expansion in the following areas:

- health and safety education;
- demand on specialist resources (legal, medical, scientific);
- negotiation over health and safety conditions.

The fulcrum of these activities has been shop floor organisation.

Original information is increasingly being generated through union-sponsored survey work. This work may take the form of research conducted by professional researchers in conjunction with shop floor structures or may, in some cases, be conducted by the workers themselves. Workers generally are surprised to realise that they are capable of producing either knowledge of an original character, or information specific to local conditions which is unattainable from the research literature. Such information is vitally useful to researchers in interpreting known or suspected hazards at work. Survey work in progress during 1983 included:

- accidents and protective clothing usage in foundries in the steel and engineering industry;
- silicosis in foundries;
- health effects of exposure to cold temperatures;
- asbestos-related diseases in the transport and fibre-cement industries;
- byssinosis in the cotton textile industry;
- effects of bleaching agents used to process dried fruit;
- respiratory effects of exposure to grain dust;
- availability and quality of work-place based health services.

A wide range of health-related problems taken up by unions during the year include:

- work in extreme temperatures;
- hazards in the textile industry;
- hazards of transport work and long-distance driving;
- handling and transporting dangerous materials;
- chemicals used in fruit packing and preserving;
- safer substitutes for asbestos-cement products;
- hazards of agricultural herbicides and pesticides;
- hazards of sewage and garbage disposal;
- hazards (besides silicosis and accidents) in the steel and engineering, construction and civil engineering industries;
- specifications and standards for protective equipment like goggles and masks;
- problems of the organisation of work, like shiftwork and high work intensity;
- specific problems of women workers, such as contraception and maternity conditions.

Broader aspects of industrial health, including health-related benefits and pensions, have also been taken up with increasing frequency during the year. Many unions have displayed interest in looking at possible concrete benefits that could be provided for their members. Such benefits include adequate sick pay and sick leave, some form of medical service and better deals with either managements or insurance companies for retirement and disability pensions. The Food and Canning Workers' Union, as a result, has employed a doctor to run a clinic since 1981.

Some industries have been organised for the first time. Black mine workers deserve special mention. They have been forcibly disorganised since the 1940s. Working in some of the worst conditions known, they are now being actively organised. For the first time, conditions and IHS problems on the mines are becoming public knowledge instead of being dealt with behind closed doors by the mine owners and government health authorities.

There have also been dramatic new developments in education during 1983. In general, not many unions have active educational programmes and where these exist they are at very different levels. This applies even more strongly to health and safety education. For instance, the NUTW has employed a doctor to run a nationwide campaign against the chest disease byssinosis in the textile industry. However the main thrust of educational activity has been at shop floor level. Most education has taken the form of shop steward committee seminars focussing on particular problems related to hazards at work, unsatisfactory conditions of employment (in particular sick leave and sick pay), and the implications for shop floor organisation of the new legislation, particularly MOSA. On occasion these activities have extended to an industry-wide level within general unions, or a regional level within a federation of unions. On the major issue of the new legislation, there were two inter-union seminars in Johannesburg and Cape Town for officials and shop stewards.

With the development of industrial health resource facilities in major centres, there have been increasing demands for educational input in the form of written materials, seminars on all aspects of health and safety at work, instruction in complaints handling, and the establishment of information bases and record systems for future negotiation and preventive actions. There has also been increasing union interest in comparative information on health and safety conditions and organisation at work in other industries and countries.

By the end of 1983, specific health and safety organisation, where it existed was not specialised, and was generally located in shop steward committees. Some unions had particular officials handling health problems and many had some form of safety agreement with their managements in the form of either specific health and safety clauses or entire agreements.

Only about 12% of workers in the country are organised and for various reasons health and safety issues are often not priorities for the emerging unions. Nevertheless, it was a year of trade union initiative in health and safety. Shop floor health and safety structures which had tentatively emerged were confronted with attempts via MOSA to redirect their growth and to place them under management control.

There were also important developments during 1983 in the legal field. For the first time, black mine workers, through the National Union of Mineworkers, participated in an inquiry into the conditions leading up to a mine disaster (Hlobane, where 68 miners were killed). In this one accident there were more deaths than in all coal mining accidents in the United Kingdom in a year.

Action through the Industrial Court resulted in some very important judgements and precedents regarding the right of workers to refuse dangerous work without victimisation. In the case of the *NUM v West Driefontein Goldmine*, where 17 workers refused to go underground due to unsafe conditions, the court decided that the work was not dangerous. However it also decided that there was a reasonable basis for the workers to believe that conditions were dangerous and that they had been given inadequate assurance that there was no danger. The court ruled that this had constituted an unfair labour practice. What constitutes an effective assurance? Unions may decide to call in arbitrators of their own choice to establish whether or not an area is safe in future.

Unions have also increasingly submitted legal and scientific comments on intended legislation and regulations to various advisory and technical committees set up under the new IHS laws. The success of the NUTW's compensation claim for a worker suffering from byssinosis was an important advance in compensation for industrial disease. This was the second case ever to be compensated in the cotton textile industry in South Africa.

Unemployed workers

The economic climate in South Africa in 1983 continued to deteriorate with some workers losing their jobs through retrenchment. The burden fell more heavily on injured or sick workers, often the first to be retrenched even where their condition results from hazardous work. With minimal state social security and little private sector provision for this aspect of worker well-being, 1983 was a bitter year indeed.

These realities are exacerbated in the bantustans where the structure and workings of what state social security systems exist are complex and confusing. Payments of pensions have always been problematic in these areas. The situation with respect to unemployment insurance benefits became even more confused last year when separate 'homeland' funds were established. Conditions of extreme repression in areas like the

Ciskei and Bophuthatswana have also had serious effects on the ability of workers in these areas to defend their health and promote their safety.

Health and safety workers

Various groups and individuals have been working in the field of worker complaints and compensation since 1974, and in industrial health proper since 1980. In the past year or two they have expanded and consolidated their operations and 1983, particularly, has seen the number of people in the field grow considerably.

The range and depth of problems tackled with the unions during the year is evidence of the skills that are becoming available to organised labour in South Africa. By the end of 1983 there were health advice and research centres in Cape Town (Industrial Health Research Group, Technical Assistance Project), East London (Industrial Health Research Group) and Johannesburg (Health Information Centre, Technical Advice Group), providing services to the unions. People working in the area include those with expertise in science, engineering, nursing, medicine, law, advice, and education. The first national meeting of groups and individuals working in industrial health took place in Durban in June.

Important services continue to be provided for unorganised workers, in the handling of complaints by independent groups such as the Industrial Aid Society in Johannesburg, and by special clinics set up by some unions. These activities revolve around worker's compensation, unemployment insurance claims and similar issues. Training courses in dealing with complaints are also provided for union personnel. The approach to the handling of worker complaints by such groups tends to minimise recourse to the law for the resolution of problems, and to emphasise the training and use of non-professional people.

Medical consultancy work with individual workers has grown during the last year. This is, in part, a result of research and consultancy work with groups of workers, revealing numbers of ill workers requiring full clinical evaluation for compensation for occupational disease. This is an important development as knowledge of occupational disease in the South African medical community is rather inadequate and many treatable and compensatable conditions are missed or inadequately handled even if identified.

During 1983, the Medical Association of South Africa and the South African Occupational Health Nurses Association devoted substantial parts of their annual congresses to occupational health, reflecting the general increase in interest in occupational health at all levels of the society. It is clear that conflict over these issues is being increasingly experienced within industry, and that professionals are unsure of how best to deal with this.

Conclusion

For organised workers in the emergent trade unions the year was one of initiatives in improving health and safety at work. Union educational activities resulted in better awareness of these issues on the shop floor and increased activity and negotiations over health and safety.

The other parties to the industrial relations equation — management, state, and health professionals — have also shown increasing interest and initiative in health and safety issues. Health and safety at work is now firmly on the bargaining table. For that proportion of the South African working class currently employed and organised into progressive trade unions, important future developments can be expected. The health care infrastructure for work-related problems will become more developed and sophisticated, and demands for safer work, better health care, rehabilitation, and compensation will increase.

For those who are unemployed, the hardships brought about by the vicious cycle of ill-health and unemployment will continue to take their toll. The plight of many workers will be aggravated by the inadequacy or absence of state welfare benefits, particularly in the bantustans.

Black Trade Unions on the Mines

Clive Thompson

During 1983 a number of black trade unions faced the challenge of organising one of the country's most segmented and controlled labour-forces, the mine workers. Worker recruitment in this industry poses peculiar difficulties. The mines are a closed system, with the labour-force typically accommodated on company premises and protected from outside influences.

The emerging unions have approached the question of gaining access to workers on the mines in different ways. Some, such as the South African Mine Workers' Union (SAMWU) and the Metal and Allied Workers' Union (MAWU), attempted to recruit without invitation and negotiate with management at mine level. Others, notably the National Union of Mineworkers (NUM), sought to reach an accommodation with the Chamber of Mines. The latter option generally meant conforming to the Chamber's detailed access provisions and initiating the bargaining process at industry rather than mine level.

Although the plant bargaining route has been used with considerable success in recent years by the emerging unions in other industries, the early indications are that the same pattern will not be repeated on the mines affiliated to the Chamber. Although the Chamber has clearly decided that a working relationship with strong and representative unions is preferable to dealing with a leaderless mass of workers, it also has settled views on what form the relationship should take.

The Chamber's new approach was highlighted by its December 1982 decision to drop registration as a recognition requirement. Several developments prompted this change of policy. Throughout the 1970s, mine managements were plagued by periodic outbursts of violence amongst workers variously ascribed to ethnic antagonisms, agitators and lack of communication channels. In 1982, Gencor and Gold Fields decided not to match the increases afforded by the other mining houses. This precipitated a wave of strikes involving over seventy thousand workers.

While the Chamber has seen the need to bargain collectively, it presently has the strength and organisation to ensure that the bargaining takes place on its terms — industry-wide bargaining. By the year's end, SAMWU had shelved its earlier approach and was talking to the Chamber.

Unions on the mines

In the last two years there has been a proliferation of black unions on the mines, although more recently there have been signs of rationalisation. MAWU seems to have held off its entry into the field pending developments in the unity talks, while the Black Allied Workers' Union withdrew from the industry after it had formed the Black Allied Mining and Tunnel Workers' Union (BAMTWU). BAMTWU is an unregistered union which has concentrated on recruiting members in the collieries of Northern Natal such as Kilbarchan, Vryheid, Coronation, Durnacol and Welgedacht. It was formally granted access to the collieries by the Chamber on 7 April 1983.

The Black Allied Mining and Construction Workers' Union was established in August 1982. Its general secretary is Tebogo Mngomezulu. It was granted access by the Chamber on 29 July 1983 but appears to have made more headway in the construction rather than the mining industry. It has concluded recognition agreements with Pioneer Concrete and LTA.

SAMWU was formed in 1983 and is run by a steering committee with members drawn from GAWU, SAAWU, MACWUSA/GWUSA, NISMAWU and OVGWU. The president of the union is Samson Ndou and Sisa Njikelana is the general secretary. It is currently recruiting members on gold mines on the West Rand and at Rustenburg Platinum. MGWUSA, which declared its intention to recruit on the mines in early 1983, has since thrown its weight behind SAMWU.

The registered Federated Mining Union (FMU) had its origin in a parallel union of the South African Boilermakers Society (SABS), with which it still retains close links. Its general secretary is Ike van der Watt and the assistant general secretary is J.H. Pieterse.

The recruitment drive of the FMU has followed both craft and industrial union lines, although it is constitutionally an industrial union. It has organised on the basis of job categories on mines affiliated to the Chamber, while at other mines it has become representative of the work-force as a whole. It has general recognition agreements with De Beers in Kimberley and Matthey Rustenburg Refinery, where it is representative of 80% and 85% of the total black labour-forces respectively. It is currently entering into recognition talks with Rustenburg Platinum mine.

The FMU was the first of the emerging unions to sign a recognition agreement with the Chamber, which it did on 12 September 1982. Like the Chamber's later agreement with NUM, this agreement was mainly facilitative in nature. It provided that as and when the union obtained a majority of workers in any specified category at a particular mine, it would be recognised as the collective bargaining agent of such workers. By the end of 1983, the FMU had been recognised at three Chamber mines, Hartebeesfontein, Vaal Reefs and Buffelsfontein for the following categories: drivers, handymen, painters and construction workers. The FMU's progress has been slow but steady and it has been intent on consolidating its gains at every step. It currently has stop order facilities in respect of some six thousand members.

The National Union of Mineworkers (NUM)

In its attempt to organise black mine workers, NUM has made the most striking headway amongst the emerging unions. An affiliate of CUSA, it began organising on the mines in August of 1982 and held its inaugural congress in Klerksdorp in December of that year. Its president is James Motlatsi and the general secretary is Cyril Ramaphosa.

As with most of the other new unions organising on the mines, NUM decided not to register while setting about the task of establishing itself in the industry. This stance is likely to assume strategic rather than principled dimensions in the years to come.

NUM decided at an early stage to apply to the Chamber for access to its member mines and, in retrospect, this course of action was probably a *sine qua non* for the massive growth in membership which the union experienced. The expedient extensively employed by unions in other sectors when faced with a hostile management − recruiting in the townships outside working hours − is not an option in an industry which barracks and oversees its work-force on company premises.

Access on the Chamber's terms carried a price. Each member mining house spelt out its conditions in elaborate detail and conspicuous amongst these were prohibitions upon mass meetings, meetings in hostels, the distribution of pamphlets without managerial sanction and the use of public address systems. Contrary to the terms of a blanket prohibition on all outdoor meetings, Rand Mines stipulated that no meeting should take place indoors but that 'meetings may be held on open areas on mine property adjacent to a hostel'. Lonrho required that 'all meetings . . . be conducted in accordance with the Terrorism and Riotous Assemblies Acts'.

As NUM's membership grew, the issue of contact with members became increasingly contentious. Very often the only way in which mass meetings could take place was by transporting members at great expense to venues in nearby townships. An organiser and a member of the union were prosecuted (and subsequently acquitted) for participating in an allegedly unlawful outdoor meeting at Vaal Reefs in May 1983.

NUM's recruiting strategy

Faced with the daunting task of breaking into an industry with over half a million potential recruits, NUM's organisers began to recruit members in areas which were more familiar to unionists. When the union signed the historic first collective agreement of 9 June 1983, a large proportion of the 6 000 members covered came from occupations such as clerks, personnel assistants, carpenters, recreation officers and stores attendants. The union was also quick to organise a majority of the workers at the recruiting arm of the gold and uranium mines, The Employment Bureau of Africa (TEBA).

With respect to underground workers, NUM's initial strategy was to aim for the team leaders — the category of black underground workers who had advanced as far up the job ladder as the Mines and Works Act would permit. Miners work in gangs comprising anything between 25–100 workers. At the head of each gang is the 'ganger' or 'miner' — the white union man. Above him is the first tier of managerial employees, the shift boss, who is responsible for the co-ordination of a number of gangs, while immediately below him will be several team leaders. The team leaders supervise and assist with the mining activities of the gang members. Although denied by statute the right to acquire the blasting certificate — the key to a number of skilled tasks and to job advancement — the black team leaders perform a range of specialised jobs in terms of and often beyond the terms of a system of exemptions. In this way the white ganger preserves his position and prestige, management redresses the skills shortage and the team leader gets short-changed.

The union reckoned that the team leaders were the route to the recruitment of the general underground workers, and channelled their efforts accordingly. It soon realised that such efforts were at least partially misdirected.

On a number of counts, the interests of the team leaders and the other members of the gang diverge. Although earning considerably less than the white miner, a team leader's wages are much higher than those of his fellow workers. His supervisory functions also serve to set him apart from them. An interesting and quite graphic illustration of this cleavage occurred in the course of a safety dispute underground at the West Driefontein gold mine (discussed below). An entire gang, including the team leader, refused to work in a particular section of the 14th level because of allegedly unsafe conditions and inadequate instruction from the shift boss. The dispute continued for some days until the workers were placed on terms: return to work or be fired. The team leaders who, according to affidavits subsequently submitted in court, shared their colleagues' grave apprehensions returned to work. The gang members were fired.

Although the team leaders remained important in terms of recruitment, the union began focussing attention on machine operators. In many senses, the general underground worker aspires to advance to the position of machine operator. This is the most demanding of all underground jobs; it enjoys an air of toughness and accomplishment, but is not tainted by supervisory duties. The machine operators are at the top of the rank and file, but they are *of* the rank and file, and NUM has increasingly been using their strategic position to swell its numbers.

Recognition negotiations

Besides the symbolic act of recognition, the collective agreement signed with the Chamber in June was essentially enabling in character. Chamber members agreed 'to recognise the union as representative of the collective views of its members . . . employed in the occupations . . . listed in the schedule'. The schedule to the agreement set out those occupations at particular mines where NUM had become representative of the persons employed there. At Vaal Reefs the agreement noted that the union was representative of boilermaker aides, builders, carpenter aides, clerks, personnel assistants, recreation officers, team leaders and vehicle drivers. Other mines included in the schedule were Elandsrand, Kloof, President Brand, and Western Holdings. The Chamber did not insist on 50% representivity in a particular occupation, but adopted a flexible criterion based on sufficiency. The bargaining unit, i.e. the clusters of employees in respect of which the union could act as bargaining agent, was accordingly based on representivity in particular occupations. Towards the end of 1983, the Chamber indicated that it wished to enlarge the bargaining unit to coincide with particular production sections (which would involve grouping a number of occupations together), and the union undertook to re-examine the situation.

The agreement also allowed for the negotiation of substantive and procedural agreements covering topics such as conditions of employment; recognition of shaft stewards (the mining equivalent of shop stewards); dismissal, grievance, retrenchment and dispute procedures. The parties have yet to settle the terms of these further agreements but clearly the conclusion of a disputes procedure must be high on the agenda.

When the union entered its first round of negotiations with the Chamber, it was bargaining nominally only on behalf of its 6 000 members actually covered by the agreement at the mines specified above. At that stage its total membership stood at about twenty thousand. As a matter of practical effect, however, the deal it finally negotiated was extended to all 460 000 workers on the gold, platinum and copper mines.

The union came in with a demand of a 30% wage raise and in the end an increase of around 15% was agreed. Although this was an adequate figure given the general state of the economy and the industry, the reaction of both union members and mine workers generally caused the union some anxious moments and has no doubt given it food for thought regarding the next round of negotiations scheduled for mid-1984.

The general attitude of the mining houses towards NUM has yet to crystallise, but there are clear indications that they are adopting an increasingly harder line. The CUSA unions had no particular reputation for militancy and at the outset management sought to encourage controlled familiarity by way of a number of gestures. One such gesture was the provision of office facilities for the union on a number of mines. By the year's end however, at least one mining house — Gold Fields — had given the union notice of its intention to withdraw office facilities.

Whatever designs the mining houses may have had, labour on the mines has demonstrated a groundswell of militancy and the union leadership has had its time cut out translating this into appropriate responses. Although the union's first recruits may have come largely from selected categories, the impetus for all major industrial action in the latter half of the year came from those at the underground rockface, and this promises to be the shape of things to come.

Disputes involving NUM

In the West Driefontein safety dispute which occurred in September 1983, it was the rank and file who refused to work under conditions perceived to be hazardous. A gang of workers had been transferred to a new area of the mine shortly after several workers had been injured there in rockfalls. They claimed that upon arrival they had been inadequately instructed by their immediate superiors in regard to the hazards they encountered there. After a series of exchanges involving ultimately the general secretary of the union and the chairman of the mining house (Gold Fields),[17] mine workers were dismissed. As a result the union had recourse to the Industrial Court for the first time. To the consternation of the industry, the court proceeded to reinstate the workers pending a later full hearing.

In the aftermath of the blast at the Hlobane Colliery in which 68 miners were killed and scores of others injured, health and safety has emerged as a crucial issue. Around eight hundred workers die in mining accidents every year and thousands more are injured. The union has attempted to focus and articulate the very widespread discontent felt by underground workers and has challenged both the safety standards employed by the mines and the manner of their enforcement. As yet no agreement exists between the union and any mine regulating matters connected with safety, although at the beginning of 1984 the Chamber invited the union to join its Prevention of Accidents Committee. The union's initial response was that the issue needed to be negotiated at mine rather than industry level.

The safety and job advancement issues combine in a manner which makes conflict in this area inevitable. The white miner is immediately responsible for the bulk of safety measures which regulate the mining operation at the rockface; it is he who is charged by regulation with checking for hazardous conditions at the commencement of every shift and 'making safe'; it is he who holds the blasting certificate and performs the blasting operation. He receives his ticket only after undergoing training in excess of a year.

Increasingly however, a large proportion of the miner's job is performed by team leaders acting under (or without) exemption. They do this after a comparatively short training period lasting several weeks. The standard exemption authorisation lays down no actual periods or standards of training but merely enjoins the mine manager to ensure that 'the competent and experienced Bantu team leader . . . shall have been specifically trained for the duties he will be called upon to perform'. The end result is that the man with the training is becoming short on experience and the man with experience lacks in-depth training. Casualty figures suggest that the blurring of job definitions and responsibilities has adversely affected the vigilance demanded by the working environment.

During 1983 and early 1984 NUM was involved in a number of disputes which provided pointers to the strengths and limitations of the union.

In August 1983 the union declared a wage dispute at Rand Refineries. On the face of it, the union was in a strong bargaining position. Nearly all the country's gold is refined at the plant and NUM was representative of 98 % of the work-force. It applied for a conciliation board — a precondition for a legal strike — and threatened that industrial action would follow a failure in negotiations. However all parties were aware that the employer was capable of replacing its labour complement, several hundred workers, in days rather than weeks. The members' skills were limited and new labour readily available.

The dispute turned out to be an exercise in brinkmanship and was settled the day before the legal strike was due to commence. The union declared itself satisfied with the negotiated package and Rand Refineries, in something of a representative capacity for employers in the industry, was prepared to compromise. This allowed a dispute which had followed the route prescribed by the Labour Relations Act to have a strife-free conclusion.

In January 1984, several workers at Impala Platinum Refineries in Springs were dismissed for alleged misconduct. The circumstances of the dismissal led to widespread worker discontent and culminated in a general work stoppage. Virtually the entire labour-force was unionised. This continued for several days until the mine management issued the workers an ultimatum. Reportedly against the union's advice, the workers decided not to return to work until their demand that the dismissed individuals be reinstated was met. With apparent Chamber backing, the mine management dismissed the bulk of its work-force, some 1 500 employees, and thereafter refused all settlement overtures on the issue.

At that stage the union was faced with the choice of escalating the dispute or abandoning all thought of industrial action. NUM decided on the latter course and by so doing furnished both its members and the industry with a frank appraisal of its current power.

The outcome of events in another dispute which occurred at virtually the same time was rather different. Two workers at the opencast Rietspruit Colliery at Witbank were killed when a pylon which they had been instructed to work on by a shift boss collapsed. The next day the entire work-force of about a thousand — mainly union members — stopped work and marched to the homes of the bereaved families in the nearby township to express their sympathies. On the second day of the inquiry into the accident under the Mines and Works Act a week later, the workers again downed tools for an entire shift. Management met with union representatives in an attempt to settle the issue and openly reproached a shift boss for his conduct in the events which led to the accident and dispute. No disciplinary action was taken against any of the workers. Subsequently the presiding officer at the inquiry found a shift boss and a more senior managerial employee responsible for the accident.

At the close of 1983 the union was claiming a membership of approximately 60 000, which would make it the biggest union in the country. There can be no doubt that the union's organisational infrastructure will be severely taxed in its attempts to service such a large and expanding constituency. At the same time, it is open to question whether it has the ability to reconcile the interests of its rank and file with those of its members in the higher grades. At its second annual congress in December 1983, the union put out the call of 'one industry, one union'. It remains to be seen whether unity amongst the emerging unions on the mines will be forged as part of wider re-alignments in the labour movement.

Bantustan Attitudes to Trade Unions

Carole Cooper

The Ciskei's banning of the South African Allied Workers Union (SAA-WU) in September 1983 and the introduction of an Industrial Concilia-tion Act by Bophuthatswana in March this year have focussed attention on bantustan attitudes towards the development of trade unions and the im-plications this has for the segmentation of the work-force.

Already, over time, sharp divisions have emerged between workers in the metropolitan areas and those at the periphery, and to a lesser extent between those within the bantustans and those on their borders. Isolated from the main urban areas and subject to a process of underdevelopment, bantustans historically have served as dumping grounds for the unem-ployed, aged and disabled.

The state's post-1976 strategy of developing a stable urban African community (earning better wages and having access to improved hous-ing) has meant a more rigorous policing of 'illegals' in urban areas and endorsing them out to the bantustans. This has contributed and continues to contribute to a rising level of unemployment and poverty in these areas. The state's success in creating rural jobs through its decentralisation poli-cy has been minimal in terms of the overall picture of deprivation. Nevertheless, this policy has led to a further segmentation of the working class at the periphery, with those living near the more developed border areas having a greater chance of gaining employment than those in the bantustans where there is little border industry. Even within border areas which have been industrialised, divisions exist between those who have access to jobs and those who remain unemployed.

Unions organising in the periphery have to contend with this complex set of circumstances. Any attempts by these unions to reshape the pat-terns of differentiation between categories of workers are controlled by

bantustan authorities intent on protecting their own economic and political interests.

Trade unionism in the bantustans is still in its embryonic stage mainly
because unions, given their limited resources, have concentrated on
organising in areas where industry is much more developed. These
comprise the metropolitan and certain border areas, for example, the
Pretoria-Rosslyn-Brits area bordering on Bophuthatswana, the East
London industrial complex bordering on the Ciskei, and the Durban-
Pinetown-Hammarsdale and Richards Bay-Empangeni areas bordering
on KwaZulu. According to BENSO, total employment (excluding
agriculture and services) in all the 'homelands' amounted to 597 505 in
1980. The breakdown was as follows: the Transkei 61 049, Bophuthatswana 107 208, the Ciskei 54 580, KwaZulu 305 240 and Lebowa 66 920
— with the numbers employed in the rest being lower than 20 000 each.
These figures are generally accepted as being inflated as a result of BEN-
SO's wide definition of the economically active population on which its
calculations are based, and thus the numbers working on a full-time basis
could be much smaller.[1] Unions have concentrated on organising in
Bophuthatswana, KwaZulu and, to a lesser extent, the Ciskei where industrial development is further advanced than in the other bantustans. In
particular two of the most successful growth points — Babelegi and
Isithebe — are situated in Bophuthatswana and KwaZulu respectively.

In the border areas the potential and actual membership of unions comprises mainly commuters who constitute the majority of the work-force
there. These workers live in the bantustans and commute on a daily or
weekly basis to work outside the borders. The total number of commuters
in 1982 was 773 000 with the most — 395 000 — from KwaZulu, followed by 173 000 from Bophuthatswana and 38 000 from the Ciskei.
Most of these commuters work in industrial areas, a lesser proportion
seeking employment on the farms. Because of the higher wages paid in
border areas and the greater possibility of union activity, these workers
generally are in a relatively better position than their co-workers within
the bantustans. Nevertheless, their position is still a precarious one.

While bantustans differ in their response to trade unions — from a
limited acceptance of their presence to an outright ban on their activities
— their overriding concern is that unions should not threaten their power
economically or politically. On the economic front, they wish to prevent
unions from undermining potential investment within their borders
which the South African state's policy of decentralisation has set out to
encourage. When initially launched in the 1960s, the decentralisation

policy was designed to attract industry to bantustan and border areas in part to stem the influx of rural Africans into urban areas by increasing the number of rural jobs. The failure of this policy led to its revision in 1983, with the government offering better incentives for businessmen in a wider range of designated areas instead of in bantustan and border areas only.

One of the main attractions offered to industrialists under both phases of the policy was the low cost of labour in bantustan and border areas. To depress wages in the former, a series of proclamations passed in 1970, 1971 and 1972 made the Labour Relations Act (then the Industrial Conciliation Act of 1956) and wage determinations under the Wage Act (1925) inapplicable in these areas.[2] Prior to 1979, although Africans were not regarded as employees under the Labour Relations Act, industrial council agreements, which set basic conditions of work (including minimum wages) within industries, could be extended to cover them. By making both this Act and wage determinations inapplicable in the bantustans, the proclamations made it possible for employers there to pay minimum wages well below those in the metropolitan areas. The only form of representation open to workers who wished to discuss their conditions of work was a system of works and liaison committees established in terms of the Black Labour Relations Regulation Act No. 70 of 1973. However, this system has long been shown to be inadequate, and, in any case, it is not clear how widely it has been implemented in the bantustans. In the border areas where the Labour Relations Act and wage determinations are still in force, employers can pay lower wages by applying for exemption from industrial council agreements. These, in any case, generally set a lower minimum rate for border than for metropolitan areas.

One of the possible effects of trade union activity in these areas would be to increase wages to a level in line with those elsewhere. In particular this would be the case where unions have organised in the same company's plants in both the metropolitan and bantustan areas. Where unions have sought recognition from companies in the bantustans, they have reported that the wage question causes the most difficulties. Discrepancies also exist between hours of work, with workers in the bantustan clothing industry working a 45-hour week as compared with a 40-hour week in the main urban areas. Attempts by unions to pressure for improved wages and working conditions could bring them into direct conflict with the bantustan authorities who, because they perceive increased investment as depending on the existence of a work-force which is both cheap and stable, wish to maintain strict control over the organisation of labour within their boundaries. Lebowa has assured businessmen that nothing will be allowed in the bantustan that will interfere with free enterprise there.

While economic considerations have played a major role in determining the attitudes of bantustan authorities to trade unions, political factors have also shaped these attitudes in a critical way. Most bantustan authorities see in the emerging non-racial and black trade union movement in South Africa a political threat to their own power and have attempted not only to prevent such unions operating within their boundaries, but some, such as the Ciskei, have attempted to harass unions which have been organising commuters in border areas. Such bantustans have not hesitated to use security legislation to detain and arrest trade unionists. Antagonism between bantustans and trade unions also has its roots in the fact that most emerging unions refuse to recognise them as separate political entities, regarding workers who live there as South African citizens. This stance has significant implications especially for unions operating in areas such as Bophuthatswana where the right of the union to organise is based on its acceptance of the territory's independence.

The varying responses of the bantustans to unionism are in part reflected in the kind of labour legislation applying in the territories. In terms of the National States Constitution Act (No. 21 of 1971) South Africa's labour legislation is frozen in the bantustans at the date of self-government or 'independence' and remains so until they amend or repeal it and introduce their own. Currently, however, there is confusion over which labour laws apply in the bantustans when they become self-governing or independent. The view of some lawyers is that because the 1970 proclamation (see above) repealed the Labour Relations Act and wage determinations in the bantustans, these no longer have force there. The Black Labour Relations Regulation Act applies instead.[3] Another view is that the National States Constitution Act could supersede the 1970 proclamation, in which case the Labour Relations Act and wage determinations would have force until otherwise amended by the bantustans. However the Labour Relations Act in its pre-1979 form (prior to the Wiehahn Commission) does not provide for registered trade unions for Africans. Thus whether this Act or the Black Labour Relations Regulation Act — which also does not make provision for unions — applies makes little real difference to bantustans such as QwaQwa, Lebowa, Gazankulu, KaNgwane, KwaNdebele and the Ciskei which have not passed their own legislation. The confusion is only of material importance where the bantustan amends the Labour Relations Act, as KwaZulu did in 1981. If the legal view is correct then its amendment is meaningless because the principal act does not apply in any case. Because of the uncertainty surrounding this issue the National Manpower Commission has asked the Human Sciences Research Council to investigate it.

Of all the bantustans, only the Transkei, KwaZulu, Bophuthatswana and Venda have passed their own legislation. The Transkei categorically refused to accept trade union activity within its borders, and its Labour Relations Act (No 13 of 1977) sets up a committee system similar to that provided for by South Africa's now repealed Black Labour Relations Regulation Act. In addition, the provisions governing strikes in the Transkei are similar to those in the repealed Act. These make it virtually impossible for workers to hold a legal strike. Venda's legislation is similar to that of the Transkei. Both Bophuthatswana and KwaZulu have shown a limited acceptance of unions and have passed their own legislation to provide for their establishment.

Currently there are no laws preventing unregistered unions from organising workers in the bantustans, and the only specific banning of a trade union is the Ciskei's banning of SAAWU.

The three bantustans where the most trade union activity has occurred — the Ciskei, Bophuthatswana and KwaZulu — are those where there has been the most industrial development. The gains and setbacks of unions organising in these areas are dependent to a significant degree on the actions of the bantustan authorities.

The Ciskei

The bantustan with the most notorious record of trade union oppression is the Ciskei which views unions as a political and economic threat and has sought to curb their influence not only within its boundaries but outside as well. Unions which it has singled out for attack are the AFCWU, the GWU and more specifically SAAWU. Its antagonism to SAAWU has been exacerbated by the union's refusal to recognise its independence. At its 1981 annual congress SAAWU denounced the bantustan system. It has been argued that the lack of a parliamentary opposition to President Lennox Sebe has meant that disaffected Ciskei citizens have turned to extra-parliamentary organisations to advance their interests and to protect them. This may explain both the degree of repression of trade unionists in the Ciskei as well as their depth of support in the townships.[4] Union activity within the Ciskei has been limited both because of the limited industrial development (in 1983 the territory had 28 040 jobs in the manufacturing industry) and because of the political problems of organising within its boundaries. The main union activity, until its banning, involved SAAWU which had members at a number of factories, notably Da Gama Textiles (one of the biggest factories in the Ciskei employing about 4 000 workers). Instead the unions have concentrated on organising in the East London industrial complex amongst commuters.

Harassment and surveillance of union activities

The Ciskei's harassment of unions has included continued detention of their leaders and members before independence under proclamation R252 (introduced in 1977), and after independence under its National Security Act (No. 13 of 1982). Proclamation R252 allowed for detention without trial for a period of 90 days renewable on expiry and placed the Minister's power to authorise detention beyond the jurisdiction of the courts. The proclamation further provided for the prohibition of all meetings without permission of the magistrate, rendered criminal 'any statement likely to have the effect of subverting or interfering with the authority of the government or any officer or anyone in the employ of the government or of any chief or headman'. It also prohibited any boycott 'with the object of causing loss, disadvantage or inconvenience to anyone or anybody'.[5] The National Security Act provides for detention without trial, bannings of individuals, prohibition and outlawing of organisations and publications, and defines security offences in broad terms.

Gatherings of more than 20 persons are prohibited unless previously authorised by a magistrate. Any person who, with intent 'to promote any industrial, social or econommic aim', interrupts any industry or undertaking, or attempts to do so, is guilty of an offence of subversion and is liable to up to 20 years' imprisonment. The Act states that a strike which is not in contravention of the Labour Relations Act is not illegal. (The assumption is being made that this Act applies ignoring the 1970 proclamation.)[6] The section prohibiting intimidation is far wider than that in South Africa's legislation, which has also been used to harass trade unions.

The Ciskei Central Intelligence Service (CCIS), formed after 'independence', has, as part of its role, the surveillance of trade unions. In 1980 the Ciskei detained at least (known detentions) 24 trade union officials (number of members harassed and detained not known), and in 1981 it detained 266 trade union members. Sixty-one of these were detained following a strike by workers at Wilson Rowntree, the remaining 205 being detained when returning to Mdantsane township after a union meeting in East London. The latter were all subsequently released. In 1982 Ciskei detained three trade union officials and an unknown number of union members, and in 1983 at least 30 union members and officials. However, very few of those detained have ever been brought to trial.[7]

The Ciskei has also attempted to gain assistance from employers in establishing a system to isolate workers who are union members or who have participated in a strike. In 1983 Lt General Charles Sebe, then commander in chief of Ciskei state security, said that he intended establishing a centralised labour information bureau which would monitor the performance and records of conduct of all Ciskei workers. If they had a record of union membership or of participation in a strike, it would be reflected in their records, and as a result they would be bypassed by the official labour recruitment channels. Sebe stated that the system was necessary to ensure that the Ciskei's prime export — its men and women willing and able to work — was the best available on the market. In keeping with this it was reported further that the Ciskei Manpower Development Centre was monitoring reports from employers on workers' performances.[8] Workers who 'misbehaved' were being marked 'unreliable'. In 1983 the Ciskei's Minister of Manpower, Chief Lent Maqoma, said that it was likely that punishment camps introducing disciplinary training on military lines would be introduced for those workers who broke their contracts for no valid reason. This was supported by Jack Roos, director of the Cape Chamber of Industries, who said it would be a 'good thing' if this form of training were to improve the 'efficiency' of workers.[9] This means that workers who demand improvements in their working conditions could, because of South Africa's labour allocation process, find themselves permanently locked into the bantustans and therefore permanently unemployed.

In its harassment of unions the Ciskei has been joined by the security police, with trade unionists detained in 'white' South Africa being handed over to police in the Ciskei and vice versa. Both have also attempted to enlist the help of employers in their attempts to crush the unions, in particular SAAWU. In 1980 the security police circulated a document amongst employers in East London advising them on how to break SAAWU.

The success of the South African and Ciskei authorities in persuading employers not to deal with SAAWU has been uneven. While many employers regard the union with hostility there are a number of companies who accept its bona fides, among these Chloride SA, Johnson and Johnson, KSM and WECCO Distributors. These have all signed recognition agreements with the union.

The banning of SAAWU
The Ciskei's repression of SAAWU culminated in the banning of the union in September 1983 following a boycott by workers living in Mdantsane (the Ciskei's biggest township) of their bus service after an 11% fare increase. The Ciskei erroneously attempted to place the responsibility for the boycott on SAAWU, whereas it had in fact been launched by a committee of community members including trade union representatives. As well as detaining hundreds of other members of the community, the Ciskei authorities detained at least 30 trade union members and officials, among them SAAWU's vice president, Sisa Njikelana. Hundreds of other workers were harassed. Anyone wearing a SAAWU T-shirt was arrested and houses were searched for union membership cards. Thozamile Gqweta, SAAWU's president, went into hiding to avoid detention. While in hiding he offered to negotiate an end to the boycott on condition that detained SAAWU unionists and committee members were released unconditionally − an offer not taken up. He reappeared in public only after the release from detention of Sisa Njikelana and other trade unionists.

Eleven unions and union federations representing 250 000 workers issued a joint statement deploring SAAWU's banning. The statement said that neither the South African government nor employers should think that they could distance themselves from the action. The unions charged that the complicity of the South African government was shown by the South African police's arrest of union officials and their handing them over to the Ciskei. They said that there could be no talk of reform of the labour laws and the new constitution while worker organisations were suppressed. They 'utterly rejected' the explanation by the Ciskei that SAAWU engaged in activities which endangered national or public safety. SAAWU and three other unions called on foreign investors to meet South African and Ciskei authorities to discuss the banning. The unions referred to the Ciskei authorities as a 'bunch of bureaucratic functionaries nurtured to rule the bantustans in the interest of racist South Africa and foreign business'.[10] In addition to the other forms of harassment which have disrupted SAAWU's organising drive, it has also been prevented from holding meetings in Mdantsane − its main way of communicating with and of recruiting members. Despite these major problems the union continues to function and is intent on consolidating its position.

Bophuthatswana

An examination of Bophuthatswana's Industrial Conciliation Act reveals that while the Bophuthatswana authorities are prepared to recognise trade unions, the latter will be subject to strict controls. Of all the bantustans, Bophuthatswana is the most industrialised, with certain industries, such as the platinum mines, being of strategic importance.

As at December 1982, of a total working population (excluding agriculture and services) of approximately 107 108, 20 055 were employed at the 161 factories in Bophuthatswana, mainly at Babelegi, its most important growth point (14 483 workers) and at Garankuwa and Mogwase.[11] Mining is the largest industry providing jobs for 46 000 people most of whom are employed at Impala Platinum (owned by the Gencor Group) and at parts of the Union and Rustenburg mines. Due to its proximity to the Pretoria/Witwatersrand/Vereeniging (PWV) area, it is also likely to experience greater industrial growth than the other bantustans.

Bophuthatswana has also seen activity by a wider range of unions in comparison with the other bantustans. Unions operating there have been the more established craft unions, which have members mainly on the mines, and, more recently, the emerging unions. The established unions include the SA Boilermakers Society (SABS), the Electrical and Allied Trades Union of SA, the Underground Officials Association, and the right-wing, all-white industrial Mine Workers Union. In the main, these unions have organised amongst the skilled, mainly white, workers, and to a lesser extent among black workers. This fact and the historical nature of their presence have meant that they have been tolerated by the Bophuthatswana authorities. It seems that this has been with some reluctance, and these unions report that they have experienced problems organising in the territory, particularly through the harassment and arrest of their organisers.

Bophuthatswana has been far more reluctant to countenance the presence of newer unions — both the emerging unions and those attached to the older established unions — who have begun more recently to organise within its boundaries. Attempts by an affiliate of CUSA, the Transport and Allied Workers Union, to organise amongst bus transport workers failed because the bus company was partly owned by the Bophuthatswana authorities who refused to deal with the union. Its other affiliates operating there — the United African Motor and Allied Workers Union, the Steel, Engineering and Allied Workers Union of South Africa, the Building Construction and Allied Workers Union, and, in particular, the National Union of Mineworkers (NUM) have all made little real progress in gaining recognition. Other unions, such as SAAWU, CCAWUSA, NAAWU, and the sister union to the SABS, the Federated Mining Union (FMU) have all experienced difficulties.

Bophuthatswana's Industrial Conciliation Act

The Bophuthatswana authorities' concern with controlling these unions and any new union activity is reflected in its Industrial Conciliation Act. One of the main provisions in the Act for this control is the requirement that both registered and unregistered unions organising in Bophuthatswana will have to have their head offices in the territory, and that their officials will have to be workers in Bophuthatswana. Even before the Act was passed this requirement was communicated to a number of unions to prevent them from operating in Bophuthatswana.

In January 1984 the NUM received notification that it would not be allowed to operate in the territory. The circular stated that trade unions were 'illegal' in Bophuthatswana, but that legislation was to be passed allowing for the operation of unions whose governing bodies would 'operate, perform their powers and have their head offices in Bophuthatswana'. It also said that no person might be employed as a union official unless he was normally employed in Bophuthatswana. It stated further that the NUM 'had no standing' in Bophuthatswana at the time, and 'nor would it have in the future'. Labour lawyers queried the validity of some of these claims, for instance, that trade unions were illegal, arguing at that time that while there was no law in terms of which they could register, nor was there any law preventing them from operating.

The effective ban on the NUM led to a strike on 23 January 1984 by about 450 NUM members employed at Union Carbide's UCAR Minerals inside Bophuthatswana. The NUM has been organising at UCAR since October 1983 and by November had a membership of 48% out of a workforce of approximately 500.

Prior to the strike, the NUM had been involved in recognition negotiations with management. The union met with UCAR's management at the Union Carbide's head office in Johannesburg on 13 December 1983. At the meeting management indicated that it was willing to recognise the union but that its problem was with the Bophuthatswana government which adopted a negative attitude towards unions. The company then held discussions with the Bophuthatswana government. Management reported back to the union that the official attitude of the Bophuthatswana government was that South African unions would not be permitted to operate in Bophuthatswana.

The union rejected a company request for a joint approach to the Bophuthatswana government on its union policy. The union said that as it did not recognise the existence of Bophuthatswana as an independent state, it would not meet with any of its representatives. The company then undertook to submit a memorandum to the Bophuthatswana government, which would be shown to the union first.

On 16 January the union received the letter from the government stating that it was operating 'illegally' in the territory. The strike followed a weekend meeting at which the contents of the circular were discussed. During the strike the workers demanded the recognition of their union as well as of their shop stewards committee, and made certain demands regarding wages and conditions of employment. They returned to work at 11.30 a.m. on the same day after management had agreed to talk to their representatives.

The workers struck again on 24 January over wages and, more significantly, over the Bophuthatswana government's intervention which had put pressure on management not to talk to the NUM — a fact which management had conveyed to the workers.

At the time, Cyril Ramaphosa, the union's general secretary, said that the union was contemplating legal action against both the Bophuthatswana government and Union Carbide for refusing to recognise the union. The industrial relations manager at Union Carbide said that the company had been attempting for some time to reach a compromise between the NUM and the Bophuthatswana government but had 'made no progress'. He said that the company was not in a position to have dealings with the NUM and was at present trying to reach a settlement with a committee of worker representatives (*RDM*, 25.01.84).

Commenting on the strike, the Bophuthatswana Minister of Manpower and Co-ordination, Rowan Cronje, denied that union recognition had been an issue. In justifying the contents of the circular he also said that no other country allowed foreign unions to operate within its borders, and Bophuthatswana would not allow this either. His claim about foreign unions is not correct. For example the American-based United Automobile Workers organises in Canada, the International Association of Machinists has about one-third of its members in the same country, and the London-based International Transport Federation has members in other countries. In addition it has been asked, why should 'foreign' unions be excluded when 'foreign' businesses are encouraged to invest in the area?

Significantly it is the emerging unions which do not recognise Bophuthatswana as a 'foreign' country and, therefore, do not accept Cronje's argument. In a statement on the strike, CUSA said that it would not become the victim of the 'Bophuthatswana regime and its misguided advisers' and in a warning to employers said that it was prepared to fight the banning of 'foreign' unions in every local and international forum (*Star*, 02.02.84).

The NUM was not the only union to receive such a circular. SAAWU, CCAWUSA, the SABS, an established union which has in the last two years begun a concerted organising drive amongst black workers, and its sister union, the Federated Mining Union which organises mainly amongst black workers, were warned against operating in Bophuthatswana. SAAWU has members at two factories in Babelegi and three in Garankuwa and has also grown rapidly in the Rosslyn area (outside Bophuthatswana) over the last year; the Bophuthatswana authorities are obviously anxious to prevent further expansion within its boundaries. CCAWUSA, which has organised at an outlet of Metro Cash and Carry and at other stores in Bophuthatswana, received a letter in 1983 from Metro Cash and Carry's management stating that the Bophuthatswana government had told it not to deal with the union because it was 'South African'.

It seems that one of Bophuthatswana's concerns is to avoid industry-based strikes, such as those which occurred at AECI in 1984, where a strike at one plant is supported by workers at other plants of the same company. Many South African companies have plants in Bophuthatswana, for example AECI, BMW, SA Breweries, Metro Cash and Carry and a number of other supermarket chains. By preventing unions which have organised a plant in 'white' South Africa from organising a sister plant in Bophuthatswana, the authorities hope to avoid labour unrest from spilling over into their territory. On the other hand, however, the creation of a situation where plants in different areas are organised by different unions, or where the South African-based plant is organised and the one in Bophuthatswana is not, can also lead to unrest particularly where the workers in 'white' South Africa receive better wages than their colleagues in Bophuthatswana.

Implications for South African-based unions
The choice now facing these unions is that they will either have to move

their head offices to Bophuthatswana or withdraw from the territory. Some of the craft unions argue that this should not be necessary as their members are employed by South African-based companies, are only temporarily in Bophuthatswana and that negotiations on their conditions of work are conducted in South Africa with the agreement being extended to cover them in Bophuthatswana.

So far a concession has been granted to the Mine Workers Union allowing it a presence in the area even though it fails to fulfil two important criteria for registration under the Act: firstly, it does not have its head office in Bophuthatswana; and secondly, its constitution discriminates on the basis of race.

However, confusion exists over what the MWU may, in fact, do in Bophuthatswana. The MWU claims that it will be able to negotiate in Johannesburg on wages and conditions of work for its members at JCI's Rustenburg Platinum Mine and Gencor's Impala Platinum. While confirming that miners in Bophuthatswana may remain members of the MWU, Bophuthatswana Minister of Manpower and Co-ordination Rowan Cronje has said that the union will not be able to represent these members, negotiate on their behalf, or enter into agreements. Agreements negotiated by the MWU in Johannesburg will have no legal standing in Bophuthatswana, he said. Only Bophuthatswana agreements published between registered employers' organisations and registered trade unions would have legal standing. He said that if miners involved in accidents wished to call on MWU officials for their expertise in an enquiry they could do so, but the union would not be able to represent workers in an 'official or semi-official capacity'.

Managements who have been dealing with these unions have also expressed concern over the new requirements, particularly the fact that they will have to respond to two different sets of labour law. Many feel that the Bophuthatswana/Rosslyn/Brits area should be viewed as a single economic region. One suggestion is to have a reciprocal registration procedure, where if a union is registered in the one territory this applies in the other.

The concern that the Act would prohibit unions organising amongst commuters from holding meetings within Bophuthatswana after work hours, has not materialised. The banning of such meetings would have seriously affected unions in the recruitment and organising of their commuters as there is a lack of alternative venues for meetings in the areas where commuters work. Workers are reluctant to stay after work in the border area for the holding of meetings, and they are not keen to commute to meetings there on weekends. The Minister had initially indicated that he would prohibit such meetings, but has since said that this decision falls outside his area of jurisdiction. In fact permission for meetings of more than 20 people must, in terms of the territory's Internal Security Act, be obtained from the local magistrate. Bophuthatswana has already, in terms of the Internal Security Act, taken action against unions holding meetings in the townships. For instance, in 1981 Bophuthatswana police broke up a union meeting held at Garankuwa for BMW workers from the Rosslyn plant and arrested three organisers of NAAWU. They were charged under the Act with attending an illegal gathering. Charges were dropped after the defence intimated that they would challenge the constitutionality of the Internal Security Act in terms of the Bophuthatswana Bill of Rights. Any legislation passed in Bophuthatswana either before or after independence which infringes the Bill of Rights is void. Nevertheless the continued possibility of harassment and arrest has placed an additional burden on unions operating in the border areas.

Controls on unions in Bophuthatswana
The Act contains other provisions designed to control activities of unions. For instance it grants very wide powers to the registrar concerning the registration of unions. Apart from other considerations, he must be satisfied that 'the applicant is a responsible body and reasonably capable of taking part in the negotiation of matters of mutual interest between employers and employees in accordance with the provisions of this Act'. There is no explanation of what a 'responsible body' is, leaving wide discretionary powers in the hand of the registrar to decide whether a union may be registered. The applicant does, however, have the right to appeal to the Industrial Court against a decision not to register it. The registrar may also cancel a union's registration on the same basis.

In addition the Act limits the number of trade unions which may be registered by stating that no more than one trade union may be registered to represent 'the same interests or any of the same interests in respect of the same area or any part of the same area'. The implication of this is that only one union will be able to represent workers in an industry or section of an industry in the same area. Already it has been reported that a Bophuthatswana-based mine workers union has been formed and, because of the Act could become the only union representing mine workers in the territory.

Apart from outlawing links between unions and political parties or organisations as contained in the South African legislation, the Bophuthatswana Act forbids a union from accepting assistance from any person, organisation or body which the Minister has specified by means of a notice in the gazette. Approval of such assistance may be sought but will not be granted if the Minister feels that the assistance is not in the public interest. 'Assistance' refers to services, donations, loans, and travel vouchers or tickets. This means that the Minister can prevent overseas organisations from paying for unionists to travel overseas.

One of the significant features of the Act is the cumbersome conciliation process which it introduces, making legal strikes practically impossible. Parties to a dispute have first either to go through an industrial board, industrial council or conciliation board. If the dispute is not settled the issue must be referred to the industrial tribunal, providing that the Minister feels that this would not lead to a change in any existing agreement. The tribunal's decision is binding. If the parties disagree with its determination they may inform the Minister of this and the determination will cease to be binding once a period of 42 days after its publication by the Minister has elapsed. Thereafter, if the workers in a secret ballot vote in favour, a legal strike may be called. However, the Act empowers the President of Bophuthatswana to intervene and declare the tribunal's determination binding in which case a strike is prohibited. Thus the President has the power to prevent any legal strike from occurring.

The Act also makes provision for an industrial court. However, this will have fewer powers than its South African counterpart, particularly because the Act does not make provision for an unfair labour practice. Its introduction in South Africa has provided workers with a means of gaining temporary relief from dismissal and other unfavourable changes in their employment conditions until a final order on the matter is made. By excluding this provision from the Act, Bophuthatswana is shutting off an avenue allowing for the quick resolution of disputes even if on a temporary basis.

Experience in the South African situation has shown that where conciliation procedures are too lengthy and cumbersome, workers will strike illegally rather than wait for the process to take its course. Thus it is likely that rather than creating a situation of industrial stability, the Act, because of this omission, could have just the opposite effect.

The organisation of labour within Bophuthatswana is being restructured. Unions which have built up some strength may be faced with having to withdraw, while other more moderate unions may comply with the new labour dispensation. This may mean slower progress regarding better wages and improved working conditions than otherwise would have been the case.

KwaZulu

As with the other bantustans, the development of industry in KwaZulu has been slow, taking place mostly outside of the bantustan in the industrial areas of Empangeni and Richards Bay in Northern Natal and to a greater extent in the Durban/Pinetown/Hammarsdale area, one of the larger industrial complexes within South Africa. In 1980 BENSO claimed that 116 420 people were employed in the manufacturing industry in KwaZulu. Isithebe was KwaZulu's main growth point with 62 factories.

Union activity within the area has been limited. MAWU has been active in organising at Vickers Lenning, FA Poole and at Henred Freuhauf's plant at Isithebe giving it representation in Henred Freuhauf's four plants. (The other three plants are situated in 'white' South Africa.) The concern of industrialists in keeping wages low is highlighted in this case as the company was only prepared to recognise MAWU in KwaZulu if parity in wages was not required for the KwaZulu plant. Until recently the minimum hourly wage at the Isithebe plant was 80c while that in Johannesburg was R1,80. MAWU has also organised workers in the construction industry and has an agreement — signed through the head office — with Grinaker Holdings. The National Union of Sugar Manufacturing and Refining Employees (NUSMRE), initially established to organise workers on the sugar mills, has begun to organise cane cutters as well as workers at the Apex Foundry. Apart from the metal and sugar industry, unions have also been active in the paper and textile industries.

KwaZulu's Industrial Conciliation Amendment Act of 1981

KwaZulu has provided for the operation of trade unions in terms of its Industrial Conciliation Amendment Act of 1981 which amends South Africa's Industrial Conciliation Act of 1956. As mentioned earlier, it is unclear whether this amendment is valid. However, it gives some indication of KwaZulu's attitude towards unions. It is similar to South Africa's present Act in that it provides for the establishment of an industrial court (at Ulundi) and the concept of an unfair labour practice. (In practice, however, this court has never sat). One of the main differences is that the KwaZulu Act places no prohibition on unions joining a political party, nor on unions granting financial or other assistance to a political party, nor influencing its members with the object of assisting any political party or any candidate for election to any office or other position in a political party or to any legislative body established by any law. It is likely that this was not prohibited to enable unions to support the Inkatha movement whose members fill all the seats in the KwaZulu Legislative Assembly. Indeed, in 1984, NUSMRE became the first union to affiliate to Inkatha. The Amendment Act also reintroduces the concept of provisional registration of unions which the South African authorities dropped after introducing it in 1979.

In terms of the South African Act, trade unions operating in South Africa are required to have their head offices there, bantustans being considered as outside of South Africa. Thus, for instance, no trade union organising in South Africa may have its head office in KwaZulu. However, there is no similar clause in the KwaZulu Amendment Act, and thus it seems that trade unions operating in KwaZulu are not required to situate their head offices there. This is significant as unions are not therefore required to view workers in KwaZulu as non-South African and thereby to give legitimacy to the bantustan policy.

At a meeting with the American Federation of Labour and Congress of Industrial Organisations (AFL–CIO) in June 1983, Chief Gatsha Buthelezi, chief minister of KwaZulu, further clarified the bantustan's approach to unions. He said that Inkatha had always adopted a stance of support for the worker movements of the country and that it has explicitly avoided and will continue to avoid any attempt to take over the role of trade unions. However, some formal interaction was needed between Inkatha and unions. Thus Inkatha wished to have trade union interests represented on its central committee. 'In this way the decision making independence of the trade union movement will be left unaffected but the movement itself would gain from the presence of trade unionists who could influence Inkatha's policy and decision making process at central committee level.' At the same time, he said, Inkatha hoped that trade unions 'in due course', would reciprocate and establish the possibilities for Inkatha's presence on their decision-making bodies. This link, Inkatha believed, would make it possible to plan effectively to bring into being strategies which would mount the right degree of pressure on employers and authorities to force industrialists to discharge their wider responsibilities.

Chief Buthelezi explained further that a 'substantial degree of collusion' was necessary between Inkatha and the trade union movement in order to provide the 'organisational and human infrastructure which would make anything the employer was persuaded to do effective at the local community and regional level'. He proposed that the Inkatha Institute should be used as a base from which negotiations could proceed to establish which course of action would best serve the joint interests of both the trade union movement and Inkatha. He pointed out that the proposal was made as a matter of urgency because Inkatha could no longer 'defer the question of what it can do for its workers which dominate its membership'.[12]

This stance raises certain questions for trade unions operating in KwaZulu, especially about their autonomy. Trade unions, in particular the emerging union movement, take varying stands on the question of joint action with other organisations and community groupings, and, even where they seek community support for activities such as boycotts against companies, they insist on remaining in control of the action.

In practice, the KwaZulu government's response to unions has been uneven, and its intervention in disputes has sometimes been problematic. In 1982 it attempted unsuccessfully to intervene in two strikes involving 700 workers at the KwaZulu Bata Shoe Company situated at Loskop within KwaZulu. These disputes highlight the problems faced by workers locked into bantustan areas. Workers residing in the Loskop area are obliged by the pass system to look for work in the nearby Mooi River-Estcourt area. Thus workers at Bata, the only company at Loskop, have few alternative employment opportunities, nor can they move freely to seek better wages elsewhere.

In 1982 workers received wages ranging from R14,00 to R28,00 per week, compared with the starting wages of a labourer of R46,55 per week prescribed in the agreement for the national industrial council for the entire footwear industry outside the bantustans. The union estimated that the company's wage bill was approximately 33% of that of equivalent competing establishments throughout the rest of the country.

The strikes centred around management's refusal to deal with the NUTW and the firing of union members. The union appealed to the KwaZulu government to intervene. However, the district chief's councillors, the chief himself and a KwaZulu labour officer all failed to engage the company in constructive negotiations. A press statement by the union claimed bitter frustration and disappointment with the labour official, Khanyile, whom they alleged had been to the factory secretly and had appointed his own committee amongst the strike breakers, thus bypassing the union. The latter lodged a complaint with the KwaZulu government.

Eventually Bata broke the strike by firing the strikers, paring the work-
force from 550 to 250, hiring non-union labour and shifting production
to factories at Greytown and Pinetown. Given the official restrictions on
the movement of workers and the lack of alternative jobs, it seems unlikely that the dismissed workers would have been able to find employment
elsewhere.[13] Again, in 1984 the NUTW called in the KwaZulu government when a renewed dispute broke out between it and the company at
the Loskop factory. Initially the authorities supported the workers, outlin-
ing their plight on the radio and in the press. However, after the company
had approached the Minister, the KwaZulu authorities again bypassed the
union and attempted to deal directly with the workers. In addition, during
all three disputes, union members and officials were intimidated, arrested and beaten up by the KwaZulu police, who supported management in
attempting to break the strikes.

It seems likely that one of the levers used by the company to persuade
the KwaZulu authorities not to support the workers is the threat to withdraw their business from KwaZulu. Thus a combination of factors —
state repression, pressure by the company, ineffectual intervention by
KwaZulu — all compounded the problem facing the union in attempting
to resolve the dispute.

The future for trade unions in the bantustans

In what ways can we expect this picture of uneven union development to
change in the future? Firstly, it is clear that bantustans such as the Transkei and the Ciskei will strongly oppose trade unions as long as their
present regimes stay in power. As a result, it is to be expected that conditions of work in these territories will lag behind those in areas where
unionism is accepted. The same situation will probably continue in
bantustans whose trade union policy is less clearly defined, where union
presence is largely absent and, because of a relative lack of industrial development, will remain so in the near future. Better gains for workers can
be expected in both KwaZulu and Bophuthatswana where unions are
accepted. However, as indicated earlier, these territories are very
concerned not to discourage investment, and union struggles to win
improvements for their members could be hampered by the intervention
of the relevant bantustan authorities.

In addition the rate at which unions can progress will be determined
by the relatively weak position of workers in the bantustans, who through

the pass system are locked into the bantustans, and who, because of the very high rate of unemployment, have little hope of finding alternative work if fired. Thus while union gains in certain areas can be expected, these will be small in comparison with the achievements in the larger metropolitan areas.

Notes

1 BENSO, *Statistical Survey of Black Development, parts I and II* (1982).
2 Proclamation R84/1970 as amended by R124/1971, R102/1972 and R94/1972.
3 A lawyer, 'Homelands' Labour Law', *South African Labour Bulletin*, 8(8) and 9(9), September/October 1983.
4 Nicholas Haysom, *Ruling with the Whip*, DSG/SARS publication (Johannesburg 1983).
5 A lawyer, 'Homelands' Labour Law'; and Haysom, *Ruling with the Whip*.
6 Ibid.
7 *Survey of Race Relations in South Africa, 1980–83*, (South African Institute of Race Relations, Johannesburg).
8 Haysom, *Ruling with the Whip*, 14.
9 *Survey of Race Relations in South Africa, 1983*, (South African Institute of Race Relations, Johannesburg, forthcoming).
10 *Survey of Race Relations, 1983*.
11 BENSO, *Statistical Survey*, table 7; figures also supplied by the Bophuthatswana National Development Corporation.
12 Memorandum by Chief Gatsha Buthelezi to the AFL–CIO, June 1983.
13 See Memorandum on the 1982 Bata Strike, prepared by the National Union of Textile Workers.

Introduction

Peter Vale

Social scientists are constantly under pressure to provide an anxious world with a glimpse of its future. On the one level, those who consider themselves serious craftsmen realise that to look beyond the immediate horizon is both a hazardous undertaking and (probably) an intellectually dishonest one. Nonetheless, deep down most in the broad social science college probably hope that somewhere, somehow, they will discover an elixir which will enable them to bridge the interval between now and what's coming.

It has become clear that what we understand as International Relations — as an academic discipline — is falsely separated from other, more substantial, social sciences. This realisation has been slow in coming. Looking back over the long, long years of tortuous debate aimed at trying to prove whether or not International Relations belonged by itself, we might wonder what the fuss was about. Indeed, the debate on these issues probably set back our understanding of the real world; for we are no closer to understanding what constitutes the discipline than two decades ago when these issues were first discussed.

This realisation does not mean, however, that our efforts have been wasted. When not trying to find ourselves at the abstract level, some useful work has been done in International Relations; especially in the conception and development of analytical techniques. Such techniques have become valuable tools in our attempt to understand and explain the world, but unfortunately, they have not enabled us to see the future. One of our number, Hans Pieter Schwarz wrote with understatement uncharacteristic of International Relations, that 'the science of International Relations has not yet developed far enough that, as in modern technology, it can formulate its predictions with 80% accuracy'.

In South Africa, International Relations has suffered from not only the debate about its very being, but also from an isolation from the mainstream. It is a fact that the regular teaching and studying of International Relations, particularly at the universities, co-incided with the first threats of international boycotts against South Africa. Thus, International Relations in this country is not only a hybrid discipline but it also suffers unique problems. These two reasons alone do not account for the fact that International Relations should be considered the weakest of all the social sciences in South Africa, and this question is interesting, although not strictly relevant here. What is relevant, however, is that − when the status quo. The techniques, fostered by the able and willing talents − for that is what they are − of many who practise and preach International Rela-

It appears necessary to explore one further theoretical point which arises from the foregoing and, by turning this on its head, a challenge will be issued to other South African social scientists. Given the roots − some would say the reason for its birth, and the timing of its introduction in this country − the techniques and spirit of International Relations have easily been commandeered by those wishing to preserve the status quo. The techniques, fostered by the able and willing talents − (for that is what they are) − of many who practice and preach International Relations have been used to support pre-ordained establishment positions. In this fashion, a quasi-academic patina has been accorded government policies. In the process, International Relations and the work of many scholars in the field have been devalued. This is important for two reasons: first, it does reflect poorly on all the social sciences in South Africa; and secondly, it paralyses our capacity − as a body of scholars − to meet the challenges of the future.

The unhappy circumstances in which the academic study of International Relations finds itself in South Africa, is in part due to its neglect by others in the social sciences. It is comprehensible that fellow social scientists do not relish participation in the passion which has been conducted over whether or not International Relations had the right to exist as a separate discipline. What is not tolerable is that they have stood by and enabled International Relations to be used to give cogency to the policies of the Pretoria government and others wishing to preserve the status quo.

The work published in this section of the *Review* represents alternative paradigms to analyse International Relations in the southern African context. It is to be hoped that this work will spawn new schools of International Relations analysis in South Africa, thereby strengthening the study of International Relations, the social sciences in general, and our capacity as a community to meet the challenges of the future.

The Botha Doctrine: Pretoria's Response to the West and to Its Neighbours

Peter Vale

Conventional analyses of South Africa's position in the post-war era have held that Pretoria has increasingly found itself isolated from the international community, primarily as a result of its racial policy. To illustrate the thrust of this mode of analysis a headcount of South Africa's exclusion from a range of international fora has been used to validate the central theme.

It is easy to appreciate, at one level, that South Africa has become isolated from the international community; that — in a fairly consistent fashion — that community has sought to put a gap between itself and Pretoria, and that the racial question has been the cardinal source of tension between Pretoria and the world at large.

This contribution, however, puts a counter-thesis; it argues that the alleged 'isolation' of South Africa has only been superficial in nature. Contrary to conventional analysis, it demonstrates that South Africa was sheltered from the anger of the international community by two sets of circumstances up until the 1975 coup in Portugal. From that moment, Pretoria has sought to re-create for itself a range of regional options which could, once again, provide the opportunities for the major Western powers to shield it. It concludes that these circumstances have been re-established by the government of P.W. Botha and that they have, in addition, provided a modicum of international legitimacy for the proposed course of domestic reconstruction by Pretoria.

The interaction between those discrete sets of circumstances provides a useful key to an understanding of the emergence — for the first time since the Boer War — of an integrated military-cum-political strategy in southern Africa; this strategy is called the Botha Doctrine and is Pretoria's response to its neighbours and the West.

The post-war period

The first set of circumstances which shielded South Africa was the role which Pretoria played in the military, economic and political designs of the Western allies in the post-war period.

•It is common cause that Africa was a neglected region in the efforts of the Western allies to restructure the world at the cessation of hostilities in 1945. Where there was concern on African questions, it coalesced around two issues, decolonisation and self-determination. Furthermore, when these issues were raised in Western capitals — especially at the onset of the Cold War — policymakers feared for the survival both of their interests on the continent and what was whimsically referred to as 'Western values'.

Given this uncertainty, it is not surprising that South Africa was seen as a valuable partner in promoting and fostering Western interests on the continent. Moreover, South Africa's importance to the West had been firmly entrenched by three factors: first, the country's pro-Western credentials had been established by her participation on the victorious Allied side in the hostilities of 1939–45. (She had also, of course, firmly endorsed the various post-war peace arrangements.) Secondly, the maritime strategic importance of South Africa had been, to a limited extent, reiterated in the wartime hostilities. Thirdly, the white minority appeared to be in effective political control in southern Africa and were seen as upholding Western values in, what was then, an accepted form of democratic government.

What is immediately apparent in reviewing this shortlist is the fashion in which, at various times during the post-war period when South Africa has been debated, one of a combination of these three issues has provided the starting point for those, in Western circles, who have sought to stress the importance of South Africa.

For its part, the Union sought to capitalise on certain aspects of its — relatively-speaking — positive international position in the immediate post-war period. She was, after all, an accepted member of the British Commonwealth and a founding member of the United Nations Organisation. Perhaps more importantly, the towering international standing of General Jan Smuts provided South Africa with an international audience which, arguably, was not commensurate with her wealth, size or strategic location. When the attacks on the Union's racial policy started in the United Nations, the South African government sought to hide behind her close links with the British crown. Successive British governments for their part were fearful of antagonising South Africa and went to great lengths to shield her when and where she was attacked in the world community.[1]

It was this 'British connection' which provided the Western allies with their *entrée* into the southern African region and which, simultaneously, ensured them access to a fairly sophisticated economy in a country which was anti-communist. This London link was crucial, for the British were tied to South Africa through both the sterling monetary area and the 1926 Ottawa Empire Trade Agreements. Moreover, certain facets of post-war British recovery were based particularly on the South African economy.

While the main proportion of South African trade was done with Britain, certain hiccoughs in the closeness of the tie appeared intermittently. One such case was the 1948 flourishing of trade between South Africa and the United States which was only of a temporary duration. Writing on this topic a British scholar has noted:

> In 1948 the Union had gone on a massive dollar spending spree, with the result that the United States had temporarily supplanted Britain as South Africa's major supplier, providing 33,5 percent of all imports into the Union . . . (but) . . . it was under pressure from Britain as a result of its own 'dollar gap' that South Africa was obliged to introduce a measure of anti-dollar discrimination during the course of 1949 (which produced) a dramatic reversal in the fortunes of British and American exporters to the South African market.[2]

This economic interest was closely interwoven with a military/security dimension which found, perhaps, its most significant expression in the Simonstown Agreement. In analysing this dimension it becomes increasingly clear that South African military strategists were always more convinced of their importance to Western security interests than the reverse position. It is, however, true that in certain Western defence circles — for example, the Royal Navy — aspects of South Africa's strategic saliency to the West were held in high regard.

Cordon Sanitaire

During the course of the post-war period, as British power and influence declined in southern Africa, so it was filled with American interest in the region. This was particularly so from 1976 onwards.

The second set of circumstances which shielded South Africa from the growing antagonism of the international community during the post-war period was the cushioning effect of the presence of colonial governments in southern Africa until 1975. These were, of course, the Portuguese in Angola and Mozambique, and the minority-ruled government in Rhodesia. Seen from the outside, this *cordon sanitaire* enhanced the stability of the white-minority regimes and, by extrapolation magnified the stability of South Africa itself.

There seems to be no under-estimating this point, for the major Western countries were prone to judge the issue of South Africa's security in a regional context. The clearest enunciation of the West's commitment to this regional package was the 1969 National Security Council Report (NSSM 39) which urged the United States government to 'tilt' towards the white-minority regimes because of the indefinite picture of stability they presented.[3]

The existence of the *cordon sanitaire* was not without an important economic aspect. During the period of rapid development of secondary industry in South Africa in the 1960s and early 1970s, a residual market for South African manufactured products lay in the adjacent states — both black and white-ruled — immediately around her. This economic aspect went, it has been argued, one step further. To offset costs incurred in importing advanced technology from the West, South Africa sought to export manufactured goods and the markets for these goods were also to be found in the neighbouring states.

Through this process, security considerations enhanced South Africa's industrial sector. The process had, of course, an important spin-off for South Africa's relations with the West. Armed with this formidable economic muscle and eager to seek markets in the hinterland, Pretoria systematically signalled her willingness to be a force for peace and stability in the region and offered to use her economic lever to provide this. By using a liberal trade argument, Pretoria has sought to convince the world that Africa, rather than she, harboured evil intent in southern Africa.

The rise of the Botha Doctrine

An understanding of the current position in southern Africa and Pretoria's role therein arises directly from reiterating that the two sets of circumstances described in the foregoing analysis provided South Africa both with a shield from Africa, and, almost more importantly, freedom of manoeuvre in the region.

The collapse of Portuguese suzerainty in its African colonies and the consequential increase in racial turbulence in the region had the effect of narrowing, rather than increasing, Pretoria's options. This was especially so between the Angolan war of 1975 and the advent of the Reagan administration in 1981. In 1983, in a fairly systematic fashion, Pretoria sought to re-establish her sphere of influence in the region under the blessing of and, indeed, with the encouragement of, the West, particularly the United States.

In charting its role in southern Africa since the withdrawal of the Portuguese presence, Pretoria initially faced a Western alliance which was less prone to view the world in an East/West divide. This circumstance changed in the late 1970s with the emergence of Western governments who were increasingly prone to use an East/West paradigm in viewing the world. This position clearly raised again the inclination in influential circles to stress some of the important aspects of South Africa's value to the West in an Africa which was seen to be crumbling. It differed, however, from country to country; for example, the Reagan administration, far more emphatically than Thatcher's Conservatives, saw southern Africa within this East/West divide.

Paradoxically, however, the increased saliency given to this East/West view on global affairs focussed attention on areas of the globe which appeared more volatile than southern Africa; the Middle East and Latin America are good examples of this phenomenon.

Thus, the Western nations, both by conviction and perception of regional self-interest, 'tilted' in the early 1980s once again toward a white minority in southern Africa. Often, for practical reasons this was necessary: for example, within the confines of Reagan's policy of constructive engagement, the willing participation of South Africa was a necessary condition for finding a settlement for the Namibian crisis.

This international climate clearly favoured the South African government, for it increased Pretoria's relative importance in Western capitals in a fashion not thought possible a decade earlier. The Botha government used this situation to re-assert its regional dominance and re-implement the *cordon sanitaire*, pushing back the threat which it perceived particularly from ANC activists.

●Whereas the early goals of Pretoria's haphazard destabilisation policies in the region were not clear in 1981 and 1982, in 1983 a full appreciation of their direction crystallised. By systematically attacking ANC activists in the neighbouring states, Pretoria emphasised again and again the high economic price which these African states would pay for their principles, i.e. active support for the ANC. In essence, the policy had two prongs: a tough and uncompromising military power, which could be accompanied by an equally effective economic muscle. The two dimensions, military and economic, would be used interchangeably as carrots and sticks.

It is also apparent that the brunt of Pretoria's concern was with ANC activists rather than with ANC refugees who might not themselves be politically active.

●The series of raids into Lesotho and Mozambique were clearly aimed at activists rather than ANC sympathisers. The Mozambican case is, in this respect, particularly instructive for it was clear that Pretoria feared the South African Communist Party presence much more than the ANC itself.

Early in 1983, the South African government made it clear that under no circumstances could neighbouring states be used as springboards against the Republic. At the same time, the Minister of Defence gave tacit recognition of South African support for 'anti-communist forces' such as Resistencia Nasional Mocambicana (MRN) and UNITA in Angola. This was the first time that South Africa acknowledged that some clandestine support was being given to these maverick liberation movements. Ironically, it is these movements which currently provide a potential stumbling block to the successful implementation of the Botha Doctrine.

A consideration of South Africa's relationship with Mozambique provides the most effective appreciation of the underlying currents which spawned the Botha Doctrine. In April, a senior MRN official was assassinated by two unknown gunmen at a farm near Pretoria (some reports have confidentially cited that the killing took place on a property owned by the South African Defence Force).

Then in May, a major bomb-blast in central Pretoria claimed the lives of a number of South Africans of all races. The South African government alleged that the act was the work of the ANC and claimed that the attack marked a change in ANC strategy from 'hard' (military installations and strategic centres) to 'soft' (civilian population) targets. The

ANC in a counter-claim stated that the incident did not mark a change in their strategy; this led observers to conclude that the bomb, planted outside the South African Air Force Headquarters in downtown Pretoria, probably went off accidently. Whatever the truth of allegation and counter-allegation, the South African Air Force responded three days later by attacking buildings in the residential suburb of Liberdade in Maputo.

This pattern of strike and counter-strike between the ANC and Pretoria threatened to embroil the region in a gathering conflict. However it came at a time when the Mozambican government was faced with severe economic and political constraints as a result of prolonged drought and the war with the MRN; on this weakness the West and Pretoria were to build.

The Liberdade raid represents a highpoint in regional conflict for, after this event, South Africa and Mozambique began a process of low-key discussions which were to culminate in a *rapprochement* between Pretoria and Maputo early in 1984.

The signs of this were evident earlier. It had become apparent during the year that the pressing economic problem in Mozambique was compelling the Frelimo government to weaken commitment to the Soviet Union and build infrastructural links to major Western countries. In February 1983, United States Assistant Secretary of State for African Affairs, Chester Crocker, *en route* from Zimbabwe to Madagascar, stopped in Maputo and held a three-hour meeting with the Mozambican leader. It is clear that this meeting provided the United States with an opportunity to stress upon the Mozambican leader the necessity for him to conduct a *rapprochement* with Pretoria. In return, it seems that the West would undertake to give Mozambique support and the extent of this support was to come later in the year when the Mozambican leader made a symbolically important visit to Britain.

Quite clearly, therefore, the Western allies had impressed upon the Mozambicans the necessity for conducting an on-going and permanent dialogue with both the West and with Pretoria. For their part, the South Africans would want the removal of ANC activists from Maputo. Faced with this economic and political plight, President Machel had no choice but to comply.

For the Botha Doctrine to succeed, the South African government will require the continued patronage of the current US administration. This circumstance is likely to endure as long as the Reagan administration commits itself to the policy of constructive engagement.

It is clear that the freedom of any US administration to move on southern Africa is considerably circumscribed by the realities of American power and American response to the Soviet Union. However, the commitment of the Reagan administration to a distinctive course in southern Africa — of which the Botha Doctrine is a by-product — means that the United States has tilted towards South Africa as far as its political system will allow. In these circumstances, a retreat on the commitment of constructive engagement will signal a fairly significant setback for South Africa's regional schema and the Western patronage upon which it has relied.

A second precondition for the success of the Botha Doctrine is that South Africa is able to provide the necessary economic and social infrastructure to sustain a state like Mozambique. Quite understandably, a series of functional economic aids will have to be accorded to Mozambique in some specific crisis areas such as drought relief, health care and economic management. It is, however, important to recognise that the resources of the South African state are finite and, as Mozambique leans increasingly towards South Africa, Pretoria may not be able to maintain the level of economic succour necessary to sustain the Machel government.

Thirdly, a major problem may arise in the inability of South Africa to put a permanent brake on the Mozambique Resistance Movement. Two hurdles stand in the path of the effective application of a damper upon this maverick liberation movement. The MNR seems to have a life of its own and appears to have support for its activities elsewhere in the international community other than South Africa. There are strong suggestions, for example, that conservative European foundations have taken to supporting the Mozambique Resistance Movement. Further, inside the Republic it is clear that disaffected elements have tremendous sympathy for the work of the resistance movement and will not be prone to withdraw their support from it.

From Washington's perspective, the Botha Doctrine has secured southern Africa in a fashion which was not thought possible in the seventies and, on the Mozambican front, has quite clearly meant a significant setback for Soviet interests in southern Africa. This clearly pleases those in the current US administration who view the world in an East/West paradigm.

Less certain, is the success of the Botha Doctrine in South Africa's relationship with Angola and with Zimbabwe. Less permanent is the likelihood of the Doctrine's survival in the inability of the constitutional proposals of the South African government to deal with the domestic racial problems facing South Africa.

In tilting towards Pretoria, the West – through the United States – has taken a calculated gamble that South Africa can be the anchor of regional stability. However, in the past decade latent volatility in southern Africa has increased, and one single racial spark could again cause the West to waver from its present course.

Notes

1 See J.E. Spence, *The Strategic Significance of South Africa* (London, Royal United Services Institution, 1970), 10–11.
2 G. Berridge, 'Economic Leverage in Interstate Diplomacy: Britain and South Africa, 1951–1964' (Unpublished PhD Thesis, University of Durham, 1977), 84–85.
3 Some of the important features of the regional dispensation offered by the cordon sanitaire have been argued in Peter Vale, 'Pretoria and southern Africa: From Manipulation to Intervention' in *Same Foundations, New Facades?*, South African Review One (SARS and Ravan Press, Johannesburg, 1983).

'Constructive Engagement': The Confused Art of Regional Foreign Policy

Bryan Bench

The United States has attempted to understand the intricacies of the Southern African region, with its delicate interplay of co-operation and conflict, in order to fit the region into the Reagan Administration's basic foreign policy parameters and priorities. The difficulties which it has experienced stem from the existence of a declining regional subsystem developing into two emerging regional subsystems — the one centres on the Frontline States (FLS) and the Southern African Development Coordination Conference (SADCC), and the other on South Africa and its Constellation of Southern African States (CONSAS).[1]

Any attempt to apportion a single and static foreign policy to an essentially divergent and transforming region, will of necessity founder on the rocks of these regional subsystems' complexities. The policy of constructive engagement, although simplistic in its theoretical assumptions and basic mechanisms, has struggled through to keep abreast of the dynamic nature of the Southern African environment by continually altering its focus at the tactical level.

Designing a new approach

The conceptual underpinnings of the policy of constructive engagement were refined by Chester Crocker, then still Director of African Studies at the Center for Strategic and International Studies at Georgetown University, in several articles published just prior to the 1980 United States presidential elections.[2]

In assessing the theoretical parameters and interest articulations made by Crocker the academic, it becomes evident that a three-dimensional interest configuration was more clearly understood than the appropriate theoretical framework within which these interests could be accommodated. The weighted averages of each of these interests, in an overall determination of United States policy to South Africa and the region as a whole, seem to have been on a declining scale from the economic, through to the military, to the moral. This quite naturally implied a conceptualisation of the region as an integrated economic entity, which was dependent on continued regional peace and unimpeded growth. Yet the realities of the political status quo in the region — and increasingly this situation determined the region's economic prospects — placed regional priorities of the states involved at loggerheads with these United States interests. Working from an assumption that greater contact with and involvement in the region was preferable to selective contact with or a staged withdrawal from the region, a recipe for the appropriate measure of rewards and sanctions was evolved.

Crocker conceded that United States leverage on the region as a whole was limited. Yet it was preferable for the United States to expand its role in the region in order to better secure its political, economic and strategic interests. The time was thought fortuitous for a more active United States involvement in the region, as Soviet isolation in the region was evident. Also, the minority government in Pretoria was embarking on what was seen as a 'moderate reformist process', while the majority-ruled states in the region were setting certain of their formidable developmental priorities within co-ordinative structures in need of international assistance. The changed power configurations in the region resulted from a settlement of the Zimbabwean civil war and the assumption to power of Robert Mugabe's Zimbabwe African National Union. These needed to be digested by all the states and interest groups within the region, and those from outside with interests therein.

The region's most immediate and vexing problem remained the settlement of the Namibian dispute under the aegis of the United Nations Security Council Resolution 435 of 1978. The beleaguered position of the Contact Group lay at the mercy of South African intransigence and the Frontline States' impatience. A satisfactory resolution of the Namibian situation would continue to concentrate the energies of states in the region and other interested parties in the foreseeable future; but renewed diplomatic initiatives were needed to inject life into the stalled process. Crocker held that the most serious situation acting against a re-establishment and enhancement of United States interests in the region, was heightened conflict. It was only through appropriate measures aimed at securing peaceful change, that such interests could be further pursued.

The South African government had shown its determination to place a variety of stumbling blocks in the way of a successful conclusion to the Namibian problem. This was attributed to the obvious domestic political implications which a too hasty South African withdrawal from Namibia would wreak on the process of 'moderate reform' within the Republic. Indeed, many influential South African decision-makers were hoping that a sympathetic Republican administration in Washington would forestall Pretoria's desperate and illogical dabbling in a 'neutral [foreign policy] option'; thereby saving Pretoria's face domestically and internationally.

South Africa, then, as the occupying power in Namibia, would need to be weaned towards an acceptance of its inevitable withdrawal from, and granting internationally acceptable independence to, the territory. As the South African government saw its involvement in Namibia as the determining variable in the equation of gauging the pace of its domestic reform process, assistance in making its withdrawal from the territory as graceful and painless as possible was needed from outside. Also the Contact Group seemed to have exhausted all possibilities in providing the appropriate bargaining environment. This dictated the immediate focus of a United States policy of constructive engagement − that a 'tilt' towards South Africa was needed if any hope of settlement in Namibia was contemplated.

The majority-ruled states of the region were likewise constrained in their efforts to press ahead with their key concerns − economic development and state formation. Without a climate of peace in the region, concerted progress in these areas seemed unattainable. This too, arguably provided a complementary reason for a policy of constructive engagement, whereby the United States could become more involved in the Frontline States as an adjunct to its influencing movement towards a settlement of the Namibian issue.

It was perceived that the Carter Administration's 'pro-African' policy had alienated South Africa to such an extent that it was forced to dig its heels in, and even contemplate a 'neutral option'. Chastising a confused, but determined South African government, had resulted in Pretoria's non-compliance with, and unco-operative stance towards, outside attempts to settle regional disputes, let alone supporting its programme of domestic reform. The negotiations surrounding the Namibian debacle were at a virtual standstill by the closing months of the Carter Administration's term of office. There was, according to Crocker, no simple choice between black and white Africans, between pro-Western and Marxist governments, or between United States interests and principles. Rather, in an article entitled: 'A US Policy for the 80s' published in 1980, he believed that 'American interests and principles cut across the shifting ideological and color lines of Southern Africa, just as they cut across the divisions within South Africa itself' (p. 3).

Crocker thought that the centrepiece of United States policy in the region was inevitably its stance toward South Africa; and as Pretoria was politically 'the focal point of intense pressure for basic change' (p. 11), it was vital for United States regional policy to 'be consistent with and based upon an understanding of where we are headed in our relationship with Pretoria' (p. 11). South Africa's regional military, economic and technological power was recognised along with the West's most important economic and strategic interests — besides its 'political and moral interests in non-violent change' (p. 11).

Crocker elaborated the need for constructive engagement on the part of the United States, if 'sustained and orderly change' was favoured for the region as a whole, and South Africa in particular. Constructive engagement had a unique feature, in that it insisted 'on serious thinking about the sequencing and inter-relatedness of change. Priority ought to be given to those arenas of change that logically lead to and make possible future steps.'[3] The United States, in his view, needed to encourage 'evolutionary change', adding that if the United States was 'to be serious in Southern Africa (probably the biggest if in the minds of those who live there), [it] must act in ways that permit the supporters of evolutionary change to gain and hold the initiative' (p. 12).

As the United States sought to pursue full and normal relations with a South Africa whose domestic order would permit this long term objective, Crocker suggested a United States policy that would 'steer a course between destabilizing the Republic . . . and aligning [itself] with the cause of White minority rule' (p. 12).

A policy of constructive engagement was therefore primarily warranted, according to Crocker, as South Africa's regional predominance at the military, economic and technological levels, made it both a regional power with which to be reckoned, and this both in a regional and international perspective. Also, by being 'part of the West', it could be expected that Western values and beliefs would be placed on any assessment of South Africa's behaviour. Indeed, he went on to posit, any guide to United

States relations with South Africa would need 'to include common sense and fundamental American principles' (p. 12). The naive assumption that white South African conceptualisations of 'Western values' concurred with those of the United States or its allies was to become evident over time, however.

'Giving up' on South Africa was not justified and 'would be an action of the highest moral cowardice' (p. 14), as a set of circumstances, including a white realisation that purposeful change was absolutely necessary and a black optimism that basic change was inevitable, existed in the country. Both sides were faced by a similar obstacle — organisational tactics for this change. Quite contrary to an expectation of domestic political disintegration, the South African economy showed a resilience as a 'firm check' on such a development and, in fact, had 'the capacity to generate resources for growth and social change' (p. 14), let alone the strength of the minority regime to control the pace of change domestically. Adding further fuel to the moral argument, Crocker saw an inherent United States interest in democratic change in South Africa, due to Washington's diverse African and international interests, in which such change would have to be moulded according to values for which the United States stood abroad.

It was United States strategic and economic interests, however, both within South Africa, and more generally within the region, which received his greatest attention. Not in so far as these interests, which he labelled 'very important tangible interests' (p. 14), dictated a United States position to be taken vis-à-vis the white minority or black majority, and change in South Africa, but that they implied a 'strong pre-emptive interest in forestalling a Soviet combat presence in Southern Africa' (p. 15) and 'the need to retain and expand US and Western access to a reliable supply of imported minerals at reasonable prices' (p. 16). This latter point too, was notwithstanding South Africa's 'potential to serve as a regional engine for development' (p. 17).

Concerning the region as a whole and its politically diverse nature, Crocker advised the United States to ape the then pragmatic approach of the states in the region in its foreign policy towards the region, and not pander to racially polarising pressures. The United States should endeavour 'to build on and strengthen linkages between [the region's states] on conditions they are prepared to accept' (p. 4). Not only was the region politically diverse, but its 'natural' economic interdependence further convinced Crocker to avoid promoting 'the "delinking" of the region's economies and infrastructures along racial lines' (p. 4), as the apparently distasteful economic hegemony of South Africa in the region was the 'basis for the survival and economic development of [the region's] highly vulnerable economies' (p. 4). In calling for a coherent policy towards each state in the region, he saw this to be conditional on a United States recognition 'that the region's substantial potential rests on such integration and on rational economic policies' (p. 4).

The regional economic focus was thus clear — that the United States should support the existing regional and subregional core-periphery relationships, and prevent by what means were available, the further fragmentation of markets and investment opportunities by the Frontline States seeking economic independence under the SADCC arrangement. This was billed as 'the triumph of ideological economics . . . the region's own folly' (p. 5). Crocker actually thought it highly unlikely, unless massive outside assistance was secured, that many of the Frontline States would be able to end their dependence on South Africa — only 'moderation' in this dependence might be possible. South Africa, it was held, was by its own technological advancement and economic dynamism, preponderant in the region — a region which was graced with the absence of 'obstacles' to development.

Crocker was looking at United States regional economic interest, in terms of South Africa's stage of economic development and this economy's ability to assure 'peaceful change' within South Africa itself and the region generally. It seemed clear to him that maintaining and/or expanding United States economic interests in the region dictated an active United States presence within a peaceful regional environment. These interests were quite clear. United States investors would be keen to continue participating in the lucrative South African market, as would an administration intent on reducing the trade deficit between the United States and South Africa.

South Africa, as the leading non-oil mineral-producing exporter on the continent, held special significance to the United States' strategic minerals interests in Africa; and Crocker thought it unrealistic to view other African, especially Southern African, suppliers of strategic minerals as alternatives to South Africa. This was so because of the obvious dominance of South Africa as a minerals supplier in the region, and the substantial reliance of many neighbouring states to South Africa on the Republic's infrastructure for their mineral exports. In the short to medium term, however, the West would still be reliant on these African minerals exports to satisfy its demands. This dictated both a broad regional and South African involvement for the United States.

The military and strategic interests of the United States became much more evident in the region as the alternative scenarios of general war and increased regional conflict were contemplated — and these related directly to United States strategic minerals and economic interests in the region. Generalised, or even limited conflict elsewhere, involving not only the Soviet Union, would emphasise these interests to a greater extent. Crocker did not view this first scenario in terms of the strategic significance of the Cape route, however, but in terms of a possible client regime of the Soviet Union coming to power in South Africa; being dependent on Soviet aid for its survival, and thus being able to control mineral exports from, and United States economic interests in, South Africa. The second scenario would involve heightened domestic and regional conflict, in which a Soviet presence would be the determining factor in securing revolutionary change. Both these scenarios implied a 'strong pre-emptive interest' on the part of the United States in the region, concomitantly reinforcing the 'political reasons for the West to oppose the militarisation of political change in South Africa' (p. 15).

It was from the comfort of academic hypothesising, clarity and rigour that Crocker would have to edge his way down uneasily into the uncertainties and complexities of policy formulation. This certainly proved to be a whole new ball game!

Making difficult choices

On his appointment as Assistant Secretary of State for African Affairs, and after a determined attempt by certain ultra-conservative interests to block his acceptance by the Senate, Crocker sought to adjust the broad sweep of his philosophies into potentially workable policies. Two principal difficulties faced the Secretary, and proved stubbornly unmalleable when it came to real choices to be made. The first concerned a choice to be made between policy priorities in Africa and those in South Africa. Here, perceptions were to prove more enduring than actual policy objectives, as were those concerning a concomitant difficulty — ameliorating the conflict between diametrically opposed actors in the region. The second concerned the handling of domestic United States pressure groups with interests in the region. Here the choice was not as simple as the first, with numerous constituencies vying for influence, and many of these were important allies of the administration in other issue-areas.

The Administration attempted to cloud over the complexities and delayed in making choices. The best of all possibilities and opportunities were virulently sought, whereby the administration could straddle the divide. The resulting confusion in policy rubbed off more on the majority-ruled states than on South Africa, and this confusion fostered what the Administration believed were misguided perceptions of the policy direction in the majority-ruled states. This scepticism was further encouraged by a lengthy policy review for the region.

Perceptions of policy priorities acted against the Administration's real policy objectives. This was the result of cumulative indications that the 'tilt' towards South Africa was preferred, and this in turn was the result of the Administration placing Cold War lenses on its African policy. Although it was recognised that successful implementation of constructive engagement hinged upon its being directed to the whole Southern African region, there was evidence of an enduring Administration 'honeymoon' with Pretoria.

Constructive engagement was believed to be a policy directed principally to the Administration's relations with South Africa. Thus, despite continual pronouncement by State Department officials and Crocker himself, that it embraced the region as a whole, the perception gained ground in most quarters. This was largely due to policy initiatives under constructive engagement focussing on the Namibian situation and contacts with South Africa in this regard; with the policies towards the majority-ruled states being the poorer cousin. Crocker believed that South Africa had accepted the inevitability of its withdrawal from Namibia. Also there were untimely leaks of policy and other documents, along with embarrassing visits by South African military officials to the United States, a tour by the rugby Springboks, and moves to repeal the Clarke Amendment, promote nuclear collaboration and review United States/South African trade restrictions. The adverse publicity received by way of this perception in both the United States and Africa, encouraged a vigorous diplomatic campaign on the part of the State Department, to clarify the central thrusts of the regional policy and attempt to dispel the adverse perceptions gained in the absence of any previous clarity. Vice President Bush was an integral part of this initiative on his well-publicised African trip. Also, Ambassador Jeane Kirkpatrick's confusing distinction between right- and left-wing dictatorships, and the predictable support of the United States for the former, enhanced a perception of a 'tilt' toward Pretoria.

The Administration's Namibian initiative was thus couched in terms primarily with reference to South Africa's acceptance of UN supervised elections and transition to independence under Resolution 435. The 'linkage' of the Angolan and Namibian conflicts was the incentive offered not only to South Africa, but to appease key elements in the Administration who were at that time still sceptical of the Crocker initiative. However, the perception developing was one supportive of the United States bending over backwards for South Africa. The inducement aspect of the 'linkage' as opposed to rhetorical or other coercion, only reinforced this belief. 'Linkage' was also indicative of the Cold War lenses through which the Administration was accused of viewing the Southern African region.

The incentive offered to Angola was eventual diplomatic recognition, but at the price of the MPLA's questionable continued control of the state. Crocker remained confident that the 'linkage' would, in the end, endure the expected criticism and instill renewed credibility and vigour into the policy of constructive engagement. This was justified partly by a belief that the MPLA was intent on reducing the number of Cubans in Angola, and partly by the belief that the 'linkage' issue would provide the South African government the necessary negotiating manoeuvreability to move ahead in earnest in the phased independence process for Namibia. Indeed Vice President Bush's Africa trip seemed to confirm this confidence, as his most uncompromising stance on 'linkage' bears testimony. It appeared to most observers that, although the Cuban troop withdrawal was to be separately negotiated to the implementation of Resolution 435, indeed it offered South Africa a further opportunity to delay progress on such implementation. This was given currency by negotiations stalling on Phase Two.

Policy reappraisals

It seems ironic that the lack of progress in settling the Namibian dispute and the understandable need to deliver some regional policy success for the Administration to carry through to the 1984 Presidential elections, convinced the State Department that a renewed effort was necessary in selling constructive engagement regionally and internationally. Not only had the earlier emphases of constructive engagement given South Africa further cause to delay on Namibia, but it had built up South African confidence to the detriment of the Administration's overall regional policy. South Africa was becoming increasingly bold in its attempts to reassert and extend its economic and military dominance in the region by destabi-

lising its neighbours. State Department diplomatic initiatives in clarify-
ing the policy had failed to overcome the negative perceptions, and an
uncompromising South Africa lurching ahead in its regional assertive-
ness, only entrenched these perceptions. This unfortunate, but hardly un-
expected turn of events brought about by constructive engagement, made
earlier perceptions change to recriminations, with the Frontline States
accusing the Administration of inept policy. There was also growing
domestic United States criticism of the policy and impending legislative
action to right this situation. South Africa was not delivering the goods,
and the policy seemed to be characterised by 'all give and no take'.

A hurried reappraisal of the policy of constructive engagement was
initiated, resulting in an important policy speech by Under Secretary
of State for Political Affairs, Lawrence S. Eagleburger, in mid-1983.[4]
Although the Administration's preoccupation with Namibia had reduced
its energies on securing its interests elsewhere in the region during the
early stages of its existence, there had been a gradual realignment with
earlier administrations' policies in the region, especially with regard to
coming to grips with changed circumstances in the region.

Cognisance had to be taken of the politically motivated regional economic co-operation being encouraged under the SADCC arrangement,
and the United States Agency for International Development could press
ahead more robustly in supporting the SADCC's sectoral project
programmes — especially transport, food, security and agricultural development. The political side of both multilateral and bilateral relations
of the United States with the Frontline States, proved thornier than ever,
with much indecision on all sides concerning the depth of commitment.

The only bilateral relationship of any consequence during the early
days of the Reagan Administration, was to move closer to Zimbabwe in
an effort to 'make the place work'. The Administration misjudged the capacities of the Mugabe government to achieve national reconciliation and
press ahead with its development objectives and programmes. Far from
these constraining the regional political confidence of Zimbabwe in as-
serting an active role in the Frontline States (let alone the SADCC), the
Mugabe government moved confidently in its striving for regional
leadership among the Frontline States. Zimbabwe-South African relations were continually deteriorating, as were relations between other
Frontline States and the Republic. This jeopardised the United States
regional interest in securing restraint and peace, and placed its policy vis-
à-vis Namibia and South Africa on the shakiest ground with the majority-
ruled states. Credibility needed to be re-established.

Eagleburger, in reaffirming the Administration's commitment to the policy of constructive engagement, placed more emphasis on the broader Southern African dimension of the policy — especially in extending options to all majority-ruled states in the region 'to diversify their external orientation and to pursue closer economic ties with the West', not only to those which warranted support from the United States. At both the bilateral and multilateral level, a change occurred in broad strategy which had earlier put United States relations with the Frontline States more at the bilateral than at the multilateral level (in line with its relations with most of the developing world). Eagleburger pressed for a greater United States involvement in, and concern for, the Frontline States. This was seen in his calling for a 'substantial commitment to the success and health of newly independent Zimbabwe' in order that it would 'not fail as a new nation' and support for the SADCC — 'while also quietly urging South Africa and its neighbours to maintain pragmatic trade and customs agreements based on mutual benefit'.

He endeavoured to encase the growing regional conflict, caused by South Africa's destabilisation tactics, more in terms of this acting against the interests of the West, and supporting those of outside 'advocates of violence'. This was followed by a statement of the necessity for regional co-operation and co-existence as 'the only path to peace and stability'. Even more specifically, he posited that 'unless there is peace and stability in Southern Africa, it will prove impossible to encourage essential change in South Africa — and by change I mean a basic shift away from apartheid'. The ire of Pretoria was awakened.

In the most forceful terms used by the Administration since its enunciation of a 'tilt', Eagleburger struck out at the domestic political system and policies of South Africa as being 'morally wrong', and that constructive engagement with South Africa involved 'both tangible and political support' to all those who were working towards 'constructive change'. The role of United States corporations, affiliates and subsidiaries operating in South Africa, received the special attention of Eagleburger, especially in so far as they were 'a force for change' and had 'considerably more experience than the US government'.

This belief in the inherent strength of the private sector (of which United States corporate interests were a part) as a positive force for domestic change in South Africa, was directly connected to domestic United States deregulatory moves and linked to earlier emphases in this regard given by Deputy Assistant Secretary of State for African Affairs, Princeton Lyman, and Chester Crocker.[5] Indeed, the concentration of attention on the part of the newly-appointed US Ambassador to Pretoria, Herman W. Nickel, pointed to his promotion of the 'magic of the marketplace' and the positive role of the private sector in promoting overall economic growth and particularly educational and labour reforms.

The bottom line of the Administration's policy towards South Africa was 'the concept of government based on the consent of the governed'. Despite virulent protests from Pretoria, the Administration's action at Pretoria's astonishment was muted.

The prime focus of constructive engagement remained settling the Namibian dispute and facilitating the 'principle of reciprocity' that Cuban troops would be withdrawn from Angola, along with a pull-back of South African forces from southern Angola. UNITA did not receive a mention, but achieving regional security became the central determinant of the Administration's bilateral and multilateral actions on Namibia, Angola, the SADCC member-states and South Africa under the changing rubric of constructive engagement. However, the 'shuttle diplomacy' undertaken by Frank Wisner to prepare the delicate negotiating grounds for Angolan-South African confidence building leading up to the Lusaka Agreement, was illustrative of a more active regional initiative by the State Department.

Eagleburger broke down the issue of regional security into a concept containing four premises. The first concerned the reciprocal nature of sovereignty in the region (except for Namibia) which related to the second premise — 'the [reciprocal] principle that all states have a duty to refrain from tolerating or acquiescing in organised activities within their territory by guerrillas or dissidents planning acts of violence in the territory of another state'. The third premise accepted the role to be played by the United States (and other outside interests) in promoting contact and communication between the states of the region, with a view to encouraging a 'structure of security'. Finally, there was a recognition of the domestic political element of fostering co-existence in the region, which tied 'peaceful domestic change' to regional security and vice versa.

Although many reasons have been put forward attempting to explain this graduation of the policy of constructive engagement, it seems from the stress of the Eagleburger speech and subsequent diplomatic activity, that the regional security dimension has been brought in as the dependent variable of the policy. This is directly related to a growing impatience on the part of the Administration, with having to play 'second fiddle' to South African policy priorities, both domestically and regionally. The boldness of South African policy assertions were proving difficult to bear in the face of a snail's pace progress on Namibia, increased suffering by the Frontline States brought about by the drought and destabilisation, and the resulting chorus of domestic and international abuse being levelled at the Administration. A greater visibility of 'sticks' being used in this regional policy proved necessary — if only this might prepare the ground for cogent arguments to be put forward in the 1984 campaigns. This was forthcoming on the forced removals at Magopa, which even received presidential censure.

The Administration certainly found that its theoretical parameters were incapable of adequately absorbing the complexities of regional realities. Rather than the simplistic East-West dichotomy being a realistic and helpful framework within which to view the United States strategic, economic and moral interests in the region, a downplaying of this dimension was essential. The Administration had to accept the domestically motivated opportunities and strictures in the regional security complex. A Cold War rhetoric and policy focus would not be swallowed by the Frontline States, nor would it be enduring to the majority of South Africans, Africans and the international community. Political and military instability was largely the reflection of internal contradictions, and not the result of conspiratorial external designs.

With this realisation, delicate feelers were put out to improve relations with Mozambique, a vital member-state in the plans of the SADCC for economic liberation from South Africa. This diplomatic initiative led by the United States, again with its appropriate dose of 'shuttle diplomacy', prepared the ground for the signing of the Nkomati Accord between South Africa and Mozambique.

Although essentially a short term diplomatic rapprochement, directly related to the difficulties resulting from the severe drought in the region, South Africa's 'pragmatic engagement' (*New York Times* 12.03.84) is designed to give a measure of success to Reagan's regional policy for the 1984 campaign. One can only agree with President Carter's United Nations Ambassador, Don McHenry, that this Accord proved that 'it now suited Pretoria to make these concessions' (*Star*, 05.03.84). Indeed, South Africa is yielding nothing important until the outcome of the 1984 election is known. United States Congressional, State and city disinvestment campaigns continue, however, unabated.

Understandably, no soft options remain, but preferences need to be expressed in a generally progressive direction, with emphasis on the positive end of the scale of United States capacities and capabilities in the region. The resort back to generalities in policy directions and implementations, will admittedly buy time for the Administration in the light of impending elections, but will necessarily be strained to the limits, given the awesome matrix of interests and priorities of the states in the region. This seems the case with a tendency on the part of Crocker for 'balanced [diplomatic] packages'. 'Crisis management' might conceivably be the only guaranteed means of assuring a continuing credible role for the Administration in the region up until such time as a second term is assured for Reagan. Recent 'shuttle diplomacy' and short term, intermittent diplomatic initiatives suggest as much.

Notes

1 See D. Geldenhuys, 'The Constellation of Southern African States and the Southern African Development Co-ordination Council: towards a new regional stalemate?' [South African Institute of International Affairs] *Special Study*, January 1981. Both the CONSAS and the SADCC, and their roles in transforming the regional subsystem, are dealt with extensively in B.G. Bench, 'The Southern African Development Co-ordination Conference (SADCC): co-operation and co-ordination leading to a new regional integration?' (unpublished BA Hons dissertation, University of the Witwatersrand, 1982), 1–61.
2 Some of these dealt more with South Africa, rather than Southern Africa as a whole. See C.A. Crocker, CA 'South Africa: strategy for change', *Foreign Affairs*, 59 (2), Winter 1980/81, 323–351; and C.A. Crocker, 'A US Policy for the '80s', *Freedom at Issue*, November-December 1980, reprinted by the South African Institute of International Affairs, *Occasional Paper*, May 1981, among others.
3 Cited in J. de St Jorre, 'Constructive Engagement: an assessment', *Africa Report*, 28(5), September-October 1983, 48.
4 This was an address to the National Conference of Editorial Writers held in San Francisco on 23 June 1983. The text was reprinted by the United States Information Service, Johannesburg.
5 Princeton Lyman had addressed a joint session of the House of Representatives Subcommittee on Africa and the House Subcommittee on International Economic Policy and Trade on 2 December 1982. A mid-term statement on the Reagan Administration's Southern Africa policy was delivered by Crocker to the House Subcommittee on Africa on 15 February 1983.

Namibian Review

Tony Weaver

'Our country abounds with traitors to the cause of a united people. Resist them!' — footnote in the *Windhoek Observer*, 19.01.84 page 25.

An appropriate footnote with which to herald the new year in Namibia. Barely two weeks after that edition of Windhoek's most outspoken and persecuted newspaper appeared, South Africa succeeded in co-opting into its own structures the territory's most outspoken and hitherto radical internal political parties, in drawing the Reagan administration further into its own ad hoc regional foreign policy, and in once again buying time and delaying the inevitable — Namibian independence.

At the time of writing (February 1984) much was being made in the media of South African Prime Minister P.W. Botha's announcement of a 'disengagement' of South African troops with those of the Peoples' Republic of Angola. Little notice was being taken of his simultaneous announcement that the Multi-Party Conference (MPC) of six internal Namibian parties had agreed to 'accept the challenge' of 'urgently' working towards a 'political and constitutional dispensation' acceptable to the majority of Namibian people.[1]

But the MPC itself was fully aware of the importance of Botha's announcement, as was the office of the administrator general, Dr Willie van Niekerk. He hailed the joint announcement of the 'disengagement' and the MPC's 'acceptance of the challenge' as 'historic events', setting the tone for a press conference later that day (31 January 1984) held by the MPC.[2]

At that press conference, the MPC confirmed months of speculation by journalists and politicians as to their intended role in the Namibian equation. They confirmed they were drawing up a 'post-independence constitution', considering as one of their alternatives the formation of an 'interim government', and that the possibility existed of them fighting independence elections as a united front.[3] Such a united front meant one thing and one thing only − an anti-SWAPO front with overt or covert South African backing, the 'moderate, credible alternative' sought by South Africa throughout all its strivings for a palatable second option to the spectre of a Namibia ruled by the South West Africa Peoples' Organisation, SWAPO of Namibia.

Before tracing the background to the events of 31 January 1984 − which will form the closing section of this paper − it is necessary to look at the parties involved in the MPC. It is also necessary to examine closely the internal political and military developments in the territory and in Angola which led to Botha's 31 January pronouncements.

Articles on Namibia usually focus on developments in the international community − particularly the Western 5 Contact Group − when analysing developments in the territory. It is, however, the belief of the writer that events in 1983 in the internal political dynamic will set the pattern for developments in 1984. Time may prove this theory wrong, but indications at present are that 1984 will see a major shift in the emphasis attached to the various elements of the 'Namibian Question'.

The Multi-Party Conference

After the dissolution in January 1983 of the Ministers' Council by Prime Minister Botha − on the grounds that it was 'not representative of the people of South West Africa' − a hiatus developed in internal Namibian politics. Direct rule by South Africa through the administrator general (AG) in the person of, briefly, Danie Hough, and then Van Niekerk, ensued. In June, Van Niekerk announced that after consultations with leaders of internal parties,

> which lasted in total more than 100 hours, unanimity was reached among the different political parties that a forum must be created for decision-making about the political development of the territory. Such a forum could be called a State Council, and be set up by proclamation. This State Council will be composed of nominated persons from the different political parties which actively practise politics in the territory. The mandate of the State Council will be to work out a system of government for the territory.[4]

The State Council was stillborn. The only internal parties with any degree of support to agree to participation were the 11 ethnic parties of the Democratic Turnhalle Alliance, the rightwing white National Party, and the outspoken, predominantly Roman Catholic Namibia Christian

Democratic Party — which made no secret of the fact that it was only there for the money.

Meanwhile, leaders of two of the three main black nationalist parties in the territory, SWAPO-Democrats and the South West Africa National Union, were busy with their own machinations. They had originally planned to launch a national convention of Namibian parties, modified to an 'all party conference', and then as support dwindled, ultimately the MPC.

Having rejected participation in the State Council on the grounds that it was a South African sponsored initiative, and therefore untouchable, SWANU and SWAPO-D continued pre-State Council talks with other internal parties in an attempt to launch an 'original Namibian initiative' which would 'lead to a common political course of action that will hasten the process of Namibian independence'.[5]

The initial signatories to the MPC founding document represented an odd coalition of political parties. SWANU, Namibia's oldest nationalist movement, under the leadership of returned exile and Swedish citizen, Moses Katjiuongua, has a long reputation of being a Maoist party with rigid Marxist ideals. But under Katjiuongua, who in 1982 ousted Gerson Veii — a close friend of Libyan president Muammar Gadaffi — the party has become a moderate, social democratic oriented movement wracked by dissent and marked in recent months by virulent opposition to Katjiuongua's watered down brand of socialism by dissidents within Namibia as well as in Botswana, London and Germany.

SWAPO-D, led by SWAPO renegade, Andreas Shipanga, has stuck to the founding black nationalist principles of SWAPO. Dirk Mudge's DTA parties represent the conservative spectrum of Namibian politics. The Rehoboth Liberation Front under Hans Diergaard is an ultra-traditionalist separatist movement which seeks autonomy for the Rehoboth Basters as a separate state within a state. Most puzzling of the lot was the participation of the Damara Raad of Justus Garöeb, long regarded as a silent ally of SWAPO, an outspoken, articulate and highly regarded opponent of South African rule and of widespread 'Security Force' repression.

The MPC was launched on 12 November amid fiery radical rhetoric, and plenty of South Africa-bashing. Also participating on this day was Hans Röhr, leader of the Namibia Christian Democratic Party, a one-person crusader against torture and detention without trial. He lasted a week before withdrawing in disgust, labelling the MPC a farce and a body with no intention of hastening independence.

The MPC's credibility took a further dive when the rightwing white National Party announced it would join in the proceedings as a full participant. The final blow to the MPC's credibility came with Botha's 31 January announcement in parliament of an Angolan disengagement, and the level of importance he accorded to the MPC, firstly by including them in talks with US assistant secretary of state for Africa, Chester Crocker, the previous weekend, and then by singling them out as being the 'leaders' charged with seeking 'urgent solutions' to the internal impasse in his parliamentary speech. The full implications of the MPC's role will be discussed in the closing paragraphs of this paper, against the background of the social, military, economic and diplomatic developments in and around Namibia.

War on three fronts

While the MPC sat in Windhoek deliberating its course of action, South African Defence Force and South West Africa Territory Force units were mustering for one of the most disastrous of all raids into Angola. Operation Askari, launched in the first week of December, saw 21 SADF and SWATF troops killed and one captured and the South African forces coming into direct conflict with a strong force of Cuban and Angolan FAPLA troops. South Africa claimed the operation was aimed at 'preempting' the by now traditional rainy season strike by guerillas of the Peoples' Liberation Army of Namibia, PLAN, SWAPO's military wing, into Namibia's white farming area. SWAPO, backed by Angola, claimed that no PLAN guerillas were either involved in or killed during the six week operation. South Africa, in turn, claimed that 324 FAPLA, Cuban and SWAPO troops were killed, at least 100 of whom were PLAN guerillas. The balance of evidence at this stage seems to be in favour of the SWAPO claims.

Operation Askari was the culmination of a year of military operations which saw major shifts in the pattern of the Namibian war. The shambolic withdrawal of the South African troops due to the onset of the rainy season and repeated attacks by seasoned Angolan troops, the high cost of the operation in terms of South African dead, and the shock to the South African public of finding themselves at war with Angola had a dramatic effect on traditionally hawkish elements of the media and the public.

There is strong evidence to suggest that the operation was brought forward by at least six weeks at the insistence of Foreign Minister Pik Botha, because of the perceived necessity of maintaining a facade of open-door diplomatic bargaining on the Namibian issue — January was the key month not only for talks with the US and Angola, but also for the announced preparedness of the Angolan government to help negotiate a 31 January ceasefire in the 17-year-old Namibian bush war. On 13 December South Africa cynically 'offered' Angola a disengagement and ceasefire when SA and SWATF troops had already been inside Angola for at least a week on the then covert Operation Askari.

Military opposition to Botha's original proposal in the State Security Council that the operation be cancelled altogether led to the operation being brought forward by six to eight weeks, launching an ill-prepared, badly informed task force into a raid on SWAPO guerillas who had not yet advanced to forward positions in readiness for their traditional February incursion.[6] The impact of the resulting political and military debacle had a significant effect on subsequent developments with the MPC and the offer by Botha of a 'disengagement', coming as it did at the end of a year when it seemed that South Africa was achieving what was thought to be militarily impossible — containing a guerilla war.

Reaction to the raid was swift. International condemnation, even from staunch allies, was universal. Even more shattering for the SA government was the reaction from its own stalwarts. Wimpie de Klerk, editor of the pro-Nationalist Sunday newspaper, *Rapport,* openly questioned the wisdom of the raid and the desirability of South Africa continuing its occupation of Namibia.[7] The liberal press demanded explanations for the raid, and abandoned their usual cautious approach to defence matters by condemning strongly what they perceived as an ill-advised and politically disastrous action. Former head of military intelligence, General H. de V. du Toit in a public statement warned that the government risked losing 'popular' (i.e. white) support for the war because of its inept handling of information related to the operation.

Botha's announcement of a 'disengagement' was clearly an attempt to appease not only local but also international dismay at the sudden escalation of the Angolan conflict. The Namibian dispute had suddenly assumed the proportions of a major war with a foreign power, a war for which South African opinion was not prepared. But they should have been. Throughout 1983, Angola had maintained a constant stream of accusations that the SADF was trampling on its sovereignty in repeated military strikes which were clearly not aimed at neutralising SWAPO bases. In addition to a claim by Angola that South African fighter jets had napalmed the town of Cangamba on 15 August, the MPLA also claimed South African paratroopers had occupied the towns of Cuiteve and Mulundo, South African regular troops were permanently stationed at Evale, Xangongo and N'Giva, and troops were staging an 'incursion' around the town of Mavinga.[8]

The claims were dismissed by the SADF as being an attempt to play down 'apparent successful offensives by (Dr Jonas Savimbi's) UNITA', widely held to be a surrogate force of South Africa.[9]

An Angolan government white paper released in London on 5 October gave extensive details of alleged South African strikes into Angola between 1975 and 1982, including alleged documentary evidence collected in the aftermath of the alleged raids.[10] The white paper alleged repeated South African and joint South African and UNITA military actions in the provinces of Cuando-Cubango, Cunene, Namibe and Huila, an area covering 401 373 square km:

> Since March 27, 1976, the date when the first big South African invasion of Angola ended, Pretoria's armed forces have never ceased to keep those regions under constant pressure, through air space violations, bombing raids, incursions of heliborne troops, acts of provocation, infantry troops supported by armoured units, artillery shelling, mine laying in fields and on bridges and highways, and the looting and destruction of varied material and means of production. ... The continuous aggression against the Peoples' Republic of Angola by the racist Pretoria regime culminated on 23 August, 1981, with the launching of so-called Operation Protea, resulting in the present occupation by the South African army of the whole of the strip north of the Cunene River, with the apparent object of creating a buffer zone, so as to make the Namibian decolonization process even more complex.[11]

The SADF has continually denied that it is occupying any areas of Angola, although the 'disengagement' offer would seem to indicate that there is some measure of armed contact between SADF and FAPLA troops on a fairly regular basis.

Although the focus of the war for Namibia has shifted into the southern provinces of Angola, the war in two main Namibian war zones — the Ovambo and Kavango-speaking regions — has also taken on a chilling new character, which had, until 1983, received scant publicity.

1983 saw the first details beginning to emerge of the hitherto top secret police special counter-insurgency unit, Koevoet (Crowbar). Credited with over 80% of violent deaths in the war zones, Koevoet has featured prominently, along with the security police, in numerous court actions alleging assaults, torture, murder and rape. In an urgent court application brought before the Windhoek Supreme Court on 22 November, 15 former security police and Koevoet detainees alleged that at various stages between 1981 and 1983, they had been tortured by either Koevoet or the security police. Evidence given by some of the detainees in sworn affidavits pointed to the existence of a secret police camp near Osire, some 100 km north of Windhoek, where they alleged they were systematically tortured.[12]

Other details of alleged and proven assault and/or torture have been emerging as more and more cases get to court. On 14 June the Supreme Court found that a security police detainee, Johannes Kakuva, had died while held at Opuwa in Kaokoland in October 1980 after being severely beaten. His body has never been found. 'Unidentified members of Koevoet' caused the death of a Kavango detainee, Jona Hamukwaya, on 18 November 1982, the Rundu magistrate's Court found on 11 October. On the same day, another Koevoet detainee, also held at Rundu, Kadima Katanga, died after being forced to run for 10 km in front of a Koevoet Casspir armoured vehicle while being beaten with sticks and clubs by 12 Koevoet men, the same court heard.

The Supreme Court in Windhoek heard evidence in the murder trial of two Koevoet members, Jonas Paulus and Paulus Matheus, that Koevoet were trained as 'killing machines' with the sole purpose of 'exterminating SWAPO'. Paulus told of how when villagers would not give information to Koevoet, they were beaten with rifle butts and fists.

In an attempt to offset the damage of evidence which emerged in the Paulus/Matheus trial, and of repeated allegations of torture and assault of civilians by Koevoet, SA Minister of Police, Louis le Grange, organised a public relations tour of Koevoet bases by a group of parliamentary journalists in January this year.

> Koevoet is a cold, calculating, efficient and totally ruthless unit as far as the enemy is concerned. As far as the local population is concerned, I ask the question: why is it that Koevoet has had such success? It is because we have the complete co-operation of the local population who give us the information, hot information, which Koevoet apples immediately. .... The local population has respect for the man with the strongest fist. If we give Swapo a good thrashing, they will vote for us, and vice versa,

Lieutenant General Vic Verster, assistant police commissioner in charge of personnel and administration told the group of journalists.[13]

The same report in the *Cape Times* confirmed previous speculation that Koevoet was deliberately formed in 1978 after the adoption of UN Resolution 435, which stipulates that 'normal' SWA police activity will continue in the territory after SADF units are confined to their bases in terms of the ceasefire proposals.

An editorial in the same edition of the *Cape Times,* commenting on General Verster's remarks, stated:

> Court cases, affidavits and allegations about (Koevoet's) activities have brought it into disrepute. Striking terror into the local population, caught between Swapo insurgents and the security forces, is no way to win hearts and minds. Respected sources, including church observers, believe Koevoet is delivering local people in their thousands to Swapo. . . . Policemen, even a highly-trained special task force, must be seen as protectors not trained killers. When this is coupled with persistent allegations of atrocities, neither the police nor the local population is served. . . . The police force should hand their crowbar to their defence colleagues and return to more peaceful civilian protection.

There is little likelihood of this happening. Koevoet has virtually taken over the war in Ovambo and Kavango, with SADF conscripts carrying out more routine functions like patrolling base perimeters, mine-sweeping, convoy protection and routine bush patrols. Koevoet is the elite reaction force which heads out into the bush immediately any activity by SWAPO guerillas is detected. Nevertheless, although there has been a drop in the intensity of the war in Namibia — largely as a result of the UNITA/SADF cordon sanitaire across southern Angola — guerilla action continues, especially in western Kavango. At an assault hearing in Rundu on 20 October, Koevoet section leader, Sergeant Jumbo de Villiers described the area as being 'rotten with SWAPO' adding that 'we get absolutely no co-operation from the local people' — a strange contradiction of General Verster's assertion that 'we have the complete co-operation of the local people'. Defence Force statistics and newspaper files show that 918 SWAPO guerillas died in 1983, 146 civilians were killed and 101 wounded, 264 civilians were 'abducted' and according to files, between 70 and 80 South African and Namibian troops and policemen died in action.

The operations of Koevoet strike a contradictory note when taken in conjunction with the SADF's 'hearts and minds' campaign in Ovambo and Kavango. Although there are sporadic, minor accusations levelled at the SADF of abuses of the civilian population, the general impression is that their conduct in the *Namibian* war zones is good. This is not to say they are welcomed by the Namibian people as either protectors or a bunch of do-gooders. On the contrary, the wearing of a uniform linked to the armed forces in the northern areas of Namibia, where over half the population live, is a risky business. There is almost universal suspicion of the SADF's brown nutria and loathing of Koevoet's camouflage outfits. But the SADF has succeeded in one limited respect in winning the reluctant support of the people. Out of necessity, the SADF now provides virtually all health care in the war zones, and has taken over administration of Ovambo's largest hospital at Oshakati. Here, there are five civilian doctors, three of them housemen, and 12 military doctors. The superintendent of the hospital is a commandant in the Permanent Force.

But the result of the SADF's control of the medical services is not always the one they expect. Doctors tell of dead SWAPO guerillas brought into the mortuary having pills issued by the hospital within a week of their deaths (in their back pockets)! The war has resulted in a massive breakdown in basic health care and in preventative medicine programmes. Malaria is currently the rampant disease, with, at the time of writing, ten cases of cerebral malaria a week being treated at Oshakati alone. Non-cerebral malaria cases are simply dosed and sent home. Bubonic plague, which reached epidemic proportions in late 1983, has tailed off significantly with the advent of the rainy season. Typhoid is deemed to be approaching epidemic proportions again, and although no weight chart tests are done on children brought in for treatment, the majority are said by doctors to be severely malnourished, with kwashiorkor and beri-beri being the most prevalent malnutrition-related diseases.

The 17-year-old bush war has also seen a severe breakdown in other essential services, although these are relatively minor in comparison with that of the health services. Law and order is virtually non-existent in some parts of the war zones, with almost 500 cases of violent death a year being attributed to 'unknown persons' in inquest hearings. This is because of the difficulties involved in investigating murders and homocides in an area where uniformed officers of the police are hesitant to venture. Deaths of 'terrorists' or people said to be 'terrorists' by the military or Koevoet are not investigated save in exceptional cases (eg. when they occur south of the war zones in the 'white' farming areas).

South Africa's statements, through Messrs Pik and P.W. Botha, that they cannot indefinitely carry the costs of Namibia, are only partly related to the ongoing war. It is against the backdrop of the war and of the generally disastrous state of the Namibian economy that the latest moves towards securing an end to the 'Namibian questions' are taking place (moves which could well have overtaken the contents of this paper, such is the fluid nature of the Namibian dynamic at present, by the time it is published).

The general state of Namibia

Other than the disastrous social conditions reigning in the northern areas of the country, Namibia as a whole is at present in a precarious economic, social and political state.

The fishing industry, mainly based at Lüderitz, Swakopmund and Walvis Bay, is virtually at a standstill, largely because of overfishing by South African and foreign trawlers — mainly Soviet, Spanish and Japanese — and unemployment in this industry is reaching crisis proportions. Walvis Bay's only canning factory, Metal Box, has ceased operations, and fish-processing plants are presently processing frozen leftovers from the 1982 catch. The total catch has shrunk from 800 000 tons in 1974 to only 200 000 in 1983.

Building and its related industries are in the midst of a severe slump, with central government projects — the only source of large scale capital projects — frozen. Agriculture, the backbone of the Namibian economy, employing over 50% of the economically active population in either commercial or subsistence farming, has all but collapsed as seven years of the worst drought in living memory shows no sign of being broken, despite widespread rains.

Mining, another mainstay of the economy, is similarly in perilous times. Oamites copper mine near Windhoek will close in 12 months laying off 110 people because of surface subsidence, while 920 miners have been retrenched at the Matchless copper mine, 40 km west of Windhoek. The mine will close down because of the depressed state of copper and lead on world markets. As Namibia has an economically active population of only 196 000, these layoffs, in the space of two months, represent a 0,52% increase in unemployment. Similarly, Rössing Uranium, mining the world's largest open pit uranium mine at Arandis, 60 km from Swakopmund, will be drastically cutting back its staff of 3 000 this year, because of a combination of depressed uranium prices and a world glut, and rapid mechanisation of the mine.

The only industry which appears to be experiencing minor boom conditions — statistics of any sort are hard to come by in Namibia — is secondary industry, because of war-related projects. Here it is mainly the engineering houses which benefit, the workshops which carry out modifications and repairs for the war machine.

Namibia at present exports around 80% of what it produces, and imports the same percentage of consumed goods. Seventy-five percent of the annual budget goes towards sustaining the ten cumbersome and often corrupt ethnic governments.

The danger signals of complete economic and social collapse are clear. In Khomasdal, the predominantly coloured and baster township outside Windhoek, 45% of adults are judged to be fulltime or 'week-end' alcoholics. In Katatura township, housing blacks from the remaining eight black ethnic groups, the figure is judged to be a staggering 65%. Khomasdal's housing statistics are on a par with those of Mdantsane. The average occupancy is around 15 per two-bedroomed house. In 1982, only nine new houses were built in Khomasdal. Eighty-six percent of Khomasdal residents live below the Poverty Datum Line of R375 for a family of five, and with 45% of adult males employed in the building industry, which has all but ground to a standstill, over 50% of this 45% are either out of work, or have been forced to migrate annually to South Africa in search of work. [14]

A Windhoek Municipality study in 1981 described Khomasdal as a 'pathological community', meaning conditions within the community were so bad, it no longer had any means of healing itself, and massive state intervention would have to be applied. The situation in the north, where over 50% of the people live, has already been described — 250 000 refugees crowd into a 30 km strip between Ondangwa and Oshakati, living in filthy squatter camps with no sanitation, and only informal sector activities to help maintain a livelihood. In the Nama-speaking areas around Keetmanshoop, rural people have reportedly taken to eating cattle fodder in an attempt to survive.

The result is massive demoralisation of the people. Trade union activity has all but reverted to tiny, clandestine cell structures because of the fear of sacking. People are more concerned with staying alive than with political mobilisation, and hence the only real political activity at a grassroots level is through PLAN in the northern areas. Guerillas penetrating to the war zones have a two-fold function here — military and grassroots political education. It would seem that the estimated 800 'resident' guerillas in Ovambo and Kavango are presently engaged mainly in politicisation — probably more through necessity, as their ammunition supply lines dry up, than in former years.

The MPC and beyond

It is against this backdrop that the present state of the Namibian question must be viewed. The economy is in chaos, the war drags on with no end in sight except perhaps South Africa's desire to topple the Luanda government, unemployment is rampant and social conditions are disastrous. Even in Windhoek itself people are dying of starvation, and repression has increased to previously unheard of levels.

At the time of writing, the whole issue was in a state of constant flux. Ceasefires in the war were being offered and rejected by both South Africa and SWAPO faster than both sides seemed able to count. But as was mentioned in the opening remarks, two major and dramatic developments have taken place. Both will no doubt be out of date by the time of publishing, but they are central to any current analysis of the Namibian issue.

The MPC is clearly on the way to becoming an interim government. Whether this will be in its present form or supplemented by other internal parties, remains to be seen. They have been charged by South Africa with the unenviable and probably futile task of establishing an anti-SWAPO front, and of attempting, in the process, to salvage something from the chaos which presently surrounds the system of government in Namibia. At the same time they have been skillfully manoeuvred by South Africa into forming a backdoor State Council.

Indications are that the ten-government second tier ethnic authorities will be scrapped or rendered powerless within the first months of 1984, and that a strong centralised government, under the MPC, will take over. (The ethnic authorities have been found by the Thirion Commission of Enquiry to be almost universally corrupt, inefficient and bungling, swallowing up 75 % of the annual budget.) The power base of a central government will no doubt be used by the MPC, as the Ministers' Council and Legislative Assemblies were previously used by the DTA, to build an internal power base from which to fight SWAPO in the event of internationally-supervised independence elections.

The MPC has already indicated it has begun work on a post-independence constitution, thereby usurping phases seven and eight of UN Resolution 435, which places this task in the hands of a post-election Constituent Assembly. This could indicate an attempt to further delay independence, or an attempt to alter the framework of 435, turning its substance into a formula along the lines of the Zimbabwean Lancaster House

Agreement, which effectively ruled out significant revolutionary changes by any post-independence government.

On the international front, the inevitability of a second-term Reagan administration continuing to hold power in the USA has strengthened the confidence of the South Africans in their dealings with Angola. It would seem that the US, through economic, political and diplomatic pressure, will continue to use the Namibian issue as a major element of its global foreign policy, and will attempt to force the Angolans into withdrawing Cuban troops stationed there in exchange for massive economic aid and diplomatic recognition. Part of the package will include the MPLA's being forced to recognise UNITA, and begin talks with them on the formation of a 'government of national unity'.

As several newspaper editorials remarked in early February, there has seldom been an international diplomatic battle fought which involves so many disparate parties — all to decide the fate of one million people living in the world's second least densely populated country.

But if all the strands can be tied together, and the political ambitions and fears of the participants satisfied to some extent at least, 1984 could be the year in which Namibia finally sees the beginning of its long-awaited independence — 100 years to the day on 7 August 1984, since it was first colonised by Imperal Germany.

Postscript (April 1984)

Since the first draft of this section was written in February, what the media are fond of describing as 'dramatic developments' have taken place in the Namibian independence issue. Pretoria has achieved hitherto unheard of political victories in the southern African region, the fruits of years of cynical military bludgeoning of its neighbours.

Although the Mozambican accord has received a higher profile coverage than the Lusaka agreement signed between South Africa and Angola — and the effects on the ANC have been more visible — the effects of the 'disengagement' of South African and Angolan troops on guerillas of PLAN and on SWAPO's overall strategy have been just as devastating.

Other 'dramatic developments' have taken place surrounding the Namibian issue, and in the process, Pretoria's revised strategy for Namibia has become more clear.

Although little information has been released on the practical effects on SWAPO of the disengagement process, what little has seeped through points towards one of the most spectacular military victories in any guerilla war. South Africa, which to an extent had managed to contain the guerilla war in northern Namibia, has now all but wiped out SWAPO's military hopes in Namibia.

Immediately after the Lusaka agreement, came the announcement by A.G. Dr Willie van Niekerk, that Angola had agreed to 'discipline' SWAPO. The methods were initially unclear, but then reports began filtering through that SWAPO bases were being closed down in southern Angola, and that guerillas had been given orders to move as fast as possible towards the Namibian border in order to establish as large a military presence as possible before the final sealing off of the Namibian/Angolan frontier by former sworn enemies, the SADF and FAPLA.

Then in mid-March, the Department of Foreign Affairs confirmed earlier reports — first denied by the SADF — that a joint force of SADF and Angolan FAPLA troops had been involved in action against PLAN guerillas. At least three guerillas were killed, and further reports indicated that a rebellion at SWAPO's Tobias Hainjeko training camp outside Lubango had been quelled by FAPLA, possibly with SADF involvement.

Since the 1974 coup in Portugal, SWAPO guerillas have been able to operate freely from Angola, and the presence of their training camps — particularly at Lubango and Cassinga — has been used as an excuse for South Africa to launch repeated attacks against Angola.

But now SWAPO has been forced — for the time being, anyway — into ·a position where they will be obliged to base their military wing inside Namibia, and not merely fight their battles in the Territory. Soon after the joint disengagement monitoring commission began its work, SWAPO was already trying out new methods of penetrating Namibia, with 14 guerillas effectively opening a new front in the first week of March when they crossed the Botswana/Namibia border near Rietfontein, clashing with police units.

The SADF announced in late February that a force of 800 guerillas had penetrated northern Namibia — and indications are that these were guerillas who had been forced out of Angolan training camps and were ordered to return to Namibia, avoiding contact with the South African occupying forces, and to instead don civilian clothing and begin grassroots political work — returning to guerilla work if and when necessary. At the time of writing, the SADF claimed to have killed 135 of this force in separate actions.

Whether the 'disengagement' will continue to hold, remains to be seen. Reports indicate there is a split in the ruling Angolan MPLA on the issue, with the military advocating a more moderate line, and the Politburo divided on the issue. At the moment the military opinion holds sway, despite repeated attacks on South Africa by senior government officials — including President Jose Eduardo dos Santos, who has continued to lambast South African aggression and support for UNITA bandits.

With the military success South Africa has achieved, the political strategy of the State Security Council, referred to in the main section of this article, has begun to take more concrete form. When first reports of this strategy were printed in South Africa on 11 March, they were greeted with disbelief and dismay by the Western Five, particularly by the US — in part, perhaps, because they had not been as well-informed by their South African allies as they believed. But the South African plan for 'independence' — never officially acknowledged, and in fact denied — is now beginning to look increasingly attractive to the West.

Briefly, South Africa hopes to evade implementing crucial elements of UN Resolution 435 not only as a face-saving measure but also as a means of ensuring that the SWAPO government which takes power in Windhoek will not be the revolutionary power so feared and caricatured by the South Africans.

One of the key elements here is that the South Africans now believe they have all but wiped SWAPO out as a significant military threat, and that without the popular mystique and popular support engendered by a movement fighting a guerilla war against a foreign occupying power, the liberation movement will be forced to enter the internal political process as 'just another political party'. Repeated attempts by South Africa to get SWAPO into the Multi-Party Conference have failed, and are not likely to succeed. But the South Africans nevertheless believe that if they can force a situation of peace onto the territory, SWAPO's popular support will gradually wither away — particularly if the MPC, as a nominal interim government, can be seen to be introducing relatively meaningful reforms.

A period of peace prior to independence — and South Africa now seems fairly keen to get rid of Namibia — would remove the necessity for a United Nations peace-keeping force having to monitor a South Africa–SWAPO ceasefire, as laid down in phase one of Resolution 435. This would remove one of South Africa's main fears about 435, namely that the blue-bereted UN troops will be seen as SWAPO support troops because of the continued stance of the UN that SWAPO is the sole and authentic representative of the Namibian people.

South African strategists would like to see the UN troops replaced by a monitoring commission made up of observers and possibly military personnel from southern African and Frontline states. This, they believe, would give the independence process even more legitimacy in the eyes of Africa than a UN presence, and help to swing an election marginally in their favour, given the background of a SWAPO debilitated politically by a lack of significant military progress.

The release of SWAPO founder member, Herman Toivo ja Toivo, while giving SWAPO within Namibia a tremendous morale and propaganda boosting, is also seen by progressive observers in the Territory as part of the South African strategy for a neutered independence. Toivo's release, South African strategists believe, will have a three-fold function. Firstly, it could have the effect of splitting SWAPO with external elements loyal to Sam Nujoma pitted against internal elements loyal to Toivo. Toivo himself has repeatedly rejected all suggestions that he is politically ambitious, but the fact remains that he has, in the short time since his release, established a large and devoted following in SWAPO ranks in Namibia.

Secondly, the South Africans believe that even with Toivo's popular standing, if he is out of gaol for a long enough period before independence elections, he will 'burn himself out', and become 'just another politician'. And thirdly, as a side-effect of the release, the South Africans are hoping to prepare white public opinion in the territory and in South Africa for independence by putting Toivo in a public position where he will be seen and heard prolifically as someone who can placate white fears of the future — and dispel South Africa's own propaganda image of SWAPO leaders being nothing but bloodthirsty 'terrorists'.

Core of the whole scenario is the effectiveness of the MPC, which South Africa has tried to promote as an anti-SWAPO front. The MPC began to fall apart in late March when the leftwing Damara Raad withdrew after alleged secret talks with Nujoma in Lusaka, labelling the MPC an anti-SWAPO front, and an attempt to bypass 435. The remnants of the motley conference are still hanging in, but their effectiveness diminishes daily, as promises of draft constitutions, sweeping bills of rights and campaigns for nationwide reform fail to materialise.

South Africa's motives may be selfish and pretty strange, but few observers doubt that the Namibian initiative 1984-model is finally the real thing. If they can force SWAPO into a position where SWAPO accepts a watered down version of 435, there is little the UN, which appointed SWAPO the sole representative of the Namibian people, will be able to do about it. There is increasing pressure from inter alia, the Council of Churches in Namibia — whose membership totals over 80% of the peo-

ple and whose senior hierarchy contains a majority of SWAPO executives
– from President Dos Santos, and from SWAPO inside Namibia itself.
Nujoma could soon be forced into adopting a position of negotiation with
parties inside Namibia, ending up with a watered down, hamstrung
SWAPO government forced into pledges which will inhibit large-scale
revolutionary change after independence.

Notes

1 *RDM,* 01.02.84.
2 Press statement by the Administrator General, Dr Willie van Niekerk, 31.01.84.
3 From own notes, MPC press conference, 31.01.84.
4 Press statement by Dr Willie van Niekerk, 06.06.83.
5 MPC launching statement, 30.09.83.
6 This section is based on information received by the writer from senior political and
  diplomatic sources.
7 *Rapport,* 15.01.84.
8 *CT,* 17.08.83.
9 General Constand Viljoen, quoted in *CT,* 17.08.83.
10 'White Paper on Acts of Aggression by South Africa', released by the MPLA Central
   Committee, Luanda, 1 October 1983.
11 White Paper on Acts of Aggression.
12 S. Nestor, M. Ausiko, A. Kabono and T. Hauwina v SA Minister of Police and nine
   others, Windhoek Supreme Court, 22.11.83.
13 *CT,* 18.01.84.
14 *Namibia Review. A Journal of Contemporary South West African Affairs,* 30, September-
   December 1983 (publisher: Dr Kenneth Abrahams).

A Comparative Analysis of Lesotho and Swaziland's Relations with South Africa

John Daniel

Lesotho and Swaziland are structurally integrated as dependencies into the South African economy and their economic survival is heavily dependent upon the 'goodwill' of the South African government. These are widely held and correct assertions which stem largely from five factors:

i the geographically tiny size by world and African standards of both countries and their landlocked condition which produces a trade-flow (import-export) dependence;

ii their membership of the Southern African Customs Union and the numerous consequent opportunities provided thereby for South African manipulation;

iii the importance of the South African labour market as an employer and a generator of national income;

iv their absolute reliance on fuel imports through South Africa and an electricity dependence varying from total to substantial;

v the increasing ownership and domination by South African capital of the commercial sectors of their economies, notably wholesale and retail trade.

These factors do not, however, affect both countries equally. Lesotho's dependence is more severe than Swaziland's. She is wholly surrounded by South Africa and 100% reliant upon South Africa's road and rail system for the movement of goods in and out of the country. Her only link to the outside world not directly involving South Africa — a twice-weekly airlink to Swaziland and Mozambique — does nothing to lessen the condition. The flights involve small (approximately 20 seater) propeller planes which carry passengers but no freight. They are nevertheless important as they offer the only means of travel/escape for those unable to transit South Africa, and have been the means by which refugees and political activists have moved in and out of Lesotho. Yet even this link is fraught with peril, for the route overflies South African territory and South Africa has a ready capacity to force down any flight. Some years back bad weather grounded a flight in Bloemfontein and a prominent ANC official fell into the hands of the South African security police. This link operates therefore by South Africa's grace and favour.

Surrounded to the north, south and west by South Africa and to the east by Mozambique, Swaziland came to independence (1968) with its only railway running to Maputo harbour. Yet this line, which entirely avoids South African territory, has been little used. In every year since 1968 more than 95% of Swaziland's imports have entered from South Africa and mostly on South African Railways' road-carrier service. Likewise, the bulk of overseas exports have exited by way of Durban. The Maputo line has been used only to carry iron ore (ceased 1981), sugar and small amounts of coal. Moreover, no attempt has been made to develop it into a major route; indeed the opposite has occurred with the construction in 1980 of a southern link off the Maputo line to Richards Bay, while work has just begun to extend this South African connection northwards to Komatipoort in the Eastern Transvaal.

Hence operationally the difference between Lesotho and Swaziland's transportation dependence is marginal. Much the same applies to their mutual revenue dependence upon the South African Customs Union (SACU). SACU constitutes the means by which South African domination of the BLS economies is institutionalised. Established as a free-trade area between the members, SACU has given South African capital free access to the markets and raw materials of BLS while South Africa has been able to use her domination of the Union to deny BLS reciprocal access. Additionally in a number of cases South Africa has blocked or delayed the BLS countries from establishing industrial enterprises (television, fertiliser, textiles, amongst others) geared to the South African market and which would have competed with established South African producers. Retaliation or even withdrawal from SACU is constrained by BLS's need for the revenue earned from the common customs pool. For Lesotho this amounted in 1982 to 71% of total government revenue while for Swaziland it constituted 63%. Annual budgets are drafted on the basis of assured annual payments from Pretoria and, as the Third World revenue crisis deepens the prospect of a BLS withdrawal from SACU remains just a fantasy of academics. Indeed, even a three-month delay in a payment by Pretoria would wreak havoc in the Finance Ministries of Maseru and Mbabane.

Swaziland and Lesotho's position is markedly different in respect of access to the South African labour pool. Only 16% of Swazis in paid employment work on the gold mines. The loss of these jobs would exacerbate a mildly serious unemployment problem but would not constitute a national crisis. To Lesotho it would be a catastrophe of unimaginable proportions. Her domestic economy generates only 40 000 paid jobs. With a population of 1,3-million, the 140 000 jobs held by Basotho workers in South Africa are vital while their earnings constitute a massive 40% of annual GNP. The realisation of an occasionally expressed threat to repatriate these workers would create a fiscal emergency and generate extreme social and political instability. As a Maseru-based diplomat put it recently, 'the government and perhaps the country would not last a week' (*International Herald Tribune*, 13.04.83).

All Lesotho and Swaziland's fuel supplies reach them by road through South Africa while Lesotho receives all its electricity from ESCOM. Swaziland presently purchases 70% of its needs from this source. She has not chosen to use the Maputo line for fuel supplies while her policy of developing her limited hydro-electric potential is geared to maintaining the dependence upon ESCOM at 66% of total needs. South Africa therefore has the capacity to plunge both countries into darkness and to paralyse their road traffic.

By African standards both Lesotho and Swaziland rank as amongst the best and cheapest nations in which to shop for basic commodities and luxury goods. This is because their commercial trade sectors have been absorbed by South African mercantile capital (OK Bazaars, Metro, Fairways, Dee Bee) or the South African subsidiaries of foreign capital (Frasers, Spar). They provide the citizenry with the good material life while being not insignificant employers. The people have become accustomed to the consumer society created by capital; disappearance via a capital withdrawal would create social discontent.

In summation, therefore, in all the vital sectors of the economy — transportation, employment, income, and the supply of food, fuel and energy — Lesotho's dependence upon South Africa is complete and there exist no viable alternatives for any significant reduction. In Swaziland's case it is heavy but not as complete and options do exist for a marked reduction in the severity of the condition, ones which however she has not chosen to develop. Indeed the tendency has been to deepen the dependence upon South Africa.

This dependency argument has been developed in detail because it conditions most analyses of the BLS-South African relationship to produce the proposition that, because of the fact of their dependence, the BLS countries have no choice but to be accommodationist in their response to South Africa's demands. Put another way, the argument is that geopolitical and geo-economic factors are the primary determinants of BLS's actions. While not wholly invalid, that view is too simple and it misses out too many subtleties in what is a far more complex scenario. By contrast, I intend to develop two major themes:

i In neither the case of Lesotho nor Swaziland is their relationship to South Africa best described as 'accommodationist'. For Swaziland 'consensual' is a more precise term while 'confrontationist' best describes Lesotho's position. The fact that Lesotho has recently fallen in line with South Africa's main regional objective (the neutralising of the ANC threat) was not a capitulation to geo-realities but a submission to massive and sustained coercion. The difference is again subtle but real.

ii It follows from this that geo-political and economic dependence is not the major influence on the LS relationship with South Africa. In the face of recalcitrance and South African flexing of its power, geo-realities will achieve for South Africa the results she desires, but different forces shape the public postures of government leaders in Lesotho and Swaziland: Lesotho's hostile public position is a response primarily to domestic pressures while the harmony in the Swazi-South African relationship is a product of the class interests of the Swazi rulers and their ideological worldview which accords substantially with that of South Africa's rulers.

It follows from the above that between Lesotho and Swaziland there are important differences both in their general foreign policy positions and in respect of South Africa. This difference can be measured along three dimensions:

i the kind of governments with whom diplomatic relations are maintained;
ii their positions on important Third World issues;
iii various aspects of the relationship with South Africa including the rhetoric employed in discussing apartheid, the attitude to the emergence of the so-called 'independent' homelands, and what it took for South Africa to gain compliance on the ANC issue.

For the first decade of its independence, Lesotho's diplomatic ties were with the Western-bloc nations and right-wing regimes like Taiwan. But with the changing geo-political pattern in Southern Africa after 1974, her diplomatic ties shifted dramatically towards the socialist group. Ties now exist with Mozambique, Cuba, the Soviet Union, Yugoslavia, North Korea and the People's Republic of China. This latter required the expulsion of the Taiwanese and the closing down of their many aid projects. Chief Jonathan has also visited East Germany and attended the 1979 Non-Aligned Conference in Havana. By contrast Swaziland's diplomatic contacts remain solidly within the anti-communist camp with the exception of Mozambique where there is an obvious necessity for mutual relations. Otherwise only the United States, United Kingdom, EEC, Israel and Taiwan have embassies in Mbabane. No formal relations exist with any radical African, Asian, Arab or East European governments.

On international issues Swaziland adopts a position far closer to that of the United States than that of the Third World. This is particularly true from an analysis of her UN voting record where she has consistently sided with the US on major issues. Swaziland is in fact regarded by the US as a reliable voting ally at the UN. She has supported the US position on Israel and the PLO and took the Anglo-American position on both the Falklands and the shooting down of the KAL airliner. After the 1973 Yom Kippur war Swaziland was the only African country not to break diplomatic relations with Israel and for nearly ten years was the sole black African nation with ties to Israel.

The Lesotho position has been rather different. Along with the shift to the left in her diplomatic contacts, there has developed a greater Third World orientation on international questions. At the UN she has a tendency to abstain or be absent from voting on issues strongly favoured by the US. She cannot afford to alienate a major donor but nor does she wish to be seen to be aligned with the United States on most issues. She has also displayed a far greater sympathy to the Arab-bloc position on Middle East issues than has Swaziland, a fact which no doubt helped her win a loan from the United Arab Emirates for the construction of the new international airport.

Sharper differences are revealed by a comparison of attitudes to the bantustans. Neither government has given formal recognition to those accorded 'independence' but Swaziland's position is more pragmatic. Swazi princesses have with the late King Sobhuza's blessing married prominent figures in both the Transkei and KwaZulu (such as King Zwelithini) while both Zwelithini and President Matanzima have made visits to Swaziland. Lesotho by comparison has been hostile to the 'homelands' and particularly to her neighbour, the Transkei. So much so that the Quacha's Nek border post with the Transkei has been effectively closed since 1977 because of a Transkeian insistence that Basotho nationals obtain visas from Umtata before entering her territory. Lesotho has refused to negotiate on this issue because to do so would imply recognition of the Transkei. Commenting on the issue of his government's refusal to deal with the 'homelands', the Minister of Information, Mr Sixishe, stated that Lesotho was 'not going to be the priest who baptises that illegitimate baby' (*Citizen*, 19.08.83). This stance has earned Lesotho considerable aid from the international community and some have suggested that this is the basis of her position rather than principle. Even so, the vehemence of Lesotho on this issue is one which contrasts with that of Swaziland.

Likewise in the whole area of rhetorical expressions on apartheid there is a definite distinction between the two countries. Since 1976 Lesotho has joined the chorus of critics who have condemned apartheid and often in language more strident than bland diplomatese. Chief Jonathan has referred to South Africa as 'the natural enemy' of Lesotho (*RDM*, 25.07.83), condemned apartheid for dehumanising and denationalising the black man, (*Sow*, 19.10.83) and denounced South Africa's regional strategy as a 'campaign of atrocities' (*Star*, 16.02.83). Both he and Minister Sixishe have used the insulting term 'Boers' to refer to South Africa's leaders (*Star*, 05.08.83), while the strength of feeling on apartheid was reflected by the recent denunciation of the opposition United Democratic Party leader, Charles Mofeli, as a 'sell-out' and 'South African agent' (*Citizen*, 22.06.83) for having had talks in Pretoria with government figures.

Swaziland's language on apartheid has never been anything but diplomatic. Where she has expressed criticism it has been on the general grounds of abhorrence of racial discrimination and denial of human rights. It has never assumed the dimension of stridency or abuse. Indeed the relationship with South Africa has in recent years become close. Foreign Minister Richard Dlamini is said to be on good personal terms with Pik Botha and recently in parliament described his government's relations with South Africa as 'friendly' (*Times of Swaziland*, 27.04.83). After the recent cyclone in January, Swaziland turned to the South African military for help. This resulted in a military convoy of 20 South African army trucks laden with white soldiers rolling into the country where they stayed for approximately two weeks. Helicopters were also provided to fly cabinet ministers and other officials around the country and the *Times of Swaziland* carried a picture of six Swazi cabinet ministers lined up with a white South African airforce pilot in front of his helicopter. It is hard to imagine a minister of any other African country voluntarily posing for such a picture but the fact that they did tells one much of Swazi pragmatism and ideological conservatism.

The most dramatic gulf between Lesotho and Swaziland is revealed by a comparison of their respective positions on both support for the ANC and in their resistance to South Africa's 'Pax Pretoria' policy. Since the mid-1970s, Lesotho has moved significantly closer to the ANC (away from its more pro-PAC stance of the 1960s) and has allowed the ANC to establish an official diplomatic presence. In addition, it has given sanctuary to a large South African refugee community. While it has not allowed ANC to have bases on its territory, it is clear that its ability to be in Lesotho played a role in the stepping up of ANC activities inside South Africa in recent years. Certainly this is the view of South African security:

> We don't say Lesotho affords the ANC bases in the sense of military camps. We accuse them of allowing the ANC to use private houses for planning sabotage and for giving instructions to trained people. Often the trained men are not armed. They may fly into Maseru from Maputo and then infiltrate South Africa — where they pick up their weapons at secret caches (taken from an undated *Financial Mail* cutting).

Security also believes Lesotho has provided ANC with a 'convenient centre for the underground's recruiting activities. South African Blacks could slip into the country easily . . . and then be flown out through Mozambique for military training' (*New York Times*, 11.10.83). It is for this reason that Lesotho has been such a particular target of South African coercion in order to achieve Pik Botha's 'Out, they (ANC) must get out. There is no compromise on this one' objective (*New York Times*, 11.10.83).

The attainment of this goal has required the employment of the whole arsenal of military and economic methods at South Africa's disposal. These have included:

  i direct military intervention as in the case of the Maseru raid of December 1982;
 ii the alleged arming, training, financing and directing of a clandestine dissident force in the form of the Lesotho Liberation Army;
iii the use of the mechanisms of manipulation provided by her domination of SACU. These have involved the delaying of revenue payments,

    the blocking of overland arms shipments from Durban and a refusal
to allow arms to be flown into the country;

iv threats to repatriate Basotho labour;

v the imposition in mid-1983 of what amounted to a virtual economic
blockade on the flow of traffic and goods into and out of Lesotho. The
effect was a massive disruption to normal life with, amongst other
things, food shortages and a drying up of tourist traffic.

All of this against a country as tiny and resourceless as Lesotho. It suggests that resistance was sustained, which indeed it was. Eventually,
however, it had to give way but not before much dragging of feet, protest
and appeals to the international community for help. Nor was it accompanied by any fanfare or the 'doublespeak' claims of victory which Mozambique used to describe its capitulation. In the course of bending to South
Africa's will, Lesotho made it clear to the United Nations and major
Western governments that it could resist no longer and that the 'painful
decision' to evacuate ANC personnel 'had been made for national survival'. Foreign Minister Sekhonyane spoke of 'an ultimatum. We have no
choice. The country is being suffocated' (*International Herald Tribune*,
13.08.83). Furthermore, the decision to ask ANC to leave was done in full
consultation with its leadership. This again contrasts with the Mozambican position where the ANC clampdown was done without explanation
or consultation with a comradely movement who had given unstinting
support to FRELIMO throughout its armed struggle, to the extent even
of fighting alongside its cadres.

    Though a lifelong, albeit low key, supporter of the ANC, it was not un-
til after Mozambique's independence in 1975 that the late King Sobhuza
allowed an official ANC presence in Swaziland. Even then, however, the
Swazi state's attitude was ambivalent and the organisation operated under
stringent restrictions and near-constant harassment from local security.
The organisation was allowed no office, possession of arms was strictly
restricted, as too was movement. Even so, by 1981 Swaziland had
emerged as a major conduit into South Africa and an increasing number
of ANC strikes (including some of the boldest like the first SASOL attack) were said to have emanated from Swazi territory. At this point (the
end of 1981) harassment of the ANC increased sharply. At the time it was
thought that this was a response to greater pressure from South Africa
as well as the 'bait' of the land deal about which details were just emerging publicly. We now know that it was a result of the signing in February

1982 of a Non-Aggression Pact — an action so out of step with the then prevailing climate that it had to be kept secret.

What followed was a series of actions, both in terms of the Pact and outside of it, which has forced what is left of the ANC operation from Swaziland deep underground. The enforced withdrawal of the veteran ANC representative, Stanley Mabizela, was followed by the murder of his deputy and his wife; then came the first of two round-ups of ANC members and the deportation of many of them, stepped up raids on ANC homes and tougher legislation on the possession of arms. Today the ANC presence in Swaziland is a shadow of what it was at the time of the signing of the Pact in 1982. And all of this was achieved with virtually none of the 'stick' to which Lesotho was subjected.

The crucial question which remains is what accounts for this major contrast between the two countries? In my view, it is insufficient to explain Swaziland's actions merely in terms of the desire to acquire the KaNgwane and Ingwavuma regions. The 'carrot' of these 'lost lands' has been a card which South Africa has played skilfully but it has only served to reinforce deeper tendencies in the Swazi state's attitude to the ANC. One of these is ideological. Swaziland is a fundamentally conservative and traditional society. Its social order is the direct antithesis to that to which the ANC aspires. The emergence of an ANC-ruled South Africa would unleash forces threatening to the essentially feudal order in Swaziland. There is thus real fear on the part of the Swazi state of the possible impact of a major advance in the struggle to liberate South Africa. The survival of the present regime in South Africa is actually in the long term interests of the present Swazi rulers. But, further than that, it serves too their class interests.

Prior to independence the traditional Swazi aristocracy which now forms the major part of the ruling class had only a base in the non-capitalist sector of the economy — the communally held non-individual tenure land (the so-called Swazi nation area). This has changed since 1968 through their control of a development and investment corporation known as the Tibiyo TakaNgwane Fund. Through the revenues acquired originally from mineral rights, Tibiyo has acquired freehold land, established businesses and purchased equity in many large and medium-size foreign companies active in the economy, and particularly in agro-industry (Lonrho, Cortaulds, Anglo-American, the Commonwealth Development Corporation, to name only the biggest). This has resulted in revenues amounting to millions of Emalangeni flowing into a Fund which operates free from public scrutiny, the control of parliament and the

Ministry of Finance. The Tibiyo board is composed of members of the Swazi Royal family and a few loyal commoner allies. Today Tibiyo is the wealthiest and most energetic locally-controlled force in the domestic economy and its style is to work closely through management contracts with international capital. And increasingly that capital is of South African origin or British capital with significant interests in South Africa. The constellation of capitalist forces in the Swazi economy has changed markedly in recent years and today South African capital dominates most sectors of the Swazi economy; and where it does not, as in banking (Standard and Barclays), there is a strong South African connection. Thus, the material prosperity and position of this royalist group, which also monopolises the post-Sobhuza political era, rests on the prosperity of South African and foreign capital. It is this above all that explains the present hostility to the ANC and the now open collaboration with South Africa. It is not insignificant that the recent disclosure of the existence of a Non-Aggression Pact with South Africa should coincide with the announcement of a decision to open trade offices in the two countries. It is this commonality of class interests which has produced Swaziland's consensual attitude to South African aggression towards the ANC.

None of these above factors applies to Lesotho. There is no such institution as Tibiyo in Lesotho. Nor has there been a tendency on the part of the Basotho state to enter into joint ventures with capital. So desperate has Lesotho been for investment that it has not posed the obstacle of equity to those willing to walk through its 'open door'. Foreign capital, pure and uncoupled, dominates the modern economy of Lesotho. The rulers of Lesotho have no class alliance therefore with capital to mitigate their hostility to South Africa. That they are so hostile in public (in private negotiations with South Africa they are said to be rather passive) can only be explained in terms of domestic political pressures.

The bulk of the Basotho male electorate has at one time or another worked in South Africa where they have experienced at first hand the degradation of the apartheid system. Nowhere is this more the case than in the experience of the underground miner. It is he who suffers the curse of enforced separation from his family as well as the indignity of working at the behest of perhaps the most racist elements in the South African working class — the white miner. He has no reason to love South Africa and this hostility acquires a political expression when he returns home. Illegitimate since its coup in 1970, the Jonathan government has tried desperately to acquire legitimacy in the 1970s by assuming a more populist position, particularly on the question of South Africa and apartheid. It is this factor which has produced the Lesotho government's confrontationist stance towards South Africa rather than the fact of its dependence.

South African Interests in Latin America

David Fig

During the course of 1983 South African troops engaged Cuban forces stationed in the People's Republic of Angola. Gold Fields of South Africa announced plans to go ahead with gold mining projects in Brazil. The port of Cape Town acted as a staging post for supplying workers and construction equipment to enable Britain to entrench its hold over the Malvinas Islands, regarded by Argentina as an integral part of its sovereign territory. The South African fishing companies extended their operations in Chile and bulk imports from Peru. The Anglo American Corporation of South Africa Limited forged ahead with its US$300-m investment in Brazil's gold mines. Attempts to set up a Brazil-South Africa Chamber of Commerce were aborted, largely at the hands of Itamaraty, Brazil's foreign ministry. British M.P.s announced their intention to question their prime minister over whether Commodore Gerhardt had provided Argentina with naval intelligence covering the movement of British ships during the South Atlantic war of 1982.

These events are some indication of the extent to which South Africa has been interacting, in the political and economic spheres, with other Latin American states. Although such interactions may be traced as far back as the early nineteenth century it is only during the past two decades that a significant and growing volume of trade and investment has occurred. Economic links have been taking place against a background of militarisation of the South African state and an increased affinity with some of the most reactionary regimes in the region.

Because of isolation and parochialism, most South Africans are spared any detailed understanding of events in the Latin American region. Despite its proximity to Africa and its common problems, we are not taught its history or its languages. Our newspapers present us with stereotyped images of Latin exuberance, gratuitous violence, economic chaos or Marxist subversion. Popular uprisings are only present in the context of the problems these may provide for Washington's foreign policy and not in terms of the struggles of people for economic and social justice in their own countries.

Hence readers may be forgiven for assuming that people in Brazil speak Spanish instead of Portuguese, for confusing the concepts of South America and Latin America (the former being only one subregion of the latter, which also includes Central America, Mexico and the Caribbean), or for pronouncing Grenada as if it was the Spanish city instead of using the pronunciation preferred by its inhabitants (Gre-nay-da).

At the same time there is a renewed concern amongst popular organisations in South Africa with events in Latin America. The tenth anniversary of the military coup against the Popular Unity government in Chile has prompted closer analysis of the lessons of the Allende period. The agony of El Salvador and the fate of the Nicaraguan revolution are both objects of intense concern, especially in the light of the invasion of Grenada. The current struggle in Guatemala deserves to receive equal attention. And the recent upsurge in the workers' movement in Brazil bears numerous lessons for its South African counterparts.

The invasion of Grenada provided significant cause for concern. It demonstrated the ease with which the United States was prepared to flout international law in the region. The treatment of the invasion in the US media helped soften up public opinion, reluctant to back foreign adventures after the defeat in Vietnam, into accepting a more aggressive interventionist US foreign policy. The invasion also helped the South African military to justify its intensified incursions into southern Angola.

Yet these issues cannot be tackled here. Our focus is, of necessity, a narrow one. The object here is to provide an overview of the role of the South African state and monopoly capital in Latin America in the recent past. The rationale for this is twofold. A knowledge of the links between South Africa and Latin America raises the possibilities of cementing political solidarity and the important task of self-education about the struggles faced by Latin Americans. Another aim of this analysis is to contribute towards the discussion on the nature and scope of direct foreign investment of South African-based firms.

The focus is on two major South African direct investments in Latin America, that of the Anglo American Corporation group in the mining and chemicals sectors mainly in Brazil, and that of the South African fishing industry's recent entry into Chile. First, however, let us examine the role of the South African state in preparing the way for and facilitating these investments.

The state as the guarantor of the overall reproduction of monopoly capital

The final years of the 1960s saw the South African state at the apex of its power. The nationalist movement had been broken at home and had yet to regroup in exile. Liberalism had lost its political momentum and became resigned to compromises with the government's policies of intensifying territorial segregation, influx control and other measures associated with Verwoerdian apartheid.

Yet the state was drifting into crisis. The costs to the economy of a high growth rate during the 1960s (6,3% between 1963–70, second only to Japan) were related to the policy of import substitution industrialisation as recommended by the Viljoen Commission in 1958.[1] To manufacture consumer goods at home it had been necessary to import vast amounts of capital goods, whose share of all imports grew from 30% in 1957 to 45% in 1970. This gave rise to balance of payment problems. In addition, uneven income distribution meant that the domestic market could not absorb the entire output of manufactures. South Africa needed new export markets.

Its natural hinterland, Africa, might have offered a way out. Yet in the 1970s, because of political changes and other factors, there was a sharp decline in the share of South African exports entering other African countries, from around 16% in the late 1960s to less than 9% by 1977. These figures include re-exports to Southern Rhodesia. In any event the bulk of South Africa's exports to the rest of Africa was comprised of primary products and not manufactured goods. This indicates the failure of the economic underpinning of what was variously known as Vorster's 'outward movement', 'dialogue' and 'detente'.

The Reynders Commission on the export trade, which reported in 1972, preferred a policy of export-led growth. It advised that

> from the point of view of export potential, South Africa should increase contact, assist-
> ance and marketing of its goods in respect of certain South American countries . . .
> the empty economies of Latin America must be regarded as natural markets for South
> African exports.[2]

Along with the crisis of markets went the problem of isolation. Apartheid became, during the 1960s, a world issue which was raised increasingly by politicised post-colonial states at the United Nations and in other international institutions. The militarisation of South Africa, a process initiated in the 1960s but which escalated geometrically the following decade, took place against the background of growing demands for a mandatory UN arms embargo, which were finally realised in 1977. Even though a number of states refused to adhere to this, Pretoria experienced increased difficulties in arms procurement. It therefore sought closer links with other likeminded regimes such as Israel, the Shah's Iran, and Taiwan, as well as the military dictatorships in the southern cone of Latin America.[3]

Through these links, Pretoria hoped to ease her diplomatic isolation and forge close ties with the military establishments in order to offset the embargo and procure armaments where necessary.

But the state still faced problems in persuading exporters to resolve the crisis of markets through a programme of trade with Latin America. In its role as guarantor of the reproduction of monopoly capital, it had a clear perception of the overall economic interests of the dominant class. Individual entrepreneurs were slow to realise their potential role in the strategy which the state favoured. Therefore the state created a number of incentives to the stimulation of expanded economic links.

1. The South African state purchased bonds issued by the Inter American Development Bank, enabling South African firms to tender for any of the numerous development projects financed by the IDB.
2. The state offered Latin American governments generous export credits through the parastatal Credit Guarantee Insurance Corporation of Africa. The Industrial Development Corporation was also involved in financing schemes for exporters of capital goods. These incentives were important for maintaining the competitiveness of South African exports on world markets.
3. The state arranged corporate participation in official government stands at trade fairs in important Latin American cities.
4. The state assisted in the immeasurable improvement of transport and telecommunications links. Air routes to Brazil and Argentina were established, and new shipping lines linked South African ports with both the east and west coasts of South America. Submarine cables and satellite links enabled telephone and other forms of communication to take place with efficiency and speed.
5. The state stepped up diplomatic contact with Latin American govern-

ments. Numerous officials crossed the Atlantic. Several new South African embassies were built in Latin America, and representation upgraded to residential ambassadors. The high point of this policy was the visit by the Paraguayan head of state to this country in 1974, a visit which the South African prime minister reciprocated the following year. There was also a setback to Pretoria: the kidnapping and assassination of South Africa's envoy to El Salvador in 1979; that country, which at the time was experiencing a short period of coalition government, broke off all relations with South Africa. The subsequent installation of General Dutton as the first resident ambassador in Chile indicated the close relationship between the security forces of both states.

6. From 1978 access to foreign exchange for the purposes of direct foreign investment was eased through the creation of the financial rand and subsequent more liberal measures of the South African Reserve Bank.

Once these infrastructural developments had taken place, the path was smoothed for South African exporters of goods and capital to consider Latin America as an appropriate destination. Let us now turn to the examination of our case studies.

Oppenheimer as Fitzcarraldo

Prior to the enormous diversification of the Anglo American Corporation's empire in the 1970s, it was essentially a mining finance house based on South African gold and diamonds. One of the constraints under which the gold mining industry operated in the middle third of the century (1934–69) was the constant price of gold, established at US$35 an ounce on the world market. With the rise in fixed costs and the rapid inflation of the latter half of the 1960s, South Africa's gold mining industry was flung into crisis. Forecasters anticipated that the industry might collapse entirely during the 1970s, if the world price for gold remained intact.

One of the strategies of the Corporation was to seek to diversify geographically, particularly into areas where costs were substantially lower than those in South Africa. A further consideration was the potentially volatile political situation in the Corporation's base country and the long term uncertainty over South Africa's future. The chairman, Harry Oppenheimer, had long been associated with liberalism and advocated the need for social transformation as the best guarantor of the survival of monopoly capital in South Africa. Yet because the pace of change was negligible, the Corporation adjudged that the further the risks could be spread, the better.

Brazil was ignored until 1973, when the Corporation established a subsidiary in Rio de Janeiro, the *Anglo American Corporation do Brasil – Administração, Participação e Comércio em Empreendimentos Mineiros – Limitada*, known familiarly as Ambrás. This was to become the holding group for most of the Anglo group's Brazilian assets.

Anglo sought to gain maximum advantage from the Brazilian government's partiality to denationalising the country's mining sector. It also took advantage of the fact that Portuguese nationals were allowed the same rights as Brazilian citizens to act commercially, and placed Dr Mário Ferreira, a Portuguese citizen, in the chairmanship of Ambrás. Ferreira had previously headed Anglo's operations in colonial Mozambique, when the Corporation formed part of an international consortium to construct the Cahora Bassa dam on the Zambezi river in the late 1960s. At the time the project was criticised for forming part of a strategic settlement scheme promoted by the Portuguese colonial government to attract white immigrants. Ferreira was also reputed to have close links with Jorge Jardim, a Portuguese businessman involved in breaking oil sanctions against the Smith government and who later helped finance the radio station of the anti-Frelimo MNR movement.

Preoccupied with gold and diamonds, Ambrás showed an interest in prospection and the acquisition of mining investments. At the time, Brazil's goldmining industry was in the doldrums. The major mine, Morro Velho, located about 325 km due north of Rio at Nova Lima, close to the city of Belo Horizonte, had experienced a turbulent history under British control between 1830 and 1960,[4] after which it was acquired by three Brazilians for the token sum of one dollar.

Despite government subsidies, the constant gold price of the 1960s made substantial investment in the mine prohibitive for the Brazilian owners. Productivity declined rapidly, the technology was backward, and the local press exposed the dangerous and unhealthy working conditions. By 1968 a former Morro Velho superintendent declared that 'in the four years necessary for its reconstruction, the mine has virtually been paralysed economically and it is humanly impossible to continue to work it'.[5]

Thus it was that the Brazilian owners invited Anglo to purchase a 49% minority holding. Here was a chance to utilise Anglo's economic expertise, vast access to capital and anxiousness to diversify geographically out of South Africa. Morro Velho, the deepest mine in all of Latin America (2,450 m), might benefit from Anglo's considerable deep-level experience on the Witwatersrand.

Despite the backing of Mário Henrique Simonsen, Brazil's finance minister who later became Anglo's major Brazilian partner, government enthusiasm towards Anglo's entry into Brazil was tempered with apprehension on the part of a number of politicians.

Two parliamentary commissions of enquiry were established in the Chamber of Deputies at this time. One sought to examine Brazil's minerals policy and the other the role of foreign capital in the country.[6] Each had the competence to examine the Morro Velho deal, and the commission on minerals summoned one of its former Brazilian owners to give evidence. Unfortunately for the historian, the key parts of his deposition which dealt specifically with the deal have been excised from the final published report, perhaps in error. No serious critique of the deal resulted, despite the intentions of some of the commission's more nationalist deputies to limit foreign acquisition of Brazilian mineral resources.

The Minister of Mines and Energy, Shigeaki Ueki's evidence, instead of being challenged, was entered piecemeal into the final report of the commission as part of the chairperson's summary, as if it were the considered opinion of the entire commission. No restrictions were placed on Anglo's investments.

Why was this the case? Firstly, substantial ignorance existed in Brazil at the time about the nature of Anglo American and its role in the South African and other national economies. Deputies, although critical, deferred easily to the technological pretext for approving the admission of Anglo into the most promising areas of Brazilian mining, failing to consider the political implications. Secondly, Harry Oppenheimer timed his visit to Brazil to coincide with the deliberations of the commission on multinationals. His reception by president Geisel spelt, in the context of an authoritarian military state, automatic official acceptance of the Morro Velho deal. Ironically, whilst Oppenheimer, a direct representative of South African monopoly capital, was able to gain access to the president, it is doubtful whether Geisel would have received any senior apartheid politician.

Under Geisel's presidency the Africa policy of his predecessor, General Medici, was continued. Brazil sought to establish and maintain good relations with West African states, which it saw as a market for Brazilian technology, often more appropriate to tropical systems and more competitive than its equivalent in the high-cost industrialised countries. With the Portuguese departure from Africa in 1975, Brazil sought to play a more significant role in Lisbon's ex-colonies. Brazil was the first capitalist country to recognise the MPLA government in Luanda. Two years later SWAPO was recognised. Relations with Pretoria were scaled down: diplomatic representation became restricted to a chargé d'affaires and Brazil's consulate-general in Cape Town closed. Brasilia's public posture was therefore one of nominal opposition to official South African policy. Yet there seemed to be no reservations on Geisel's part in welcoming the Anglo American investment in Brazil's major gold mine.

The Morro Velho deal was to form the springboard for further Anglo investments in Brazil. Anglo also acquired a vast expanse of land in the interior of the north-eastern state of Bahia, close to the town of Jacobina, 1 300 km from Rio. This holding, rich in gold, was later consolidated into the Morro Velho company. Capital has been thrust into both mining investments, amounting to a total of US$306,8-m by the end of 1988. Of this figure $70-m has already been spent on the Jacobina mine, and $197,5-m is earmarked for the extension of the Morro Velho project to the nearby Cuiabá-Raposos mines. These figures were announced by Morro Velho's superintendent at a mining industry conference in May 1983.[7]

In a similar manner, despite close questioning of witnesses, the commission on multinationals failed to tackle fully the question of the entry of South African capital into Brazil.

The Minister of Mines and Energy, Shigeaki Ueki, was cross-examined on the deal, putting forward the technological imperative as an argument for accepting the new South African presence:

> It's really only Anglo American which has the best knowhow for exploiting gold at this depth . . . so this national group thought that this association was convenient. We hope that with this association gold production will increase. The deal was signed a year ago (in 1975). I believe that the Brazilian group made the deal on excellent terms, because gold has since dropped in price from 200 to 130 dollars.[8]

Anglo's partner in Morro Velho is no longer the original Brazilian group, but has been replaced by the Bozano Simonsen group led by Mário Henrique Simonsen and Júlio Bozano, a good friend of Mário Ferreira. All sorts of complicated shareholdings have been arranged to disguise the full extent of Anglo's minority ownership of Morro Velho, yet the company is operated by Anglo personnel to all intents and purposes. In addition, Minorco, Anglo's holding company for the Americas, owns significant and growing percentages of the Bozano Simonsen group and its bank, through other subsidiaries based in Liberia. In 1983 Ambrás announced it had received a dividend of $1,6-m from these interests, contributing to its own dividends of $5,5-m for the same period.[9]

Working conditions on Anglo-run mines have come under great criticism in Brazil. In Jacobina, the miners complain about dangerous working conditions, bad transport and inadequate food. There is no danger pay or social security supplement. Wages are low and with overtime (normal shifts last ten hours) the 800 workers receive just over the minimum wage of around $50 per month. The company, according to testimonies of workers, has attempted to cover up the cause of a worker's death in a mining accident in order to avoid having to compensate the family. The company has also threatened workers with dismissal for attempting to form an association.[10]

At Morro Velho average wages are between two and three minimum salaries (between $90 and $140 per month) depending on overtime worked. Because of the deep level of the oldest part of the mine, there are substantial refrigeration problems. Very high temperatures force the miners to work in shorts and sandals and with scarves over their faces instead of protective headgear. Because of the drilling, fine silicon dust enters both through the respiratory system and through the unclad pores of the skin. The high incidence of silicosis (one in three workers are affected according to union officials) testifies to the poor working conditions. The company has closed down its hospital and workers depend on their union and inadequate state provision for medical services. Although a company town, the mayor, himself a doctor, claims that the company has failed to assist the municipality with any social service payments. He alleged that none of the taxes paid by the company reached the municipality.[11]

Social responsibility for the poverty of the community of Nova Lima, dependent on mine incomes since the last century, must lie to a large extent with the company.

From official statistics it is evident that the Morro Velho group is by far the most important source of underground gold in Brazil, providing 97% of total underground production in 1981. Until 1979, underground production was far greater than opencast and alluvial production, but this pattern has changed substantially since then.

BRAZILIAN GOLD PRODUCTION, 1978–1982 (metric tonnes)

Year	Total	Morro Velho	Opencast/ Alluvial	Other
1978	8,6	3,8	4,5	0,3
1979	4,3	3,1	0,9	0,3
1980	13,8	4,0	9,6	0,2
1981	24,1	4,2	19,7	0,2
1982	33,8	4,2	29,3	0,3

Source: *Brazil, Ministry of Mines and Energy, Departamento Nacional de Produção Mineral.*

Nevertheless whilst Morro Velho has declined in relative importance, the question of gold has become strategically crucial to the Brazilian economy, whose national debt approaches $90-billion. The escalation of gold production is a key element in paying off the debt. Eager to acquire as much gold as possible, the Brazilian government is offering producers a higher price than is obtainable on the world market. There is also substantial interest in the establishment of a national gold regulating authority and growing criticism of any foreign participation and control over gold production. Both these factors are likely to constrain Anglo expansion into further areas of gold production.

Because of this, Anglo has tended to spread its investments into other areas of mining and industry, as well as the banking field mentioned earlier. Through its De Beers subsidiary AECI, it has acquired interests in a number of explosives companies in Brazil. Its Brazilian partners in this venture used to have formal associations with one of Salazarist Portugal's finance ministers, Prof. Texeira Pinto, responsible for advising the Champalimaud family on their investments in Mozambique. Although public links with Texeira Pinto are no longer acknowledged, AECI's Brazilian partners are backed by a mysterious Swiss company, *Dex Holdings*, which experts believe is a cover for Texeira Pinto, who transferred his investments out of Portugal before they could be nationalised in the wake of the 1974 revolution.

One of the explosives factories owned by the joint venture is called *Companhia de Explosivos Valparaiba — CEV*. According to the Brazilian specialist defence press, CEV, based at Lorena in the state of São Paulo, supplies the Brazilian armed forces and numerous export customers with 'various types of hand grenades, smoke grenades, smoke markers, smoke gas grenades for anti-riot use, fuses for various types of heavy ammunition, rockets for bazooka-type launchers, aircraft rockets of different types' as well as the M1 submachine-gun, soon to be launched.[12] CEV uses the logic of 'security reasons' to avoid divulging the names of countries to whom it sells its products.

Neither Anglo nor AECI have ever made mention of their participation in the Brazilian explosives industry in their annual reports. Shareholders are kept ignorant of the workings of the partnership, *IBEX Participacões SA*, which had a capital of 1,4-billion cruzeiros at the end of 1982. Anglo's involvement in the lucrative Brazilian arms export industry raises numerous sensitive questions about the Corporation's image and activities.

Further inroads into the Brazilian mining industry were made in December 1981, when Anglo and its associates purchased a 40% interest in *Empresas Sudamericanas Consolidadas SA*, the holding company for all the South American assets of the Panama-based Hochschild group. Through this deal Anglo extended its Latin American holdings to Peru, Chile and Argentina and has set up its own subsidiary companies in Buenos Aires and Santiago.

Most recently, in November 1983, *De Beers do Brasil* started operating its Brazilian industrial diamonds division in São Paulo, with the object of marketing its product in the country's industrial heartland. It intends, according to the chairman Jorge Salomá Minguell, to market a million carats and do a turnover of $2-million during 1984. By the time of its official inauguration at the end of January, it had already acquired a market share of 50%.[13]

The 14 000 km sardine run

Fishing is a predatory industry, somewhat akin to hunting. It is also an industry subject to rapidly oscillating business cycles. As such it involves high risks and occasionally very high profits. In South Africa the industry is highly monopolised, with half a dozen major fishing corporations and a small number of more modest-sized independent companies. Monopolisation means that there are prohibitive costs involved for new companies attempting to enter the industry. Some of the larger fishing groups are subsidiaries of even larger, more diversified food sector companies. Marine Products, for example is part of Fedfood in the Federale Volksbeleggings stable. Others such as Ovenstones or Saldanha Bay have their origins in family firms and have not yet been acquired by the giant corporations.

The fishing corporations have their headquarters in Cape Town, and operate fleets and processing plants along the west coast as far north as Walvis Bay. Until the 1980s the Namibian fishing grounds ranked amongst the most lucrative in the world. They attracted fleets not only from South Africa, but from Eastern and Western Europe, Japan, South Korea, Israel, Iraq and Cuba. In 1976 the fishing resource began to collapse, owing to overfishing and the killing off of plankton due to unusually cold water temperatures. A reduction in quotas controlling the amount of fish caught was applied to the fishing corporations. The quota on pilchards fell to zero by 1981, and the 1982 quota was filled within two months of the opening of the pilchard season.

A number of the corporations had to develop strategies of survival. They had been left with redundant fleets, canneries, processing plants and warehouses in Walvis Bay and Luderitz. Some companies joined forces in order to rationalise their assets in Walvis Bay (for example Ovenstone and General Development Corporation). Other solutions were to put factories into mothballs, or to transfer plant to other installations. A third solution to the Namibian crisis was to establish subsidiaries abroad.

Certain fishing executives were interviewed as to the choice of available investment destinations. Australia was rejected due to its high-tax regime and hostility to South African investment, Britain due to the militant reputation (often imaginary) of its trade union movement, and Argentina owing to the 'chaos and instability' there around the time of the fall of Isabel Peron. Ovenstone had encountered problems in attempting to sell its fishing factory-ship to an Argentine group. Peru had decided to nationalise its fishing fleet, thus there were no openings there for capital investment.

The ideal choice for most companies was Chile. Firstly, there had been a historical precedent, in that the Ovenstone group participated in a joint venture with a Chilean company over twenty years ago. In July 1963 a factory was established at Iquique to process 50 tons of fish an hour. Most of the machinery and equipment for the factory was manufactured in South Africa, and Ovenstone supplied the technical staff for its construction and for training local workers. South Africans were also brought in to run the small fishing fleet.[14] The Ovenstones were appointed honorary consuls for Chile in Cape Town. Their holdings in Chile were nationalised by the Popular Unity government which came to power in 1970. Once this government had been toppled, the military junta invited the Ovenstones to resume their fishing activities in Chile and to increase their investment if they so wished. Ovenstones took up this offer in 1979, shipping a cannery partly to Iquique and partly to Talcahuano.

Secondly, Chile offered South African investors a favourable investment environment. Unlike other choices, Chile's firm military government had seen to it that there were no inconvenient trade unions demanding high wages or cushy working conditions. The economic nationalism of the Allende period was put aside, and Chile made it easy for foreign firms to obtain local investment finance. The tax regime was favourable, allowing foreign corporations to choose their own level of taxation with only two possibilities for minor upward revision. Profits will be allowed to be repatriated subject to a relatively low tax of 30%, although at present they will be used for loan repayment, reinvestment and offsetting of losses.[15]

Thirdly, Chile's relations with South Africa have been stepped up gradually over the past decade. At first Pinochet attempted to distance himself from contacts with Pretoria in order to create a good impression at the UN and offset the junta's isolation. However this tactic failed, and closer contact with South Africa was developed precisely because of the junta's continued isolation. Diplomatic relations were raised to ambassadorial level and Pretoria dispatched one of its top military men, Lieutenant-General Jack Dutton, as its first resident ambassador in Santiago in 1981.[16] Prior to this the envoy to Argentina had also been accredited to Chile.

General Dutton had previously been Chief of Staff (Operations), the number two position in the South African Defence Force. He had also been an ideologue for what became known as the Total Strategy.[17] Within South Africa, his appointment to Santiago was regarded as something of a sideways promotion, to eliminate him from any further rise to power at GHQ — apparently a common way of dealing with ambitious Anglophones. Outside South Africa, the appointment drew attention to the close military links between the two states.

According to the International Institute for Strategic Studies, South Africa had sold Chile 12 Cactus surface-to-air missiles, equivalent to the French Crotale system produced locally under licence.[18] Close naval links were manifested in the visits of the four-masted barquentine *Esmeralda*, normally used as a training ship. In 1973, immediately after the coup, this vessel had been used for the internment and alleged torture of sailors loyal to the Popular Unity government. In 1981 its visit coincided with the twentieth anniversary of the Republic. Chilean sailors and midshipmen goose-stepped through the streets of Durban in the official military parade, and visitors to the ship included Mrs Botha who 'was visibly moved' when the crew sang 'Die Stem' in Afrikaans.[19]

Given this context, the South African fishing companies found a warm welcome in Chile.

Ovenstones' return in 1979 prompted other companies to consider investments in Chile. A deal was struck between Fedfood (the parent company of Marine Products) and another fishing group Kaap-Kunene, whereby R6-million would be committed to a joint venture with a Chilean fishing company, Empresa Pesquera Tarapaca. Investments were made in a cannery at Iquique, Pesquera del Norte, and a fish meal concern, Pesquera Caldera, at Caldera itself, which received dismantled reduction plant equipment from the General Development Corporation at Luderitz. Trawlers were also sent from Namibia to supplement the fleet at Caldera. However this investment has run into trouble owing to the financial difficulties of the Chilean partner and the general conditions of recession in Chile. Although the canning plant has begun to operate, the fish meal project at Caldera had to be delayed. About R1-million had to be set aside in 1982 to cover anticipated losses.[20]

The same Chilean partner, Humberto Camélio, also struck up a deal with a consortium known as United Fishing Enterprises. This is made up of three shareholders, Swafil, Seaswa (Oceana group), and Sarubar (jointly run by Sarusas and Willem Barendsz). With the bankruptcy of Camélio, Seaswa and Willem Barendsz moved in to acquire the Chilean assets, such that the company, Pesquera Coquimbo, is now wholly South African-owned. Coquimbo is the site of a cannery and reduction (fish meal and oil processing) plant, shipped from Walvis Bay, and installed during 1980–1. The 1983 Oceana annual report stated that the company was not anticipating further operating losses but that R220 000 was being set aside to cover possible exchange losses on the outstanding foreign loan. This loan was contracted to assist with the purchase of the company's share of Camélio's assets.

The canned fish and fish meal is sold on the world market and much of it finds its way to South Africa, such that a new shipping line was initiated in March 1982 to cover the Peru-Chile-South Africa route. Peru provides the largest quantities, and the canned fish products are imported through the industry's sole marketing agency Federal Marine, jointly owned by the fishing companies themselves. Imports began in 1978 after domestic production had fallen below public demand. Federal Marine sent quality control personnel to Peru and Chile to upgrade production and packing to South African standards. In Peru this was later formalised when Federal Marine set up a company staffed by nationals of Peru; in Chile South Africans are still in supervisory roles.

The Peruvian fish canning industry at Chimbote was recently exposed in the world press for its scandalous working conditions by Dr Jenny Amery of the Catholic Institute for International Relations, who works on a health project in the shanty towns surrounding the town.[21]

The boom in the industry has drawn people to Chimbote's 30 canning plants at such a rate that the small port of 5 000 people in 1940 has grown to an urban slum of 300 000. The canneries employ mostly women workers (80%) who are paid less than men, are less aware of their rights, less organised and easier to exploit. Almost all are casual workers, have unstable shifts and compulsory overtime, earning around R2 a day (1 450 soles) regardless of the shift's duration. The factories do not comply with health standards and there is no protective clothing, so that hands are exposed to knife wounds and fish spines during gutting, as well as painful burning for those packing pilchards in hot chile sauce. Women have begun to organise themselves in a Union of Cannery Workers and are beginning to articulate demands for better paid and healthier work.[22]

The chain from sea to table is one which involves the labour of thousands of people, not simply in our own country, but increasingly from all over the world. A decision to relocate production in other countries has a devastating effect upon local fishing communities and processing workers. But this also applies to the workers in the fishing factories of Peru where minimum wages are inadequate and health and safety legislation is scantily enforced. The South African companies involved in buying cheap Peruvian tinned fish and fish meal for resale in South Africa and Europe do not have any impetus to ensure that these workers receive living wages or that elementary health and safety conditions are met during production. Conditions in Chimbote would be very familiar to low paid food industry workers in South Africa.

Conclusion

This analysis has concentrated on two major South African investments in Latin America, that of the Anglo American Corporation, mainly in Brazil, and that of the fishing industry, mainly in Chile. It has attempted to place these investments in their political and social contexts.

South Africa's entry into Latin America was largely motivated by state policy, creating the conditions for future commercial opportunity. Much of the policy was designed by and linked with former foreign minister Hilgard Müller. Since his departure from the portfolio, there has been a reduction in the emphasis on the importance of developing these relations. Yet there have also been real constraints operating on both sides.

For South Africa's part, the emphasis of official foreign policy formation has shifted, of necessity, to a preoccupation with the immediate southern African region. Organisationally, the Department of Foreign Affairs has introduced structural changes and has established an entire section to deal with the immediate region. Strategic issues have come to outweigh considerations of trade and foreign exchange balances. Latin America is still regarded, however, as a useful trading area, and a potential source for the procurement of armaments.

As for the Latin American countries, the attitude to South Africa varies considerably. In recent years, Mexico, Nicaragua, El Salvador, Colombia, and Venezuela have broken diplomatic or commercial relations with Pretoria. Argentina and Bolivia have both reverted to civilian rule and are likely to take a less favourable attitude towards the apartheid state. In particular, Argentina has taken a dim view of South African logistical support for the construction by Britain of a military airport at Port Stanley, and of South Africa's acceptance of the credentials of the torturers Chamorro and Astiz as military attachés for Argentina. In Brazil's case the evenhanded commercial relationship will continue despite some African objections, but on a cultural and diplomatic level, relations will continue to be scaled down. Much will depend on the shape of the presidential contest in 1985; if this takes the form of a direct election, the first civilian president since 1964 would be likely to adopt a firmer anti-apartheid posture than any of his military predecessors.

These constraints on the development of political relations seem not to affect the continued expansion of an economic presence for South African corporations which regard Latin America as a challenging new area for profit-taking.

Notes

1 Union of South Africa, *Report of the Commission of Enquiry into Policy Relating to the Protection of Industries*, UG 36/1958 (Government Printer, Pretoria, 1958).

2 Republic of South Africa, *Reports of the Commission of Inquiry into the Export Trade*, 2 volumes, RP 69/1972 (Government Printer, Pretoria, 1972), 166.

3 Rightist military regimes took power in Paraguay in 1954, Brazil in 1964, Chile and Uruguay in 1973, and Argentina in 1976. Prior to 1972 Argentina also laboured under a military dictatorship. During 1983 Argentina reverted to civilian rule.

4 On the history of Morro Velho, see Marshall Eakin, 'Nova Lima: life, labour and technology in an Anglo-Brazilian mining community, 1882–1934', (History PhD, University of California, Los Angeles, 1982); Douglas C. Libby, *O trabalho escravo na mina de Morro Velho*, (tese de mestrado, Universidade Federal de Minas Gerais, Belo Horizonte, 1979); and the excellent account of worker organisation researched under conditions of great danger: Yonne de Souza Grossi, *Mina de Morro Velho: a extração do homem, uma história de experiencia operária*, (Paz e Terra, Rio de Janeiro, 1981). The author wishes to thank Professora Grossi for kindly sharing many of her research experiences and contacts.

5 Guido Jacques Penido addressing the XXth Week of Mining and Metallurgy Studies, September 1968, quoted in Sérgio Danilo, 'A venda da mina de Morro Velho', *Opinião*, 11 April 1975, 9.

6 Republica Federativa do Brasil, Congresso, Camara dos Deputados, Commissão Parlamentar de Inquérito para investigar o comportamento e as influencias das impresas multinacionais e do capital estrangeiro no Brasil, Relatório e conclusões, *Diário do Congresso Nacional*, (Seção I – Suplemento), 1 July 1976; and Commissão Parlamentar de Inquérito destinada a evaluar a política mineral brasileira, *ibid*, 7 March 1978.

7 Juvenil Tibúrcio Felix, 'Ouro – um bem mineral que se confunde com a história do Brasil. Os 150 anos da Mineração Morro Velho: estágio atual e programa de expansão em curso', Lecture given to the National Meeting on Mining and Brazil 83, Instituto Brasileiro de Mineração, 17 May 1983 (mimeo).

8 *ibid*, 1 July 1976, 989–990.

9 Anglo American Corporation of South Africa Limited, 66th Annual Report 1983 (Johannesburg, 1983), 11–12.

10 Prof. Mauricio Tragtenberg, writing in *Notícias Populares*, São Paulo, 8 September 1982.

11 Interviews conducted in Nova Lima, 24 June 1983.

12 *Tecnologia e Defesa*, 3, São Paulo, May 1983, 15–17.

13 *Istoé*, 1 February 1984, 57.

14 See *Finance and Trade Review*, 5(2), Pretoria, June 1962.

15 Interview with fishing company accountant, Cape Town, 21.12.83.

16 David Fig, 'Chile gets the full treatment', Third World Review, *The Guardian*, London, 17.06.81.

17 Lieutenant-General Jack Dutton, 'The military aspects of national security', in Michael H.H. Louw (editor), *National security: a modern approach*, Papers presented at the Symposium on National Security, Pretoria, 31 March – 1 April 1977, Institute of Strategic Studies, University of Pretoria (Pretoria, 1978), 100–121.

18 See International Institute for Strategic Studies, *Military Balance, 1981–82*, IISS, (London, 1982), 94.

19 *Armed Forces*, Johannesburg, June 1981, 17–21.

20 *SA Shipping News & Fishing Industry Review*, 36(8), August 1982, 26–27.

21 See Third World Review, *The Guardian*, London, 25.01.83.

22 See Graciela Cosvalente Vidarte, *Desarrollo capitalista de la indústria conservera en Chimbote: sus repercusiones sociales* (Chimbote, 1982), and various other publications of the Instituto de Promoción de Educación Popular.

Section 4: Rural Areas and Bantustans

Introduction

Alan Mabin, Gerhard Maré, David Webster

In *South African Review One* there were significant silences on developments in the non-metropolitan areas of South Africa. It is, of course, hard to categorise those areas. Beyond the cities are the rural parts of South Africa, but those rural areas are divided between the bantustans, with over half of the population of the country, and the remaining 80% of the land. Nor are the bantustans purely rural: an increasing proportion of their residents commute to work on a daily basis in nearby towns and cities outside their boundaries like Durban, East London and Pretoria. In this issue of the *Review* we have chosen to include in one section eight papers on issues which affect the non-metropolitan areas of the country, both 'rural' and 'bantustan'.

There is an increasing awareness in South Africa of the 'reality of power' in the bantustans, as Streek puts it in the first paper in this section. Although they are not recognised as political entities by any government other than South Africa, the four bantustans which have been given legal 'sovereignty' by the South African state, and the other six, all exercise an enormous impact on the lives of their 'citizens and residents'. Streek's analysis demonstrates the political divisiveness of the existence of the bantustans as well as the necessity to confront their growing power.

One aspect of the divisions introduced through the bantustans which has hitherto received little attention is the growth of the commuter population, referred to above. De Clercq's paper addresses the question of the way in which these commuters reflect a shift in the utilisation of bantustan labour by South African employers. The paper focusses on the restructuring of education in the bantustans, which is intimately connected with this issue, and examines Bophuthatswana, in which a very high proportion of the population is involved in daily commuting to work across the bantustan boundary.

The extent of the divide and rule strategy represented by the bantustans has gained new attention over the past year, reflected in the first two papers in this section. Another topic relating to bantustans and to rural areas in general which has occupied much attention is drought. The widespread low rainfall in the past few seasons has affected almost the whole summer rain area of southern Africa — the whole subcontinent except the Western Cape. Food production has been very badly affected and many commercial farmers face huge losses, extending in some cases to the loss of their farms. Nevertheless, access to state assistance and private borrowing provides most white commercial farmers with protection against disaster in time of poor rains. Among workers on those farms, who have been unable to supplement incomes by growing food and who have been made redundant, the effects are more severe. In the villages, relocation camps and other rural areas of the bantustans, the drought has also proved crippling. But the drought is not the sole cause of catastrophic conditions in rural areas of South Africa. Its effects must be 'understood against the abject poverty of "normal" conditions' in those areas, as Muller and Bolus put it in their article below. That contribution is one of two case studies of the impact of the drought; it deals with the Transkei, while Freeman's paper examines conditions in two villages in rural Bophuthatswana. In both cases it is concluded that forced removals, overcrowding and unemployment have been the real causes of rural poverty, while drought has been an additional problem, the severity of which is related to the lack of alternative means of support for most rural South Africans.

The conditions of production in rural South Africa have not changed merely by neglect and decay, however. On the contrary, enormous capital investment in agriculture has been transforming the face of many areas of the country over the past few decades. Budlender and De Klerk both address this process of capitalisation in agriculture and its effects on the people who work in that sector. Budlender's contribution surveys the nature of technological change in a variety of areas, while De Klerk's paper is based on detailed research in one region — the western Transvaal maize belt. Together these articles convey a sense of the rapidity of technological change in recent years and its enormous impact on farm workers — including unemployment and a high death rate in accidents involving machinery (*Rapport*, 12.02.84).

Such capitalisation is not restricted to agriculture outside the bantustans. In the latter parts of South Africa, a complex combination of the central state, the bantustan governments and capital has given rise to 'agribusiness' engaged in a wide variety of different capital intensive agricultural projects. Keenan examines the nature of this development, while Roodt analyses one such project in Bophuthatswana.

The changes taking place in the rural areas of South Africa and in the bantustans are directly affecting the lives of a majority of people in the country. The articles in this section of the *Review* begin to address some of the ways in which rural and bantustan residents are being affected by these changes. A substantial amount of material on forced removals has appeared over the past year, including the report of the Surplus People Project, and we have chosen to exclude further consideration of that issue here. That is not to imply that the book on removals is closed: indeed, the connections between the factors leading to mechanisation on the commercial farms, the drought and the politics of bantustans as well as forced removals are little researched. It need scarcely be emphasised how vital further detailed contemporary research on the subjects touched upon in this section of the *Review* is.

Disunity through the Bantustans

Barry Streek

The strategy of divide and rule in South Africa has long been reflected in the creation of ten separate bantustans where African people are meant to exercise their political rights and most are forced to reside. Through the establishment of governments in these areas — now officially called 'national states' — some power was transferred to a group of conservative politicians with strong links to tribal and chieftainship structures. In every one of the bantustans this group, with strong support from the South African government, has entrenched itself with power, control and interests. It also has the backing of an entrepreneurial group, many of whom have done well out of the system, and of growing civil service bureaucracies.

The degree to which this divide-and-rule strategy has succeeded has been underlined by a number of recent incidents. It goes beyond the mere geographic separation of African people into ethnic groups. There has been competition between the various bantustans for land, resources and people; the exploitation of tribal and ethnic 'loyalties' has resulted in pressure and victimisation of outsiders; the undemocratic consolidation of power within a particular elite group has seen in every bantustan the suppression and restriction of opposition and dissent; and the bantustan governments have all taken steps against groups such as trade unions and other organisations who usually have their bases in the urban areas outside the bantustans.

This article looks at the divisive effect of the policies of separation as generated by the creation of these ten bantustan governments. It does not analyse the division caused by broader government policy, such as the citizenship laws and influx control measures, but rather how the power of the bantustans has served to divide and disorganise black people, particulary African people.

Bantustan power

Bantustan leaders are frequently dismissed as 'puppets' and the 'independence' of four of the ten bantustans is not recognised by any government other than the South African one. The undemocratic base of the bantustan governments, all rooted in the support of nominated and paid chiefs, and the rejection of 'independence' should not, however, obscure the reality of power in those areas. In legal terms, the four 'independent' bantustans have complete sovereignty, with their own police and defence forces to administer laws operative in those areas.

Two incidents in the Ciskei, which was granted its 'independence' in 1981, emphasised the reality of this power in 1983. In July, Lieutenant-General Charles Sebe, the head of state security in the bantustan, and his adviser, Major-General Tailefer Minnaar, were detained along with other senior members of the Ciskei Central Intelligence Services, allegedly on the grounds that they had been involved in planning a coup against President Lennox Sebe, the brother of Charles. Until his detention, General Sebe had wide-ranging power over much of what went on in the bantustan. In terms of the 1982 Ciskei National Security Act, he had the most extraordinary powers ever held by a policeman in South Africa without even the nominal control of a cabinet minister. He could ban organisations and publications; he could prohibit any song, slogan or statute; and he alone was responsible for compiling a consolidated list of members and office-bearers of banned organisations, of people convicted of certain offences and of people restricted by him.

Shortly after their detentions, Generals Sebe and Minnaar applied to the Ciskei Supreme Court for their release, using lawyers often hired by opponents of government policy. Despite allegations of bad faith and invalid law, the court found against them, ruling that Ciskei's detention laws − in fact drafted by the two generals − were valid.

Another widely publicised detention was that of Father Smangaliso Mkhatshwa, secretary of the Southern African Catholic Bishops Conference, who was detained at the end of October after he had spoken at a Fort Hare (Ciskei) commemorative service for the victims of the clashes on the Ongoye University campus in KwaZulu. He had been in the bantustan for about three hours before his detention there, eventually appearing in court three months later to face charges of 'terrorism'. Despite worldwide appeals and protests from Christian leaders, as well as pleas to the South African minister of foreign affairs, Father Mkhatshwa was not released. An urgent court application failed as well.

These two incidents show what hundreds of people involved in the Mdantsane bus boycott in 1983 experienced: the Ciskei government has the power to implement laws and detain people, even in the case of a family feud involving the bantustan's president and head of security.

All the 'independent' bantustans have this kind of power. The Transkei, for instance, reimposed a state of emergency with extensive powers not subject to any judicial control in July 1983, prolonging a situation which has been in force since the Pondoland revolt in 1960–1 except for a brief period after 'independence' in 1976. In Venda, the government agreed to pay R150 000 to the family of Isaac Muofhe who died in detention from severe bruising and internal bleeding while in the bantustan in November 1981. Although at the inquest the magistrate had held two security policemen responsible, they were acquitted of murder in the local supreme court.

In Bophuthatswana, the leader of the opposition Seoposengwe National Party was charged with publicly violating the dignity of President Lucas Mangope whose political dominance over the bantustan makes criticism impossible. In the Phokeng area of Bophuthatswana, an emergency was declared after Chief Lebone Molotlhegi refused to fly the bantustan's flag and he was accused by President Mangope of holding meetings where the chief 'despised and humiliated the Bophuthatswana government'.

In the non-independent 'self-governing' bantustans, the security laws are the same as those applied in the rest of South Africa, but in some cases, the control of the police within the bantustan has been transferred to the local government. Control of the police in KwaZulu, was, for instance, transferred in 1983 to the minister of police, Chief Gatsha Buthelezi, who is the bantustan's chief minister.

Besides the control of security, all the bantustan governments, whether 'independent' or not, have been granted substantial powers of resource allocation. Continuing reports have been published that a membership card of the ruling party in one or other bantustan is the quickest and safest way of acquiring housing, land, business rights, jobs, pensions and disability grants — and that known opponents of the various governments are often victimised and frustrated in acquiring these rights. Moreover, within tribally controlled areas, chiefs wield inordinate control usually requiring both allegiance and subservience as well as bribes. For example, in 1983 a University of Zululand survey, conducted by Paulus Zulu, found that 88% of respondents in certain tribal authority areas had to pay from R5 to R50 for a site of land, 35% stated they had to pay an annual fee of R2 or more before being allowed to plough their fields, and 40% said they had to pay some fee to the local induna along with an application for pension and disability grants (*Star*, 19.09.83). Little research into this aspect of bantustan government has been conducted before, but these findings confirmed reports about the effect on ordinary people of tribal rule in the bantustans.

These incidents show that for the people in the bantustans the local governments do wield substantial and important powers — and in the use and protection of those powers division is often the result.

Ethnic mobilisation

Central to the South African government's rationale for separate development has been the alleged need for ethnic and 'national' identification and homelands. Government spokespeople have argued that there is no homogeneous African population in South Africa, but rather different nations, each of which needs its own national base. The Xhosa and Zulu people could never live peacefully together in one state, it is frequently argued. The creation of two states for the Xhosa 'nation' and the existence of sizable minorities of a different 'national' group in all the bantustans contradicts government theories but the dominant groups have been quick to exploit ethnic identification in attempting to mobilise support for the local governments and leaders.

The Inkatha Cultural Movement, headed by Chief Buthelezi, which now claims membership of over 800 000, is an obvious example. Although it claims to be spearheading the liberation of South Africa, its power base is rooted in the KwaZulu bantustan and government, and its operations are founded on the Zulu 'nation'.

Other bantustan leaders have not developed such extensive ethnic organisation and mobilisation, but all have latched onto shrines and symbols, as well as the chieftainship structure, to bolster and reinforce their regimes.

The divisiveness of this ethnic mobilisation will be examined later, but its significance needs to be recognised. As Saul Dubow has argued elsewhere,[1] it is real. Progressives, he said, dismiss at their peril the emergence of ethnicity as 'false consciousness'.

> False it is in the sense that the real source of misery and oppression – the South African state – becomes obscured. But this false consciousness is not a mere ephemeral ideology which can be ignored. Its basis is distinctly material; rooted on the one hand in the class interests of the new African petty bourgeoisie, and on the other hand in the struggle for survival by the ordinary mass of exploited and oppressed people,

he concluded.

Moreover, it could well have long term implications. The deliberate fostering of ethnic power and ethnic divisions could make greater unity in the future more difficult. In other parts of Africa, ethnic consciousness and suspicions have fuelled division and hostility after independence. With the deliberate fostering of these feelings in South Africa, similar tensions may be easier to exploit in the future than if they had not formed a key part of the government's strategy of control.

Fighting for the spoils

The KwaNdebele minister of interior, Piet Ntuli, appeared in the Nebo Magistrate's Court in December 1983 on a charge of murdering a Lebowa M.P., Andries Mahlangu, nearly three years before. This fuelled persistent rumours in the Moutse area that the M.P. had been killed to reduce the opposition to the transfer of Moutse to KwaNdebele, which is the next bantustan scheduled to get 'independence'. Mahlangu, regarded in the area as a spokesperson for Ndebele-speaking people in Lebowa, had been a strong opponent of the move to transfer Moutse, which, it seems, will be incorporated into KwaNdebele. This is despite the strong opposition of the Lebowa government, which saw the South African government's move as a reward to KwaNdebele for agreeing to 'independence'. It had also been told that some 70 000 people would have to be resettled elsewhere in Lebowa.

In the Ciskei, the house of the foreign minister was shot at before Generals Sebe and Minnaar, and their alleged cohorts, were detained. President Sebe later said there had been a plan to kill him. At the time of writing, the outcome of the case against General Sebe was still to be resolved, but what was clear was that the two brothers and their supporters were engaged in a battle for power. No hint of any political or ideological differences was made: it was a fight for control of the Ciskei government.

In Durban, after violent clashes in Lamontville following the announcement of rent increases, the South African government announced

that it intended transferring the area to the control of the KwaZulu
government. No consultation with the people of Lamontville had taken
place and a meeting of a thousand residents rejected the move. Chief
Buthelezi said he had informed the South African government he did not
want 'rowdy elements' in Lamontville, who had murdered, maimed and
destroyed property, to be part of KwaZulu and that KwaZulu had nothing
to gain if Lamontville were incorporated into its jurisdiction.

In Gazankulu, the Sotho-speaking staff and patients at the Douglas
Smit Hospital at Shiluvane were summarily withdrawn by the Lebowa
government after the area was declared part of the Gazankulu bantustan
in 1981. Sotho-speaking patients, some of them on drips, were
transported to a hospital inside Lebowa 15 kilometres away.

What these incidents show is that there are indeed conflicts over the
spoils of separate development. These conflicts may be for more land or
people for a particular bantustan or for office (although apart from the
ousting of the then chief minister of the Ciskei, Chief Justice Mabandla,
in 1973, the bantustan leaders have succeeded, so far, in maintaining their
power). The people concerned are rarely consulted although they are
directly affected. Ethnic mobilisation is often resorted to in an attempt
to bolster a particular cause and tensions rise. The result is division.

Another form of this type of division is manifested by the tensions between different bantustans. When the Matanzima brothers suspected that
Buthelezi and Inkatha were fomenting dissent among Zulu-speaking people in the Transkei and QwaQwa's ruling Dikwakwentla Party was
agitating among Sotho-speaking people in the Transkei in 1980, they
were banned. Yet, three years later the bannings were quickly undone as
the leadership of these three bantustans joined the heads of the other non-
independent bantustans to form the South African Federal Union in opposition to the government's constitutional plans.

The conflict between the Ciskei and Transkei governments has existed
ever since Lennox Sebe, who named his party the Ciskei National Independence Party after Matanzima's Transkei National Independence
Party and who called for unity between the two bantustans until his election as chief minister in 1973, decided to go it alone and keep the two bantustans separate.

Many strongly worded statements have passed between the two governments over the years, but in 1983 the Transkei government cast itself in
the mould of supporting the people against the Sebe government: the
Transkei parliament condemned a move to transfer the University of Fort
Hare to the Ciskei and the Transkei minister of foreign affairs said some

Transkeians had been the victims of 'callous murders which had been going on in Mdantsane' during the attempt to smash the bus boycott there. Prime Minister George Matanzima said South Africa had a moral duty to intervene in Mdantsane. The Ciskei government, in turn, detained a Transkei 'consul' who went to the Mdantsane hospital to check up on people injured in the boycott and the papers of a Transkei citizen were torn up at a road block. It also snubbed the Transkei government by not inviting it to its annual independence celebrations.

Transkei's President Kaiser Matanzima has long dreamt of a Greater Xhosaland uniting the two bantustans, increasing his power base, and putting pressure on the white-owned corridor separating them. However, in 1976 thousands of residents of the Herschel and Glen Grey areas left for the grim Thornhill area in the Ciskei rather than submit themselves to his rule, giving an indication of what the people thought about his dreams.

Similar tensions have developed in the Northern Transvaal, as evidenced by the Douglas Smit Hospital incident, where a hotchpotch of borders between different pieces of Venda, Gazankulu and Lebowa have produced conflict, as they have further south between Lebowa, KwaNdebele and Bophuthatswana and in the Free State in the Thaba 'Nchu and Onverwacht areas.

All in the family

The alleged ethnic (or 'national' in government language) differences among black people and the need for each of those groups to have a 'national state' is still used as the theoretical basis of Nationalist policy. It is also used in just about every speech by party spokespeople about the relationships between black and white people. The translation of that belief into practice has meant the relocation of, according to the Surplus People Project, some 2,5-million people into their different ethnic compartments. It has led to some remarkable actions.

Thus, after a 'scientific' investigation by a government ethnologist — his findings were even published in the *South African Journal of Science* — the Riemvasmaak community near the Augrabies Falls in the Northern Cape was relocated in 1973–4 from what was regarded as a 'temporary native reserve', although they had lived there for 60 years and had intermarried. Those classified as 'Xhosa' were settled at the bleak Welcomewood camp near Mount Coke in the Ciskei; those classified as

'Damara' were relocated 1 300 km away to a place near Khorixas south of the Etosha Pan in Namibia; and those classified as 'coloured' were allowed to stay in the area. A settled community was forcibly prised apart.

In 1983, another settled community was faced with the same sort of choice: the people living in the Driefontein 'black spot' in the Transvaal were told that the Zulu-speaking people should go to KwaZulu, the Swazi-speaking people to KaNgwane and the Sotho-speaking people to QwaQwa. The experience of a 77-year-old grandmother, Rosta Milo, who was ousted from the Evangelical Lutheran Church's Hermansburg Mission farm at Luneberg near Piet Retief after a long dispute with the church authorities, was instructive: regarded as a 'Zulu' she was taken to a relocation area, Compensation, 400 km away in Natal, and left there without her family and without knowing any other person in the area.

The division caused by this process of ethnic separation is extensive enough, but it has been exacerbated in the bantustans where ethnic identity is exploited by the authorities. Three different incidents in Bophuthatswana illustrate this. The tensions in the Thaba 'Nchu area have been outlined before[2] but, basically, with the 'independence' of Bophuthatswana in 1978 the local police were accused of harassing 'illegal foreigners' (that is, non-Tswanas), with the result that the QwaQwa government complained that South Sotho people were being discriminated against in respect of work permits, residence rights and language of instruction in the schools. It, in turn, was accused of interfering in the internal affairs of Bophuthatswana. Eventually, two separate residential areas were created: Thaba 'Nchu under Bophuthatswana and Kromdraai, afterwards called Onverwacht, under South Africa. Onverwacht, where QwaQwa citizenship documents are required for housing, is scheduled for incorporation into QwaQwa. Ironically, because Sotho identity is not an indispensable credential for obtaining QwaQwa citizenship, there is a significant Xhosa-speaking minority in Onverwacht.

In the Winterveld area, similar practices have taken place. According to Laurine Platzky of the Surplus People Project, non-Tswanas have fled to KwaNdebele 'in their thousands. Non-Tswanas cannot get work permits, pensions or their children taught unless it is in Tswana. Their only legal alternative is to go to another bantustan and then it is claimed they come in their hundreds of thousands voluntarily "streaming back to their homelands".'[3]

In the Phokeng area tribal police under Chief Lebone Molotlhegi — who, as discussed earlier, has been accused of disloyalty to President

Mangope — were reported to have raided villages, 'hunting down non-Tswana people and those harbouring them'. Non-Tswanas, often wives visiting their Xhosa and Sotho husbands who work at the local mines, were loaded onto a bus and taken to the tribal court. Fines were said to be R30 per person and R100 for local people who harboured them (*E Post*, 02.02.83).

Reports of this kind of pressure have appeared in other bantustans — Transkeians, for instance, in Mdantsane face similar problems from the Ciskei authorities. They show that ethnic mobilisation, perhaps ethnic 'nationalism', has contributed to the process of division.

'Democracy'

The methods adopted within the bantustans to restrict dissent and opposition are extensive, but it is not intended here to do more than to highlight trends.

In every bantustan, one of the key methods of control is through the chiefs, who, as has been pointed out, wield inordinate power over the people under their jurisdiction in tribal authorities. These nominated and government-paid chiefs form at least half of every bantustan parliament and dominate the various cabinets in them. The Matanzimas in the Transkei, Sebe in the Ciskei, Buthelezi in KwaZulu, Mphephu in Venda, and Mangope in Bophuthatswana are all chiefs, and all the ruling groups have formed alliances with the chiefs in the bantustans. This in itself is substantial restraint on democratic opposition to the system.

But other less subtle measures have been adopted. Detentions of opposition politicians have been regular in the Transkei, the Ciskei and Venda. It was in Venda where the opposition party 'won' two elections in a row, but through the chiefs and the detention of opposition M.P.s, Chief Mphephu made sure he became the first president after 'independence' in 1979. It is an offence in the 'independent' bantustans to insult the dignity of the presidents although they are all the central political figures in them. In the Transkei, it is an offence to say anything against the bantustan's 'independence'.

Through the chiefs and an armoury of security laws backed by police (who have earned a reputation for heavy-handedness), consent has been engineered in the 'independent' bantustans. The leaders in these areas all profess support for 'democracy' but the reality is something else.

In the non-'independent' bantustans, effective controls are also extensive although, perhaps, more restrained than in the other four. In KwaZulu, however, 1983 saw the open emergence of Inkatha as an instrument of force: in spite of the known opposition to Buthelezi on the Ongoye University campus, the chief minister was determined to assert his authority there, resulting in violent clashes between the students and Inkatha supporters. A commission of inquiry has been appointed into the incidents, in which five students died, but the message was clear: either accept the dominance of Inkatha or face the consequences. It was a message reinforced by the beating up of UDF supporters in Hammarsdale, the beating up outside the R14-million parliament of an M.P. who dared to defy Buthelezi, the demand that students with KwaZulu government bursaries sign a pledge of loyalty, and the decision by a group of church leaders to move their meeting outside the bantustan because they feared Inkatha 'discipline'.

Certainly such a display has not been matched in other non-'independent' bantustans but, to varying degrees of efficiency, methods and inducements to restrict opposition and promote subservience to the governments exist.

With this approach, power has been consolidated in each of the bantustans, causing huge divisions between those who have been prepared to work within the system of separate development and those totally opposed to any form of participation.

Patronage

Another method of encouraging 'loyalty' has been the allocation of jobs, houses and other rights to party supporters in the bantustans. In nearly every bantustan there have been allegations of favouritism, often accompanied by allegations of bribery and corruption.

One incident, early in 1984, at Imbali near Pietermaritzburg illustrated this. At a meeting, a community councillor, Abdool Awetta, was reported to have told residents that if they wanted houses for their married sons they should join Inkatha — and 35 of the 100 people present immediately did so. The chairperson of the Imbali Inkatha Constituency, Be Jele, publicly objected to Awetta's promises. 'Imbali falls under Pretoria and for Mr Awetta to entice stranded people with a housing bait is against the spirit of Inkatha. This will also jeopardise the name of the movement when people don't get the carrot they were promised, after parting with money for joining Inkatha' (*Echo, NW*, 20.01.84). Whether the people in Awetta's area were convinced by this rebuke is, however, doubtful.

There is in any event little doubt that it is believed in all the bantustans that 'loyalty' to the ruling group is an important way of access to limited resources.

Division

These methods of entrenching power and control in each of the bantustans have not only created division between them and between African people, where mere survival frequently ensures subservience, but they have also stimulated significant division between the bantustans as a whole and democratic movements outside these regions. These organisations, whether legal, such as the United Democratic Front and the National Forum, or illegal, such as the African National Congress and the Pan Africanist Congress, have all condemned the policies of separation and the people who work within government structures. This in itself has meant substantial and obvious division.

But the bantustan governments have often taken it further, forcing popular movements to curtail or severely restrict their activities. Thus, the SA Allied Workers Union was banned in the Ciskei in 1983 and blamed for the bus boycott in Mdantsane. Trade unions operating in Bophuthatswana have been told to register in the bantustan or cease operating. In 1980, the Transkei banned a number of organisations, including the ANC and PAC. Most bantustan leaders have publicly declared their opposition to the ANC. Buthelezi has accused the UDF of plans to bomb houses of Inkatha supporters.

The evidence is beyond dispute: the bantustan policy has succeeded in creating major division, beyond the mere geographic separation of African people into ten separately governed areas and beyond the definitions of 'citizenship'. Divide and rule is the name of the game — and the central government, so far, is winning it.

In December 1983, Buthelezi said the UDF 'seems to be another force of disunity' and seemed 'destined to destabilize the black political struggle in this country' (*CT*, 05.12.83). From his point of view, this interpretation is correct. Others — and history — may assess the causes of disunity somewhat differently.

Notes

1 Saul Dubow, 'Ethnicity and Class in Gazankulu', *Work In Progress*, 22, April 1982.
2 'Onverwacht: "ethnic" division and oppression', *Work In Progress*, 15, October 1980.
3 Laurine Platzky, paper at University of Cape Town Summer School, January 1984.

Some Recent Trends in Bophuthatswana: Commuters and Restructuring in Education

Francine de Clercq

A great deal has been written on the political and economic restructuring taking place in South Africa. A central plank of present state strategy is to divide the 'insiders' or those with residential rights in 'white' South Africa from the 'outsiders' or those originating from the bantustans and the rural areas. According to these analyses,[1] urban Africans are becoming the target for class and occupational differentiation while the bantustan population experiences tighter influx control and exclusion from the central economy. The bantustans, reservoirs of cheap migrant labour, are now seen as dumping grounds for the surplus population no longer needed in the central economy.

These analyses leave out a fast-developing section of the African population, namely those workers who live in the bantustans and commute daily to work in 'white' South Africa. How do these commuters fit into the reformulated apartheid policies and to what extent do they represent a shift in South Africa's utilisation of bantustan labour? This study of Bophuthatswana addresses itself to these questions.

Most analyses view the bantustan population in a homogeneous way, subject to the same undifferentiated control and repression by the central state. The bantustan population is, and for a long time, has been subject to class and social differentiation. Furthermore, restructuring is also taking place in certain areas of the bantustans leading to further divisions within the bantustan population.

From the early 1960s the central state has tried to undermine African unity and nationalism by fragmenting the African population into ten different ethnic groups. The bantustans also became growth poles for African class formation when such a process was unthinkable amongst the urban African population of 'white' South Africa. The limited but real economic and political development of the bantustans gave rise to a class of African traders, petty bureaucrats, administrators and professionals who, together with the traditional chiefs, developed a stake in the 'homeland policy'.

Urban population in the bantustans and the origin of commuters

The central state has been looking for ways to curb African urbanisation in 'white' South Africa and redirect it towards the bantustans. Sometimes, political boundaries were drawn to include municipal African townships within the bantustans (eg., KwaMashu which falls now under the jurisdiction of KwaZulu). New African townships were planned and developed in the bantustans either to house those workers employed in the border industries or to resettle African workers who used to live in the 'white' urban areas and still work in these 'white' industrial complexes. In short, influx control, forced removals and new housing policies created a large urban population in the bantustans. In 1960, there were 33 500 Africans living in the bantustan 'proclaimed' towns. In 1970 the number rose to 595 000 and reached 1,5-m by 1981.[2] To these figures one should add the urbanised Africans from the unproclaimed towns as well as the large number of 'illegals' who, in search of employment, have moved to the sprawling squatter camps at the outskirts of the African townships situated close to the 'white' metropolitan centres. This growing bantustan population put these urban Africans high on the political and economic agenda of South Africa. Today, this urban African population represents nearly 20% of the 7-m urbanised Africans.

The majority of the urbanised labour-force commutes to the 'white' suburban industrial parks located in the border areas or in areas close to the 'white' metropolitan centres. By 1981, the number of commuters was 739 000 (compared to 1,3-m migrants) or 12% of the 6-m economically active African population.[3] These figures do not include all the 'illegal' commuters who manage, by virtue of their proximity to industrial complexes, to bypass the influx control machinery and find work in 'white' South Africa. Of the total number of commuters in 1981, 384 200 (or 55%) came from KwaZulu, 54% of whom were employed in the Durban-Pinetown-Pietermaritzburg area; the second largest proportion came from Bophuthatswana (162 200), 60% of whom were employed in the Pretoria-Rosslyn area.

To what extent does the commuter labour-force in the urbanised bantustan areas adjacent to the 'white' industrial complexes differ from the permanent urban Africans of the 'white' areas of South Africa? According to Greenberg and Giliomee,[4] Administration Boards treat the residents of some bantustan townships (like Umlazi near Durban or any other townships located near the 'white' metropolitan centres) as 'administration section 10s', i.e. local workers with preferred access to housing and employment. These workers from commuter areas are given access to job opportunities before workers from more remote areas in the bantustans. Although part of the 'white' industrial set up, these commuters tend to have no residential rights nor any legal claim to political rights in 'white' South Africa. They also fall under a tighter section of the influx control machinery at a time when the permanent urban African population is being given more intra-urban freedom of movement and employment.

Following the Riekert recommendations, the urban Africans do not have to register as work seekers before looking for a job, nor do they have to report to the labour bureaux in between jobs, whereas the commuters are not allowed to enter unless they get a written contract of employment, endorsed by the Administration Board. However, commuters do sometimes manage to bypass the labour bureau system and find work themselves in 'white' South Africa.

In practice, employers adopt similar criteria of recruitment towards the commuters and the permanent African workers. Africans get hired, at least in the 'white' metropolitan centres on the grounds of their skill, productivity and overall quality. A survey done in the Pretoria area in 1981[5] reveals that employers do not see any significant difference between their commuter and permanent African workers in terms of occupation, wage, skill, level of education and training and the use of, and time spent on, transport. However, commuters encounter more severe problems in other areas such as how to get their pensions, UIF and other benefits back from the bantustan administrations which are known to be inefficient.

Commuters do not distinguish themselves too sharply from the permanent Africans. They are subjected to the same kind of pressures at work and the fact that the central state has delegated some of its administrative and repressive powers to the bantustans does not make a big difference to their socio-economic situation. In some cases like the Ciskei, their daily situation is worse because of continuous harassment and policing. In other cases it gives them some advantages such as access to better housing, plots and security of leasehold tenure, all practicalities which affect the commuters' living conditions (workers of the Pretoria area are given access to better housing in Mabopane in Bophuthatswana than in the municipal townships around Pretoria). For the workers of KwaMashu, the change in their legal political status has had, until now, very little effect. On the whole, commuters consider themselves South African workers, working in, and contributing to the wealth of, South Africa. In the future though, things could change and become tougher for the commuters, precisely because their rights to work in 'white' South Africa are sanctioned administratively, rather than legally. This makes them more vulnerable to the changing labour needs of the central economy.

Commuters and the regional development strategy

In the previous *Review*, Zille[6] shows how the revamped version of the industrial decentralisation policy is based on economic co-operation between the central state and the bantustans. This strategy aims to promote decentralisation within eight defined regions which happen to cut across political borders. Regional, more than 'homeland', development is sought. Eleven deconcentration points (closely integrated with the metropolitan centres) and 49 developments (both in the 'homeland' and 'white' areas) were chosen to become alternative growth points to counterbalance the concentration of economic activity in the four main metropolitan centres.

The government think-tank, according to Zille, is split over the viability of the new regional development strategy of the 1980s. One strand warns against decentralisation to far remote points on the ground that it is not viable. What is more important according to this thinking is deconcentration points, integrated with the existing metropolitan centres (and the PWV complex in particular). In contrast, the other group adopts a more rigid interpretation of separate development and calls on the government to promote decentralisation and development points deep in the bantustan boundaries so as to prevent further African migration to the 'white' areas of South Africa.

In the past, industrial decentralisation policies have failed to generate development in the bantustans. Most firms are very reluctant to move to remote areas with bad physical and social infrastructure irrespective of the generous incentives and subsidies attached to the deal. Most of the firms who did decentralise were 'black' labour intensive and tended to rely on a mass of undifferentiated cheap unskilled labour. These kinds of firms do not generate substantial development nor do they attract many other firms into the area; instead they create small pockets of industrial activity in relatively underdeveloped regions of South Africa.

Some capital-intensive firms did decentralise but mostly to areas close to the metropolitan centres. A good example is the Rosslyn area north of Pretoria which today has become one of the main sites of the motor industry in South Africa. Because of the nature of their business, these firms depended on a sophisticated infrastructure and could therefore not move to remote points. These firms tend to constitute a healthier core for development than the ones which moved to more remote points in the bantustans. Most of these capital-intensive firms 'import' their skilled labour-force and the question arises to what extent some bantustans could supply a local skilled labour-force to these points near their borders. In other words, could the bantustans supply these decentralised points with the 'other leg' of the regional development strategy, namely the quality and differentiated labour required by big firms?

Let us now concentrate on a case study of Bophuthatswana to examine how the restructuring in certain areas is geared towards the labour requirements of the regional development strategy. Could the commuters become a target of the restructuring in education in Bophuthatswana and if so, is it correct to imply that a new form of labour dependency is developing between the central state and this bantustan?

Bophuthatswana is not necessarily a typical example of what is happening in the bantustans. Each bantustan exhibits its own specific political, social and economic configuration which makes it unique in its relationship to the central state. The purpose of this case study is to encourage debate and stimulate further research in these often neglected areas so as to get a fuller picture of the restructuring process at the level of education, training and labour utilisation in the whole of South Africa.

276 _Rural Areas and Bantustans_

A case study of education in Bophuthatswana

With its formal independence received from South Africa in 1977, Bophuthatswana inherited a system of education which had suffered from the cumulative effects of 25 years of Bantu Education, i.e., poor buildings and equipment, overcrowded classes, underqualified teachers and poor academic standards. Independence, however fraught politically, unleashed genuine forces committed to break from the stranglehold of Bantu Education and introduce reforms to improve the quantity and quality of education. Very soon after independence, the Bophuthatswana authorities commissioned a report, Education for Popagano, to outline educational priorities. Two main factors were emphasised: on the one hand the people in Bophuthatswana demanded a better education which they saw as a symbol of social status and mobility; and on the other hand, given the shortage of a qualified manpower needed to assist in the development of the area, the education system had to be geared to produce the vitally needed manpower.

Bophuthatswana is far from being a self sufficient area especially in the field of employment. Although the statistics differ widely, it seems that around 70% of the Bophuthatswana labour-force is employed in 'white' South Africa, the proportion of migrants being slightly higher than the commuters.[7]

This labour dependency means that any restructuring in education is bound to be influenced by the labour needs of South Africa. The Manpower Department in Bophuthatswana, set up in 1983 to identify the manpower and training needs of the region, acknowledges Bophuthatswana's labour dependency on South Africa as an inevitable long term phenomenon. However, determined to make the best out of this state of affairs and in particular out of Bophuthatswana's close proximity to the PWV industrial complex, the Manpower Department concentrated on training and upgrading the commuters of the 'exported' labour-force. On the basis of a BENSO survey on manpower planning,[8] the authorities in Bophuthatswana identified the manpower and training priorities of employers both of the border industries and of the public and private sector in Bophuthatswana. The plan was to identify the shortages and come up with the labour quality and quantity required by the above-mentioned employers, thereby ignoring the migrants and all the workers living in the subsistence sector.

Bophuthatswana is in a favourable position to put that intention into practice. Money is needed to revamp a very underfinanced education and training system. Bophuthatswana's financial position is relatively healthy with its incoming mining revenues and the strong financial backing it receives from South Africa who is determined to support this 'homeland' which appears to be the most viable. At another level, South Africa is interested to use Bophuthatswana as a laboratory for testing ways in which to modernise its own system of education and training and do away with the more dysfunctional aspects of apartheid.

At the moment South Africa is in the process of negotiating a restructuring in black education and training. The 1981 De Lange Report, set up to investigate the educational provisions in South Africa, called for a streamlining of apartheid education. It recommended a more differentiated system of career-oriented education to answer the changing labour needs of the economy (see Chisholm and Christie in *Review One*). It also proposed that black education be brought into the South African mainstream to provide a solid foundation for equal educational provisions and standards for all races and ethnic groups. Accepting the principles of the De Lange Report, the Government White Paper (published in November 1983) rejects the idea of a single ministry of education and calls instead for different government departments to be responsible for white, coloured, Indian and African education in accordance with the recent constitutional terms. The main opposition to a common system for all groups came from the politically significant class of white teachers, petty bureaucrats and craft unionists. This section of the white petty bourgeoisie will always be reluctant to consent to any change which uplifts a section of the African population in South Africa. But, de facto, it looks as though the government will gradually implement the various changes as formulated in the De Lange proposals.

In contrast, Bophuthatswana has more political freedom to introduce educational reforms. With its non-racial constitution and policies, Bophuthatswana is unlikely to meet the same kind of opposition. For a start, it does not have to deal directly with the lower and middle level of the 'verkrampte' bureaucracy of the Department of Education and Training and the Department of Co-operation and Development. Secondly, given the bantustan ideology of self-determination, African advancement in these areas is seen as legitimate and necessary. However, a white petty bourgeoisie exists in Bophuthatswana and holds a strategic position in education and training. They should not be totally disregarded because they may become instrumental in carrying the strategy through.

The Bophuthatswanan authorities have the commitment, money and relative freedom to experiment with their system of education and training and Bophuthatswana is in a favourable position to embark on a new educational strategy. Whether it will be successful and in what areas in particular is difficult to predict. But the implementation of such a strategy is likely to encounter serious obstacles to do, inter alia, with the bureaucracy, the lack of solid organisational structure in education and training, the lack of clear and detailed guidelines and, above all, the fact that the people at whom the strategy is targetted haven't been consulted sufficiently.

Educational changes in the context of South Africa's restructuring

The regional development strategy selects development points in areas in and around Bophuthatswana which are partly developed while it ignores the more underdeveloped areas. The development points most likely to attract capital are situated in the eastern regions of Bophuthatswana in areas close to 'white' industrial complexes, namely Mogwase near Rustenburg, GaRankuwa and Babelegi in the Pretoria-Rosslyn area (Mafikeng is also likely to develop, but mainly as an administrative growth point). The unequal distribution of educational provisions in Bophuthatswana tends to reflect the regional and local bias of its economic development. Furthermore, the changes introduced since independence, far from redressing these inequalities, have reinforced them. A better quality and quantity of educational provisions tend to develop in the areas marked for development. For instance, let us compare the changes in two regions: the more urban eastern region of Odi-Moretele where 40% of Bophuthatswana's de facto population lives and the rural region of Ganyesa-Thlaping Thlaro, east of Vryburg where 9% of the population ekes out a living.

In the first region in 1977 there were 11 high schools with 30% of the high school population. By 1982 there were 30 high schools with 46% of the total pupil population. In contrast, in the second region, in 1977 there were three high schools with 5% of the high school population and in 1982 the same number of high schools had 3% of the total high school population. Plans to build more schools in the first region confirm the intention of the Bophuthatswanan authorities to concentrate on the areas marked for development. However, this region of Odi-Moretele is politically sensitive given large numbers of 'illegal' squatters and non-Tswana citizens. This might well be another reason explaining the Bophuthatswanan authorities' concern with the area.

The unemployment of school leavers is a large scale phenomenon in Bophuthatswana and acquires dangerous political dimensions particularly in the densely populated eastern region of Bophuthatswana. The Popagano Report, like the De Lange Report, attributes the school leaver unemployment problem to the inadequate content of schooling which, it is argued, is too academic and unrelated to the labour requirements of the economy. Popagano stresses the need for more technical and vocational schools and the importance to enhance the value of technical education and technical work. Since then, plans have been made to build more technical schools (at the moment there is only one technical high school near Rustenburg); to replace some academic subjects at middle school level with technical subjects and to use community education to build a more positive image of technical work. A technikon is also planned at the Mmabatho University to train technically better qualified manpower. Technical education which fell under the Education Department was recently brought under the Manpower Department in an attempt to reorganise technical education and gear it more closely to the labour needs of the economy.

The reorganisation of technical education in Bophuthatswana is influenced by the needs of the industries in and around Bophuthatswana and in particular by the PWV industrial complex. Very little is done to promote, as in the Transkei, self employment through technical education and traditional craftsmanship. The thrust of technical and vocational education reflects the aspirations of those who want to develop Bophuthatswana by drawing it into the orbit of its most powerful industrial neighbour.

Training and changing labour requirements

Another area earmarked for changes is the field of non-formal or on-the-job training. These industrial training programmes which are directed at all employees — whether managers, supervisors, artisans or operators — are designed to impart employees with supplementary skills needed on the job.

Over the last decade employers have complained of skills shortage and the need to upgrade the skills of black workers. Their argument, which is increasingly endorsed by government agencies, is that whites are no longer able to provide the whole economy with a large enough supply of skilled labour. Blaming the inferior Bantu Education system and the lack of technical training for blacks, the private sector took the initiative in educational and training provisions for blacks. In terms of skill training, employers are trying to phase out the rather expensive, out-of-date apprenticeship system which produces high wage workers with a strong control over their work. Instead, employers want a more flexible and cheaper system which will be in line with their changing labour requirements. The Building Industry Employers Association, for example, has designed a new and cheaper system of skill training which, at this stage, will supplement the traditional apprenticeship system which, it is argued, doesn't produce enough skilled builders. One can question the extent of skills shortage in the building industry but the interesting point is that the employers want to introduce a more flexible and cheaper form of skill training based on a combination of formal and non-formal training. These changes in skill training, which are bound to be resisted by the white unions and the white petty bureaucrats in the Department of Manpower, are planned to be introduced at the same time as employers are bringing African workers into more skilled jobs.

In Bophuthatswana, skill training is being reorganised as is the whole non-formal industrial training system. The Manpower Department is threatening to scrap the apprenticeship system in Bophuthatswana before unions get formally registered under the pending labour legislation. A new form of modular skill training is being designed which will train workers in bits of the trade as well as the full trade depending on the labour needs of the employers. This modular approach to skill training allows for more flexibility. Questioned on the possibility of such a scheme to dilute skilled jobs, an official of the Manpower Department said

> It must be understood that these categories of workers (who do not complete the full module set- FdC) will not displace artisans but supplement them instead, allowing the artisans to tend to more productive and sophisticated tasks while properly trained assistants can carry out the elementary routine tasks.[9]

What is not said, though, is that employers reorganise their labour process in an attempt to cheapen their labour and undercut the artisan unions by deskilling their jobs and introducing black workers at lower wage rates.

These newly designed training programmes, which will be housed in the renamed Manpower Development Centres (old trade colleges) will mainly cover the technical trades but also a few commercial, catering and clerical trades. Unlike in South Africa, the Bophuthatswanan government wants to be in charge of all forms of non-formal training to monitor and regulate in its infancy. The authorities hope to convince employers to release their workers in these new schemes rather than initiating their own in-house training schemes. The financial arrangements for these training courses are not finalised yet but it looks as if the Manpower Department will offer generous incentives in the form of cash payments to employers operating both in Bophuthatswana and outside (although priority is to be given to Tswana workers).

Whether this new form of modular skill training will work is difficult to assess at this stage (the first Manpower Development Centre was opened in March) but will mainly depend on the relationship between the Bophuthatswanan authorities and the employers. Such a scheme is also being planned for 'white' South Africa and will ultimately be tested by its efficiency in producing the appropriate skilled manpower required by the employers.

Finally, when talking about skill hierarchy and skill training, it is important to define these concepts. Too often skill is used to refer to technical knowledge and competencies and skill training to the teaching of technical skills which will improve the ability of workers to perform more sophisticated tasks. However, skill is a socially-constructed concept whose full meaning can only be gauged in its context. In the same way, skill training is not only the teaching of neutral skills but also the teaching of a certain form of work discipline, work ethic and attitudes. Skills, as Chisholm argues, have an ideological and social dimension:

> the skills that are demanded . . . are concerned as much with labour discipline and with the inculcation of the values of free enterprise as with increasing technical competencies . . . the purpose is as much to intensify ideological control over workers and wed them more firmly to capitalist principles as it is to provide for South Africa's manpower requirements.[10]

The Manpower Department adopts a very technicist approach to training. According to them, these courses are about technical knowledge with the view to improve workers' productivity 'for their own good and the good of the employers'. In short, they are concealing the social dimension of these training programmes to depoliticise the arena of training and technical education.

Efforts are also put into improving the quantity and quality of the teaching staff which will carry through this new education and training strategy. The University of Bophuthatswana is taking on not only the training of a more qualified teaching force but is also in charge of the re-organisation and co-ordination of all teacher training colleges. Technical teachers and trade instructors are in great demand throughout South Africa and will constitute a major brake on the re-organisation of technical and industrial training.

Conclusion

Although some of the changes planned for Bophuthatswana are unique, most of them run parallel to similar plans formulated in respect of 'white' South Africa. In comparison, the latter has a great capacity to set this process in motion on a large scale but will also encounter greater obstacles in the implementation of some changes and reforms. The changes intended in Bophuthatswana are geared towards its powerful industrial neighbour. The Bophuthatswanan authorities appear keen to respond in their own real but limited way to the changing nature of the central economy. At this stage their commitment can only be taken at face value, but the changes envisaged will only apply to a tiny minority of the population of Bophuthatswana. The restructuring process is by definition aimed only at a section of the bantustan population and will most probably lead, if successful, to the furthering of divisions within its population.

Notes

1 See *South African Review One* (SARS and Ravan Press, Johannesburg, 1983); and *'Homeland' Tragedy: function and farce*, DSG/SARS Information Publication 6, August 1982.
2 In *Statistical Survey of Black Development* (Benso, Pretoria, 1979 and 1982).
3 *Statistical Survey of Black Development*, parts 1 and 2.
4 S. Greenberg and H. Giliomee, 'Labour Bureaucracies and the African Reserves', *South African Labour Bulletin*, 8(4), February 1983.
5 C.C. Mastoroudes, 'The Transfrontier Commuting System in South Africa: a comparative review', *Development Studies of Southern Africa*, 5(4), July 1983.
6 H. Zille, 'Restructuring the Industrial Decentralisation Strategy', *South African Review One*, (SARS and Ravan Press, Johannesburg, 1983).
7 According to the Bophuthatswana Statistics, 1980, the total labour-force was 406 000, with 140 000 employed internally (35%); 162 000 migrants (40%); and 103 000 commuters (25%). The Benso figures for 1980 were respectively 469 000 with 110 000 employed internally (35%); 197 000 migrants (40%); and 103 000 commuters.
8 D. de Klerk and C.C. Mastoroudes, *Manpower Planning for Bophuthatswana* (Benso, Pretoria, March 1982).

9 De Klerk and Mastoroudes, *Manpower Planning for Bophuthatswana*, quoted 21.
0 L. Chisholm, 'Redefining Skills: black education in South Africa in the 1980s', *Comparative Education*, 19(3), 1983, 360.

Drought and Agricultural Decline in Rural Bophuthatswana

Claire Freeman

The 1982/83 drought has been given continual and prominent coverage in the media during the last year. This coverage has perpetuated the myth of drought as the most significant and in many cases the sole cause of the catastrophic conditions prevailing in rural African societies in South Africa. The following article offers some suggestions on identifying the broader processes underlying and leading to the present rural crisis in which drought, rather than being seen as the sole variable, can more realistically be seen as an added component compounding and intensifying the problems existing and inherent in the socio-political situation within which rural black communities in South Africa are located.

Though the severe physical conditions of the prevailing drought cannot be denied, at least in some areas of the country, it can be argued that drought is just one of a series of factors contributing to the present agricultural and economic recession facing African villagers. In an effort to identify the factors leading to the prevailing agricultural decline and culminating in the present 'drought' crisis, an investigation is being undertaken to assess, firstly, the impact of drought, and secondly, the processes contributing to the present state of impoverishment existing in two 'traditional' villages in the Molopo and Ditsobotla districts of Bophuthatswana, located close to the old Cape/Botswana/Transvaal border area near the town of Mafikeng.

Investigation of two villages

The two villages studied are both long-established Tswana settlements (dating back to the period of early Tswana occupancy of the highveld). This facilitates the identification of the long term factors leading to the present deterioration of these communities' agricultural bases. The two communities place heavy dependence on agriculture: 103 out of 134 villagers interviewed were either directly or indirectly dependent on agricultural and livestock farming. Neither village has been involved in any recent betterment or resettlement scheme which could be held accountable for the changes occurring in these villages. The selected communities are therefore representative of the problems of South Africa's less prominent rural areas, communities which once exhibited a vibrant agricultural economy. According to informants:

> In the past people here had everything, they could plough and cultivate crops, had enough meat and milk so people were not totally dependent on money.
>
> Years ago this area used to be beautiful and productive. The river would now be flooding. We were not used to buying mealie meal from the shops. We did not buy milk as we had cattle to milk. Our children were healthy and very happy. The land was green everywhere. We used to drink good brew because there was sorghum our wives could use.

Agricultural decline

In 1976 the communities experienced the start of a period of agricultural decline, a renewed decline similar to that identified by Simkins as occurring in the reserves from 1955 onwards. The villagers perceive the drought and the decline to have begun around the same time, therefore seeing drought in its wider context as agricultural failure rather than just as a statistically low rainfall aggregate.

Drought
Several reasons can be put forward to account for this apparent recession in agriculture, one of which is the present drought. The seasons of 1978/79, 1981/82 and 1982/83 have been characterised by having relatively low rainfalls. Though the rainfall levels did not fall below 70% of the mean annual rainfall (the cut off point for severe drought is perhaps 60% of mean annual rainfall), they are of heightened significance occurring in a marginal region. The 1982/83 rainfall levels were not exceptionally low in terms of aggregate rainfall levels but were abnormal in terms of rainfall distribution through the season. Slightly below average rainfalls were received in December and February (approximately 70% of the

mean monthly rainfall). In January, however, all but two rainfall stations
in the general area of the villages studied received below average rainfalls
(approximately 50% of the mean monthly rainfall). These rainfall figures
do not constitute any significantly abnormal deviation from the normal
rainfall regime of the area, certainly nowhere near the claimed once-in-
two-hundred-year drought. In fact, the 1979/80 and 1980/81 seasons were
more anomalous in terms of their exceptionally high rainfall levels (about
820 and 760 millimetres respectively). It is impossible to account for the
present crisis by reference to rainfall levels alone; other factors have to
be taken into account.

Change in the economy

The communities have experienced an increasing need to participate in
the wage economy, through factors such as tax, transport costs (particularly important since the Bophuthatswana government undertook the
shooting of untethered donkeys during 1983), school fees, church collec-
tions, medical fees, and more specifically at present, money for milk and
other staple foods. Production of crops and livestock at a subsistence
level is no longer sufficient. An excess for sale purposes is essential, but
such an excess is beyond the carrying capacity of the limited land available and beyond the means of the majority of the villagers.

Employment and migrant labour

Eighty-five percent of the villagers interviewed regarded employment as
the main problem confronting them. Other problems mentioned (in order
of significance) were schools, transport, migration of strangers into the
area, lack of land and lack of clinics. One of the main local employment
opportunities, casual labour on white farms, has declined substantially
in recent years through the introduction of mechanised farming (see De
Klerk's article on farm mechanisation in the Western Transvaal below).

The decline in agricultural opportunities within the village coupled
with the lack of local employment has led to a massive increase in the
entry of members of the local work-force into the migrant labour market
(Table 1), such that 'presently people are going out seeking jobs, lands
aren't ploughed. The place is deserted by young people.' This situation
perpetuates the vicious cycle of agricultural decline by removing the most
vital sector of the labour-force. Migrant labour and prayer were seen as
the only survival strategies open to the villagers in the face of the present
crisis. The rural push has not only affected the mature labour force, but

involved a large percentage of the youth: 13% of families interviewed had sent young children outside the village to seek work.

Table 1. EMPLOYMENT OF THE HOUSEHOLD HEAD (PERCENT)

	Molopo village	Ditsobotla village
Migrant labourer	16	30
Farmers	26	19
Pensioners	26	20
Employed locally	18	15
Not employed	12	16

Village problems

The conditions prevailing in the two villages are those of extreme deprivation and impoverishment. No family succeeded in producing sufficient maize to meet their needs. Most livestock-owning households experienced loss of stock, notably of cattle and donkeys. As occurred during the 1978/79 drought in Botswana, the hardest hit were those comprising the 'rural service sector', the most vulnerable of the rural community. These include those having no access to rural production, the stockless, the permanently unemployed, female headed households (many of whom receive no remittances) and numerous old people either not eligible for or not receiving a pension. With the large number of farmers both full and part time who have reaped no harvest this year, and in many cases for several years (in some cases since 1976), there is now a significant percentage of the community with no effective income and/or food supply.

The problems facing villagers such as lack of work, inadequate land availability, poor harvests, ill health, disease and malnutrition are not peculiar to drought years but have long existed within the communities and have been exaggerated by lower water availability. The drought and the steadily deteriorating socio-economic circumstances of the area are indivisibly linked, with drought intensifying the difficulties already being faced by these 'marginal' societies.

In an attempt to overcome the present impasse, a variety of measures were taken by individual villagers, the community and the Bophuthatswana government. The most significant measures adopted by individuals were migrant labour, sale of cattle, applications for government aid (including pensions) and sending children out to seek work. Community measures included digging boreholes and prayer; both were regarded as insignificant by most residents in alleviating drought damage. Government drought relief programmes were of little consequence as neither village formed a focal point for any drought relief scheme. Small amounts of food and milk were made available at the clinics for the extremely needy. Similarly small amounts of cattle fodder and salt were available to those with large herds, along with transport to collect the feed from the government distribution centres. The most notable omission by all concerned with the drought (understandable in the villages in terms of the day-to-day struggle for survival) was any attempt to identify the broader processes such as farm mechanisation, the economic recession, entrenched migrant labour, inadequate land and processes going beyond one year's rainfall deficits.

Outlook and future prospects

The necessity to go beyond the rainfall constrained approach to the drought is evidenced when one looks at future prospects for villagers such as those interviewed in this study. Even if good rains were to fall in the coming year few villagers see any real prospects for the revival of agricultural productivity and for the progress of the economy in general. The people are trapped into the migrant labour cycle. Casual farm labour, though exploitative, was previously a central source of income; its reduction from previously high employment levels has removed this prop. The area's population continues to grow to levels beyond the available agricultural support, in part as a product of in-migration, some of which is a by-product of forced population removals elsewhere. Overgrazing and overcropping have depleted the land's reserves, the land is denuded and suffering from severe soil erosion.

On an individual level the seed normally stored for planting in the next season has already been utilised, the able-bodied adults needed to plant and harvest are invariably absent, and the donkeys necessary for ploughing and transport have been shot. The people are also losing hope and are unwilling to embark on what have previously proved to be useless projects; for example, seeking employment when there is often none to be had. Many families will not plant next year even if it does rain as previous harvests have a record of failure — and the lack of labour and seed will in many cases prevent planting.

Finally, the area offers no future to the youth, which is felt most bitterly by those with education. Prospects in general are at best bleak, with the only possibilities being the dubious opportunities offered by agricultural schemes such as Mooifontein (see Roodt's article below) and the migrant labour job market.

> It is difficult to feed the children. There are no jobs where one could work to buy food. In the past food from the previous year could be used during the drought. It is also difficult to visit friends in the nearby villages to ask for help as the only means of transport away from the road was the donkey, these are now killed.

> I would rather move to urban areas and seek a permanent job and so would leave the children at home and seek a job outside.

> Life has stopped; the place is dry, no food, the death of livestock in large numbers. People suffer from diseases. We pay much money for food.

Conclusion

From this initial investigation several points have emerged. The physical climatological conditions cannot on their own account for the severity of conditions existing in the two Tswana villages studied. The roots of the present crisis have to be found in the increasingly stringent and strangling influence of the wider South African socio-economic and political system within which the rural African communities are situated. The present drought and agricultural crisis has acted as yet another catalyst in furthering the transformation of Tswana society, increasing its dependence on migrant labour, and decreasing the ability of the agricultural base to support even a small segment of the community on the land.

The outlook for the future is poor, with few prospects for an improvement in the job situation and little chance of any significant agricultural revival.

> Life today is unbearable, there is no access to the basic need of the people. . . . The life of the villagers has changed. They want to go back to their previous life where they all lived harmoniously. . . . This year will be the same as next year; I don't think that there is any hope for next year and conditions will worsen.

The Drought and Underdevelopment in the Transkei, 1982–83

R. Bolus and Neil Muller[1]

This article describes the drought conditions in Transkei. Trends in subsistence production, livestock deaths, and health as well as the two largest drought relief programmes are outlined. A number of tentative hypotheses are advanced about the likely long-run impact on the rural areas. The major point of departure, however, is that while the drought has certainly worsened conditions in the bantustans, they can only be understood against the abject poverty of 'normal' conditions.

Population, production and rural poverty in Transkei

Ninety-five percent of the estimated 3,2-m inhabitants of Transkei live in the rural areas. These areas contain some of the worst victims of South African 'polarised' development. As in the other 'labour reserves', ecological and human degradation is extreme as can be seen from the following characteristics.

- 66% of the adult population is illiterate;
- Two-thirds of rural households had cash incomes below the estimated household subsistence level of R1 509 in 1982;
- Tuberculosis is perhaps the greatest killer with five times as many open adult sufferers as the next highest 'homeland', KwaZulu;
- Two-thirds of the male labour-force is permanently absent, working as migrant labourers in the major urban areas of South Africa;
- The mortality rate in children up to five years of age ranged up to 261 per thousand in Tabankulu and averaged 190.

Statistics such as these, which show the poverty of human existence, cannot in themselves explain the complex processes of underdevelopment and repression which combine to lock rural Africans into a world of hopelessness. An adequate account would require an examination of the process by which pastoral cultivators were transformed into wage dependent households (Southall, 1983: 67). Such a task lies beyond the bounds of this report although three aspects of this history are of particular relevance to the approach adopted here.

Firstly, as Beinart (1982: 3–4) noted in his study of Pondoland, peasant 'underdevelopment in the context of Southern Africa, meant not a skewing of production in the rural economy through the necessity to produce cash crops, but mass dependence on wage labour'. Through a variety of measures such as the poll and hut tax, land legislation, and biased state agricultural policies, the 'effort price'[2] of migrant labour and agricultural labour were manipulated in favour of the former. Increasingly rural production fulfilled the subsistence needs of the non-productive (from the point of view of the industrial capitalist economy) population rather than providing fulltime employment for primary workers. Bembridge (1982: 44) observes that:

> The small gross income from farming (estimated at R246 per annum) comprised less than 20 percent of total household income and, as in the past, more than 80 percent was used for home consumption, indicating that the farm economy in Transkei is still largely subsistence based.

The above quotation illustrates the relative unimportance of 'subsistence' production in satisfying the consumption requirements of rural households. Consequently the term 'subsistence production' which often implies 'self sufficient' is somewhat of a misnomer in Transkei.

Secondly, the function and magnitude of rural production have changed continually. In the early stages of capitalist development subsistence production was more or less sufficient for the household requirements of rural households. As a result, by maintaining the rural population on the land, the capitalist sector enjoyed increased profitability as it only had to support the individual migrant. Over time the various methods designed to extract labour from the 'reserves' undermined this subsistence base and encouraged the urbanisation of African households. Between 1946 and 1951 the annual average rate of African urbanisation reached 6,4%. This generated new pressures for tightened influx controls after the accession of the Nationalist government in 1948.

Thirdly, African urbanisation and settlement patterns have been in-

creasingly controlled. Although its content has changed with the changing nature of capital accumulation in South Africa, African settlement
has been ruled by the two principles of the so-called 'Stallard Doctrine':
the temporary nature of African settlement outside the bantustans; and
its limitation to the population directly required for capitalist production.

The role of the rural areas in the political economy of South Africa can
be periodised with regard to tendencies in both urban and rural areas.
Each phase has its particular forms of attraction and repulsion of the
African population. As the real economic function of rural production
declined, the bantustans have increasingly taken on ideological and political functions of control.

Hemmed in by an increasingly repressive set of 'influx' controls and
subject to over a century of underdevelopment, the population in these
areas suffer from endemic under- and unemployment and are largely dependent on migrant remittances and pensions for their survival as can be
seen in Table 1.

TABLE 1: SOURCES OF RURAL TRANSKEIAN CASH INCOME BY INCOME LEVEL 1982

Income Interval (R)	% House-holds	Wages	Pensions	Remit-tance	Home Produc-tion	Total
– 500	23,90	10,65	19,40	67,05	2,90	100,00
501 – 1 000	26,42	12,10	14,30	71,10	2,50	100,00
1 001 – 1 500	13,21	15,36	17,11	65,75	1,78	100,00
1 501 – 2 000	6,69	26,52	21,40	48,08	4,00	100,00
2 001 – 3 000	6,96	37,67	13,89	46,17	2,27	100,00
3 001 – 4 000	6,47	74,40	4,24	19,86	1,50	100,00
4 001 – 5 000	5,36	80,61	4,22	13,22	1,95	100,00
5 001 – 10 000	7,31	69,90	4,43	22,95	2,72	100,00
10 000+	3,68	83,05	8,16	6,08	2,71	100,00

Source: IMDS Income and Expenditure Survey (Unpublished Results).

It is against this background of ghetto conditions that the drought must
be located.

Impact of the drought

In this section the impact of the drought on subsistence agricultural production, livestock, and health is considered.

Subsistence agricultural output

The point has already been made that subsistence agricultural production is relatively unimportant as a source of rural consumption. Nevertheless, rural households will be affected by a decline in output − especially at the margin. Table 2 contains estimates of subsistence output of major crops for 1980–82.

TABLE 2: TOTAL SUBSISTENCE AGRICULTURAL PRODUCTION 1980–1982

| Crop Type | Harvest (tonnes) | | | % Change |
	1980	1981	1982	1980 − 82
Mealies	139 263	205 175	204 750	+ 47
Sorghum	22 204	20 364	21 976	− 1
Pumpkins	121 865	34 312	44 928	− 63
Potatoes	73 276	11 978	8 411	− 89
Cabbages	77 969	10 984	13 368	− 83
Beans	15 336	14 083	2 774	− 82
Peas	113	69	202	+ 79
Wheat	192	n.a.	738	+284
Carrots	69	14	4	− 94

Sources: Abedian (1981, 1984).

Two contradictory trends are identifiable. Firstly, as might be expected, there is a drastic decline in output for most crops. Secondly, however, the production of maize, peas and wheat increased. The most probable explanation for this phenomenon is that as conditions become drier, households move away from vegetable crops towards the less water intensive maize. In the case of peas and wheat they are winter crops and perhaps less disturbed by dry summers.[3]

Total subsistence output is the sum of three types of farming: homestead production on the allocated plots which measure 50m by 50m and are available to most households; communal garden production which concentrates on vegetables; and dryland production. Fewer households have access to fields than to homestead gardens and the impact on the less powerful households can best be seen by examining trends in homestead production as in Table 3.

TABLE 3: HOMESTEAD AGRICULTURAL OUTPUT 1980–1982

Crop Type	Harvest (tonnes)			% Change
	1980	1981	1982	1980 – 82
Mealies	47 797	45 486	24 795	−48
Sorghum	11 949	15 418	10 685	−11
Pumpkins	85 356	34 239	27 280	−68
Potatoes	51 206	11 884	8 396	−84
Cabbages	54 626	10 654	13 352	−76
Beans	8 548	10 199	−	−

Source: Abedian (1984).

Table 3 reveals a decline in production for all homestead crops over the period. As these gardens are the major source of fresh vegetables, the implications for already inadequate rural diets are severe.

Livestock deaths

Cattle deaths provide perhaps the best index of the severity of the drought. Firstly, cattle are perhaps the most valuable single resource of most rural households and thus give an immediate index of loss. Secondly, because of their value, it is likely that cattle will only be allowed to die when all resources have been exhausted. Thirdly, it seems that cattle deaths are reported regularly and that records are fairly accurate.

Based on cattle death figures it seems that the drought has been most severe in the central plateau area around Umtata (61,3%) and Idutywa (65,5%). The least affected areas seem to be the districts lying against the mountains and the coastal areas of the North East.

Cattle deaths also indicate the period of greatest crisis. Between April 1982 and November 1983 a total of 555 691 cattle were reported dead, i.e. 36,2% of the Transkeian herd of 1 537 155 cattle. Sixty-one percent of these deaths were in the period between April and November 1983.

Health

One effect of the drought has been to increase the incidence of waterborne diseases. The number of cholera cases increased 600% in 1983 over the 109 cases reported in 1982. There was also an outbreak of typhoid at Sulenkama in the Qumbu district. Although figures are not available, discussions with a number of doctors at rural clinics and a births and deaths registrar in one district seem to imply an increase in infant and child mortality due to kwashiorkor, measles and gastro enteritis.

Drought relief programmes in Transkei

The two most important drought relief efforts in Transkei were the efforts by the state based on a grant of R6,7-m from the RSA treasury, and Operation Joseph run by the Transkei Council of Churches. In each case we sketch the basic organisation and extent of the programme before moving on to a preliminary assessment.

The official drought relief programme
The programme is under the control of the Civil Defence Unit with administrative responsibility held by the Transkei Department of Social Welfare. A drought relief coordinator is appointed for each of the 28 magisterial districts in Transkei and is responsible for monitoring water, livestock, and health conditions and for selecting 'needy' families in consultation with local headmen.

There are three sub-programmes each of which received about one third of the R6,7-m budget:

A *food* programme was run to counter starvation. It was divided between a food voucher scheme where needy families were given vouchers of R25 for three months to be spent at local trading stores, and a Pro Nutro distribution programme through hospitals and clinics.

The *water relief* programme attempted to provide water to the worst hit areas through the use of tankers provided by the Department of Agriculture and the South African Defence Force.

The *stock feed* programme consisted of providing stock feed at distribution points in Viedgiesville, Qamata, Ndabakazi, Mt Ayliff, Umzimkulu, and Libode. This feed was then available to buyers who had to provide their own transport. The first 25 bales sold were given a 50% subsidy while any further bales were sold at full price.

Operation Joseph
The largest programme outside government was 'Operation Joseph' run

by the Transkei Council of Churches. This programme ran from August 1983 to January 1984. Monthly relief packages of 25 kg of maize and 8 kg of beans were distributed to needy families identified by the pastors of local churches. The programme was run in ten districts and involved 1 600 families.

The programme was organised through member churches who were asked to identify 30 needy families who would receive aid for the duration of the programme. Once the families had been identified, the churches were authorised to buy the necessary package elements at selected local stores. The churches were responsible for distribution to the families. A total of R123 000 was spent in this manner. In addition 14 350 bags of maize were donated by Operation Hunger. At an average cost of R4,50 per 12,5 kg bag, this increased the total value of the programme to R187 575.

Impact of the drought relief programmes

It is still too early to draw hard conclusions on the impact of the drought relief programmes on rural communities as the drought is still not over and information is scanty — especially on the official programme. However, from the information available a number of issues are raised.

Selection of recipients. The generalised poverty in Transkei makes it very difficult to select the most needy families. Neither programme laid down 'objective' criteria and relied on local decision makers (headmen in the official programme and priests in Operation Joseph) to make final decisions. While this does have the advantage of involving locals, it does open the door to nepotism. This is especially true in the case of the official programme where problems of bribery and corruption are known and the temptation is there to add drought relief to the armoury of rural social control.

Price controls. Both programmes relied to some degree on food voucher systems. While this has the advantage of minimising on costly transport infrastructure, if it is not linked to a system of rural price controls, the most likely consequence is price inflation and the distribution of relief towards store owners through increased profit margins.

Social impact. The stock feed programme is perhaps most controversial here. As a start it excludes the poorest third of the population that do not have cattle. Furthermore, when linked to the necessity of supplying one's own transport, it is clear that such a programme will prove of benefit only to the richer people.

Ideological effects. A more general point, however, concerns the ideological effects of drought relief. While it would be pointless to deny that drought relief programmes are of benefit to the rural population they ameliorate rather than alter the fundamental conditions of rural poverty. While the success of Operations Joseph (in Transkei) and Hunger (South Africa) has revealed that the more affluent sections of the population can be shocked into donations, there is a danger that they will attribute too much to the drought. As the 'normal' characteristics of Transkei's rural areas outlined earlier have shown, nothing could be further from the truth.[4]

The drought and social crisis: some longer run trends

It is impossible to separate the effects of the drought from the more generalised processes of underdevelopment and rural poverty. The most likely effect will be to accelerate existing trends. As the head of the Transkei Appropriate Technology Unit put it: 'The present drought shows you the conditions in ten years time.' In this section we consider some of the trends emerging in the rural areas, both ecologically and sociologically.

The most obvious impact of the drought is environmental. Erosion and general deterioration of the land will continue at an accelerated rate. As top soil is exposed and removed, lower layers become more impermeable to water, less nutritious grasses proliferate and karoo vegetation colonises. Secondly, as the more permeable top soil washes away, the rate of water run-off increases. Over the long run this will affect the water table. As most rural communities are dependent on springs and underground water supplies this is critical.

In areas such as the south-west where ecological collapse was general before the drought, 1983 was a year harsher than normal. However, the greatest danger would appear to lie in areas usually regarded as more fertile and well watered. The veld has been badly damaged here and the lack of rural organisation means that it is unlikely that damage will be minimised by allowing time for recovery.

As the ability of the veld to sustain cattle declines, rural communities are swopping towards smaller livestock such as sheep and goats which are seemingly also more drought resistant. Due to their different grazing patterns this further debilitates the veld.

By damaging resources in an area where they are already scarce, the drought has increased the level of social conflict. Divisions caused by competition have been in evidence for some time. During the drought conflict sharpened noticeably, especially over grazing and water rights. Desperate to keep their animals alive, people trespassed on other lands. Some even attempted to drive their cattle to the coastal areas. This led to confiscations, finings, assaults, and the introduction of new laws allowing for criminal prosecution of the owners of cattle found on 'agricultural schemes'. Historical and ethnic differences overlay the struggle for survival and allow easy lines of rural division unless people become more aware of the macro processes to which they are being subjected. Although there are no statistics, there are strong impressionistic grounds for believing that banditry and theft, symptoms of social disintegration, are increasing.

Perhaps most importantly, the drought has impressed on people the risks of rural life, eyes turn to the urban areas and the rural 'home' is seen as an area of retirement (if anything). While much will depend on the mode of mobilisation, it is possible that the dispossessed rural people may become another force demanding the restructuring of apartheid South Africa.

Summary and conclusions

This article has attempted to sketch the major impact of the present drought in Transkei. Brief descriptions and evaluations of the drought relief programmes were made. What then are the major lessons of the drought?

Firstly, the drought and its effects have to be located against the background of rural underdevelopment and population influx controls which have resulted in a sustained rural crisis. The drought has accelerated all the symptoms related to poverty whether they be lawlessness or malnutrition but it has not 'caused' them. These must be traced to the structural characteristics of racial capitalist development in South Africa which concentrates poverty along racial, spatial, and sexual lines.

Secondly, a lesson is to be learnt from the role of relief programmes. Relief in minute amounts to millions of Transkeians is a token gesture. Given the underdevelopment of Transkei, the poverty, overcrowding, land shortage and limited agricultural potential, relief (sometimes) fills stomachs but not aspirations. Until influx controls are removed and some pressure is taken off the land, the structural poverty of the rural population will continue. In this context rain might alleviate circumstances somewhat but it will not cure the evils that already exist.

Finally, the accumulation of structural poverty in the rural areas of Transkei is giving rise to new crises and new forms of rural conflict. The relevance of these struggles to broader political events will turn importantly on whether or not they lead to increased internal conflict ('faction fights') or link up to other attempts to restructure the fundamental imbalances of apartheid South Africa.

Notes

1 Acknowledgement is given to Iraj Abedian for the as yet unpublished 1982 production figures and to Bob Herr.
2 The term is Arrighi's. Southey (1983) claims that a person working on the mines could earn more in three weeks than the average annual gross maize yield per family.
3 The statistics must be approached with considerable caution as the margin of error can be large. Furthermore, these figures do not include 1982/3 when the drought was at its worst. In many areas absolutely no crops were harvested, while in better areas harvests declined by 50%–70%.
4 According to one drought relief officer 'there has always been a drought in Transkei because the people are poor'. Indeed it seems that one of the major problems of drought co-ordinators was not deciding who was needy, but who was not.

References

C. Bundy, *The Rise and Fall of a South African Peasantry* (London, 1979).
W. Beinart, *The Political Economy of Pondoland* (Johannesburg, 1982).
N. Muller, *The Political Economy of Labour and Development in Transkei* (Umtata, 1983).
C. Simkins, *The Economic Implications of African Resettlement* (Cape Town, 1981).
R. Southall, *South Africa's Transkei* (London, 1983).
C. Southey, *Land Tenure in Transkei* (Umtata, 1983).
W. Thomas, *Socio-Economic Development in Transkei* (Umtata, 1982).
P. Wakelin, *Demographic Characteristics in Transkei 1982* (Umtata, 1983).

Technological Change and Labour on 'White' Farms

Debbie Budlender

> There are 4,4-million blacks in white rural areas. We have no policy for them. But we do have a homelands policy and an urban policy. And when the blacks in the white platteland become sophisticated enough to bother about it they usually go to the cities, where we have a policy (A 'very senior government official', *S.A. FRONTLINE*, November 1983).

> The reaping machine will finally become an institution here and lessen the demand for labour, which article is of the scarcest and worst description (Beaufort West farmer, quoted in *Standard and Mail*, 05.12.1872).

It is over a hundred years ago that the farmer noted the effects of the introduction of technology on employment in agriculture. Over the last few decades there has been a speeding up of this process in South Africa.

The late 1960s and early 1970s saw the publication of the three-volume Report of the state's Commission of Inquiry into Agriculture.[1] One of the themes which came strongly out of these reports was the need for rationalisation and modernisation of agriculture. No longer, it appeared, was agricultural capital the favoured son of the state. The modern, mechanised sectors of farming were held up to the more backward and uneconomic sectors as the model to emulate.

The pronouncements of the state cannot be taken at face value. This paper examines mechanisation of agriculture on 'white' farms, what the factors are which affect the process, and what the consequences are for the people most affected — the agricultural workers.

Agriculture, and South African agriculture in particular, is characterised by extreme diversity which makes generalisation difficult. This diversity is caused by an interplay of economic, political as well as purely physical factors. On the physical side, there is the difference between pastoral and arable farming, and within this between different crops and livestock, and different climates and terrains. On the economic and political side there are factors such as labour supply and the relationship between agricultural capital and the state. Capital and state often operate in tandem. To take only one example, labour supply in South Africa is often related to proximity to bantustans. There are also more overtly political factors such as the call for development of the northern border areas, in order to provide protection against 'terrorist incursion'.

These physical, economic and political factors are related to each other. One of the chief motivations of the bantustan policy has been an adequate labour supply for white farms. Likewise, in deciding which areas were to be allocated to Africans, the state often chose the less fertile, and thus more pastoral areas, rather than choice arable land.

A second difficulty in generalising is that mechanisation was introduced for different crops at different times. The wheat harvest was mechanised before maize. Today on many fruit and vegetable farms harvesting is still done by hand.

Broad generalisations also ignore the fact that political and economic conditions change with time. State policy with regard to influx control and bantustans depends not only on the needs of agriculture, but also on those of the rest of the economy. For example, population change in the 'white' rural areas can be correlated strongly with proximity to bantustans. In the 1950s the new Nationalist government was introducing its policy of stricter influx control. The population of farming areas far from bantustans grew more slowly than that of areas near these regions, as the state tried to force 'surplus' people out of the 'white' areas. In the 1960s and 1970s the state had already achieved it spurpose in most areas. In these two decades population grew more slowly in the more pastoral areas — the type of farming appears to have been more important in determining population change.[2]

Changing technology

Until the mid 1950s, apart from the Western Cape wheatlands, technological innovation was virtually synonymous with tractorisation, as farmers replaced animal-drawn ploughs with motorised tractors. This change caused a major revolution, not only in the labour process, but also in the position of many squatters and labour tenants. The area under cultivation was extended and stock reduced. Both these trends encourag-

ed the (forced) conversion of the more independent forms of rural existence to wage labour. As former labour tenants remember:

> There first came the tractors and the big ploughs. The threshing machines came later.
> (People) were reduced as a result of those machines. They were rendered redundant
> because the machines had taken over.
> Ever since they started cultivating with tractors and planting wheat, they told us to sell
> our cattle. They are using tractors only now.[3]

In the last few decades mechanisation has entailed much more than tractors. Starting in the wheat-growing areas, the move has been towards both
bigger and more powerful tractors, and more advanced and specialised
machinery, such as mechanical harvesters. In 1966 it was estimated that
only 2% of tractors purchased were over 61 KW, while 41% were under
37,5 KW. By 1980 the percentages were 25% and 10% respectively. All
these machines, together with more efficient irrigation and fertilisation,
have meant that the land has been more extensively cultivated and the
area of 'unused' bushveld greatly reduced. Cultivated land as a percentage of total farm area increased from 8,3% in 1946 to 15,1% in 1976.[4]
This increase was accompanied by the large-scale removal of first squatters and then labour tenants as farmers began to cultivate the land on
which these people were living.

Farmers have also introduced science in other forms. Herbicides,
pesticides, fungicides, fertilisation and irrigation are important com-
ponents of 'modern, scientific' farming. Many of these innovations
facilitated the further expansion of farming, both in making formerly in-
fertile or marginal land cultivable, and in increasing the incentive to
enlarge farming units to take advantage of economies of scale. Tractors
laid the necessary base for these innovations — indeed many of the new
instruments are mounted on, or drawn by, tractors, while chemicals, fertilisers and irrigation equipment are applied from them. In this sense
tractors provide a basis for and a fairly good index of technology in
agriculture.

The ratio of tractors to 'farming implements' rose slightly from 1,3 in
1926 to 4,0 in 1937 and by 1955 had reached 39,4, giving some indication
of the importance of tractors in comparison to other tools. Even in the
later period 1964 to 1977, when more sophisticated mechanical equipment was being introduced, the number of tractors, expressed as a
percentage of the real value of machinery and implements, continued to
rise slightly (from 18,7% to 22,0%). If we take into account the increase

in the size of tractors, this probably understates the increasing importance of tractors.

A second complication in looking at mechanisation is the interrelationship of different processes. Farming consists of a series of processes such as land preparation, planting, weeding, harvesting. Conceptually, and even technically, each process can be considered separately. In practice when a farmer decides to introduce mechanisation in one process he must also at the same time introduce it in another process.

This interdependence can be clearly seen in the case of horticultural crops where adequate mechanical harvesting methods have often not yet been introduced. In Western Cape viticulture, while the weeding and irrigation processes can and have been mechanised, thus cutting down on the demand for labour, during the harvest period the farmers still need extremely large teams of workers. To cope with this peak demand period, the farms have resorted either to employing more women, or otherwise employing contract labour, but cut-throat competition between farmers with regard to labour remains the order of the day during the harvest. Many farmers have diversified into other crops with complementary cycles so that the workers are kept at full production throughout the year.

Interdependence can also be of a more technical nature. In citrus the change-over from 'flood' irrigation to microjet, reduces the labour requirement from three teams, each of seven people, to one single worker who controls the system. But the elimination of the banks which retain the water under flood irrigation has also facilitated tractor usage, thus allowing greater usage of chemical weedkillers instead of handhoeing. This has led to a further reduction in labour requirements.

Labour is not the only factor considered in the decision to mechanise. Farmers will also be influenced by the available technology, prices of both inputs and products, the availability of finance, politics, the terrain of their particular farm, and harvests. Where labour is scarce or perceived as a problem, there is an obvious motivation to introduce labour-saving technology – '. . . labour is more difficult to handle than a chemical'. But to some farmers it is still the case that '. . . labour requires less supervision than machines'.

Consequences of technology

There is no doubt that the application of labour-saving technology has often made work less arduous. In terms of sheer physical strength, the many changes which have allowed increasing employment of women have also meant that the work is less strenuous. The planting of trellis vines rather than bush vines has meant that the women working in the field are able to stand upright while working rather than working with their backs continually bent. Mechanical loading in maize and sugar farming has obviated the need for men to lift extremely heavy bags. Farm work is usually not easy work, and insofar as machines can eliminate the need for hard work, they have a potential benefit for some workers.

There are also less pleasant aspects to the application of technology. The dangers of the increasing use of pesticides have been well documented overseas, yet they are not at all adequately recorded or controlled in South Africa. The official figures for pesticide poisonings are the tip of the iceberg. Even deaths are not properly reported. A study in the Western Cape shows that in 1977 the government pathologist received 34 notifications of death from pesticide poisoning while the official Department of Health figure was only seven.[5] The position with regard to non-fatal poisonings is almost certainly much worse.

Pesticides which are banned in overseas countries are registered for use in South Africa. Yet the illiteracy, malnutrition and general poverty of the farm population here can only mean that the effects are more severe.

Work is also sometimes harder when technology is applied. Harvesters with headlights permit longer working hours, mentioned as a benefit by some farmers. For the farmer this is rational as it means either greater utilisation of the expensive capital equipment over a larger area, or completion of the same amount of work in a shorter period, cutting the casual labour demand. For the workers it means intensification of the work process.

The application of technology has also seen minimal increase in skills among the farm population. Farmers in all areas are loath for workers to acquire heavy-duty driving licences for trucks and other delivery vehicles as this means they are more able to find jobs in the town. Tractor driving (where the licence is confined to private roads), however, is a non-saleable skill in the urban setting. Farmers are quite prepared to send workers on a tractor driving course, as shown by the fact that this is the most 'popular' course at the Kromme Rhee school, the training school for coloured farm workers. Most skills are acquired on the job. Very few of them are of use in acquiring a job in the towns. Where they are, the lack of a formal certificate makes it more difficult for the worker. The lack of saleable skills also makes it more difficult for the farm worker to demand higher wages.

The most obvious problem with technology, however, is the question of employment, which in the South African context also means housing. Whereas overseas the application of technology in agriculture has been accompanied by movement to the cities, in South Africa the 'surplus' population finds itself restricted to the bantustans.

Expulsion of labour

There has been an absolute decrease in the number of agricultural workers on 'white' farms since 1970. The number of regular workers in agriculture increased from 845 400 in 1947–8 to 1 005 700 in 1955 but since then has remained fairly constant or even declined. Statistics for casual employment are very unreliable, but what evidence there is shows an even greater relative decrease in the number of casual workers. Farmers usually deny having actually retrenched workers because of mechanisation. They will admit a saving in labour in certain processes, but claim that the labour is still being employed on the farm for other tasks.

There are several possible explanations for this seeming contradiction. There has been a noticeable concentration and centralisation in farm ownership, and it is almost always the bigger farms which have most finance and most justification for mechanisation. It seems that very often when a farm is taken over and consolidated with another one in the same area, the work-force of the newly acquired farm is retrenched, and the workers on the original farm work on both farms. Thus the farmer does not retrench what he sees as 'his' workers, but people certainly lose their jobs. An alternative strategy, especially where peak demand still exists, is that of diversification of farming operations into other crops, allowing greater production and profits with the same labour force. Because of the range of jobs in agriculture, and the almost complete lack of job specialisation, agriculture is still able to absorb labour to a much greater degree than industry.

A second explanation suggested by the larger relative decrease in casual labour, is that it is perhaps not the workers resident on the farms who are losing their jobs, but those in the reserves who are no longer being employed on a casual or longer term basis. De Klerk's case study, which follows, shows clearly the transfer of jobs from annual migrants to a reduced permanent on-farm population. The effects of mechanisation are felt in the bantustans, where the formerly employed casual workers and their families are forced to live, rather than in the white agricultural areas.

Thirdly, people who have left white farms rarely see their removal as being caused by mechanisation as clearly as the tenants of the 1920s saw the reduction of their stock. They usually see their leaving the farm as the result of a personal difference with the farmer, or personal dissatisfaction with the farmer. But obviously these things are not unrelated. The farmer who has a smaller labour need is much freer to sack workers who do not behave as he would like them to behave. As one farmer put it, mechanisation makes it 'makliker om arbeiders uit te skakel'. The work-force can thus be decreased by attrition in a more inconspicuous way.

Finally, the change to female labour could account for the farmer not reporting retrenchments. The males resident on the farm, who formerly worked there, might be moving more and more into work in the towns. The farmer will often, however, have no desire to force the family off, as the women and children form an ever larger proportion of his workforce. A decrease in the number of people working fulltime on the farm as a proportion of people resident on the farm suggests that this is indeed happening. The men live on the farm and work elsewhere — almost a new form of labour tenancy, where the time not spent working for the farmer is spent in the town, rather than on the worker's own land. Women, classified almost exclusively as 'casual' labour, continue to both live and work on the farm. As one farmer remarked, women 'will always be there', at least as long as the farmer has use for them. They have few other alternatives in terms of employment and accommodation.

The move towards female labour is accompanied by lower wages. Although women might be earning more than before, they will still be earning less than would male workers doing the same job. The farmers can justify the wages on the basis that the woman has her husband to support her and thus does not need a family wage. From the farmers' point of view, however, there are still on the whole too many women and children on the farms. Family planning is a compulsory additional course for all students at the Kromme Rhee Training School. Knowledge of and access to contraception is very important, but the farmer also has a vested interest in smaller families and fewer dependants on his farm.

However, even with respect to the use of women, generalisations are impossible. In some areas mechanisation appears to have encouraged greater use of the women already resident on the farms. In other areas the increasing overcrowding and poverty in neighbouring homeland areas has led to a reliance on off-farm women and children, who are recruited on a daily basis. Similarly, whereas mechanisation is usually seen as encouraging the establishment of a more permanent work-force, in the Western Cape greater use is now made of contract workers from the Transkei as the traditional coloured work-force becomes ever more reluctant to stay in farm jobs. While the contract workers are in many senses permanent, in that they return each year, they are still not permitted to bring their families with them.

While in general the trend is towards ever-increasing mechanisation, especially in the early 1970s when labour everywhere had become more militant, when more and better jobs were available in the towns, and when there had been a run of good harvests, in Natal a short period of intense mechanisation has been followed by one of absolute 'demechanisation' once the labour pressure eased. The mechanisation of loading is the only process where there are not signs of slackening, perhaps because reversion to old loading methods would exclude the possibility of using women. In the other processes the farmers have either stopped introducing new machines, or, in some cases, actually packed away their new machinery.[6]

Conclusion

Farming in South Africa is very diverse. The easy availability of cheap and exploitable labour has weakened incentives to mechanise. Many agricultural processes are still performed by largely manual methods. Yet over the last few decades technology in its various forms has been introduced more and more as farmers strive to rationalise their operations, improve control and increase production. In the process many workers and their families have suffered. Many of them have joined the ranks of the unemployed in the bantustans.

Notes

1 RP 6/1968, RP 84/1970, RP 19/1972.
2 Forthcoming paper for Carnegie Commission Conference.
3 Interview, African Studies Institute, University of Witwatersrand.
4 Calculations based on figures in *Agricultural Census No. 49*, 1976 Part I, 06-01-13, Table 2.3 and *Abstract of Agricultural Statistics*, 1979, 5.
5 G.J. Coetzee, 'The Epidemiology of Pesticide Mortality in the Western Cape' (unpublished paper, Department of Community Health, University of Cape Town).
6 Jane Nelson, 'A Survey on Technology and Employment in the South African Cane Industry' (unpublished B.Sc. dissertation, University of Natal, Pietermaritzburg, 1983).

Technological Change and Farm Labour: A Case Study of Maize Farming in the Western Transvaal

Mike de Klerk

Nowhere are the effects of recent changes in farm technology on employment clearer or more far-reaching than on maize farms. This study was carried out in 1982 on 61 farms in six magisterial districts of the Western Transvaal.[1] Maize farming almost certainly provides more employment than any other sector in South African agriculture and the Western Transvaal in turn produces more maize than any other region in most years. Information was gathered about harvesting, delivery of the harvest and weeding for the years 1968–1981. In 1968, these were the last three tasks for which the large numbers of seasonal workers were still employed.

Changes in technology

Technology has changed radically in recent years. Combine harvesters, which both reap and thresh in one mechanical operation, have largely replaced the seasonal workers who for decades reaped by hand and threshed by machine. Only gleaning, i.e. collecting the maizeheads or 'blaarkoppe' left behind by the combine, is done manually on most farms nowadays. In 1968, between 25 and 30% of the area planted with maize was being harvested by combine. By 1981 this had risen to about 95%, the greatest part of this change occurring between 1973 and 1977 (see figure 1).

Farmers used to deliver the crop to co-operative depots in sacks. On farms, 200-pound sacks were filled from the threshing machine, weigh-

FIGURE 1

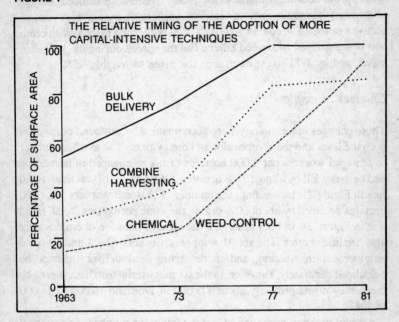

THE RELATIVE TIMING OF THE ADOPTION OF MORE CAPITAL-INTENSIVE TECHNIQUES

ed, topped up or emptied a little, sewn closed and loaded onto a trailer for transport. At the depot, the sequence was: weighing the trailer with its full cargo, off-loading, sampling for grading, weighing the empty trailer and stacking the sacks. Almost all of this was done by hand — a back-breaking task — and required many young, able-bodied men. Nowadays bulk handling and storage systems have virtually eliminated this work. Threshed grain is poured directly into bulk trailers. These are emptied into a grain-elevator chute at the depot by simply opening sluices built into trailers or by letting down the sides. Silos are used for storage. The use of bulk handling and storage techniques was more widespread than combine harvesting in 1968: by that stage, more than half the crop — 54% — was already being delivered in bulk, and by 1977 virtually the entire crop was reaching silos in this way.

The main activity between planting and harvesting is weeding. Early weeding can be done by ploughing lightly. But when the maize has grown taller, weeds can only be controlled in this way where the rows have been planted seven feet or more apart. Partly, for this reason, later weeding was mostly done by hand by women and children with hoes. Chemical weed sprays became available in the 1960s. These have reduced, but not eliminated the employment of seasonal workers since spraying is not effective against all weeds. In 1968 only 15% of the area planted with crops was being sprayed with weed killers. But the spread during the 1970s was rapid, and by 1981 the sprayed area had risen to roughly 95%.

Changes in employment

These changes in technology were accompanied by profound changes in both the level and the composition of employment. The average number of seasonal workers per 1 000 hectares of maize engaged in harvesting and delivery fell by almost 70% between 1968 and 1981 (see 'total' trend line in Figure 2). In weeding, the number of seasonal workers per 1 000 hectares declined by about 60% during the same period (see 'total' trend line in Figure 3). In both instances, the average duration of employment also became shorter. The actual number of workers who found seasonal employment in weeding and/or harvesting and delivery cannot be calculated accurately. However, in the six magisterial districts covered by the survey it was probably about 105 000 in 1968 and 40 000 to 45 000 in 1981.

Agricultural censuses suggest that the fall in the number of permanent farm workers was much smaller — from about 30 000 in 1969 to 26 000 in 1978. Yet, between 1968 and 1981, the survey showed a drop of nearly 50% in the number of permanent workers per 1 000 hectares harvested and delivered. The difference can be explained by the fact that harvesting and delivery are only two of the full annual cycle of farming activities.[2]

The decline in the number of seasonal jobs between 1968 and 1981 can be ascribed to the following causes:

— about 37% to the replacement of hand by mechanical harvesters,
— about 32% to the adoption of chemical weed sprays,
— about 24% to the re-organisation of hand harvesting prior to the introduction of combines,[3]
— about 7% to the introduction of bulk handling and storage techniques,
— less than 1% to the replacement of tractor-drawn by self-propelled combines.

These estimates conceal two major changes in the composition of employment: the transfer of seasonal jobs from people living in African rural areas to the families of permanent workers living on white farms, and the substitution of children for men in seasonal teams. In 1968 workers drawn from 'external' sources — mainly what is now Bophuthatswana and to a lesser extent the Transkei, Botswana, white towns and 'black spots' — could count on about 100 workplaces per 1 000 hectares of maize harvested. By 1981 the number was less than 20. But even workers from 'internal' sources, i.e. who lived on white farms, benefitted little in practice, despite a large increase in their share of employment: from 10 jobs per 1 000 hectares in 1968, the actual number increased to only 16 in 1981 (see figure 2).

The picture is noticeably different for seasonal workers employed to hoe. Even in 1968, between 60 and 65% were members of the families of permanent workers, and by 1981 this had grown to between 70 and 75%. In terms of jobs, 36 internal and 22 external workers were employed per 1 000 hectares weeded in 1968. In 1981 this had dropped to 17 internal and six external workplaces (see Figure 3).

FIGURE 2

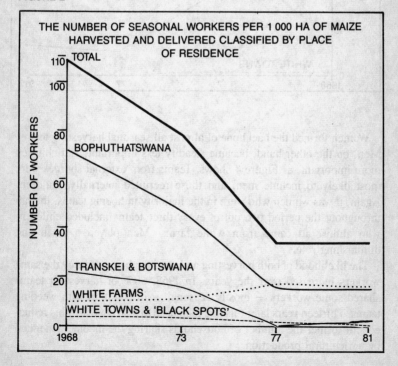

THE NUMBER OF SEASONAL WORKERS PER 1 000 HA OF MAIZE HARVESTED AND DELIVERED CLASSIFIED BY PLACE OF RESIDENCE

FIGURE 3

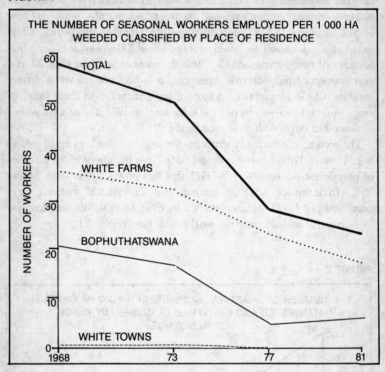

THE NUMBER OF SEASONAL WORKERS EMPLOYED PER 1 000 HA WEEDED CLASSIFIED BY PLACE OF RESIDENCE

Women formed the backbone of almost all seasonal harvesting teams. Men, on the other hand, became steadily less important, and children more important, as Figure 4 shows. Teams from external sources were most likely to include men, and those recruited internally, children. Again, it was women who were in the majority in hoeing teams, though throughout the period two out of every three teams included children, who almost all came from white farms. Men played a small and diminishing role.

The likelihood of both harvesting and weeding being done by the same workers increased over the years. In 1968, 60% of harvesting teams shared some workers − mostly seasonal − in common with weeding teams. Thirteen years later this had increased to nearly 90%. This reduced still further the number of households sharing the income generated by agricultural production.

FIGURE 4

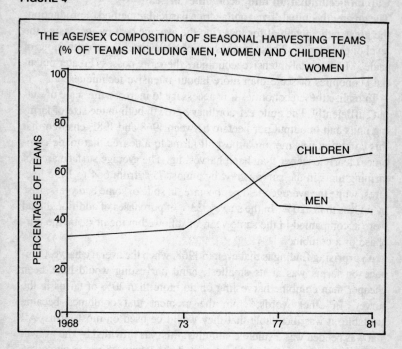

THE AGE/SEX COMPOSITION OF SEASONAL HARVESTING TEAMS
(% OF TEAMS INCLUDING MEN, WOMEN AND CHILDREN)

Relatively little information was collected about the characteristics of permanent workers. The great majority appear to have been men who lived with their families on the farm where they were employed. Surprisingly, harvest mechanisation seems to have done little to alter the 'skills-mix': in 1968 roughly 60% of permanent workers were machine operators and 40% manual workers. Thirteen years later these percentages were virtually unchanged, though the numbers of both had fallen considerably.

In keeping with mechanisation, the greatest part of all these changes occurred between 1973 and 1977.

Causes of technological change

From questions answered by farmers and from other sources, there appear to have been four main causes of the changes in farming techniques.

Capital accumulation and 'economies of scale'

The greater the initial, fixed outlay for a particular method of production, the greater the potential for lowering the average cost by increasing the level of production. These savings are often referred to as 'economies of scale'. More capital-intensive techniques therefore possess greater potential economies of scale than more labour-intensive techniques.

To realise these economies it is necessary to increase the scale of output sufficiently. The quite extraordinary growth both in the size of farming units and in output per hectare between 1968 and 1981, ensured that this condition was met on almost all farms to a degree that made combines clearly cheaper than hand harvesting. The average surface area of farming units in the survey grew by almost 75% from 664 to 1 155 hectares, while the average yield per hectare, in spite of some bad years, rose by no less than 120%. In the survey, 23% of purchases of additional land were accompanied in the same year, or followed in the next, by the purchase of a combine.

A surprising finding is that even in 1968, when the average harvest tonnage on farms was at its smallest, hand harvesting would have been cheaper than combine harvesting on no more than 10% of farms in the survey. In other words, from the moment that combines became available, it was inevitable that they would be used on most farms. All that was needed was a suitable stimulus: this was provided by the growth in the size of farms and yields – and in the labour shortage perceived by farmers (see below). So, in the end, it is chiefly to the development of new technology abroad that harvest mechanisation should be ascribed.

Control over the labour process

Almost all of the main reasons for purchasing combines given by farmers can be seen as attempts to increase the degree of their control over the labour process. The many tasks performed by hand, which were subsequently taken over by machines, represent only one aspect. The change in the composition of seasonal teams is another: women and children are less fractious than men, and the families of permanent workers living on or near the farm a more accessible and dependable source of labour than independent communities living far afield. To this one can add the shortening of the harvest period.

Furthermore, when traditional techniques were still in use, farmers had no option but to go to the bantustans to negotiate for the men they needed in substantial numbers and who could not be recruited on their own farms. With the introduction of bulk handling and combines, men were no longer essential and the bargaining position of communities in black rural areas was undercut.

On the other side of the coin, many machine operators who remain have acquired skills which are in demand in urban areas — mainly heavy vehicle drivers' licences and a knowledge of machine maintenance. These create more than a little leverage, which partly accounts for the rise in the real wages of permanent workers.[4] Organising labour — which many farmers expect in the foreseeable future — may be less difficult in these circumstances.

Technological interdependence

Though combines made it possible for farmers to reduce the size of seasonal teams, without the prior introduction of bulk handling it would still have been necessary to go to the bantustans to find men to handle sacks. The silos that one can see from so far away in the flatness of the Western Transvaal were therefore the key to the profound changes in employment patterns in the 1970s.

To a lesser extent, mechanical harvesting in turn encouraged the use of chemical weed sprays. With the spread of combines there was a tendency to plant maize in three-foot rows, which makes part hand, part mechanical weeding difficult. So weedicides applied at planting time were a natural complement to the use of combines fitted with three-foot intakes. Both of these examples suggest that, to a degree, technological change is a cumulative, interdependent process.

Labour shortage

Farmers said they had experienced increasing difficulty in finding reliable workers. Though there are grounds for questioning the validity of this complaint, there is evidence to support it.

During the crucial years of the early and middle 1970s, when most mechanisation was taking place, the real wages (i.e. allowing for inflation) of both permanent and seasonal farm workers did rise — quite substantially for the former though less so for the latter.[5] At the same time, the employment of both groups fell. This combination of events does suggest an increasing reluctance on the part of workers to accept farm jobs, for whatever reason.

Furthermore, real farm wages rose less than real wages in mining, manufacturing and construction — the sectors which were the main alternative sources of employment for men from rural areas. And, during this period, employment opportunities in these sectors expanded rapidly.[6] In other words, at least for men employed on farms, urban jobs became more attractive. To a significant extent then, agricultural mechanisation does appear to have taken place in response to an increasing 'urban labour pull'.

Unexpectedly, perhaps, institutional factors do not appear to have been a significant cause of mechanisation. In particular, the state's population relocation policy seems to have played little part: labour tenancy was not widespread in the Western Transvaal, at least in the 1960s, and few of the residents of 'black spots cleared' appear to have been employed on farms. Rather, structural changes on farms led to relocation. Though farmers say they are reluctant to dismiss workers on their own farms who are made redundant by mechanisation, there is no such hesitation where other workers are concerned. When additional land is purchased, the general practice appears to be not to re-employ workers previously employed on that land. Such workers, if they are unable to find jobs on other farms, then have no (legal) choice but to move to an African rural area.

Four conclusions emerge clearly:

– that rapid and extensive mechanisation took place in one of the most important farming sectors during the 1970s,
– that, directly, or indirectly, this made the greater part of the seasonal labour-force – and a smaller proportion of permanent workers – redundant,
– that those permanent workers who retained their jobs benefitted,
– and that African rural areas bore the brunt of these changes, both in terms of lost jobs and in terms of population inflow.

Notes

1 Full details may be found in the author's MA (Economics) thesis: 'Technological Change and Employment in South African Agriculture: the case of maize harvesting in the Western Transvaal, 1968–1981' (University of Cape Town, unpublished, 1983).
2 1969 and 1978 are the years closest to 1968 and 1981 for which census data is available. No data on weeding was collected for permanent workers.
3 This involved having one central threshing point rather than moving the threshing machine from field to field.
4 The average all-inclusive annual wage (i.e. in cash and kind) for permanent workers increased from R220 in 1970 to R1 737 in 1981 (or to R550 at constant 1970 prices).

5 The average cash-only daily wage for seasonal harvest workers increased from 39c in 1969 to R1,54 in 1981 (or to 47c at constant 1969 prices). In practice, the real increase was greater than is shown by these figures because women and children were progressively replacing men, and because an increasing proportion of workers were employed to glean rather than harvest by hand. Women and children were almost certainly paid less than men, and gleaners were certainly paid less than hand harvesters.
6 Total employment in mining changed little, but recruitment in Bophuthatswana increased from 6 000 in 1970 to 33 000 in 1976.

Agribusiness and the Bantustans

Jeremy Keenan

Since 1977 there has been a rapid development of commercial agriculture in the bantustans. Prior to 1977 commercial agriculture was limited to a few 'plantation' schemes, producing such crops as sisal, tea, citrus, etc., and run by the agricultural sections of the Department of Co-operation and Development or the local bantustan administration itself. A small number of African farmers were producing on a commercial basis, and it is possible that small areas may have been leased to white farmers. A few co-operatives, usually centred on small-scale irrigation schemes, were producing limited amounts of cash crops for sale, but in most cases, attempts to encourage African farmers, whether independent or producing co-operatively, to produce for a commercial market, were unsuccessful in that they were reluctant to abandon their subsistence base.

In 1977 the Promotion of Economic Development of Bantu Homelands Act 1968 was amended in two very significant ways. While changing the name of the Bantu Investment Corporation (BIC) to the Corporation for Economic Development (CED), the amendment made provision for whites, coloureds and Asians to become shareholders in 'Bantu companies' which were previously controlled by Africans only. Secondly, the amended Act abolished racial prescriptions which in the original Act set a limitation on the undertakings of the BIC. Whereas previously, the corporation could only acquire undertakings from non-Africans and sell to Africans, it could now buy undertakings from, and sell to, any racial group.

The lifting of the racial prescription covered virtually all other activities of the CED, such as the establishment of industrial concerns, the regulating of loans, debentures, stocks and other monies, the guaranteeing of contracts, its functions as a director or agent and its capacity to lend money with or without security. In other words, the amendment enabled the CED to fulfil these functions in respect of persons who no longer had to be African and who wished to undertake business in the bantustans. The amendment made the way clear for an unprecedented flow of capital into commercial agricultural production in the bantustans.

Since the 1960s there have been profound changes in the structure and form of capitalist production in South Africa. During this period South African capitalism has evolved from the conditions of small-scale competitive capitalism to large-scale monopoly capitalism. Although many of the important changes in the structure of the South African economy that have led to this transition occurred during and immediately after World War II, the real growth of monopoly capitalism did not occur until the 1960s with the major transition to a monopoly phase only taking place during the last decade.

This transformation in capitalist production has led to significant changes in the demand for certain forms of labour-power and the conditions of its reproduction. Although the majority of the African working class still occupies unskilled and semi-skilled positions, there has been a considerable increase in demand for and movement of Africans into both petty bourgeois and skilled/semi-skilled occupations.

The evolution to a monopoly phase of production has also led to an acceleration in the rate of structural unemployment. During the 1970s the percentage of unemployed has doubled, rising from 11,8% in 1970 to 21,1% in 1981, with the figure for 1983 probably being about 25%.

These twin processes, the demand for a more skilled labour-force and the expulsion of labour from production, in conjunction with certain political developments, have led to major changes in the supply, reproduction and relocation of labour. The recommendations of the Riekert Commission were orientated towards the creation of a more skilled, mobile and 'stable' urban proletariat, the tightening up of influx to the urban areas, and the relocation of the surplus population to the bantustans.

The major division in the African working class now is between those with permanent urban rights and those who are excluded from the urban areas. Some of these latter may be 'worker-peasant' migrants, but most are workers either commuting from the 'border-urban' areas or migrating from resettlement camps and other more distant areas in the bantustans. Whereas in the past the bantustans functioned to reproduce a cheap labour supply for the capitalist areas, this is no longer the case. Under the conditions of monopoly capitalism the reproduction of the

African component of the active work-force is taking place primarily in the urban areas.

Of the various elements of the African working class located in the bantustans, those in the border-urban areas receive similar wages and maintain living standards like those of their urban counterparts. This element of the bantustan population is fully proletarianised and its reproduction is assured, albeit somewhat precariously, through wages. Most of the other elements of the African working class in the bantustans are largely dysfunctional for capital. They comprise, for the most part, the ever-growing surplus population, many of whom have been relocated there, and whose reproduction is neither needed nor taken care of. In the case of 'worker-peasants' their subsistence/peasant activities are irrelevant to capital.

With this collapse of peasant-subsistence cultivation, the political and class barriers to the penetration of 'white' agricultural capital have dropped. With no strong class of peasant landowners left, capital has met no resistance in taking over control of the rural means of production.

State or private capital

It is extremely difficult, if not impossible, to ascertain whether the capital invested in many of these agricultural 'development' schemes is of state or private origin. Not only are most schemes surrounded in secrecy, but private capital is frequently closely intertwined with the state through various forms of agency, tripartite and other agreements catered for in the 1977 amendment. The situation is further complicated by differences in the administrative and financial structures of 'independent' and 'non-independent' bantustans. The agricultural 'development' schemes are usually closely tied up with local tribal authorities, political parties and other quasi-state/bantustan authorities. Capital can be invested into bantustan agricultural schemes in the following ways:

a) State capital

State capital can be invested directly through the CED, or in the case of 'independent' bantustans, directly through the agricultural corporation, or, if the state does not want to account for the purpose of such capital flows, it may channel funds through the Department of Foreign Affairs (as seems to be the case of Bophuthatswana).

Alternatively, state capital channelled through the CED, may combine with the national development corporation concerned to form an agricultural company, as for example in the case of Gazankulu Fruit Farming (Pty) Ltd, and Saringwa Estates (Pty) Ltd, both of which are citrus estates.

b) Private capital

Private capital may involve itself in the bantustans in any number of ways, and given the secrecy surrounding such involvement one can do little more than speculate on certain possible channels of investment. The 1977 amendment also allows for almost any possible permutation of agency system, with either the CED acting as agent for private capitalist interests, or private capital acting as agent for the CED.

Tripartite arrangements, where equity is held by the 'white' company, and the CED or Development Corporation both on its own behalf and on behalf of the people of the bantustan, are quite common in some bantustans (eg. KwaZulu). But in many cases, such as with several of the sisal, tea, coffee, citrus, and sugar schemes, it is difficult to ascertain whether investment is on a tripartite or agency basis.

There is now an increasing tendency for both companies and individual farmers to lease land directly from the bantustan for their own use. In Bophuthatswana, for example, much of the better land now being incorporated will be leased back to individual farmers and companies. The benefit to the farmer/company is that he will be able to produce without being under any of the controls of the local farming co-operative; his ground rent may be lower; and taxation in the bantustan will almost certainly be lower than in South Africa.

The attractions of the bantustans

Land in the bantustans is not uniformly bad, there being several areas suitable for commercial agriculture. These more agriculturally attractive parts of the bantustans can become economically viable in the context of the very specific advantages that the bantustans have to offer capital. In very general terms we can identify the following advantages to capital:

1) Differential ground rent

Land is usually made available to agricultural development projects at extremely low or nominal ground rents. Where the project is state run and on Trust land there may be no rents at all. In addition to the obvious contribution towards profit, low ground rents enable the extension of capitalist agriculture into hitherto marginal areas. This is an important consideration in the development of the large maize projects set up by the Agricultural Development Corporation of Bophuthatswana (AGRICOR).

2) Cheap labour
Wages in the bantustans are low. This is an important consideration in the development of certain crops such as tea, sisal, cotton, citrus etc., whose production is very labour-intensive.

3) Controlled labour
The close association between nearly all types of agricultural project and both the tribal authorities and the state, in conjunction with the fact that capital in the bantustans is exempt from just about all labour legislation, make the projects relatively safe from labour unrest and strike action. (However, resistance can often be of a more subtle nature.)

4) Various forms of subsidy
These may take several different forms:
a) Capital receives a subsidy when the production risk is borne not by capital itself but by members of a co-operative, or the bantustan or central government authorities.
b) Private capital is usually subsidised by assistance from the CED. The principle of this form of subsidy is similar to that offered by the South African government to industrial concerns wanting to set up in the de-centralised 'growth points', and involves such things as tax concessions, transport subsidies, provision of capital infrastructure, etc.
c) A direct subsidy may be obtained from the state for political and ideological reasons. The ideological importance of showing the viability of bantustan economies is such that it may be more advantageous for the South African government to subsidise the losses of certain projects rather than let them go bankrupt. This is the situation with nearly all the agricultural production undertaken in Bophuthatswana by AGRICOR.
d) Subsidies may be obtained through transfer pricing agreements. Although no direct evidence for such agreements has been found during the course of this research, which is not surprising as any such agreements would be kept very secret, it would seem that they probably do take place.

5) The development of large scale high-technology agribusiness in the bantustans

This provides guaranteed captured markets for a host of agricultural inputs. Such markets involve tens of millions of rands per year. The largest such market is that provided by the Mooifontein and Shiela-Verdwaal cooperatives in Bophuthatswana.

General tendencies in bantustan agricultural development

At a very general level there are three tendencies in bantustan agricultural 'development' which are becoming increasingly apparent, namely the increasing capital intensification of production; the increasing involvement of private capital; and the increasing tendency for tribal land, as distinct from Trust land, to be taken over for 'development' by the bantustan authorities.

a) Capital intensification

This trend is best illustrated in the Mooifontein scheme. Indeed, one of the reasons for its financial failure has been the excessive overcapitalisation of production in a climatically marginal area. The overall tendency, in nearly all schemes, whether private or state developed, is for increased mechanisation and capitalisation. Even in those crops which have hitherto been labour-intensive (eg. sisal, cotton, tea, coffee, citrus, etc.), the movement towards agribusiness is clearly visible.

b) Privatisation

The recommendations of both the De Waal and Swart Commissions for Venda and the Ciskei, respectively, as well as other bantustan reports, are for the increased involvement of private capital and the free enterprise system. This is now being seen with several private organisations and companies, such as Murray and Roberts, leasing land in the bantustans for commercial production. One of the most apparent forms of privatisation is through the involvement of so-called agricultural consultancy firms.

The normal pattern is for such companies to take over the running of projects once they have been satisfactorily established by the state. The take-over of projects by private management 'consultants' is usually associated with a considerable increase in mechanisation and more technically advanced forms of production, as well as marked increases in the rate of exploitation of labour. Measured Farming, for example, in taking over certain sisal projects provoked strike action leading to the rehiring of workers at up to 40% decreases in wages. In certain citrus schemes under their 'management' they have reduced wages, extended working hours and increased the work load. At the Champagne citrus project in Lebowa, where Measured Farming took over at the end of 1982, sprinkler irrigation replaced the flood system; the number of workers was drastically reduced; the length of the working week was increased by 15–20%; and workers (women) had to increase the number of trees 'cleaned' per day from 20 to between 100 and 200. Needless to say, Measured Farming has become the focus of resistance in the area, with organised theft of crops being the way the population 'gets its own back' on the company.

c) Tribal land and tribal authorities

Before we see how tribal land is being taken over more and more by the bantustan authorities, it is necessary to have some knowledge of the role played by the tribal authorities in the agricultural 'development' of the bantustans.

Most agricultural 'development' projects, except some of those on state or Trust land, are aligned with the local tribal authority. As it is widely assumed that tribal authorities are representative of the people, the impression is fostered that such schemes have a basis of local support and participation.

Tribal authorities vary considerably within the same bantustan and between different bantustans in the extent of their authority, effectiveness and popular support. They range from relatively weak ineffectual bodies to fairly sinister organisations consisting of corrupt and despotic chiefs and their associates.

The establishment of development projects on tribal land is nearly always with the approval and collaboration of the tribal authority. In most cases the establishment of a 'development project' involves extensive dispossession of peoples' land rights. The people who are usually most affected are those who are known members of opposition parties, the poor, migrant workers and the small-scale subsistence producer elements.

For example, at the villages of Bethanie, Manqwe and Berseba, in Bophuthatswana, the best tribal land in the area, covering more than 3000 ha., was taken over by AGRICOR in 1979, allegedly on the initiative of the tribal authority, for a proposed wheat and sunflower project. Hundreds of residents in these villages were dispossessed of their traditional rights of access to relatively fertile land which had hitherto provided them with a comparatively good subsistence base. Many families had twelve or more hectares with an annual production of 200 bags of mealies being commonplace. The land has been divided into 34 100 ha. farms which have been allocated at R5 per ha. rent by the tribal authority to people whom most residents claim to be known supporters and associates of the chief, several of whom had little or no farming experience. The chief himself has little or no popular support, is well guarded and rarely accessible to his people. Since the villagers were dispossessed of their land there has been only minimal production on these 3000 ha. of prime arable land.

In the recent past there has been a clear trend whereby chiefs who are closely tied to the bantustan governments have allowed their lands to be taken over directly by the agricultural or development corporations. TRACOR (Transkei Agricultural Corporation) has recently taken over several large areas of tribal land with disastrous consequences for the local population. Such schemes are being developed on large-scale highly mechanised production lines, similar to the Mooifontein scheme in Bophuthatswana. Apart from people losing access to their land there have been reports of livestock dying from contact with pesticides, etc.

The implications of agricultural 'development'

These few examples illustrate what is now becoming a widespread tendency in the 'homelands'. Agricultural land must be put under profitable production, regardless of the consequences for the local population. Indeed, many of these schemes, as seen in the case of Mooifontein in Bophuthatswana, are very unprofitable, but serve an important political and ideological use.

The bantustan authorities concoct quite meaningless statistics which serve to show the viability and growth of the bantustan economies. Notwithstanding the massive indebtedness of AGRICOR, Bophuthatswana claims to be one of the few food exporting countries in Africa. The Ciskei is portrayed as the only economy in Africa that is growing while all others are in a state of recession. Many of these schemes have served to foster a class of small-scale privileged producers. Not only is this class dependent on its subservience to the tribal authority, but it is both numerically small and economically frail. Worse still, it is at the expense of the proletarianisation and physical removal of thousands of small-scale subsistence producers for whom their stake in the land, albeit impoverished and unviable in capitalist terms, provided some slight measure of support against the vicissitudes and vagaries of employment in the capitalist sector.

Perhaps the most significant implication of this form of development is that resistance, albeit not always very overt, is widespread. Many of the bigger plantation schemes (eg. tea, citrus, etc.) have been subjected to strikes, while even in some of the most impoverished regions people have refused to sell their labour to such schemes. Frequently, as in the case of cotton, the crop is deliberately damaged, while as in the case of Champagne mentioned above, large-scale theft of the crop is organised on a community basis.

Capitalist Agriculture and Bantustan Employment Patterns: Case Studies in Bophuthatswana

Monty J. Roodt

The creation of employment in the rural areas of Bophuthatswana

AGRICOR has calculated that if all available arable land were utilised in Bophuthatswana for commercial agricultural purposes, the potential production could be worth in the region of R127-m. At present, agricultural production stands at R12,7-m.[1]

AGRICOR has set a norm of R5 000 income per year per farmer, a figure calculated as necessary to keep a full time farmer on the land and to prevent him from migrating to the urban areas. The sum of R3 000 was considered sufficient by AGRICOR until recently.

At R5 000 per year per family and a potential production figure of R127-m., we see that 25 000 families could find employment in the agricultural sector. At R3 000 per annum 42 000 families could be accommodated. If we take average household size to be 6,84 persons in the rural area,[2] 25 000 families means 171 000 people can rely on agriculture for their livelihood. If the second figure of 42 000 families is taken, the equivalent number of people will be 287 280.

Considering that there are approximately one million people living in the rural areas of Bophuthatswana,[3] it is clear that many would not be able to be absorbed in the agricultural sector. At R5 000 per family per annum (25 000 households) this would mean 841 741 people or 123 062 households who would have to find an income from some other source. At R3 000 (42 000 households) the equivalent amount is in the region of 725 461 people or 106 061 households.

Over 80% in the first case (at R5 000 per annum) and over 70% of the people in the second case (at R3 000 per annum) cannot find a livelihood from agriculture.

AGRICOR has decided to use the Israeli moshavim as a model for its rural development projects, and recently sent a team of its top management to Israel on a study tour. AGRICOR has also appointed an Israeli expert on agriculturally-based industry in an attempt to provide more employment in the rural areas.

Employment in rural Bophuthatswana is illustrated by the case of the Ditsobotla region to the south-west of Mafikeng. Agriculturally this region is important as it is the site of AGRICOR's two biggest dry-land maize projects. Further agricultural development is planned for the Kunana tribal area to the south of the Mooifontein project, as well as for the western sub-region.[4]

The Ditsobotla region

The region comprises 239 579 ha. (2 533 km²) of flat plain broken by a series of low, rocky hills in the Kunana area. Roughly 30% of the region is regarded as being arable given suitable climatic conditions. The natural vegetation is extensively and severely overgrazes.

Climatically the area is semi-arid and receives an annual average rainfall of 507,6 mm, although this can vary by up to 200 mm either way.

There are two planned towns, Itsoseng (population approximately 25 500) and Atamalang (population approximately 3 000). Approximately 25 other 'closer settlements' and roughly 52 traditional villages are situated on potentially productive arable land. Both towns are situated near the border and have a high percentage of commuter workers and migrant workers. The main railway line from Cape Town and Kimberley to Mafikeng runs through the region. The population of the Ditsobotla area has a farming population of 2 640 full-time and 2 550 part-time — a total of 5 190 farmers. Barely one out of four economically active persons resident in Ditsobotla finds work in the area, most of the people working as migrants in Mafikeng, Lichtenburg, Klerksdorp and in the Johannesburg area.

Roughly 70 000 ha. of high potential land (about 30% of the total) has been identified as sutiable for dry-land, summer grain crops, especially maize. There are four types of land ownership in Ditsobotla, namely:

1. Tribal land;
2. Reserved land — belonging to the state, but the tribe living there administers it;
3. Private land;
4. State-owned land — includes land transferred to Bophuthatswana.

In 1976 the Department of Agriculture appointed Noordwes Koöperasie as a Management Agent to finance, plan and manage the Shiela-Verdwaal project. The Shiela scheme adjoins the town of Itsoseng. It occupies ten state land farms, the land being allocated by the community authority. Since then further areas have been included comprising a total of 6 511 ha. with a total of 429 farmers.[5]

The Shiela project began with the 'contractor' system, where certain farmers were chosen and given a mechanical 'package' (i.e. tractors) on the understanding that they plough for the other farmers as well. To enable them to pay off the package they were allocated 30 ha. each instead of the usual 15 ha per farmer. This system has not worked well and some of the ploughing is now done by the co-operative. The average yield for the project was 2,73 tons per ha. until 1981/2.

The Mooifontein summer grain scheme in the Ditsobotla district commenced production in 1977/8 under the management of the Corporation for Economic Development (CED) and has expanded into the largest dry-land maize project in southern Africa with 1 264 'farmers' registered and a total of 23 340 ha. under mainly maize. It is situated on 27 state land farms. Each participant is a member of one of the 14 primary agricultural co-operatives of the scheme, which are in turn affiliated to the Ditsobotla Secondary Agricultural Cooperative (DSAC) with its headquarters on the farm Mooifontein.

The land was bought from white farmers in terms of the 1936 Land Act and held as trust land. The former employees of the white farmers were joined by families from the Western Transvaal and were given land tenure rights on small plots for crops along with communal grazing rights at nominal annual rentals. Because of overcrowding and the high population density these allocations barely served subsistence needs. The area was also planned as a 'betterment scheme' in the 1950s.

Mooifontein Project does not use the 'contractor' system. Instead, the machinery is owned by the Co-operative which employs drivers to operate the tractors at hire-charges to the farmers. The costs were shared by AGRICOR and the CED. AGRICOR is also responsible for the financing of seasonal crop production inputs such as seed, fertilisers, weed killers and fuels.

The Mooifontein Project

An average ten-year cycle for the Mooifontein area would be:

- 1 bad year
- 4 poor to average years
- 3 good to average years
- 2 excellent years

Taking the average yield in metric tons per ha. for the project since it started, we find a figure of 2,18 tons per ha. This is in line with the South African average of 2,1 tons per ha. Using these averages the following distribution over a ten-year cycle could be probable:

- 1 bad year = 0,5 metric ton per ha.
- 4 poor to average years = 2 metric tons per ha.
- 3 good to average years = 3 metric tons per ha.
- 2 excellent years = 3,5 metric tons per ha.

This distribution coincides with an average yield of 2,25 metric tons per ha. At the 1982 price of R135 per ton, a gross income over ten years of R49 612 for a farm of 15 ha. emerges as R4 961 per year. Subtracting the total inputs for one year (at 1982 prices), the average nett earnings for one year for a 15 ha. farm is R731, or R49 per ha. The average farmer, to achieve a nett income of R5 000 at R49 per ha. therefore needs *102 ha, with the present amount of inputs*, especially fertiliser. To achieve a nett earning of R3 000 the farmer has to have 61 ha.

Fertiliser costs may be as much as 60% of production costs, and may be over R103 per ha. If one considers that rainfall in the Ditsobotla area is variable, it becomes a major factor in deciding the yield potential. Overcapitalisation therefore, could be one of the major reasons why the total amount spent on inputs at Mooifontein often exceeds the gross income.

It appears that the Foreign Affairs Department of South Africa, one of AGRICOR's major investors, has realised this, as it has requested AGRICOR to calculate production costs for new projects in the area on yields of 2,4 tons and to reduce the fertilisation programme, to be closer to the real potential of the area.

This has in fact been done and AGRICOR is planning a project for the western sub-region of Ditsobotla where farmers would receive 71 ha. to achieve a yearly income of R5 000. If mixed with groundnuts (3 years maize, 1 year groundnuts) 55 ha. is needed.

Implications for employment

The present size of 15 ha. per farmer is insufficient for the farmer on Mooifontein to earn a living, and in many cases is putting him into debts of thousands of rands which he has very little chance of repaying.

We have seen that with a realistic fertilisation programme based on the real yield possibilities of the area a farmer needs at least 71 ha. to achieve an annual income of R5 000. Using AGRICOR's projection for the new project, we see that to earn R3 000 per annum a farmer needs 42 ha. for maize only.

This means that far fewer farmers can be accommodated on the existing arable land in the Ditsobotla district than if 15 ha. allotments had been a feasible idea. With 70 000 ha. of arable land available in Ditsobotla at 71 ha. (R5 000 per annum), 986 families can be accommodated in full-time crop farming. At 42 ha. (R3 000 per annum), 1 666 families can do the same.

Potgieter estimated that, based on the achievements of the Shiela Project, some 2 000 families can be accommodated in full-time crop farming in Ditsobotla. He also calculated that under optimal conditions 27 000 livestock units can be kept on the remaining 166 000 ha. of land not suitable for ploughing, giving a further 90–100 cattle farmers an income of R3 500 per annum at 1979 prices. This gives, in terms of Potgieter's figures, a total potential farming community of 2 100 households.[6]

Agriculturally-based industries, as a means of providing further job opportunities for the rural population, are not very promising. A recent feasibility study for Ditsobotla shows that agriculturally-based industries would create only another 483 *basic* job opportunities. This shows the difficulties of establishing industry in remote rural areas far away from the main market centres.

To sum up briefly: at R5 000 per annum per crop farming household, *986* families can be accommodated. At R3 000 per annum the number of families is *1 666*. If we add to this Potgieter's cattle farmers and the basic employment created by agro-industries we get a total of *1 569 households* who can find definite employment in the rural areas of Ditsobotla for the first amount, and *2 249* for the second. By calculating the discrepancy between total population and those households in employment, we are left with *14 904* households which cannot find a livelihood in the rural sector. Our alternate formulation of R3 000 per annum per household gives us *14 224 households* unable to be sustained within the area.

This means that between 66% and 69% of the rural households are unable under optimal conditions to survive in the rural areas of Ditsobotla without having resort to migrancy. Yet this region is considered to be one of the better areas in agricultural potential and that many other areas of Bophuthatswana are less centrally situated and even more arid. The situation is worsened by the massive influx of people through the South African state's policy of relocation of people, from so called 'white spots', the resettlement of entire communities into dormitory townships (as in the case of the Itsoseng community's removal from Lichtenburg to within the borders of Bophuthatswana) and the movement of people off white-owned farms because of increasing mechanisation.

The capital-intensive project

The capital intensive Shiela and Mooifontein Projects are a relatively recent phenomenon in rural development in South Africa. Until very recently AGRICOR has relied on management from the CED and the Noordwes Koöperasie to run its projects. Given the political task facing AGRICOR, that is to make Bophuthatswana self-sufficient in maize production, and the background of its management, the projects were linked into the highly capital-intensive multi-national agri-business network. There is no doubt that this link has had a considerable influence on the type of rural development that has occurred on the AGRICOR projects — a highly capital-intensive and production-orientated approach.

A major element in this process is VETSAK, the huge South African central co-operation organisation which acts as a retail outlet in South Africa for multi-national giants such as Fiat Trattori, Claas, the biggest harvesting machinery manufacturing concern, Amozonen, the industrial giant Allis-Chalmer, Hobbs Incorporated, and Kuhn in France. VETSAK also markets a large range of chemicals and other assorted agricultural equipment, and owns 50% of the newly formed TEMO-VET. AGRICOR owns the other 50%. The only products they do not supply are fertiliser and fuel, which are both controlled products. Fertiliser is supplied by companies such as Triomf, Omnia, and Bonus. Through demonstrations, training courses, etc., these companies continuously make their presence felt.

The production figures for Mooifontein for two years demonstrate the trend towards capital-intensity. In 1980/81 the total cost of inputs per ha. was R282. Of this amount R165 (59%) was spent on fertiliser, pesticides, weed killer, tractors, implements and phosphates. In 1981/82 this figure went up to R198 which represents 70% of the total expenditure on inputs. The companies which supply these commodities cannot lose as they are guaranteed their money irrespective of the yield, unlike the farmer, who as the last person in the vast chain, is dependent on what is left over after all the costs have been paid.

The above figures, contrasted with the nett income of the farmer, are revealing. Above these amounts, the farmer still has to pay for the seed, transport, packing, labour, interest and a management fee. In 1980/81, which was an excellent year climatically, the farmer at Mooifontein made on average R60,81 per ha., giving him a total of R912,15 for the year. The following year was not quite as good, farmers made a loss of R172,36 on average per ha., giving him a debt of R2 585 for his 15 ha. The project participants call it a 'blank cheque'.

This kind of technology requires a certain kind of approach to agriculture. It requires a highly centralised and skilled management core, but in the rural areas of Ditsobotla, most of the farmers have never been involved in this kind of farming, have small pieces of land, and are to a large extent illiterate.

Although there was an attempt to involve farmers in the decision making process when the project first started this is no longer the case. Many of the primary co-operatives have become superfluous as management have centralised the running of the project. The reasons given by the management for this centralisation are that they do not have sufficient trained staff to run the primary co-operatives and the necessity for speed in the implementation of the project.

From a survey done at Mooifontein, it emerged that the participants are farmers in name only. Consultation as to fertiliser application, weeding, crop spraying, and harvesting is virtually non-existent. Up to 70% of registered farmers are away working as migrants in the urban areas.

In an attempt to remedy the situation AGRICOR has taken over the management of the projects from the CED, and will in future be implementing its TEMISANO concept of 'farming together'. TEMISANO is a rural development programme which goes beyond the production process and will include elements of community development, training and secondary industry.

AGRICOR is operating in an extremely difficult situation due to the complexity of the different factors involved. To provide an adequate productive base for farmers to remain in the rural areas on a full-time basis requires the provision of larger land holdings and a scaling down of the capital inputs to a more manageable size. This entails a careful look at the land tenure system in conjunction with the existing rate of unemployment and overcrowding in the rural areas — making it ultimately a political question which needs urgent attention.

Land redistribution cannot take place in Bophuthatswana, or any of the other bantustans, without confronting the political question of the 70–80% of the people who cannot be employed in the rural areas. The failure of the 'Betterment' policy bears adequate witness to the resistance in the rural areas to the redistribution of land. It is here where the real resistance to the changing of the land tenure system lies and not in some inexplicable clinging to tradition.

Notes

1 J. Graaff, unpublished paper (Unibo, 1982).
2 F.J. Potgieter, 'Developing Ditsobotla' (1980), 11.
3 J. Graaff, unpublished paper (Unibo, 1982).
4 Planning section of AGRICOR, feasibility study (June, 1983).
5 Pretorius, *Agricultural Schemes and Projects*, AGRICOR, 40.
6 F.J. Potgieter, *Agricultural Schemes*.